Anonymus

Ceremonial for the use of the Catholic churches in the United States of America

Anonymus

Ceremonial for the use of the Catholic churches in the United States of America

ISBN/EAN: 9783741183942

Manufactured in Europe, USA, Canada, Australia, Japa

Cover: Foto ©Lupo / pixelio.de

Manufactured and distributed by brebook publishing software (www.brebook.com)

Anonymus

Ceremonial for the use of the Catholic churches in the United States of America

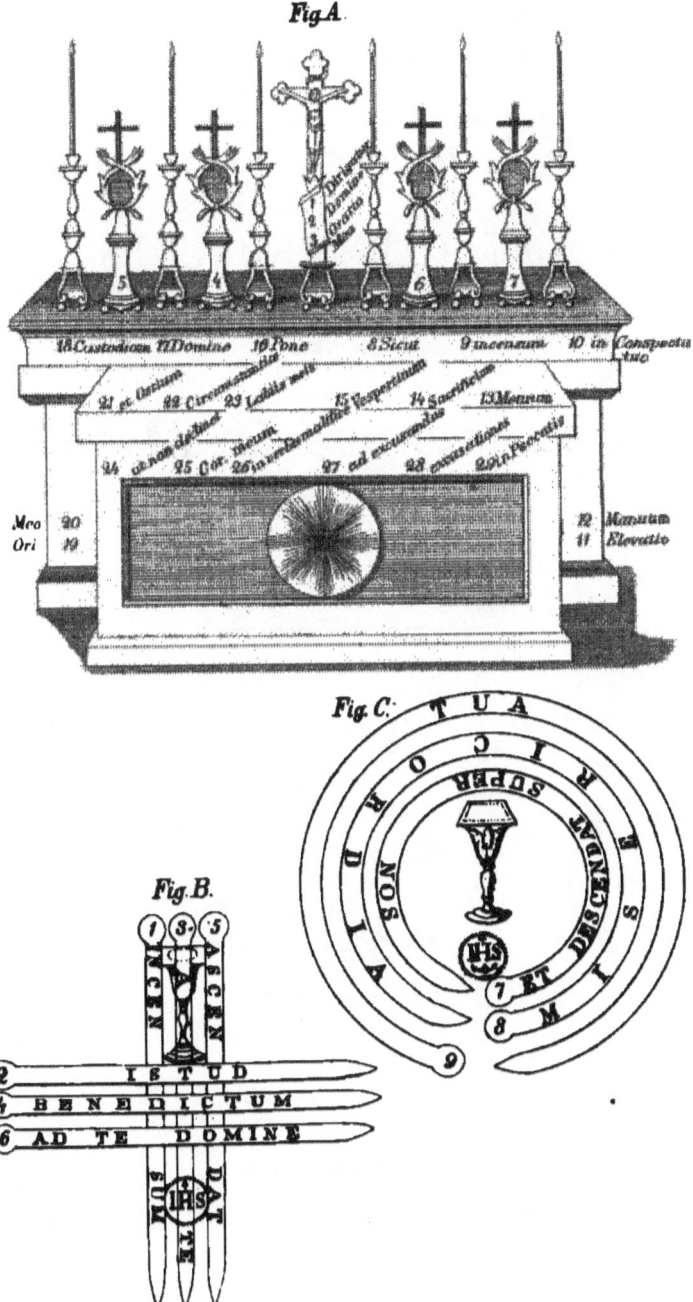

CEREMONIAL

FOR THE USE OF THE

CATHOLIC CHURCHES

IN THE

UNITED STATES OF AMERICA.

FIFTH REVISED EDITION.

BALTIMORE:
PUBLISHED BY JOHN B. PIET & CO.
1882.

This edition of the Ceremonial, for the use of the Catholic Churches in the United States of America, having been carefully revised and corrected, is hereby approved of.

Given at Baltimore this 4th day of May.

†JAMES GIBBONS,
    Archbishop of Baltimore.

Feast of St. Monica, A. D., 1882.

PREFACE TO THE FIFTH EDITION.

This volume of the Ceremonial is something more than a mere reprint from former editions. While it cannot be expected that any novelty should be found in a work treating of the ritual of the Church, yet it is quite possible to make many changes in the order of the material; and this volume affords evidence of the feasibility of correcting mistakes.

With regard to the arrangement of the matter, it has been deemed preferable to place together the various articles treating of ceremonies in which the priest is not assisted by deacon and sub-deacon; and hence the first and second parts of the present volume treat of the ceremonies of Low Mass, Missa Cantata, Vespers and Benediction, and the ceremonies for Holy Week and other occasions as given in the small Ceremonial of Benedict XIII. In the article on Missa Cantata will be found the ceremonies of the *Asperges*, which should take place every Sunday, unless the Bishop officiates.

The former editions placed the directions for the *Asperges* after the ceremonies prescribed for Holy Saturday, and made no reference to it in the article on Missa Cantata; and in consequence the *Asperges* was omitted in many churches, whilst in others a lack of uniformity in carrying it out was found.

Among the many corrections in the first part is one concerning the singing of the Epistle in a Missa Cantata. The Missal prescribes that in such circumstances a lector in surplice shall sing the Epistle, and the former editions of this work contained the provision that the first acolyte should at the proper time sing the Epistle. This was scarcely, if ever, observed; and in some churches the celebrant sang, whilst in others he read, the Epistle. The Roman authorities being consulted on this point, replied (in an informal answer received through the Propaganda) that in case the rubric of the Missal could not be observed, the celebrant might read the Epistle. The same reply contained the following decisions, which have been used in preparing this edition:

I. The Missal may be left on the altar beforehand at a Low Mass, where such is the custom; though the rubrics require that the server should carry it to the altar when accompanying the celebrant.

II. When the sacristy is behind the altar of the church, the celebrant enters the sanctuary by the Epistle and leaves by the Gospel side.

III. The salutations prescribed in the *Cæremoniale*, and elsewhere, need not be made to mere sanctuary boys.

IV. When the Blessed Sacrament is not kept at the altar where Mass is celebrated, the server on arriving, or when passing before the middle of the altar, should not genuflect, but bow profoundly.

The article on Votive Masses in the first part has been entirely rewritten.

The ceremonies for Solemn High Mass, Solemn Vespers and Solemn Benediction have been left in the third part, but many corrections and additions have been made; all of which are in consonance with Roman custom, especially as interpreted by the latest Roman liturgical writer, Mgr. Martinucci.

No alteration, so far as the order is concerned, will be found in the fourth, fifth and sixth parts, nor in the Appendix; but many corrections have been made and some new matter introduced.

Writers on liturgical questions have differed and will continue to hold divergent opinions on minor points regarding which neither the *Cæremoniale Episcoporum*, the Missal nor the Pontifical give definite instructions. In treating such, it has been considered that the safest plan was to follow the approved Roman writers. By deferring to the authority of Mgr. Martinucci, the present edition, it is believed, has attained that end.

The closest fidelity to approved Roman custom will insure perfection in carrying out any ceremony, and for this reason it is expected that the present edition of the CEREMONIAL will prove even more acceptable than its predecessors.

As in duty bound, this volume is published with due submission to Ecclesiastical authority, and especially the Sacred Congregation of Rites.

CONTENTS.

PART I.

CEREMONIES OF LOW MASS, MISSA CANTATA, VESPERS AND BENEDICTION.

CHAP.		PAGE
I.—ART. I.	What is to be prepared,	1
II.	On the Preparation for Mass by the Priest,	3
III.	On Leaving the Sacristy,	6
IV.	On Approaching the Altar,	8
V.	From the Commencement of the Mass to the Introit,	9
VI.	From the Introit to the Epistle,	11
VII.	From the Epistle to the Offertory,	13
VIII.	From the Offertory to the Canon,	15
IX.	From the Canon to the Consecration,	20
X.	From the Consecration to the Pater Noster,	24
XI.	From the Pater Noster to the Communion,	26
XII.	From the Communion to the End of Mass,	32
XIII.	On Votive Masses,	34
II.—Order to be observed in celebrating two Masses on the same day,		40
III.—Low Mass for the Dead,		42
IV.—Low Mass when the Blessed Sacrament is exposed,		44
V.—Of Low Mass in the presence of Prelates,		46
VI.—Giving Communion,		48
ART. I.	Giving Communion during Mass,	48
II.	Purification of the Ciborium,	51
III.	On giving Communion at other times,	51
VII.—Manner of Serving a Priest at Low Mass,		54
ART. I.	General Remarks,	54
II.	Of the Vesting of the Priest,	55
III.	From the beginning of the Mass to the end of it,	56
VIII.—Manner of Serving a Bishop at Low Mass,		60
ART. I.	Things to be prepared,	60
II.	Of the preparation and Vesting of the Bishop,	60
III.	When there is but one Chaplain,	65
IX.—Manner of Celebrating High Mass without Deacon or Sub-deacon; the Asperges,		67
ART. I.	Things to be prepared,	67

xii   CONTENTS.

CHAP.	PAGE
X.—Vespers sung without Cope-bearers,	72
ART. I. Things to be prepared,	72
II.	73
III. When Benediction follows,	78
XI.—Benediction of the Blessed Sacrament	79
ART. I. Things to be prepared,	79
II. When there is but one Priest,	80
III. When another Priest, or a Deacon assists,	83

PART II.

CEREMONIES FOR HOLY WEEK AND OTHER FESTIVALS.

I.—Blessing of Candles on Candlemas Day,	86
ART. I. Of what is to be prepared,	86
II. Ceremonies to be performed on Candlemas Day,	87
II.—Of the Benediction of Ashes on Ash Wednesday,	92
ART. I. Things to be prepared,	92
II. Of the Sacred Rites to be performed,	93
III.—Of Palm Sunday,	96
ART. I. What is to be prepared,	96
II. Of the Ceremonies to be performed,	97
IV.—Of Maunday-Thursday,	103
ART. I. What is to be prepared,	103
II. Of the Sacred Rites,	104
V.—Of Good Friday,	110
ART. I. Of what is to be prepared,	110
II. Of the Sacred Rites,	111
VI.—Of Holy Saturday,	123
ART. I. What is to be prepared,	123
II. Of the Sacred Rites,	125

PART III.

CEREMONIES OF HIGH MASS, SOLEMN VESPERS AND SOLEMN BENEDICTION.

I.—Rules to observed by the Clergy in Choir,	135
ART. I. The order of going to the Choir,	135
II. The order to be observed in Choir,	136
III. Internal dispositions,	139
IV. The order to be observed in receiving Holy Communion,	139
V. The order in going from the Choir,	140
II.—Instructions for the Officers,	141
ART. I. Things to be prepared,	141
II. Instruction for the Censer-bearer,	142
III. Instruction for the Acolytes,	146
IV. Duty of the Master of Ceremonies,	150

CONTENTS. xiii

CHAP.		PAGE
V. Instruction for Sub-deacon,		158
VI. Instruction for the Deacon,		166
VII. Instruction for the Celebrant,		176
III.—High Mass for the Dead,		183
Art. I. Things to be prepared,		183
II. What is to be particularly observed,		183
IV.—Solemn Vespers,		186
Art. I. Things to be prepared,		186
II. General Rules to be observed,		187
III. Instruction for the Acolytes,		188
IV. Instruction for the Censer-bearer,		190
V. Instruction for the Master of Ceremonies,		192
VI. Instruction for the Cope-bearers,		195
VII. Instruction for the Celebrant,		198
V.—Solemn Benediction when the Celebrant is assisted by Deacon and Sub deacon,		200
VI.—Of Solemn Vespers, and of the Procession on Corpus Christi,		202
Art. I. Of Solemn Vespers, the Blessed Sacrament, exposed,		202
II. Of the Procession on Corpus Christi,		206
VII.—Vespers for the Dead on the 1st of November,		208
Art. I. Things to be prepared,		208
II. Ceremonies peculiar to these Vespers,		209

PART IV.

CEREMONIES FOR THE PRINCIPAL FESTIVALS.

I.—Feast of the Purification,		211
Art. I. Necessary Preparations,		211
II. From the Vesting of the Ministers to the Distribution of the Candles,		212
III. From the Distribution of the Candles to the Procession,		213
IV. The Procession,		215
II. Ash Wednesday,		217
Art. I. Necessary Preparations,		217
II. Of the Blessing and Distribution of the Ashes,		218
III. Of the Mass,		221
III.—Sundays Lætare and Gaudete,		222
IV.—Palm Sunday,		222
Art. I. Preparations,		222
II. From the Beginning of the Ceremony to the Distribution of the Palms,		223
III. Of the Distribution of Palms,		226
IV. Of the Procession,		227
V. Of the Mass and Passion,		230
V.—Office of the Tenebræ,		233
Art. I. Preparations,		233
II. From the Commencement to the End of the Office,		233

CONTENTS.

CHAP.		PAGE
VI.—Maundy-Thursday,		235
ART. I. Preparations,		235
II. Of the Mass,		236
III. Of the Procession,		239
IV. Of Vespers, and of the Stripping of the Altars,		241
VII.—Of Good Friday,		243
ART. I. Preparations,		243
II. From the Vesting of the Ministers to the Uncovering of the Cross,		244
III. From the Uncovering of the Cross to the Procession,		247
IV. Of the Procession,		250
V. Of the remaining Part of the Office,		252
VIII.—Holy Saturday,		256
ART. I. Things to be prepared,		256
II. From the Benediction of the New Fire to the Exultet,		258
III. From the Exultet to the Prophecies,		261
IV. From the Prophecies to the Benediction of the Baptismal Font,		263
V. From the Benediction of the Font to the Beginning of Mass,		264
VI. The Mass,		267

PART V.

CEREMONIES FOR MASS AND VESPERS, SOLEMNLY CELEBRATED BY THE BISHOP, OR IN HIS PRESENCE.

	PAGE
I. Solemn Pontifical Vespers,	270
ART. I. Things to be prepared,	270
II. From the entrance of the Bishop and Clergy to the beginning of Vespers,	271
III. From the beginning to the end of Vespers,	272
IV. Benediction of the Blessed Sacrament given by the Bishop,	275
II. Solemn Vespers, in the presence of the Bishop,	276
III. Complins, when the Bishop officiates,	277
IV. Matins, when the Bishop officiates,	278
V. Lauds, when the Bishop officiates,	280
VI. Solemn Pontifical Mass,	281
ART. I. Things to be prepared,	281
II. Of the Vesting of the Clergy and of the Bishop,	284
III. The Pontifical Mass,	288
VII. Solemn Mass, celebrated in the presence of the Bishop, dressed in Cope,	300
VIII. Solemn Mass in presence of the Bishop, in Rochet and Cappa,	304
IX. Vespers for the Dead, celebrated by the Bishop,	305

CONTENTS.

CHAP.		PAGE.
X.	Matins and Lauds for the Dead, celebrated by the Bishop,	306
XI.	Solemn Pontifical Mass for the Dead,	307
	ART. I. Things to be prepared,	307
	II. From the beginning to the end of Mass,	308
	III. The Absolution after Mass,	310
XII.	Solemn Mass for the Dead, in the presence of the Bishop,	312
XIII.	Particular Instructions for the Officers who attend the Bishop,	313
	ART. I. Instruction for the assistant Priest,	313
	II. Instructions for the two assistant Deacons,	318
	III. Instruction for the officiating Deacon,	321
	IV. Instruction for the Sub deacon,	328
	V. Instruction for the inferior Ministers,	332

PART VI.

OTHER DIFFERENT SOLEMNITIES AT WHICH THE BISHOP OFFICIATES OR IS PRESENT.

I.	Commemoration of all the Faithful departed,	336
II.	Sundays in Advent,	337
III.	Christmas,	338
IV.	Festivals between Christmas and Candlemas,	339
V.	Candlemas,	340
VI.	Ash-Wednesday,	343
VII.	Sundays in Lent,	345
VIII.	Palm Sunday,	346
IX.	Matins of the Tenebræ,	349
X.	Maunday-Thursday,	350
XI.	Good Friday,	361
XII.	Holy Saturday,	369
XIII.	Ceremonies to be observed in Provincial Councils,	376
	ART. I. What is to be done before it opens,	376
	II. How the Metropolitan Church is to be adorned and arranged,	377
	III. The opening of the Council,	378
	IV. Mode of Procedure of the Council,	384
	V. Second Solemn Session,	385
	VI. Third Solemn Session,	387
XIV.	Ceremonies to be observed in Diocesan Synods,	390
XV.	Solemn administration of the Sacrament of Confirmation,	395
	ART. I. Things to be prepared,	395
	II. The administration of the Sacrament,	396
XVI.	Episcopal Visitation of Parishes,	399
	ART. I. The Bishop's Reception when he visits the Parishes,	399

APPENDIX.

CHAP.		PAGE
I. Forty Hours' Exposition,		406
ART. I. Things to be prepared for the Mass of the Exposition,		406
II. Of the Mass of the Exposition,		407
III. Of the Procession for the Exposition,		409
IV. Of the Mass *pro Pace*,		413
V. Things to be prepared for the Mass of the Reposition,		414
VI. Of the Mass for the Reposition,		414
VII. From the Litany to the end of the Forty Hours,		418
II.—Different Intonations for Vespers and Solemn Mass,		422
Elenchus Defectuum,		430

NOTE.—The following foot note was inadvertently omitted on page 137:

Mgr. Martinucci, following the directions of the *Cæremoniale Episcoporum*, prescribes that the clergy, with the exception of Prelates and Canons in their own church should kneel while the *Incarnatus* is being sung. A contrary custom prevails in many places, even in some churches in Rome; hence it has been thought better to leave the text as in former editions, and insert this note.

CEREMONIAL.

PART I.

Ceremonies of Low Mass.

CHAPTER I.

ARTICLE I.

WHAT IS TO BE PREPARED.

On the Altar.

1. THE altar, which should be of stone or marble, consecrated by the Bishop, or, at least, having on it an altar-stone consecrated by the Bishop, should be covered with three clean altar-cloths. The first two, long enough to cover the whole top, and the uppermost should reach the base of the altar on both sides. (*Rub. Miss.*, part i, n. **xx**.)

2. In the middle of the altar, a crucifix sufficiently large to be distinctly seen. (*Rub., ib.*)

3. At least two candlesticks, with wax candles, which should burn during the whole time of the Mass.*

4. In front of the altar, the antipendium of the color of the vestments.† This does not seem strictly necessary, especially when the front of the altar is handsomely ornamented. (*Rub., ib.*)

---

* All priests (even prelates, who are not Bishops) should have at their private Mass only two candles and one server. (*S. R. C.*, 27th Sept., 1659.)

† As the word antipendium is generally accepted to signify altar-veil, or frontal, it shall be made use of in this manual.

5. If the Blessed Sacrament is in the tabernacle, the veil covering the tabernacle should also be of the color of the vestments, unless black vestments be used. No veil is needed over the tabernacle when the canopy is of marble or stone. (*Cær. Ep., lib. I*, c. xiii, n. 3.)*

6. The altar cards.

7. At the Epistle side, the book-stand.

8. On the *credence*,† or any suitable place, the cruets‡ with wine and water on a plate, the finger-towel and the hand-bell. Should the priest be obliged to celebrate Mass without the assistance of a server, the plate with cruets and towel should be placed on a stand near the altar, at the Epistle side, not on the altar.

In the Sacristy. §

1. The sacred vestments, of the color prescribed. They should be placed on the sacristy table, ‖ or vestment case; they should be so disposed that the priest may find them in order as he vests. The chasuble should be adjusted first, so that the lower half of the front part will hang down, and the lower part of the back be folded over the upper. Next, the stole, folded in four parts, should be laid across the chasuble, and the maniple across the stole. The girdle, in a serpentine form, should be placed on the maniple. The upper part of the alb should lie on the vestments, and over it the amice extended, the strings of which may be arranged on the amice itself.

2. The Missal, unless it be already on the altar.

---

* "Tabernaculum, in quo assidue Divinissima servatur Eucharistia conopeo serico, vel simili materiæ vestiri debet, ejus item coloris cujus est altaris Pallium; quanquam pro colore nigro violaceus congruentior erit in honorem Christi viventis." (*Merati*.)

† Credence, generally used for the side table near the altar.

‡ Cruets should be of glass, not of silver. (*Gavan.*, P. 1, 7, xx.)

§ If there is no sacristy, the sacred vestments are prepared on a table near the altar, or, if there is no table, on the Gospel side of the altar itself; not in the middle of it, unless a Bishop is to celebrate. (*Rub. Miss.*)

‖ St. Charles Borromeo recommends that the table or vestment case, on which the sacred vestments are laid, be covered with a white linen cloth.

3. The chalice,* and paten with particle, the purificator, the chalice-veil, the pall, and the burse with the corporal in it.

4. The priest's cap near the vestments; not on them, nor on the chalice.

5. A surplice for the server.

6. A place for the priest to wash his hands.

Article II.

On the Preparation for Mass.

1. The priest, wishing to celebrate the most Holy Sacrifice, should prepare himself by prayer. *Aliquantulum orationi vacet.* (*Rub. Miss.*) He should also have said matins and lauds.

2. The suitable prayers for the occasion are those suggested by the Church, and laid down in the Missal, that is, the anthem, *Ne reminiscaris*, with the psalms and prayers that follow them. Should the priest say these prayers, he will take notice that the anthem above named is said entirely on feasts of double rite; and during Paschal time the *Alleluia* is added to it.

3. It is well not to omit the pious protestation, *Ego volo celebrare Missam.* By reciting this, not only he can gain the indulgences annexed to it, but he may then also direct his intention.

4. The priest, clad in his cassock, opens the Missal, and marks the places of the Mass and prayers, that he may not lose time at the altar. (*Rub. Miss.*) After which he washes his hands, saying at the same time, in a low voice, *Da Domine*, etc.

---

* The chalice ought not to be carried to the altar, and fixed on it by any person before Mass, but the priest ought to carry it himself to the altar, not before he goes thither to begin Mass, but when vested with the sacred vestments he goes from the sacristy, or from the place where he put on the vestments, to the altar, as directed. (*Ib.*, tit. ii, n. 1.) "Sacerdos omnibus paramentis indutus accipit manu sinistra calicem ut supra præparatum, quem portat elevatum ante pectus, bursam manu dextra super calice tenens, et facta reverentia cruci, et capite cooperto accedit ad altare cum ministro, cum Missali," etc.; any contrary custom is to be looked upon as an abuse, which should be abolished. (See *S. C. R.*, n. 4285.)

5. Having washed his hands, he prepares the chalice by placing on it a clean purificator,* in such a way that it will hang equally on both sides. On the purificator he places the paten, and on the paten the large bread, which should be round, entire, and free from loose particles, to remove which the priest will pass his thumb and forefinger around the edge.† (*Rub. Miss.*) Then he puts on it the pall,‡ which he covers with the veil. If the veil is not large enough to cover the whole chalice, he will arrange it so that it will hide that part of the chalice that will be towards the people while going to the altar. Last of all, he places the burse, containing the corporal,§ on the veil. The opening of it should be towards himself as he proceeds to the altar. Nothing should be laid on the burse. (*S. C. R.*, 1st Sept., 1703.)

6. Everything being prepared, the priest proceeds to vest. He will do well to make the sign of the cross,

---

* The purificator should be of plain linen, neither coarse nor very fine. It may be about thirteen and a half inches square, with a very small cross worked in the centre. It requires no special blessing, but after use should not be handled by laics, until washed by some one in major orders.

† Some authors recommend that a slight line be traced on the large bread before Mass, so that the priest may more easily break it. There is nothing for or against this in the Rubrics.

‡ According to the Rubric, the pall should be of linen. Formerly the pall formed a part of the corporal, which was large enough to cover the chalice. The inconvenience of its being too light can be obviated by having it made out of a piece of linen which when folded is about six inches square, including large edging if there be any. "In sacrificio missæ uti non licet palla a parte superiori drapo serico cooperta." (*S R. C.*, 2d Jan., 1701.) Nevertheless, by a late decision of the S. R. C., the pall may be of silk cloth, ornamented on the outside, while the inside is of linen; but it should not be black. "Permitti posse dummodo palla linea subnecta calicem cooperiat, ac pannus superior non sit nigri coloris, aut referat aliqua mortis signa." (*S. R. C.*, 10th Jan., 1852.)

§ The corporal should be of fine white linen, very clean, and starched. It should have a small cross worked in the middle of the front part, but not with gold or silver. It is generally folded by bending first one-third of it over, so as to cover the second third part; again, the other third folded over the first. Then one-third of its length over the middle third part, and the last part bent over the rest. A corporal will be found sufficiently large if it be from twenty-two to twenty-four inches square. The corporal is blessed as well as the pall.

although the Rubric does not say so. If he does, he should make it without the amice in his hand. He then takes the amice by the two corners where the strings are connected, raises it so that he may kiss the cross in the middle; he puts it on his head, saying at the same time, *Impone, Domine*, etc.; and as he continues the prayers, he adjusts the amice around his neck, so that every article of his neck-dress be entirely covered by it; and after crossing the strings upon his breast, the left being under the right, he passes them behind, and ties them in front with a loose knot.* (*Rub. Miss.*)

7. He puts on the alb (without kissing it) by passing it over his head; then he puts his right arm into the right sleeve, and his left into the other. He adjusts it about his neck, and fits it around so that it descends about one inch above the floor all around, at the same time saying, *Dealba me, Domine*, etc. (*Rub. Miss.*)

8. As he girds himself with the cincture,† he says, *Præcinge me*, etc. (*Rub. Miss.*) The common practice is to leave the tassels hanging down as low as possible, to be able afterwards to fasten the stole with the two ends of the cord.

9. He takes the maniple and kisses the cross on it, and passing it over his left arm, fastens it half way between the hand and the elbow, saying, *Merear, Domine*, etc.

10. Then having taken the stole, he kisses the cross on it, and, with both hands, he passes it over his head, fits it around his neck, so that both ends of the stole hang

---

* In putting on the amice, he ought not to forget that the object of it is to cover entirely the usual dress, and that part of the cassock which is near the collar, and the collar itself; and, therefore, he ought to put it on so as to answer this purpose as directed. (*Ib.*, tit. 1, n. 3.) "Ac primum accipiens amictum circa extremitates et chordulas, osculatur illud in medio ubi est crux et ponit super caput, et mox declinat ad collum, et eo *vestium collaria circumtegens*," etc. The first Council of Baltimore has strictly enjoined the observance of this Rubric. Indusia vero privati apparatus sub amictu et alba lateant, ita ut non indecoro vel mundano more appareant. (*Con. Balt.* 1, Decr. 24.)

† Cinctures may be made of either silk or cotton, and of any color except black. Congruentior est uti cingulo lineo. (*S. R. C.*, n. 3436 ad. 7.)

down at equal distances. Afterwards he crosses both ends of the stole, first passing towards his right the end that hangs on his left side, and drawing over it the other end which hangs upon his right. Then he confines the stole with the extremities of the cincture, which he allows to hang on each side under his arms, and not behind his back. In the meantime he says, *Redde mihi, Domine,* etc.

11. Lastly, he puts on the chasuble without kissing it, saying, *Domine, qui dixisti,* etc. He will take care to fit it around the neck and shoulders, and tie it in front with the strings. He may then fasten a clean white handkerchief to the cincture, but it should not be visible.

ARTICLE III.

On Leaving the Sacristy.

12. The priest being vested, puts on his cap. Then, taking with his left hand the chalice *per nodum,* he lays his right, flat on the burse, holding the chalice before his breast, neither too far nor too near himself, but in a natural position. He makes a low bow * to the cross or image in the Sacristy, and, preceded by the server, who carries the Missal, he proceeds to the altar with a grave and modest deportment, his mind and heart occupied with the great mystery he is going to celebrate.

13. It is a laudable custom for the priest to take holy water and make the sign of the cross going to the altar. (*S. R. C.,* 9th April, 1808.) Nevertheless the Rubric does not prescribe it.

14. If the priest passes before the tabernacle containing the Blessed Sacrament, he will make a genuflection†

---

*Rubricians distinguish three kinds of bows—the low, the moderate and the simple. A low bow is made by bending the head and the shoulders, so that the person making it could touch his knees with the extremities of his fingers. The moderate is made by sufficiently lowering the head, and somewhat bending the shoulders. The simple bow consists in simply bending the head, without perceptibly moving the shoulders.

† A simple genuflection is made by bending the right knee to the floor, as near as possible to the left foot.

without removing his cap. If he passes before the high altar, he makes a low bow to the cross. Should he pass before an altar where there is a relic of a saint whose feast is celebrated, or some other remarkable relic, he makes a low bow without taking his cap off. (*Rub. Miss.*) If it be a relic of the true cross, he will make a genuflection with his head covered. (*S. R. C.*, 7th May, 1766.)

15. If he should pass before the Blessed Sacrament exposed, or at the time of the elevation, or when Holy Communion is given, he will take off his cap, and kneel on both knees, being careful, in the last two named instances, not to rise until after the elevation, or before the priest giving Communion has returned to the altar, and placed the ciborium on the corporal. (*Rub. Miss.*) If, however, in the latter case, the communicants should be too numerous, a genuflection on both knees will be sufficient, without remaining until the end. (*S. R. C.*, 5th July, 1698.)

16. When, on these occasions, the priest takes off his cap, either he will give it to the server to hold until he is to put it on again, or he will hold it between his thumb and forefinger, with the opening of it towards himself, and with the last two fingers holding the burse, that it may not fall.

17. While the priest is going to or coming from the altar, he should salute no one except his Bishop or other great prelates, or some distinguished person, and then he should do so by a simple bow. He will do the same on meeting another priest clad in sacred vestments, going to or returning from saying Mass. If the two priests meet in a narrow passage, the one going to celebrate will give way to the one returning.

18. If, perchance, the priest should go to or return from the altar without the chalice (whenever he is to bow or make a genuflection), he should take off his cap.

Article IV.

On Approaching the Altar.

19. The priest, having reached the foot of the altar on which he is to celebrate, stops in the middle, takes off his cap, gives it to the server, and makes a low bow to the cross. If the Blessed Sacrament be in the tabernacle, he makes a genuflection on the floor, not on the step. (*Rub. Miss.*, Part ii, Tit. ii, n. 2.)

20. Then he ascends the steps, and, having arrived in front of the middle of the altar,* without making any bow, he places the chalice on the Gospel side. If the veil, being large, is turned over the burse, he will lower it immediately, with both hands. Then he takes the burse, brings it to the middle of the altar, holds it with his left hand, and with his right he takes the corporal from it, which he lays on the altar; after which, with his right hand, he will place the burse at the Gospel side, against the *gradus*, so that the aperture of it be towards the tabernacle, unless some figure be marked on it, requiring another position. His left hand he will keep on the altar.†

21. Then with both hands he will spread out entirely the corporal in the middle of the altar, sufficiently, but not too near the edge, that neither the maniple nor the chasuble may disturb it.‡

22. Having spread the corporal, with his left hand he will take the chalice *per nodum*, and, putting his right on the chalice covered with the veil, he will place it in the middle of the corporal at such a distance that he may

---

* Some Rubricists direct that the priest, upon arriving at the altar, should make a bow to the cross. Nevertheless, neither the Rubrics of the Missal, nor any decree of the Sacred Congregation, makes such a prescription.

† As a general rule, when only one hand is employed, the other is kept on the altar; before the consecration and after communion, off the corporal; from the consecration to the communion, on the corporal.

‡ If there be an altar stone set in the table of the altar, the priest should be careful to find out its dimensions.

afterwards conveniently kiss the altar* without touching the chalice. He will be careful to extend the lower extremities of the veil, that the chalice may not be seen. (*S. R. C.*, 12th Jan., 1669.) After this, without making any bow, having his hands joined, he goes to the Epistle side,† opens the Missal where the Mass of the day is to be found (*Rub. Miss.*, n. 4), and then returns with his hands joined to the centre of the altar, where, having bowed moderately to the cross, he moves a little towards the Gospel side, in order to avoid turning his back to the cross, and descends to the foot of the altar, still keeping his hands joined. (*Rub. Miss.*)

Article V.

From the Commencement of the Mass to the Introit.

23. Having arrived in front of the last step, the priest turns on his right to the altar, and makes a low bow to the cross, or, if the Blessed Sacrament is in the tabernacle, he makes a genuflection on the last step, without making any other bow. Then standing modestly erect, he will commence Mass, by making on himself the sign of the cross (*Rub. Miss.*), pronouncing the words distinctly, and sufficiently loud to be heard by the faithful near the altar.

---

* Some writers on Rubrics are of opinion that the front part of the corporal should be laid over the foot of the chalice, giving as a reason, that there might remain on the corporal some consecrated particles; but the Rubrics of the Missal, Part 2, Art. 2, speaking of the corporal, says, *quod extendit super altare*. The general practice in Rome and Italy is to spread it entirely. The Church supposes that every priest will follow exactly the Rubrics prescribed, and that, consequently, no consecrated particles will be left on the corporal.

† To join the hands, the palm and the fingers extended, of both hands, should be brought together, the thumb of the right to be crossed over the thumb of the left, except from the consecration till after the ablution. The hands, thus joined, should not be kept either too near or too far from the breast, nor too much turned towards the face, nor towards the floor, but naturally directed upwards. The elbows should recline gently towards the sides.

24. Having signed himself,* he says, in the same tone of voice, the antiphon, *Introibo*, and the psalm, *Judica me Deus.* While he says the *Gloria Patri*, he inclines his head, and stands erect at the *Sicut erat.* At the *Adjutorium nostrum*, etc., he makes the sign of the cross.

25. At the *Confiteor*, he inclines profoundly, still keeping his hands joined. At the words, *Vobis fratres* and *Vos fratres*, he does not turn towards the server, this being only done at Solemn Mass. In saying *mea culpa*, he strikes gently and unaffectedly his breast with the extremities of the fingers of his right hand, while he holds his left extended below his breast. (*Rub. Miss.*)

After the *Mea maxima culpa*, he rejoins his hands, and remains inclined until (the server having said *Misereatur tui*, etc.) he answers, *Amen*, upon which he resumes his former attitude.

26. The server, having terminated the *Confiteor*, the priest says, *Misereatur vestri*, etc.; and while he says *Indulgentiam*, etc., he makes the sign of the cross. (*Rub. Miss.*) Then, inclining moderately, he says, *Deus tu conversus*, etc., and remains in that attitude till *Oremus* inclusively, which he says in the same tone of voice, extending his hands† and immediately rejoining them, and standing erect, he ascends the steps slowly, saying at the same time, in a low voice, *Aufer a nobis.*‡

27. Having arrived in front of the altar, he inclines moderately, puts his hands joined on the edge of the altar, so that the little fingers, joined and extended, touch the front of it, and the other fingers, being also

---

* He makes the sign of the cross by putting his left hand extended under his breast, then he raises his right to his forehead, and, touching it with the extremity of his fingers, he says, *In nomine Patris;* then, with the same hand, touching his breast, says, *Et Filii;* touching his left and right shoulders, *Et Spiritus Sancti;* and again joining his hands, he says, *Amen.*

† In extending the hands, the priest should not allow them to pass the width of his body.

‡ The Missal (with many Rubricists) does not prescribe any elevation of the hands in this case. The ceremonial of Bishops, however, enjoins it, perhaps only for Bishops; nevertheless, it would seem that priests could also do so.

joined and extended, rest on the top. (In this manner the hands are to be placed, whenever the Rubric prescribes them to be joined upon the altar.) In this position he says, *Oramus te*, and at the words, *Quorum reliquiæ hic sunt*, he extends his hands upon the altar, on either side of the corporal, and kisses the altar.* After which, standing erect, he joins his hands and turns towards the Epistle side, to which place he goes to commence the Introit, without making any bow to the cross.

Article VI.

From the Introit to the Epistle.

28. Having arrived opposite to the Missal, he commences the *Introit* aloud, making on himself the sign of the cross, and then, having joined his hands, he continues in the same tone of voice;† as he says *Gloria Patri*, etc., he makes a simple bow to the cross, turning himself a little towards it, without, however, moving his feet.

Should the holy name of *Jesus* occur during the Introit, he bows to the cross. If the name of *Mary* is mentioned, or the Saint whose feast is celebrated on that day, he bows towards the book. After the *Sicut erat*, he repeats the Introit, but does not make the sign of the cross.

29. At the end of the *Introit*, he returns to the middle, having his hands joined; and, facing the chalice, he says alternately with the server, the *Kyrie*. (*Rub. Miss.*)‡

---

* It is to be remarked, that whenever the priest kisses the altar he does so in the middle, not on one side nor on the edge of it; and that to do this properly he should neither be too near nor too far from the altar, lest he be awkward or affected. Neither is it sufficient in these cases to put the fingers on the altar, and it is too much to place the wrists there; yet it is required to lay the hands on the altar-cloth.

† Sufficiently loud so as to be heard by the faithful who assist near the altar.

‡ Should there be no server the celebrant will recite all.

30. After the last *Kyrie*, if there are no Prophecies to be read, and the *Gloria* is to be said, he will disjoin his hands, and raise them as high as his shoulders, and without raising his eyes, he says, *Gloria in excelsis*, etc., and in the same tone of voice, in saying *Deo*, he joins his hands again, making a simple bow to the cross, and remains in that position till the end of the *Gloria*. At the words, *Adoramus te, Gratias agimus tibi, Jesu Christe, Suscipe deprecationem nostram, Jesu Christe*, he makes a simple bow to the cross. Whilst he says *Cum Sancto Spiritu*, etc., he makes the sign of the cross on himself, and having said *Amen*,* he kisses the altar in the usual way, joining his hands afterwards.

31. If there are Prophecies to be read, as is the case on the Ember days, the priest, after the *Kyrie* (without making any bow), returns to the Missal, and says *Oremus*, etc. He reads the Prophecies in the same tone of voice, having both his hands either on the Missal or on the stand. The Prophecies being concluded, he returns to the middle of the altar to say the *Gloria*.

32. After having kissed the altar, the priest standing erect, turns on his right, facing the people, and extending his hands and rejoining them again, he says *Dominus vobiscum*.† (*Rub. Miss.*)

33. Then he returns towards the Missal as before, extends his hands, and rejoining them he says *Oremus*, at the same time making a simple bow towards the cross; and again extending his hands not higher than, nor beyond his shoulders, as has been already said, he says the prayers.‡

---

* The priest is not to join his hands after making the sign of the cross after the Gloria, Credo and Benedictus qui venit, S. C. R., in una Marsorum, 12th Nov. 1831 (4520).

† Whenever the priest says *Dominus vobiscum*, he does not look at the people, nor does he raise or lower the hands, and in extending them, he does not bring them beyond the limits of his body, but simply opens them so that the palm and fingers of one hand face the other, and rejoins them again. Neither does he bend the head towards the people, nor does he rest his back against the altar.

‡ The same thing is to be done whenever *Oremus* is to be said, unless something else is prescribed. Also, in pronouncing that word, care should be taken not to prolong the letter O, nor should it be said in any way affectedly.

84. At the conclusion of the prayer or prayers, when *Per Dominum nostrum* is to be said, the priest joins his hands and bows simply to the cross, while saying *Jesum Christum;* he remains erect, with hands joined, till the end of the conclusion of the prayer. If, however, the prayer concludes with the words, *Qui vivis et regnas,* or, *Qui tecum vivit et regnat,* without making any bow, he joins his hands while saying, *in unitate Spiritus Sancti.* (*Rub. Miss.*)

35. When there is more than one prayer, he says *Oremus* only at the commencement of the first and of the second; so, also, the conclusion is said at the end of the first prayer and of the last.

If, during the prayers, he pronounces the holy name of *Jesus,* or of *Mary,* or the Saint whose feast is celebrated that day, or the name of the Pope, he makes a simple bow, in the first case to the cross, in the others towards the Missal.*

Article VII.

From the Epistle to the Offertory.

36. At the end of the prayer or prayers, the priest reads the Epistle in the same tone of voice, having his hands on the book or book-stand, in such a manner, however, that he touches the Missal. (*Rub. Miss.*) If, in reading the Epistle, he happens to pronounce the holy name of *Jesus,* he will bow as was said before. If he is to make a genuflection, as is the case when he says, *In nomine Jesu genuflectatur,* etc., or, *Adjuva nos Deus,* he bends only the right knee to the floor, placing his hands meanwhile on the altar. The last words of the Epistle he may say in a lower tone, as an indication to the server that he is to answer, *Deo Gratias,* but he should not turn his head towards him. After which, he reads, in the former tone of voice, the Gradual, the Tract, or the Sequentia, if these are to be read.

---

* In the prayer, *A cunctis,* the Patron Saint to be named is that of the place in which he celebrates.

37. This done, he goes, with his hands joined, to the middle of the altar, where, having raised his eyes to the cross, he inclines profoundly, keeping his hands joined between his breast and the altar, and in that attitude he says, *Munda cor meum.* Then, *Jube, Domine,* etc. (*Rub Miss.*)

38. Should there be no server, the priest will move the Missal to the Gospel side, so that the opening of it be somewhat towards the middle of the altar. In moving the book, he makes a simple bow to the cross, and having adjusted it in its place, he returns to the middle to say the prayer above named. (*Rub. Miss.*)

39. The prayer being over, standing erect, and, having his hands joined, he goes to the book, his face turned partially towards the Gospel side, and in the same loud tone of voice he says, *Dominus vobiscum.* In saying *Sequentia,* or *Initium Sancti Evangelii,* he disjoins his hands, and, with the thumb of his right, the fingers extended, he makes a cross on the commencement of the Gospel he is to read, at the same time keeping his left hand extended on the Missal. (*S. R. C.,* 17th Sept., 1816.) Then he forms a cross with the same thumb on his forehead, his lips, and his breast, holding his left hand on his breast. (*Rub. Miss.,* n. 2.)

40. After this, he joins his hands, and continues to read the Gospel in the same tone of voice. Should the holy name of *Jesus,* or any other name at which (according to what has been said before) he is to bow, be mentioned, he does so towards the book. So, also, should he be required to make a genuflection, it is to be made towards the book, his hands supported on the altar. (*Rub., ib.*) The Gospel being read, he raises the Missal with both hands, at the same time bending a little over it, and kisses the commencement of the same Gospel, saying, in a low voice, *Per Evangelica dicta,* etc.

41. When he is to read the *Passion,* he makes a simple bow to the cross, as he goes from the Epistle side to the Gospel; he reads the Passion in the same attitude as at the Gospel, without, however, making any sign of the cross. At the words, *Emisit Spiritum,* he kneels on

both knees, his hand supported upon the altar, and again joins his hands, in which position he meditates for a few moments on the passion of our Lord. Then, resting his hands on the altar, he rises, rejoins the hands, and continues to read until where he is to say the *Munda cor meum*, which he says in the middle of the altar, in the same attitude prescribed above. After the *Munda cor meum*, he returns to the book, his hands being joined, and finishes reading the Passion; at the end of which (except on Good Friday) he kisses the Missal as above, saying, *Per Evangelica dicta*, etc.

42. Having kissed the Missal, he replaces it on the stand, and, with both hands, he places it nearer to the corporal, so that he may conveniently read in it thereafter, and having rejoined his hands, he returns to the middle.

43. There (if the *Credo* is to be said) he extends his hands, raises them (not higher than his shoulders) at the word *Credo*, and joins them again at the words, *In unum Deum*, making at the same time a simple bow to the cross. In this position he continues the *Credo* to the end, in the same tone of voice, except that at the words, *Et Incarnatus est*, having placed his hands upon the altar, on either side of the corporal, he makes a genuflection on his right knee only (*S. R. C.*, 22d August, 1818), in such a manner that, by commencing it at the *Et Incarnatus*, he touches the floor with his knee at the words *Et Homo factus est;* as he makes the genuflection, he does not bend his head. He makes a bow at *Jesum Christum, Simul adoratur;* whilst he says *Et vitam*, etc., he makes on himself the sign of the cross, as at the end of the *Gloria*.

Article VIII.

From the Offertory to the Canon.

44. After the *Credo*, if it has been said, or after having arranged the Missal, the priest kisses the altar; and, turning towards the people, he says, *Dominus vobiscum*. He turns again to the altar, and, with the usual moving

of the hands and bowing of the head, he says, *Oremus*, and, keeping his hands joined, he reads the Offertory. (*Rub. Miss.*)

45. At the end of the Offertory, he removes the veil from the chalice with both hands, folds it, and places it at the right hand, near the corporal (on which he may afterwards place the pall, if he chooses), or, without folding it, he gives it to the server. Then, having placed his left hand on the altar, near the corporal, he takes the chalice *per nodum* with his right, and places it outside of the corporal.* Then, with the same hand, he removes the pall from the paten, and places it on the folded veil, or on the corporal against the altar-card.† Then, taking the paten, upon which the large particle is, between the thumb and the forefinger of his right hand, he brings it opposite to him, over and in the middle of the corporal, at the height of his breast, and there he takes it also with the thumb and forefinger of his left hand, in such a manner that the paten is supported by the named four fingers at equal distances from each other, and that the other fingers are extended and joined underneath it; after this, he raises his eyes, immediately lowering them on the large particle, and says, *Suscipe, Sancte Pater*, etc. (*Rub. Miss.*)

46. The prayer being entirely finished, still holding the paten in the same manner, but nearer to the corporal, he forms a cross in straight lines of about eight inches in length; then bending the paten towards the corporal, he causes the large particle to slide on the middle of the front part of the corporal. Then he puts the paten somewhat under the corporal at the right, placing at the same time his left hand on the altar.‡ (*Rub. Miss.*)

---

* If the chalice is not purified, he puts the pall first, where the chalice is to be placed.

† It is always with the right hand that the priest uncovers and covers the chalice.

‡ It is not permitted to make *any marks* with the paten, or anything else, on the large bread during Mass.

If there are small particles to consecrate, either in a ciborium* or on the corporal, he directs his intention to the offering of them, having previously opened the ciborium, and drawn it nearer towards the middle. After saying *Suscipe*, etc., he covers it, and places it in its former position, having previously put the paten under the corporal. If he should be presented with any small particles after coming to the altar, he puts them on the corporal, a little higher up than the large particle, at the Gospel side.

47. Next, having joined his hands, he goes to the Epistle side. Thence he takes the chalice *per nodum* with the left hand, brings it before him, and, with the fingers of his right hand, he puts a portion of the purificator in the cup of the chalice, and purifies it, while he holds it with his left hand.

48. Then, holding the chalice, with his left hand on the altar, he places the purificator between the cup and the thumb of his left hand, that it may serve to catch any drops, which might fall from the cruets.

Then, with his right hand, he receives the cruet with wine from the server, and pours a sufficient quantity of it in the Chalice.† Then, having returned the cruet to the server, he forms with the same hand, extended, a cross over the cruet containing water, saying, *Deus qui humanæ substantiæ*. He takes the same cruet, and pours a little water in the chalice,‡ saying at the same time, *Da nobis per hujus aquæ et vini mysterium* (*Rub. Miss.*, n. 4), he returns the cruet to the server, continuing the prayer, taking care to make a simple bow towards the cross, at the holy name of *Jesus*. It is advisable to

---

* According to *Gavantus, De Mensuris*, the ciborium should have a veil, or cover made out of rich materials, either of silk or silver, or even gold cloth, through respect for the Blessed Sacrament.

† It is generally supposed, that the quantity of the wine should cover the bottom of the chalice, or such quantity that the priest, in consuming it, may be able, without effort, to take it all at one draught without lowering the hand (*uno haustu*).

‡ The quantity of water poured in the chalice should be very small, three or four drops of it are sufficient. (See *Pope Eugenius IV*, in *Decreto pro Armenis*.)

absorb with the purificator the drops within the chalice, that might have gathered around the cup. (*S. R. C.*, 7th Sept., 1816.)

49. This done, he places the chalice sufficiently near the corporal with his left hand, goes to the middle of the altar, and lays the purificator, folded in two, on that part of the paten that remains outside of the corporal. Then, having placed his left hand on the altar, he takes with his right the chalice *per nodum*, carries it over the corporal, and places his left hand under the foot of it; then, holding it raised, so that the top of it may not be higher than his eyes, he says, *Offerimus tibi, Domine*, etc., looking at the cross the whole time of the offering. (*Rub., ib.*)

50. After the *Offerimus*, the priest forms with the chalice a cross over the corporal, without passing over the particle. Then, having placed the chalice in the middle of the corporal, behind the particle, he covers it with the pall. (*Rub., ib.*)

51. Then he inclines moderately, and places his joined hands on the edge of the altar, and says, *In Spiritu humilitatis*, etc. (*Rub., ib.*) Having finished the prayer, standing erect, with his eyes raised to the cross, he extends his hands, and, having raised them as high as his eyes, he joins them again, in the meantime saying, *Veni Sanctificator*, etc. Then he forms a cross with his right hand over the chalice and the particle together, saying, *Et bene ✠ dic hoc sacrificium tuo Sancto nomini preparatum*,* while he holds his left hand on the altar near the corporal.

52. After this, he joins his hands again, and goes to the Epistle side, where, a little beyond the altar, he

---

* When the priest is to make a cross over the offerings, the hands are first joined before his breast, and, in forming the cross, the left hand is placed on the altar, and the right should be straight, and the fingers united, according to the decree of the S. R. C., 24th July, 1683. Also, when the cross is made on the chalice and Host conjointly, the first line is commenced from the middle of the pall, and, without lowering the hand, it is drawn over the Host; and the second, or the transversal line, is drawn between the Host and the chalice, from one side of the pall to the other, or not any longer than the first line.

washes the extremities of the thumbs and forefingers of his hands, at the same time saying, *Lavabo*, etc. Having washed his fingers, he turns towards the altar, meanwhile drying them, and concludes the Psalm.

53. At the *Gloria Patri* he bows to the cross, and, may conclude it, going to the middle of the altar.

54. Having reached the middle of the altar, with his hands joined, he raises his eyes to the cross, and, having lowered them immediately, he puts his hands, joined, on the edge of the altar, inclines moderately, and says, *Suscipe, Sancta Trinitas;* at the end of which, extending his hands on the altar, he kisses it.

55. Then, standing erect, and rejoining his hands, he turns to the people, and, extending and joining the hands, as at the *Dominus vobiscum,* with a voice a little louder, he says, *Orate, Fratres;* and, having rejoined his hands, he turns to the altar by the Gospel side, making a complete circle, and saying, at the same time, in a low voice, *ut meum ac vestrum sacrificium,* etc. (*Rub., ib.*) The server having answered *Suscipiat,* etc., the priest answers, to himself, *Amen.*

56. Here he extends his hands, as at the prayers, and, without saying *Oremus,* he reads the *Secrets* in a low voice. The number of these should equal that of the prayers said before the Epistle. If there is only one of them, he does not read the conclusion, but stops after having said *Spiritus Sancti, Deus.* If there are more than one, he will say the conclusion of the first, saying, also, *Amen;* and at the conclusion of the last *Secret,* he stops at the above-named words, which are considered as the commencement of the Preface. Then he turns the pages of the Missal for the Preface with his left hand, whilst his right is laid on the altar, off the corporal, unless, through necessity, he should be obliged to use both hands to find the Preface.

57. Having found the place for the Preface, he lays both hands on the altar, and says, with a loud voice, *Per omnia sæcula sæculorum, Dominus vobiscum,* etc. At the *Sursum corda,* he raises his extended hands as high as his breast, so that both palms face each other.

At the *Gratias agamus*, he rejoins his hands without raising them any higher. At *Deo nostro*, he looks at the cross and bows. (*Rub., ib.*)

58. When he commences *Vere dignum et justum est*, he opens his hands again, and holds them as he did during the prayers until he reaches the *Sanctus*, etc., whereupon he rejoins his hands, inclines moderately, and says, in a moderate voice, *Sanctus, Sanctus*, etc., without, however, placing his hands upon the altar. At the words, *Benedictus*, etc., he stands erect, and makes on himself the sign of the cross in the usual manner.

Article IX.

From the Canon to the Consecration.

59. After the sign of the cross, the priest raises his hands as high as the shoulders, and his eyes to the cross, lowering them immediately. Then, joining his hands, places them on the edge of the altar, and inclines profoundly, whilst he says, *Te igitur*, in a low voice. (*Rub. Miss.*) At the words, *Ac petimus*, he extends his hands upon the altar, and kisses it. Then, standing erect, and with joined hands, at the words, *Hæc dona*, etc., he makes three signs of the cross on the offerings conjointly, saying at the first, *hæc ✠ dona*, at the second, *hæc ✠ munera*, and at the third, *hæc ✠ sancta sacrificia illibata*; and, having extended his hands without joining them, he continues, *In primis quæ tibi offerimus*, etc. (*Rub. Miss.*) In pronouncing the name of the Pope, he makes a simple bow toward the Missal, but does not bow at the name of the Bishop in whose diocese he says Mass; or if the See is vacant, he does not say *Papa nostro* nor *Antistite nostro*.* (*Gav.*, p. 2, Tit. viii, n. 2.)

---

* The Bishop named is that of the diocese in which the priest celebrates, although he may not be his Bishop. In case he does not know the name, it is sufficient to form his intention to pray for him. In Rome, the words *Et antistite nostro* are omitted, as the Pope is the Bishop of Rome.

60. In saying *Memento, Domine*, he raises his hands only as high as his breast or face, and joins them slowly, and having somewhat bent his head (it is not requisite to look at the large particle, it not being consecrated), he prays in silence for a short time, making his *Memento* for the living. Then, having extended his hands, he continues to read, in a low voice, *Et omnium circumstantium*, etc., till *muniamur auxilio*. (*Rub. Miss.*)

61. During *Communicantes*, he makes a simple bow towards the book, at the name of the Blessed Virgin, and towards the cross, at that of *Jesus;* he also bows towards the book at the name of the Saint whose Mass he says, or of whom he makes a commemoration. (*Rub. Miss.*)

62. At the conclusion, *Per eundem Dominum*, etc., he joins his hands without bowing. Then, on commencing *Hanc igitur*, etc., he extends his two hands over the particle and chalice together, without touching the pall, the thumbs still crossing each other above the hands, and the forefingers being united. (*S. R. C.*, 4th Aug., 1663.) At the conclusion of the prayer, he joins his hands, closing them without separating them previously, and draws them to himself before his breast, at the same time continuing to read, *Quam oblationem*, etc., till the words *Benedictam*, etc. (*Rub. Miss.*)

63. Then, having placed his left hand on the altar, near the corporal, he makes three crosses on the offerings, in the same manner spoken of in n. 56. The first, as he says *Bene✠dictam*, the second at *Ad scri✠ptam*, and the third (which is to be made slowly) during the words, *ra✠tam, rationabilem, acceptabilemque facere digneris;* and as he continues, he makes another cross on the large particle at the words, *ut nobis Cor✠pus*, and another on the chalice whilst saying *et San✠guis;* and immediately after, raising and joining his hands before his breast, he continues, *fiat dilectissimi Filii tui Domini nostri Jesu Christi*, bowing at the same time that he pronounces the sacred name. (*Rub. Miss.*)

64. If there are particles to be consecrated, he uncovers the *Ciborium*, and moves it a little in advance of the

chalice; should they be upon the corporal, and not in a Ciborium, he does not move them.

65. After this (if need be, says the Missal) the priest purifies his fingers, which is done by rubbing the thumbs and the forefingers on the front of the corporal, while he says, *Qui pridie quam pateretur*. He takes the large particle between the thumb and the forefinger of his right hand (*Rub. Miss.*), pressing it a little for that purpose with the forefinger of his left (which he should do, Baldeschi says, whenever he is to take it up), and immediately after, taking it on the other side with the thumb and forefinger of his left, extends and joins the other fingers together; and, standing erect, holding the large particle somewhat raised above the corporal, he says in the meantime, *accepit panem in sanctas ac venerabiles manus suas* (*Rub. Miss*).

66. In saying, *Et elevatis oculis in cœlum*, he raises his eyes to the cross, and lowers them immediately. At *Tibi gratias agens* he bows, and at *bene✠dixit* he makes with his right hand a cross on the large particle; while he still holds it with his left, he takes it again with the right hand, continuing, *fregit, deditque discipulis suis*, etc. (*Rub. Miss.*)

67. In this position of the hands, having ended the said words, not before, he leans with his elbows on the edge of the altar, in an unaffected manner, bends his head, and distinctly and reverently, without any twisting of the body or of the mouth, without at all raising his voice, or breathing violently on the particles, he pronounces the words of consecration, saying, *Hoc est enim Corpus meum*. (*Rub. Miss.*)

68. After pronouncing these words, continuing to hold the Sacred Host in the same manner, he stands erect, drawing his hands a little more towards the edge of the altar, bends his right knee to the floor and adores the Blessed Sacrament in silence. (*Rub. Miss.*) After the genuflection, following the Sacred Host with his eyes, he raises It respectfully in a perpendicular line over the corporal, a little higher than his head, that the people may adore It; then, without stopping, he lowers It slowly towards the

corporal, on which he places It, with his right hand, in Its former position;* and, having placed his hands on the altar, the thumbs and forefingers being united, he makes another genuflection.

69. After rising, he uncovers the chalice, taking the pall with the fore and middle fingers of his right hand (in this manner he covers and uncovers the chalice hereafter), and having purified his fingers by rubbing them over the cup of the chalice, he says, *Simili modo postquam cœnatum est;* then, with both hands taking the chalice between the cup and the *nodum*, he raises it a little over the corporal, and replaces it immediately, saying, in the meantime, *accipiens et hunc præclarum calicem;* and without taking his hands off, he will make a bow to the consecrated Host, at the words, *Tibi gratias agens.* In saying, *bene✠dixit*, he makes a cross over the chalice with his right hand, still holding it with his left, and immediately holding it with both hands, he continues, *deditque discipulis suis.* (*Rub. Miss.*)

70. Having finished saying these words, he leans his elbows on the edge of the altar, and holding the chalice *per nodum* with his right hand, and supporting it at the foot with the last three fingers of his left, without bending it (as some do) having his head inclined, he devoutly pronounces the words of consecration, *Hic est enim calix*, etc. (*Rub. Miss.*)

71. After the words of consecration, he places the chalice upon the altar, stands erect, and, in a low tone of voice, says, *Hæc quotiescumque feceritis*, etc., then he makes a genuflection, his hands being placed on the altar as at the consecration of the Host, and adores the Precious Blood. Standing erect, he takes the chalice with his right hand *per nodum*, and, with his left at the

---

*From this moment until after the ablution, the thumb and the forefinger of each hand are kept united, and are not separated, unless to touch the consecrated Host; consequently, in turning the pages of the Missal, he does so with the fore and middle fingers. Neither are the hands placed out of, but on the corporal (as was said before), except when they rest against the edge of the altar as before, with the exception that the thumbs and forefingers continue to be united together.

foot, and following it with his eyes, he raises it above his head, that the people may see it; then he puts it back on the corporal, in its former position, covers it with the pall, holding the foot meanwhile with his left hand, and makes a genuflection (*Rub. Miss.*), paying attention in this, as in any other case, that the maniple may not touch the Host.

Article X.

From the Canon after the Consecration to the Pater Noster.

72. Standing erect, and, having extended his hands as before, he says, in a low voice, *Unde et memores*, etc. (*Rub. Miss.*), to the words *de tuis donis ac datis*, when he joins his hands. Then, having placed his left hand on the corporal, at the Gospel side, he makes three signs of the cross over the chalice and Host conjointly, saying, *Hostiam* ✠ *puram, Hostiam* ✠ *sanctam, Hostiam* ✠ *immaculatam;* then he makes one on the Host only, saying *Panem* ✠ *sanctum vitæ æternæ*, and one on the chalice alone, saying, *et Calicem* ✠ *salutis perpetuæ;* after which, he extends his hands, and in that position he continues the Canon, in the same low tone of voice, saying, *Supra quæ propitio*, etc.

73. After the words, *immaculatam hostiam*, he inclines profoundly, and puts his hands joined on the edge of the altar, and in that attitude he says, *Supplices te rogamus* (*S. R. C.*, 7th Sept., 1816) till *ut quotquot;* and in saying, *ex hac altaris participatione*, having extended his hands on the corporal, he kisses the altar in the middle, being careful not to touch the Host. (*Rub., ib.*) Then, standing erect, and joining his hands at the words *sacrosanctum Filii tui*, he places his left hand on the corporal, making with the other a cross on the Host at the word, *Cor*✠*pus*, and another immediately after, on the chalice alone, at the words, *San*✠*guinem sumpserimus;* then, having placed his left hand under his breast, so that the thumb and forefinger do not touch the chasuble, he makes with his right hand a sign of the cross on himself, saying *omni benedictione cœlesti, et gratia repleamur;*

and immediately after, he joins his hands before his breast, while saying, *Per eundem Christum Dominum,* etc. (*Rub. Miss.*)

74. In saying, *Memento, Domine,* etc., he extends and closes his hands slowly, so that they be joined at the *in somno pacis.* Then, thus joined, he raises them as high as his chin, without touching it, and somewhat lowers his head, and, his eyes being fixed on the Blessed Sacrament, he makes the *Memento* of the dead for whom he desires to pray.

75. After the *Memento,* he raises his head; and, having extended his hands as before, he continues, *Ipsis Domine,* etc. At *Per eundem Christum,* he again joins his hands; and, in this particular case, although the holy *Name* is not mentioned, he makes a simple bow. (*Rub. Miss.*)

76. Then, having raised his head, and placed his left hand on the corporal, with the last three fingers of his right he strikes his breast, saying, in a moderate voice, *Nobis quoque peccatoribus;** then extending his hands, he continues in the low tone *famulis tuis.* (*Rub. Miss.*) Should the name of the Saint, whose feast he celebrates, occur in this prayer, he will bow on reading it.†

77. At *Per Christum Dominum nostrum* he joins his hands as usual, without saying *Amen;* continuing with joined hands, *Per quem,* etc., to *creas,* after which he places his left hand on the corporal, and with his right he forms three crosses on the chalice and Host conjointly; the first at *sancti✠ficas,* the second at *vivi✠ficas,* and the third at *bene✠dicis et præstas nobis.*

78. Then holding the foot of the chalice with his left hand, he uncovers it with his right, and having placed his hands on the corporal, he makes a genuflection. Standing erect, he takes the Host at the lower part, with the thumb and forefinger of his right hand, and having

---

* In this case, as well as at the *Agnus Dei,* and *Domine non sum dignus,* when again he is to strike his breast, he should take care that the thumb and the forefinger shall neither separate, nor touch the chasuble. (*Durandus,* Lib. IV, cap. 46.)

† The Sac. Cong. Rit. has decided the St. John, here mentioned, is St. John, the Baptist. (Mar. 27, 1824.)

brought It over the chalice, he forms with the Host, within the cup, and without touching It, three crosses, holding, at the same time, with his left hand the chalice *per nodum*, saying, *Per ip✠sum, et cum ip✠so, et in ip✠so;* and immediately bringing the Sacred Host out of the chalice, but still with his left holding the chalice, he makes two more crosses at the words, *Est tibi Deo Patri ✠omnipotenti, in unitate Spiritus✠Sancti.* (These crosses are formed between the chalice and himself.) Then bringing the Host over the chalice, and leaning the thumb and the forefinger on the edge of the cup, he raises the chalice a little with his left hand, at the same time saying, *Omnis honor et gloria.* Then having replaced the chalice and the Host in their respective places, he lightly rubs his fingers over the chalice, which he covers immediately after with the pall, at the same time holding the chalice with his left hand. After which having placed his hands extended on the corporal, he makes a genuflection.

ARTICLE XI.

From the Pater Noster to the Communion.

79. The priest having risen, with his hands still on the corporal, says aloud, *Per omnia sæcula sæculorum.* The server having answered *Amen*, the priest joins his hands as usual, and says, *Oremus*, at the same time bending his head somewhat to the Blessed Sacrament. Having raised his head, he continues, with hands joined, the prayer till *Pater Noster*, when, having extended his hands before his breast, he continues it to the end, at the same time keeping his eyes fixed on the Blessed Sacrament. (*Rub. Miss.*)

80. The server having answered *Sed libera nos a malo*, the priest says in a low tone, *Amen.* Then he takes the purificator in his right hand, and cleans or wipes the paten drawn from under the corporal; afterwards he places the purificator at some distance from the corporal at the Epistle side. During this action his left hand is held on the corporal. Then, having taken the paten

between the fore and middle fingers, he holds it upright, its edge resting near the corporal, and the concave part towards the Sacred Host, at the same time saying, *Libera nos*, etc. (*Rub Miss.*) In pronouncing *Mariæ* he bows to the book.

81. In saying, *Petro et Paulo*, he places his left hand under his breast, and with his right, holding the paten, he makes with it the sign of the cross on himself, at the same time that he says, *Da propitius pacem in diebus nostris*. After the sign of the cross he kisses the paten, not in the middle, but on the border (*S. R. C.*, 24th July, 1683), where it is not to touch the Sacred Host. Then, as he continues, saying, *ut ope misericordiæ tuæ*, he places the paten under the Host, using to that effect the forefinger of the left hand. (*Rub., ib.*) Then, in the usual manner, he uncovers the chalice, and makes a genuflection. Having risen, he takes the Host with the thumb and forefinger of his right hand, raises It over the chalice, and with the help of the thumb and forefinger of his left hand carefully and reverently breaks It in the middle, commencing from the upper part, and saying in the meantime, *Per eundem Dominum Nostrum Jesum Christum Filium tuum.** Having divided the Host, he places the portion remaining in his right hand on the paten, still holding the other half over the chalice; then with the thumb and forefinger of his right hand, he breaks a small piece from the lower part of the second half, at the same time saying, *Qui tecum vivit et regnat;* and holding the small piece over the chalice, he places the portion that is in his left hand on the paten, near the other half, saying. *In unitate Spiritus Sancti Deus.* Then, with his left hand taking the chalice *per nodum*, he says in a loud voice, *Per omnia sæcula sæculorum. Amen* being answered, he makes three crosses within the cup of the chalice with the small piece of the Host,

---

* To break It properly, It should be gently bent in and out two or three times, commencing at the top, then in the middle, and lastly at the end; and returning to the middle, bent again carefully, till It separates. In this manner there is less danger of causing small particles to break off.

saying, *Pax ✠ Domini sit ✠ semper vobis✠cum.* In forming these crosses he should not allow the Particle to touch the chalice. The server having answered, *Et cum spiritu tuo,* the priest lets the Particle fall into the chalice, at the same time saying in a low voice, *Hæc commixtio,* etc. Then having purified his fingers as usual, within the cup of the chalice, he covers it, holding his left hand on the foot of the chalice, after which he makes a genuflection.

82. Having risen, he inclines moderately before the Blessed Sacrament, his hands being joined between his breast and the altar; and, in a loud voice, he says, *Agnus Dei qui tollis peccata mundi;* and, having placed his left hand on the corporal, he strikes his breast with the three fingers of his right hand that have not touched the Sacred Host, at the same time saying, *miserere nobis.* In the same manner (without joining the hands), he strikes his breast again at the second *miserere nobis,* and at the *dona nobis pacem.* (*Rub. Miss.*) Then, having joined his hands, and placed them as usual on the edge of the altar, but not on the corporal, according to the decree of the Sacred Congregation (7th Sept., 1816), he says, in a low voice, the three prayers prescribed before Communion, his eyes being fixed at the same time on the Sacred Host. (*Rub. Miss.*)

83. Having said the prayers, the priest makes a genuflection, saying, as he rises, *Panem cœlestem accipiam, et nomen Domini invocabo.* (*Rub. Miss.*) Then, with his right hand he takes both parts of the Host at the upper ends, from the paten, and places them between the forefinger and the thumb of his left hand, in such a manner that the Host preserves its round appearance as much as possible. After this, he takes the paten between the index and middle finger of the left hand, and holds it between himself and the chalice, a little above the corporal, and under the Host, and being somewhat inclined towards the middle of the altar, without resting the left elbow on it, he says three times, in a moderate voice, *Domine, non sum dignus,* etc., slightly striking his breast

with the last three fingers of his right hand as many times. Then he continues, in a low voice, *ut intres*, etc. (*Rub. Miss.*, n. 4.)*

84. Standing erect, he places one part of the Sacred Host on the other; then, with the thumb and forefinger of his right hand, having taken both parts of the Host, thus joined at the bottom, he forms a perpendicular cross, at the same time holding the paten under It. He does not raise the Host so high as to allow the people to see It, nor does he pass the limits of the paten in drawing the transverse line; while he forms the cross, he says, *Corpus Domini Nostri Jesu Christi* (inclining at the word *Jesu*) *custodiat animam meam in vitam æternam. Amen.* (*Rub., ib.*) After this, he inclines moderately, rests his elbows on the edge of the altar; and, thus inclined, and holding the paten under the Host, he reverently receives the Sacred Body.† Should the Host adhere to the palate, he must use his tongue, not his fingers to loosen It.

85. Having received the Sacred Host, the priest stands erect, lays the paten on the corporal near the edge of the altar, and joins his hands, which he raises toward his chin, without touching it, and, his head being a little inclined, he meditates for a few moments. (*Rub., ib.*)

86. After a short meditation, he lays the left hand on the foot of the chalice, and, with the right, takes the pall from the chalice, saying, in a low voice, *Quid retribuam Domino pro omnibus quæ retribuit mihi?* and makes a genuflection. Then, having taken the paten between the first and the second fingers of the right hand, and holding it inclined, he passes it gently several times from right to left over the corporal, to gather the

---

* To give himself time to pronounce these words, the priest may lay his right hand on the corporal, immediately after striking the breast, or he may move the hand slowly as he pronounces the words. (*Baldeschi.*)

† Rubricians differ in describing the method of communicating. It would be extremely difficult to reduce to practice what some of them prescribe on the subject. It is sufficient to say, that such an action is to be done with as much respect and reverence, and, at the same time, as unaffectedly, as possible.

fragments that might have fallen on it, for that purpose, raising, with his left hand, the extremity of the corporal. (*Rub., ib.*)

87. Having gathered the fragments, he brings the paten over the chalice, and, holding it there, sufficiently inclined, he takes it between the first and second fingers of his left hand, as near as he can to the place where he held it with his right hand; then, with the thumb and forefinger of his right, rubs the paten from top to bottom, so as to bring all the fragments into the chalice; then rubs the same thumb and forefinger together in the middle of the chalice-cup, in order to remove any particle that may have remained on them. (*Rub., ib.*) Here the priest places his left hand (still holding the paten) on the corporal, and with the three free fingers of his right, he takes the chalice under the *nodus*, saying, *Calicem salutaris*, etc., till *salvus ero*, inclusively. Then he raises the chalice until the top of it reaches as high as his forehead, and with it he forms a perpendicular cross, in the same manner as he did with the Sacred Host, saying, at the same time, *Sanguis Domini Nostri*, etc., bowing at the word *Jesu*. (*Rub., ib.*) He then raises the paten under his chin, and brings the chalice to his mouth to take the Precious Blood, which he does *uno vel duplici haustu*, together with the Particle previously placed in the chalice. It is well to remark, that it is more becoming to hold the chalice steady to the mouth than to move it off and replace it again while the priest consumes the Precious Blood.

88. Having received the Precious Blood, or after the communion of the people,* the priest having placed on

---

* Attention should be paid to renew frequently the Sacred Species preserved in the Ciborium. St. Charles Borromeo ordained that they should be renewed every eighth day. The Sacred Congregation (3d Sept., 1662) prescribed the same thing. "In renovatione quæ quolibet octavo die fieri debet de Augustissimo Sacramento," etc. Clement VIII (Const Sanctissimus, 31 Maii, 1595) says, that the Sacred Species should be renewed at least every fifteen days, and more frequently in damp places. "Hostiæ consecratæ post quindecim dies ad summum (quod in locis humidis, præsertim pluvioso aut hiemali tempore, frequentius fieri debet), una cum minutissimis fragmentorum particulis,

the corporal his left hand holding the paten, presents the chalice to the server, in order to receive wine for the purification, and at the same time he says, *Quod ore sumpsimus*, etc. Then he takes the wine, holding the paten under his chin, as he did in consuming the Precious Blood. If the Sacred Particle should adhere to the chalice, it may be brought near the mouth of the same, with the finger, or taken with the first purification. (*Rub., ib.*)*

89. After receiving the purification, he puts the chalice and the paten on the corporal, so that the chalice be in the middle, and the paten a little towards the Gospel side; then taking the chalice below the cup with the last three fingers of both hands, he puts the thumbs and forefingers, still joined, over the cup of the chalice, and in this manner he carries the chalice to the Epistle side, where, holding it a little raised above the altar, the server pours on the fingers wine and water, while the priest says, *Corpus tuum Domine*, etc. It is well to remark that the Rubric says, *abluit pollices et indices*, therefore the priest not only washes the extremities of the fingers, but the fingers, by rubbing them against each other, as the server pours wine and water on them. Then holding the chalice in the same manner, he carries it near the purificator, where he places it; and still keeping the thumb and forefinger of the left hand on the cup, he takes the purificator with his right, and places it on the fingers of his left, and as he goes to the middle of the altar he dries his forefingers with the purificator.

---

quæ in ciborio remanserunt, a sacerdote consumentur, et in ipsum ciborium, aut pyxidem ab illis fragmentis et particulis mundatam, novæ hostiæ consecratæ reponantur; nec unquam illæ recentes cum his vetustioribus misceantur." The same thing is to be observed regarding the Sacred Host which is kept for Benediction.

* From a letter of Pius V, 8th January, 1571, quoted by Benedict XIV (*de Sacrif. Miss.*, lib. 2, ch. 21), we gather that the quantity of wine poured in the chalice for the purification should at least be equal to that consecrated; also that the purification should be received at that part of the chalice where the Precious Blood was taken. Should, however, the wine for the purification happen to be less, it will suffice to move the chalice gently, so that it may touch the parts where the Blessed Sacrament reached.

90. Having reached the middle of the altar, he places the purificator between the thumb and the forefinger, so as to cover the fingers of the left hand, and with his right he takes the chalice *per nodum*, and takes the last ablution, at the same time holding the purificator under his chin. Then he puts the chalice in the middle of the corporal, wipes his lips gently with the purificator, and with the same in his right hand wipes the interior of the cup of the chalice, holding it by the *nodus* with his left.

91. Lastly, the chalice being dried, he places it at the Gospel side (but not on the corporal); he extends the purificator over the cup as before, and places on it the paten and the pall. Having folded the corporal with both hands, and taken the burse with his right hand, he puts the corporal in it, which he lays on the middle of the altar. Then he covers the chalice with the veil, on which he places the burse, and taking the chalice with both hands, he puts it in the middle of the altar, and adjusts the veil in front as at the commencement of Mass. (*Rub., ib.;* and *Sac. Con.*, 5th March, 1698.) Then he joins his hands and goes to the Epistle side, to which the server should have removed the Missal.*

Article XII.

From the Communion until the End of Mass.

92. Having arrived at the Epistle side, the priest, with his hands still joined, reads the Communion in a low voice; then he returns to the middle of the altar, kisses it, turns to the people and says in a loud voice, *Dominus vobiscum*. He rejoins his hands, returns to the Missal, and reads the prayer (or prayers) in the same manner and order in which he had previously read at the commencement of Mass.

---

* The Sacred Congregation, consulted by the Bishop of Puy: "An in Missis privatis, permitti possit ministro si fuerit sacerdos, vel Diaconus, vel Subdiaconus, ut præparet calicem, et ipsum extergat in fine post oblationes sicut in Missa solemni?" Answered: "Negative, et serventur Rubricæ." (7th Sept., 1816, no. 4526, ad 12.)

The above refers to private Masses of priests.

93. At the end of the last prayer (unless there is a proper Gospel to be read), the priest closes the book in such a manner that the leaves be turned towards the chalice.

94. Then he goes to the middle of the altar, kisses it, and turning towards the people, he says, *Dominus vobiscum ;* and having rejoined his hands, he says, *Ite Missa est*, or if the season or particular Mass requires it, he says, *Benedicamus Domino.* And in this case he says it turned towards the altar.

95. Having said *Ite Missa est*, he turns to the altar, inclines moderately with his hands joined on the edge of the altar, and says in a low voice, *Placeat tibi Sancta Trinitas.* (*Rub. Miss.*)

96. Then he kisses the altar, and having risen, he raises his eyes, extending his hands (which he has elevated as high as his shoulders), and then joining them again before his breast, he says, *Benedicat vos omnipotens Deus ;* at this last word he inclines his head and turns by the Epistle side towards the people, having his hands joined and his eyes modestly lowered. Then having placed his left hand extended below his breast, he blesses the people with his right hand, by forming a cross and saying in a loud voice, *Pater et Filius, et Spiritus Sanctus.*

To give the blessing properly and unaffectedly, he extends his right hand, having all the fingers united, and the little finger turned towards the people; then without haste drawing a straight line from his eyes to his breast, he says, *Pater et Filius ;* he raises his hand vertically to his shoulders, and crosses the first line transversely from left to right, saying, *Et Spiritus Sanctus.* Then he rejoins his hands, and turns towards the Gospel side to the altar corner to say the Gospel of St. John.

97. The last Gospel is read in the same tone of voice, and with the same ceremonies as the first Gospel, except that, when the Gospel of St. John is read, in saying *Initium Sancti Evangelii*, the priest forms the cross on the altar, or on the card instead of the book. At the *Et Verbum caro factum est*, he makes a genuflection, having

the hands extended, and laid on the altar. He also makes a genuflection, if on reading other Gospels there are words requiring it, as is the case on the feast of the Epiphany.

98. The Gospel being ended, the priest goes, with his hands joined, to the middle of the altar, takes the chalice by the *nodus* with his left hand, puts his right on the burse, and, turning on his right, he descends to the foot of the altar, where he makes a profound bow, or a genuflection on the floor, if the Blessed Sacrament be in the tabernacle. Having risen, he takes the cap presented to him by the server. As he leaves the altar, he says the anthem *Trium Puerorum*,—the whole of it when the Mass is of double rite, or only commences it, when the Mass is semidouble, to which, in Paschal time, he adds Alleluja. Then he says the *Benedicite*, (*Rub. Miss.*)*

99. On arriving in the sacristy, he makes a low bow to the cross or other image; then he places the chalice on the sacristy table, or press, takes off his cap and unrobes. In taking off the vestments, he observes the contrary order from that observed in vesting; for in removing the alb, he draws off the left sleeve first, then passes the alb over his head, and, lastly, draws off the right sleeve. He kisses the cross on the stole, maniple, and amice, as he did when vesting.

100. Finally, having washed his hands (a praiseworthy practice, not ordered by the Rubric, but recommended by most Rubricists), without speaking to any person, he goes to make his thanksgiving. If he vested at the altar, he unvests there also, at the Gospel side, as soon as he has read the Gospel, without previously returning to the middle of the altar.

Article XIII.

On Votive Masses.

101. By a *Votive Mass*, is generally understood one which does not conform to the office of the day.

Votive Masses are of two classes: Solemn and Private.

---

*If the sacristy is behind the altar, the priest enters the sanctuary at the Epistle side and leaves at the end of Mass at the Gospel side.

102. A solemn votive Mass is one which is said *pro re gravi, vel pro publica Ecclesiæ causa.* The S. C. R. having been asked to declare the significance of these words, replied as follows (May 19, 1607, in Placentina): *In omnibus casibus propositis potest dici res gravis quando ab Episcopo et Universo Clero et Civitate Missa votiva solemniter celebretur cum interventu Magistratus et populi.*

The cases proposed to the S. C. R. were: *propter pluviam pretendam, pro serenitate, pro quacumque necessitate, pro Principe infirmo, et similibus.*

103. A solemn votive Mass can be said on any day except doubles of the first class, Sunday of the first class, Ash Wednesday, during Holy Week, and on the vigils of Christmas and Pentecost. (S. C. R. Mar. 27, 1779.)

104. A private votive Mass may be said on any day on which a low Mass for the dead is allowed.

More latitude is accorded by the Church with regard to the Mass *pro sponso et sponsa*, which can be said any day except Sundays and feasts of precept, doubles of first and second class, during the octaves of Epiphany, the vigil of Pentecost and during the octave, the octave of Corpus Christi, and days which exclude doubles of the second class. Neither the *Gloria* nor *Credo* is said; three prayers are said, the first of the Mass and the second and third of the day as prescribed in *Rub. Miss. tit. VII de commem. No.* 3. *Benedicamus Domino* is said, and at the end of Mass the Gospel of St. John. (*Dec. Gen.*, 28*th Feb.*, 1818.)

On days which do not allow the Mass *pro sponso et sponsa*, the Mass of the day is said with the commemoration of the nuptial Mass, *non sub unica conclusione sed post omnes commemorationes a Rubrica præscriptas.* (*April* 20, 1822, *and General Decree, Dec.* 20, 1783.) The Sacred Congregation has also decreed (*Mar.* 3, 1761, *in Aquen ad* 4): *Si mulier est vidua, non solum debet omitti benedictio nuptiarum sed etiam Missa propria pro sponso et sponsa.*

105. In a solemn votive Mass one prayer only is said, but in the Mass *pro gratiarum actione* (which is that *de*

SSma Trinitate, vel de S.Sancto, vel de B. Maria Virgine) the prayer, *Deus, cujus misericordiae* is added *sub una conclusione*. When the conventual Mass (the Mass which is sung each day in cathedral and collegiate churches is so called) is not celebrated, if the solemn votive Mass take its place, the commemoration of the day is added.

In a solemn votive Mass, *pro re gravi* or *pro publica Ecclesiæ Causa* the *Gloria* is said, unless the Mass be celebrated in purple vestments. (*Rub. Miss., tit. VIII, No.* 4). The *Credo* is said in such Masses, even though the Mass be said on Sunday and in violet vestments. (*Rub. Miss. tit. XI de Symbols.*)

The proper Preface (if there be one) is said; otherwise the Preface *de tempore*, of the octave, or the common. The Gospel of St. John is said at the end of Mass.

106. In private votive Masses, including nuptial ones, three prayers are said; the first of the Mass, the second of the day and the third the one which would have been said in the second place in the Mass of the day. In votive Masses of the B. V. M., however, the third prayer is that *de Spiritu Sancto*; on Saturdays when the office is de B. V. M., the second prayer is *de Spiritu Sancto* and the third *Ecclesiæ vel pro Papa*. In votive Masses of the Apostles when the third prayer would be *a cunctis*, in its place is said the prayer *Concede nos;* and in any case if there is a commemoration of a simple, the third prayer prescribed above is not said, but in its place the commemoration of the simple. In votive Masses of the B. V. M. on Saturday, when her office is said the commemoration of the simple is put in the second place and the third prayer is *de Spiritu Sancto*. The *Gloria* is never said unless in Masses B. V. M. on Saturday, and in Masses *de Angelis*. The *Credo* is always omitted. The Preface is as in solemn votive Masses. The Gospel of St. John is said at the end. The vestments are of the color prescribed for the Mass which is said.

107. The S. C. R., by order of Pope Paul V, has declared that certain Masses cannot be said as votive ones, in which the prayers, etc, have regard to certain fixed days; as for example, the Masses of Christmas, Circum-

cision, Epiphany, Easter, Ascension, the Nativity, Purification and Assumption of the Blessed Virgin, the feast of St. John the Baptist and others having proper introits or collects. These Masses can only be said on the day assigned to them or during their octaves.

Votive Masses of other festivals not having this objection, may be used, yet it would be better that priests should only say those Masses which are classed as Votive in the Missal.

108. A priest, who on Saturday, within the octave of some feast of the B. V. M. has recited the office of a saint occurring on that day, desirous of saying a votive Mass of the B. V. M., must say the Mass of the feast of the B. V. M. (Dec. 1, 1684). This Mass is said with *Gloria* but without *Credo*. If a priest have the office of double rite and celebrates Mass in a church where a semidouble occurs, he cannot say a votive Mass. (Sept. 7, 1816.)

109. The three Masses which a newly ordained priest is directed to say must be said on days when the Rubrics permit. For a reasonable cause their celebration may be delayed. The *quality* of the Mass and not the application is prescribed, hence the priest may apply them for whomsoever he pleases. (St. Alphonsus, lib. iv, Tract 5, de Ord. §829.)

110. Requiem Masses may be classed among votive insomuch as they do not conform to the office of the day, but the Missal distinguishes between the two: "*Extra ordinem Officii, potest esse votiva vel defunctorum.*"

Requiem Masses cannot be said at an altar where the Blessed Sacrament is exposed, nor in a church where It is exposed (21 June, 1670 ; 12 Sept. 1671.) If the exposition, however, is not *pro re gravi*, a requiem Mass can be said at another altar in a church where the Blessed Sacrament is exposed (n 4181 ad 9 die 7 Maii, 1746). If the Blessed Sacrament is exposed for the Forty Hours' Devotion on All Soul's day, it is allowed to celebrate solemn and even private Masses of the dead. (n. 4477 ad. 1 die 16 Sept. 1801.)

111. Requiem Masses, both private and solemn (the

body not being present) are forbidden on all doubles; Sundays; the vigils of Christmas, Epiphany and Pentecost; within the octaves of Christmas, Epiphany, Easter, Pentecost and Corpus Christi; Ash Wednesday and Holy Week.

112. Solemn Requiem Masses, even though the body be present, are not allowed on doubles of the first class which are feasts of precept.

The S. C. R. has declared (*die* 23, *Maii*, 1835 *in Namurcen*) that such Masses, the body being present, are also prohibited on the suppressed festivals.

If the body has been already buried, Solemn Masses are forbidden on doubles of the first and second class and feasts of precept.

In those places where *only one* Mass is said on Sundays and feast days, even though the body is present, a Requiem Mass cannot be sung in place of the usual Mass; but the Mass of the day must be sung, and the Requiem Mass may be said on the first day on which it is allowed. (*n.* 4448 *ad.* 7, 26 *Jan.* 1793.)

A Solemn Requiem Mass, the body being present, can be said on doubles of the first class, which are not of precept, unless the feast be that of the titular of the church. (*April* 8, 1808.)

Solemn Masses of Requiem, then, the body being present, can not be said on the following days: Easter, Pentecost, Christmas, Epiphany, Ascension, Corpus Christi, Assumption and Immaculate Conception B.V.M., Nativity of St. John the Baptist, SS. Peter and Paul, All Saints, the titular saint of the church, the principal patron saint of the place, the last three days of Holy Week, and when there is Exposition of the Blessed Sacrament *pro re gravi.*

113. On the day of the death or burial of a person, though the body is not present, a solemn Mass of Requiem may be said on greater and less doubles, not of precept, on Ash Wednesday, Monday, Tuesday and Wednesday of Holy Week, and the vigils of Christmas and Pentecost. Before the burial of the body a solemn Mass may be said—the body being present—on Sundays

and feasts of precept and doubles of the second class. In which case a catafalque should be erected in church with some symbol or mark that the body is not yet buried. (25 *April*, 1781, *in Florentina*.)

114. On the third, seventh and thirtieth day from the death or burial a Requiem Mass may be sung on any day except Sundays and feasts of precept, doubles of the first and second class, the eves of Christmas and Pentecost, within the octaves of Christmas, Epiphany, Easter, Pentecost and Corpus Christi, Ash Wednesday and Holy Week. The same rule holds with regard to anniversary Masses.

115. We may add under this heading a few particulars with regard to the Mass which a priest ought to say in a church when a different office occurs.

As a general rule, the Mass should conform to the office of the day, but this cannot always be followed. Hence, a priest saying Mass in a church where the office is different, should according to circumstances either follow his own *Ordo* or conform to that of the church in which he celebrates.

116. If the office of the church does not allow votive and requiem Masses, all the Masses should conform to the *color* of the office. (*S. C. R. Sept.* 4, 1845.) An exception is made in favor of privileged requiem Masses, nuptial Masses and votive Masses, which the priest might be privileged to celebrate on forbidden days. A priest, who in virtue of a special permission, says the Mass of the Blessed Virgin every day, should use white vestments.

117. If he say Mass in a church, where a festival is celebrated solemnly and with concourse of people, for instance, on the feast of its patron or on the day of its dedication, he ought to conform to the rite and to the color of this church. He would even do better to say the Mass of such church, without taking any notice of his own office, unless on a Sunday or a privileged feria, a commemoration of which is never omitted. If he celebrate High Mass, on a day of obligation, or even on a day when devotion attracts a concourse of

people, he is obliged to follow, exclusively, the rite of the Church where he is, without paying any attention to the office he has recited.

118. If he go, through devotion, to say Mass in a church, where the festival of a saint is solemnly celebrated, he can say the proper Mass, if it have been granted to the whole Church; or, if not, he can say the common. This has been decided, with some exceptions, by many decrees of the Congregation of Sacred Rites.*

119. On other days, not celebrated with such solemnity, if the color be the same as that of his own church, he can say Mass conformably to his office.

If his own office be of double rite, he cannot say a votive Mass, although the office of the place be compatible with it; nor a *requiem* Mass, unless there be in the same church, on that day, solemn *Exequies* for the dead.†

CHAPTER II.

ORDER TO BE OBSERVED IN CELEBRATING TWO MASSES ON THE SAME DAY.

1. WHEN a priest is authorized to say two Masses (which can only be done on Sundays and feasts of obligation), in order to afford an opportunity for a considerable number of people to comply with the precept of assisting at the Holy Sacrifice, he may be much perplexed as to how he should act with regard to the chalice and the ablution of the fingers, especially if he has to say the second Mass in another church, and at some distance. The Sacred Congregation of Rites, in an

---

* See *Traité des SS. Mystères*, ch. 12, n. 5.

† All these rules have been extracted from several decrees of the Congregation of Rites; 11th June, 1701; 4th Sept., 1745; 7th May, 1746; 29th Jan., 1752; n. 3437, ad 2, et 3; 4026, ad 8; 4032, ad 13; 4074, ad 10, et 11. See also Romsée, tom. i, art. 5, and tom. v, n. 39.

instruction approved by Pope Pius IX the 11th day of March, 1858, prescribes that when a priest is obliged to celebrate Mass in two different churches on the same day, he should, in consuming the Precious Blood (during the first Mass), use the utmost diligence to take the whole of It. Then he places the chalice on the corporal, covers it with the pall, and with his hands joined, standing in the middle of the altar, he says, *Quod ore sumpsimus*. After which, drawing towards him the little water vase, he washes his fingers, saying at the same time, *Corpus tuum Domine*, etc., and then wipes them. The chalice being still on the corporal, removing the pall, he places on the chalice the purificator, then the paten, the pall, and lastly the veil. He then continues the Mass, and having finished reading the last Gospel, goes to the middle of the altar, where, uncovering the chalice, he examines whether any of the Precious Blood has collected at the bottom, which often happens, for although the Sacred Species were at first carefully consumed, nevertheless, in the very act of consuming, drops are spread around the surface, and will not collect at the bottom, until the chalice is again in its position for awhile. If, then, there still remains a drop of the Divine Blood, he will carefully take It from the same side of the chalice, from which he had consumed It. He should by all means do so, as the sacrifice still morally lasts, and by divine precept is to be completed by the consummation of the species still existing. After this, the priest will pour into the chalice at least as much water as he had before poured wine, and by gently moving the chalice cause the water to pass around, and then empty it in the vessel used for that purpose by the same side of the chalice from which he received the Precious Blood. Then, wiping the chalice with the purificator, he covers it as usual, and leaves the altar.

2. The priest having unvested and made his thanksgiving, if he is to say Mass on the following day, in the same place, he will preserve that water, and pour it in the chalice at the second purification; or he will cause it to be absorbed by raw cotton, or tow, which he burns;

or if it be left to evaporate, he puts it in the *Sacrarium*, or in the *Piscina*.

3. This chalice having been used by the priest, being now purified, if he needs it for the second Mass he can take it with him, or he can use another. (*S. R. C.*, 11th March, 1858.)

4. When a priest is obliged to say two Masses in the same church, he may observe the rules given above, or at the first Mass reserve the purification in a vessel used for that purpose and take it at second Mass.

CHAPTER III.

LOW MASS FOR THE DEAD.*

1. In a Requiem Mass there is no change to be made in the psalms and prayers which are a preparation for Mass. The Amice, Maniple, and Stole should be kissed as usual.

2. At the commencement of Mass, the priest having made the sign of the cross and said the anthem *Introibo*, omits the psalm *Judica* and the *Gloria Patri*, etc., and says, *Adjutorium nostrum in Nomine Domini*, making at the same time the sign of the cross.

3. He does not make the sign of the cross at the Introit, but having placed his left hand on the altar,† with the right extended, he makes the sign of the cross on the Missal, without, however, touching it. Instead of the *Gloria Patri*, he says, *Requiem æternam*, etc. The *Gloria in Excelsis* is not said. (*Rub. Miss.*, part ii, rit. xiii.)

---

* Low Mass for the dead, even *præsente cadavere*, cannot be said on Sundays, festivals of double rite, nor during the octaves of Christmas, Epiphany, Easter, Pentecost, and Corpus Christi, nor on the vigils of Christmas, Epiphany, Pentecost. or on Ash-Wednesday, nor during Holy Week. "Missæ privatæ de requiem, etiam corpore præsente et insepulto, dici non possunt diebus quibus fit de officio duplici, vel aliis a Rubrica exceptis." (*S. R. C.*, 29th Jan., 1752.)

† S. R. C., Sept. 7th, 1816.

4. At the *Munda cor meum*, the *Jube Domine*, with *Dominus sit*, etc., are omitted. After the Gospel he does not kiss the book, nor does he say, *Per Evangelica*, etc. (*Rub., ib.*)

5. While saying *Deus, qui humanæ substantiæ*, he does not bless the water; at the end of the Psalm *Lavabo* he omits the *Gloria Patri*, without saying anything in its place. (*Rub., ib.*)

6. At the *Agnus Dei*, instead of saying *miserere nobis*, he says, *Dona eis requiem;* and at the third he says, *Dona eis requiem sempiternam*. He does not strike his breast in pronouncing these words, but keeps his hands joined before him, without touching the altar.

7. He omits the first of the three prayers before Communion. (*Rub., ib.*)*

8. At the end of the Mass, instead of *Ite missa est*, he says, *Requiescant in pace*, turned towards the altar, not to the people. (*Rub., ib.*) Having said the prayer *Placeat*, he does not say *Benedicat vos*, nor does he give the blessing to the people (even had he given Communion during Mass), but having kissed the altar, he goes to the Gospel side, where he says, *Dominus vobiscum*, and the Gospel of St. John.

9. It is to be remarked, that as often as only one prayer is to be said, the *Dies iræ* should be said; and this occurs, 1st, on All Souls' Day; 2d, on the day of the death or interment; 3d, on the third, seventh and thirtieth day after interment, and on the first anniversary, which are called privileged days for the dead. When more than one prayer is said, it is *ad libitum sacerdotis*.

10. Although the Requiem be celebrated for one person, the *Introit, Gradual, Tract, Offertory, Communio* and *Requiescant in pace*, are to be in the plural.†

---

* Communion may be given at Masses for the dead, either with particles consecrated at the same Mass, or with others which had been reserved in the tabernacle.

† In Missis quotid. quæ pro defunctis celebrentur possunt quidem plures dici orationes quam tres, sed curandum est ut sint numero impares, et aliquando pro illa: *Deus veniæ largitor*, impune subrogabitur alia v. gr. *pro patre, matre* etc., dummodo ultimo loco dicatur illa: "*Fidelium omnium.*" *S. R. C.*, 2d Sept., 1741.

CHAPTER IV.

LOW MASS WHEN THE BLESSED SACRAMENT IS EXPOSED.

1. It should be remarked, that it would be better not to celebrate Low Mass at an altar on which the Blessed Sacrament is exposed, according to the ceremonial of Bishops (lib. i, ch. xii, sec. 9), which states, that the discipline of the Church is very ancient, to which the practice of the Patriarchal Churches of Rome, and of the best regulated churches, is conformable. Nevertheless, when there is a just reason to celebrate at such an altar, the following ceremonies should be exactly observed.

2. In going to the altar, as soon as the priest comes in sight of the Blessed Sacrament, he takes off his cap, and gives it to the server. When he comes to the foot of the altar, he kneels on both knees, and bows profoundly; he then goes up to the altar, sets the chalice thereon, makes a genuflection only on one knee (which kind of genuflection is made when it is to be made on the platform), and arranges the corporal and chalice. He again makes a genuflection, goes to the Epistle side, opens the Missal, returns to the middle, makes a genuflection, and turning a little towards the Gospel side, he descends to the foot of the steps, makes a genuflection on one knee only, and, without bowing, begins Mass.

3. After the confession, without making a genuflection, he goes up to the altar, and makes there a genuflection, before he commences the *Oramus te Domine*. After the *Oramus*, he again makes a genuflection, and goes to the Missal for the *Introit*.

A General Rule.—A genuflection is to be made whenever the celebrant goes from the middle to either side of the altar; the same when he goes from either side to the middle, with this difference only, that when he goes from the middle, he first kisses the altar or performs any action prescribed, and then makes the genuflection, this being the last thing to be done. When he leaves any side to go to the middle, the first act on arriving there is to make the genuflection, then to kiss the altar, or perform any other duty.

4. At the *Dominus vobiscum*, he turns back a little towards the Gospel side; and only half turned towards the people, he says, *Dominus vobiscum*, which must be observed whenever he turns towards the people.

5. When he is about to wash his hands, he makes first a genuflection, then goes down the steps by the Epistle side, and taking care not to turn his back to the altar, turns so that his right side be next to the corner of the Epistle, and his face towards the people; and there he washes and wipes his hands, then returns to the middle of the altar, and makes a genuflection.

6. He says *Orate fratres* in the same way as the *Dominus vobiscum*, without completing the circle. The remaining part, till Communion, is the same as in other Masses.

7. After the first ablution, without removing from his place, he receives the second ablution, having his face turned as much as possible towards the Blessed Sacrament. (*Bauldry*, part iv, ch. ix, art. ii, n. 12.) Then he wipes his fingers, takes the ablution, and adjusts the chalice as usual.

8. He then continues the Mass, observing the genuflections prescribed, and the manner of turning himself at the *Dominus vobiscum*, and *Ite, missa est*. Should he have to say, *Benedicamus Domino*, instead of the *Ite, missa est*, he turns round to the altar, and makes a genuflection before he says it.

9. After the *Placeat tibi*, he kisses the altar, says *Benedicat vos omnipotens Deus*, and, instead of the usual bow, makes a genuflection, and turning towards the people, he gives his blessing. He does not, however, complete the circle, neither does he make another genuflection; but turning to the Gospel side, he says, *Dominus vobiscum*, and reads the last Gospel as usual.

10. At the *Verbum caro factum est*, as on all other occasions without exception, he turns a little toward the Blessed Sacrament when he makes the genuflection.

11. At the end, he goes to the middle, makes a genuflection, descends, a little on the right, to the floor, makes a genuflection on both knees, and bows. He then returns to the sacristy, putting on his cap at the place he had taken it off when going to the altar.

CHAPTER V.

OF LOW MASS IN PRESENCE OF PRELATES.

1. By Prelates, are here understood Cardinals in every part of the world, Archbishops throughout their whole province, Bishops in their dioceses, and Apostolic Delegates in the countries to which they are accredited. Others are not so considered; neither are the above when they are *incogniti*, or not in their robes.

2. If possible, the priest should be vested, and at the altar, before the arrival of the Prelate, and should be standing on the floor of the sanctuary, at the Gospel side, with his hands joined, waiting for him, having previously prepared the chalice and Missal on the altar.

3. On the arrival of the Prelate, the priest salutes him with a low bow, and on receiving the sign to begin Mass, he again bows to him; then turns a little towards the altar, makes a low bow, and begins Mass in the same place and position. (*Rub. Miss.*, part ii, tit. iii, n. 2.)

The practice introduced, is to commence Mass immediately after the salutation, without waiting for a sign from the Prelate.

4. If the Prelate arrive before, at the altar, the priest, whether he has the chalice or not, salutes him from a convenient place; then, bowing to the altar, he arranges on it whatever is necessary, descends on the floor to the place above mentioned, and after bowing to the Prelate, he commences Mass.

5. At the *Confiteor*, instead of saying, *et vobis fratres, et vos fratres*, turning and bowing to the Prelate, he says,

et tibi Pater, et te Pater. (*Rub., ib.,* n. 8); if there be more than one, *et vobis Patres, et vos Patres.*

6. After the confession, having said *Oremus,* he bows to the Prelate, then ascends to the altar, and continues Mass as usual. (*Rub., ib.,* n. 10.)

7. At the end of the Gospel he does not kiss the book, neither does he say, *Per Evangelica dicta.* The attendant takes the book to the Prelate to kiss. (*Rub., ib.,* tit. vi, n. 2.) Even should the Prelate not kiss it (which happens when there are many, no one kisses it), the priest should also omit to kiss it.

8. After the *Agnus Dei,* except in Masses for the dead, when he has said the first prayer before communion, he kisses the altar, then the instrument of peace (which the attendant presents, kneeling at his right hand), saying *Pax tecum,* the attendant answers, *Et cum spiritu tuo* (*Rub., ib.,* tit. x, n. 3), and takes it, covered with a cloth, to the Prelate to kiss; or, to several, saying to each one, *Pax tecum;* they answering, *Et cum spiritu tuo.* He makes a bow to them after they have kissed it, not before. (*Cærem. Episc.,* lib. i, ch. xxix, sec. 8.) The priest continues the other prayers.

9. In giving the blessing, after having said *Benedicat vos Omnipotens Deus,* he bows to the cross; then turning to the Prelate, he makes a low bow, as if requesting permission to bless the people, and says, *Pater, et Filius, et Spiritus Sanctus,* blessing the people only on the side opposite the Prelate. (*Rub., ib.,* tit. xii, n. 3.) If the Prelate should be in the middle, he blesses on the Gospel side.

10. After the last Gospel, without going to the middle of the altar, he turns to the Prelate, and makes a low bow (*Rub., ib.,* ii, 5), and remains there until the Prelate leaves.

11. Should the Prelate remain, the priest goes to the middle, takes the chalice, descends from the altar, makes a low bow to the cross, and another to the Prelate, puts on his cap, and proceeds to the sacristy.

12. The instrument of peace is not presented to Prelates out of their diocese. A bow is made to them

in going to and coming from the altar, and, according to the opinion of some Rubricists, at the end of the Gospel. In other respects, everything is done as if they were not present.

CHAPTER VI.
GIVING COMMUNION.
ARTICLE I.
Giving Communion during Mass.

1. THE practice of giving Communion to the people during Mass, being more conformable to antiquity, is preferable to that of giving it before or after Mass. A quantity of small particles should be prepared, corresponding with the number of persons to receive. If there are many, it is better to make use of a ciborium; if only a few, they may be placed on the corporal at the left side; but, in all cases, they should be on the altar before the Offertory. In making the Offertory, the priest extends the intention also to the small particles, which, unless in a ciborium, should be on the corporal, and *not on the paten* (as the rubric clearly prescribes).

2. If the ciborium is used before the Offertory, he brings it nearer to himself and uncovers it. After the Offertory, he covers it again, and places it a little in the rear of the chalice, but not off the corporal.

3. At the consecration, if the small particles are on the corporal, he does not touch them. If the ciborium is there, he uncovers it before pronouncing the words of consecration, as was said above for the Offertory; and after the elevation of the Sacred Host, having made the genuflection, he covers it, and puts it in its place.

4. Having consumed the Precious Blood, and placed the chalice on the corporal, he covers it with the pall. If the small Hosts are on the corporal, he makes a genuflection before touching them, and then he reverently places

them on the paten, and again makes a genuflection. Meanwhile the server says the *Confiteor;* after which the priest turns to the right, and, facing the corner of the Epistle, says, in a loud voice, *Misereatur vestri* (not *tui*, although there may be only one communicant). The server having answered *Amen*, he says, *Indulgentiam*, etc., at the same time making a sign of the cross with his right hand over the communicants, in the same manner as he gives the blessing at the end of Mass. If the small Hosts are in a ciborium, after having covered the chalice with the pall, he places the ciborium between himself and the chalice, uncovers it, makes a genuflection, and turns towards the people to say *Misereatur*, etc.

5. Having said *Indulgentiam*, etc., he turns to the altar, makes a genuflection, and takes the paten between the middle and forefinger of his left hand, or the ciborium by the *nodus;* and, having taken one of the Hosts with the thumb and forefinger of his right hand, he raises It a little above the paten or ciborium, and in that position turns to the people. Then, having his eyes modestly fixed on the Blessed Sacrament, he says, in a clear and unaffectedly devout tone of voice, *Ecce Agnus Dei, ecce qui tollit peccata mundi;* and then, three times, *Domine non sum dignus, ut intres sub tectum meum, sed tantum dic verbo, et sanabitur anima mea.* (*Rub. Miss.*, part ii, tit. x, 6.)

6. Having said these words, he descends by the middle of the altar, not by the side (*S. R. C.*, Sept., 1737), and approaches the communicants, beginning at the Epistle side. Before giving Communion, the priest makes, each time, a sign of the cross with the Host, above the paten or ciborium, taking care not to pass the limits of either; while he says, *Corpus Domini Nostri ✠ Jesu Christi*, bowing at these last words, he puts the Host on the tongue of the communicant, saying, *custodiat animam tuam in vitam æternam. Amen.* In giving Holy Communion, the priest will be careful to lay the Host on the tongue of the communicant in such a manner that It will adhere to it; at the same time he will carefully avoid touching the communicant's lips or tongue with his

fingers.* When there are many communicants, and the first row have received, the priest should not continue to give Communion by retrograding, but should recommence at the Epistle side; and, as he passes by the middle of the altar, he makes no genuflection, even should the Blessed Sacrament be exposed.

7. Having given Communion, the priest returns to the altar, without saying anything, keeping the thumb and forefinger of his right hand united over the paten or ciborium. If any Hosts remain, and there is no place to put Them, he makes a genuflection and consumes Them. If They had been on the corporal, he gathers the fragments with the paten, and causes them to fall in the chalice; then, receiving the purification, continues Mass as usual.

8. Should the priest give Communion with Hosts already consecrated, having consumed the Precious Blood, he puts the chalice at the Gospel side, on the corporal, and covers it with the pall. Then, having removed the altar-card, he opens the door of the tabernacle, and makes a genuflection. Then he takes out the ciborium, places it in the middle of the corporal, closes the tabernacle door, uncovers the ciborium, and makes another genuflection. Meanwhile the server says the *Confiteor*, after which the priest says, *Misereatur*, etc., and then continues as described above.

9. After having given Communion, he returns to the altar, makes a genuflection, covers the ciborium, opens the tabernacle, and places the ciborium within, makes another genuflection, closes the door, and replaces the card before it. Then he receives the purification, and continues Mass.

---

* If there are ecclesiastics in surplice to receive Holy Communion, they kneel on the top step of the altar. If there are priests or deacons, they should wear a stole, and receive first. Lay persons should kneel at the railing, or any other place where the communion cloth is prepared. It is not permitted to use the chalice veil or finger-towel for a communion cloth.

Article II.

Purification of the Ciborium.

10. The priest having received the Precious Blood, and given Holy Communion (if it had to be given), he consumes the small Hosts that remain in the ciborium. Then, taking with his left hand the ciborium by the *nodus*, brings the opening of it over the chalice, and, with the forefinger and thumb of his right hand, causes the particles to fall from the ciborium into the chalice. If necessary, a little wine is poured into the ciborium, and he gently moves it in such a manner that the wine may pass all around, and detach the small particles that may still remain. To do this more thoroughly, he may use the forefinger of his right hand; and then he pours that wine into the chalice, after which he wipes the interior of the ciborium with the purificator. If newly consecrated Hosts are to be placed in the ciborium, he does so; after which he makes a genuflection, covers the ciborium, and replaces it in the tabernacle. Otherwise, he covers the empty ciborium, and puts it off the corporal. This being done, he presents the chalice to the server, to receive wine for the purification, and continues Mass.*

Article III.

On giving Communion at other times.

11. When circumstances require that Communion should be given immediately before Mass, the priest proceeds to the altar, clothed in the vestments in which he is to celebrate (provided, however, that they are not black); he places the chalice on the Gospel side, the veil

---

* Quarti, Murati and other Rubricists remark that, in purifying the ciborium, such particles as may be found in it should not be brought to the mouth with the fingers, nor received with the mouth at the edge of the ciborium; for, besides the impropriety of so doing, there is danger of losing some of the particles. It is better, however, not to use any wine in purifying the ciborium, especially when newly consecrated Hosts are to be immediately put in it.

concealing it from the people, and then, having taken the corporal from the burse, extends it upon the altar. After which he opens the tabernacle, makes a genuflection, takes the ciborium, places it on the corporal, and proceeds as directed in Nos. 4, 5 and 6. Communion being over, should he perceive any particle on his fingers, he must let it fall into the ciborium. Then he makes a genuflection, purifies his fingers in the little water-vase, which is kept near the tabernacle for this purpose, wipes them with the purificator, and says during this time, "*O sacrum convivium in quo Christus sumitur, recolitur memoria Passionis ejus, mens impletur gratia, et futuræ gloriæ nobis pignus datur.*" During the Paschal time, *Alleluja* is added to the above anthem. Then he says, *Panem de Cœlo prestitisti eis*, and the server answers, *Omne delectamentum in se habentem*, with *Alleluja* in Paschal time and during the octave of *Corpus Christi*. Then adding, *Domine exaudi*, etc., and *Dominus vobiscum* (*S. R. C.*, 24th Sept., 1842), he says, *Oremus.*

"*Deus qui nobis sub sacramento mirabili Passionis tuæ memoriam reliquisti; tribue quæsumus, ita nos Corporis et Sanguinis tui sacra mysteria venerari, ut redemptionis tuæ fructum in nobis jugiter sentiamus. Qui vivis et regnas cum Deo Patre,*" etc., and the server answers, *Amen*. During Paschal time, instead of the above prayer, the following is said: *Oremus.* "*Spiritum nobis, Domine, tuæ caritatis infunde, ut quos Sacramentis Paschalibus satiasti, tua facias pietate concordes. Per Christum Dominum nostrum.*" The server answers, *Amen*. After this he replaces the ciborium in the tabernacle, makes another genuflection, closes the door, locks it, and removes the key. (Should the priest foresee that he is to give Communion during Mass, or immediately after, the key may be left in the door of the tabernacle.) Then he places the chalice in the middle of the altar, on the corporal, and gives the blessing (to those who received Communion) in the following manner:

12. The chalice being arranged, the priest extends, elevates, and rejoins his hands, raising his eyes at the

same time, and says, *Benedictio Dei omnipotentis;* at these words bowing to the cross. Having turned to those who received Holy Communion, he continues, *Patris, et Filii, et Spiritus Sancti,* and he makes the sign of the cross, adding the words, *descendat super vos, et maneat semper.* The server answers, *Amen.* Then, without turning to the altar, he descends the steps, and having made the requisite genuflection or bow, he commences Mass.

13. When Communion is given immediately after Mass, the priest, having finished the last Gospel, goes to the middle of the altar, and puts the chalice on the Gospel side; then, taking the corporal from the burse, opens the tabernacle, and proceeds as in No. 11. The ciborium being replaced in the tabernacle, the door of it should be locked, and the key placed on the altar. After the blessing, the corporal is again put in the burse, which the priest places on the chalice, and on the burse he puts the key of the tabernacle, and returns in the usual manner to the sacristy.

14. When Communion is given at other times, the priest washes his hands, puts on a surplice and a stole of the same color as that used for the day, or white; should the priest wear a cape, he takes it off for the occasion. (*S. R. C*, 12th July, 1628.) He goes to the altar with his head covered and his hands joined, being preceded by the server, who should have lighted the candles previously, and carried to the altar the burse, with the key of the tabernacle and the communion cloth, unless the latter had been already prepared. If the server be a layman, the priest will carry the burse before his breast, and take along also the key of the tabernacle. Having arrived in front of the altar, he gives his cap to the server, and makes a genuflection before ascending the steps. Then he goes up to the altar, unfolds the corporal, and places the burse against the step as at Mass. He opens the tabernacle, makes a genuflection, takes the ciborium from the tabernacle, and places it on the corporal; he uncovers the ciborium, places the cover on the corporal, and again he makes a genuflection. He con-

tinues the rest as before noticed in No. 11. After Communion he replaces the ciborium in the tabernacle, gives the blessing to those who have communicated, puts the corporal into the burse, bows to the cross, and, after descending the steps, he makes a genuflection, and puts on his cap; the burse is carried either by the priest or the server. He returns to the sacristy, where, having bowed to the cross, he takes off the stole and surplice, and the server returns to extinguish the lights.

CHAPTER VII.

MANNER OF SERVING A PRIEST AT LOW MASS.

ARTICLE I.

General Remarks.

1. THE server should consider himself highly honored, being permitted to attend on a priest offering the most Holy Sacrifice. He should therefore perform this important office with great purity of conscience, rectitude of intention, devotion, and decorum.

2. In making the sign of the cross, he should put his left hand a little below the breast, and touching the forehead, the breast, and the left and right shoulders with the fingers of his right hand, he should say: *In nomine Patris, et Filii, et Spiritus Sancti. Amen.*

3. A simple inclination is made by bending the head moderately. A simple bow implies an inclination of the head and a moderate bending of the body. A low bow is made by bending the head and body profoundly, yet not so much as to render the action unseemly. A bow is considered sufficiently profound when the person that makes it, being in that position, can reach the knee with the extremity of his hand.

4. To make a genuflection, one should bring the right

knee down to the floor near the left foot, without inclining the body, and then rise up again naturally, without too great haste.

5. A genuflection on both knees is made by first bending the right knee to the floor, then the left likewise to the floor; and having made a low bow, the person rises by lifting the left knee first, and then the right.

6. To join the hands properly, the palm of one hand should be applied to the palm of the other, and both held upwards against the breast. The thumb of the right hand should cross the thumb of the left. During the Holy Sacrifice, whenever the hands are not necessarily employed, they should be joined.

7. The server should make an inclination whenever he hears the priest pronounce the holy name of Jesus, of Mary, or of the saint whose festival is celebrated, and on other occasions marked in the third article.

8. In answering, he should take care to pronounce distinctly, and not too loud, nor too quickly. His manner should be grave, without affectation. He should hold his head a little inclined, and his eyes modestly lowered.

9. To put on the surplice in a proper manner, the server should open the lower part of it, and with both his hands pass it over the head upon his shoulders. Afterwards he puts first the right arm in the right sleeve, and then the left in the other sleeve; and having adjusted it about his person, fastens it in front. In taking it off, he should first loose the strings, then withdraw his left arm from the sleeve, and lifting the surplice from the left side above the head over his right shoulder, he takes it off from the right arm.

Article II.

Of the Vesting of the Priest.

1. At the appointed time the server puts on the surplice, and if no one is appointed to prepare the cruets, light the candles and make other necessary preparations, he should attend to it. Then he places himself at the left of the priest and, if it be the custom, helps him to

vest. Whilst the priest puts on the amice, the server prepares the alb, and then puts it on him and assists him by holding up first the right sleeve of the alb and then the left. Afterwards he takes the girdle (keeping the tassels at his right) and gives it to the priest, so that he may easily gird himself. He should take care to adjust the alb in such a manner as to let it hang equally around, about an inch from the floor. After that he presents to him the maniple to kiss, and fastens it on his left arm. Then he hands him the stole, and finally he assists him in putting on the chasuble. After the priest is vested, he takes the Missal (unless it be already on the altar), holding it with both his hands before his breast, having the back of it to his right. He makes a low bow to the cross or chief image in the sacristy, with the priest, and goes before him to the altar.

ARTICLE III.

From the beginning of the Mass to the end of it.

1. Having arrived before the lowest step of the altar, the server places himself at the right of the priest, from whom he receives the cap. He makes a genuflection on the floor with the priest, or (if the Blessed Sacrament be not there) a profound bow; and raising a little the priest's vesture, he ascends the steps with him. He places the book on the stand, so as to have the back of it turned to the right. (The server does not open the book.) Then he puts the cap at a suitable place, and goes to the Gospel side, kneels on the floor at the left of the priest, a little in the rear, and joins his hands.

2. He makes the sign of the cross with the priest, and answers at the confession. He bows at the *Gloria Patri.* After the priest has said the *Confiteor,* the server, inclining a little towards the priest, says *Misereatur tui,* etc.; then, bowing profoundly towards the altar, he says the *Confiteor.* At the words *et tibi Pater, et te Pater,* he turns his head somewhat towards the priest. He strikes his breast when he says *mea culpa, mea culpa, mea maxima culpa.* When the priest has said *Misereatur vestri,* etc.,

the server raises his head. At the words *Deus tu conversus*, he inclines a little. At the words *Dominus vobiscum*, he rises and raises a little the priest's alb, while he ascends the steps. Then he kneels on the lowest step, and remains there till the end of the Epistle.

3. He says the *Kyrie eleison* alternately with the priest. If the celebrant says *Flectamus genua*, the server answers, *Levate*. If there be more than one epistle, he answers, *Deo gratias*, at the end of each of them. The Epistle or Epistles being read, he rises, makes a genuflection or a bow in the middle, and goes to the book. If the priest makes a genuflection, as happens during Lent, the server makes also a genuflection. When the priest has done reading, the server carries the book with the stand to the Gospel side, making a genuflection or a bow in the middle, as he passes. Having placed the book on the altar, he turns it a little to the right, and goes below the platform near the book. He answers at the *Dominus vobiscum;* and at the words *Sequentia Sancti Evangelii* he puts his left hand on his breast, and with the thumb of the right he makes a cross on his forehead, lips, and breast. As the priest pronounces the name of *Jesus* in the beginning of the Gospel, the server bows towards the book, and goes down on the floor to the Epistle side, making a genuflection or a bow in the middle. If the name of *Jesus* be not mentioned, then he bows to the priest, and goes to his place, and there he stands during the Gospel, at the end of which he answers, *Laus tibi Christe*, and kneels down.

4. If the *Credo* be said, the server kneels down during it, and makes a low bow at the words, *Et incarnatus est*, etc. Having answered at the *Dominus vobiscum*, he rises and goes to the side-table, takes the cruets, and carries them to the altar on the Epistle side. (He folds the veil of the chalice, if the priest leaves it unfolded.) When the celebrant approaches the corner of the Epistle, the server bows to him, and presents the cruet with wine to him, after first kissing it; he receives it back, kissing it, and presents to him the cruet with water, kissing it both before giving it and after receiving it. (He does not kiss the priest's

hand.) At the words *Veni sanctificator*, he takes in his right hand the cruet with water, and the plate in the left, holding the towel on his left arm, and pours water on the priest's fingers, bowing to him before and after.

5. Having placed the cruets on the side-table, he kneels on the first step in front of the altar at the Epistle side; bowing slightly he answers at the *Orate fratres;* afterwards he answers at the Preface, and moderately rings the little bell at the *Sanctus*. It is the custom here to ring the bell at the *Hanc Igitur*.

6. At the words, *Qui pridie*, etc., the server goes up and kneels on the edge of the platform, at the right of the priest. He inclines during the consecration of both species, and makes a low bow when the priest adores the Blessed Sacrament. At each elevation the server raises a little the extremity of the chasuble with his left hand, and with his right gives three strokes of the bell.

7. The elevation being over, he rises, and goes to kneel at his place. He strikes his breast at the words, *Nobis quoque peccatoribus*. He answers at the *Per omnia sæcula sæculorum*, and at the end of the *Pater Noster*. He answers again at the *Per omnia*, etc., and at the *Pax Domini*, etc. When the priest says *Domine non sum dignus*, the server inclines, and rings the bell moderately, that if there be persons to go to Communion, they may approach the holy table. When the priest uncovers the chalice after receiving the Sacred Body, the server rises, goes to the side-table, takes the cruets, carries them up to the altar, and inclines when the priest takes the Sacred Blood; after which he ministers wine and water with the usual bows and kisses. When the server goes from the credence-table to the altar, he genuflects on the floor at the Epistle side. He stands on the platform to minister wine at the first ablution, and returns to the highest step for the second.

8. If there are communicants, after the priest has received the most Precious Blood, the server, kneeling on the step at the Epistle side, bows profoundly, and says the *Confiteor*. He inclines and answers at the *Misereatur vestri*, and makes the sign of the cross at the words *In-*

dulgentiam, etc. The Communion being over, he raises the priest's alb while he ascends the steps, and kneels again until the priest has closed the tabernacle; after which he presents the cruets as is said above.

9. Having placed the cruets on the side-table, the server goes to the Gospel side; thence he takes the book and carries it with the stand to the Epistle side, making a genuflection in the middle as he passes; after which he kneels on the lowest step at the Gospel side. He answers the prayers, etc. When the priest gives the blessing, the server, remaining at his place, bows and makes the sign of the cross, at the end of which he answers, *Amen*. Then he rises, answers at the *Dominus vobiscum*, and at the beginning of the Gospel signing himself, as mentioned in n. 3. Towards the end of the Gospel, he goes for the priest's cap; he bends the knee at the words *Et Verbum caro*, etc. Then he goes up to the altar, takes the book, bows to the cross with the priest, and with him he goes down and makes a genuflection on the floor, or a bow. He gives the cap to the priest, and goes before him to the sacristy. There, after making a low bow to the cross or image with the priest, he bows to him. After that he puts the book in its place, and, if customary, helps the priest to disrobe. Finally, he takes off his surplice, and retires.

10. If there be a last Gospel peculiar to the day, after the priest has said *Ite, missa est*, the server takes the book to the Gospel side, taking care to kneel when the priest gives the blessing. When the priest has done reading, he carries the book back to the Epistle side.

11. Should the Mass be celebrated in presence of the Blessed Sacrament exposed, the genuflection in going to and leaving the altar, is made on both knees. The server pours water on the priest's hands, standing on the floor at the Epistle side, with the towel on his arm. The cruets are not kissed.

12. When Mass is for the dead, the psalm, *Judica me*, etc., is not said. The usual kisses are omitted: At the end of Mass, the priest, instead of *Ite, missa est*, says, *Requiescant in pace*, to which the server answers, *Amen*.

CHAPTER VIII.

MANNER OF SERVING A BISHOP AT LOW MASS.

ARTICLE I.

Things to be Prepared.

1. THE vestments for saying Mass, viz., chasuble, stole, cincture, alb, and amice, should be prepared on the middle of the altar. Near the vestments on the Epistle side, the pectoral cross on a plate, and the maniple on the Gospel side. The Missal open at its place. (The altar-cards should be removed, if the Canon * be used.) On common days only two candles need be lighted; on festivals, four or more. On the side-table two large candles should be placed, to be lighted at the end of the Preface.†

2. On the side-table should be prepared the chalice, the cruets, and the basin and ewer, with a towel.

3. In the sanctuary, towards the middle, the kneeling-desk, covered with a green or violet cloth; also, two cushions, one placed on the upper part of the desk, the other on the lower part. On the kneeling-desk should be placed the Canon, and the hand candlestick with lighted candle.

4. If the Blessed Sacrament is exposed, the vestments should be prepared in the sacristy, or on a side-table in the sanctuary; as on such occasion the Bishop does not vest at the altar.

ARTICLE II.

Of the Preparation and Vesting of the Bishop.

1. Two chaplains, at least, are requisite to serve a Bishop's Mass.

---

* A book containing the Canon and some other parts of the Mass, is so called. It is placed on the altar instead of the Missal during the most solemn part of the Mass, when a Bishop celebrates.

† Vid Cer. Episc., lib. i. c. 29, n. 4; Martinucci, lib. 5, c. 5, 21.

2. At the appointed time the two chaplains put on their surplices, and go to receive the Bishop at the door. They bow to him when they meet him, and walk before him towards the middle of the sanctuary, where they bow to the cross, or make a genuflection if the Blessed Sacrament be in the tabernacle. The Bishop goes to the kneeling-desk; the first chaplain takes the hand candlestick, and stands at his left, whilst the second at his right turns the leaves of the Canon.

3. After the preparation, all go to the lowest step of the altar, where they bow or make a genuflection. When the Bishop has finished, the second places the Canon open in the middle of the altar, against the tabernacle, and the first puts the hand candlestick to the right of the Missal on the altar. The first takes the pectoral cross and cape from the Bishop, and places the latter on the kneeling-desk. He takes the ring from the Bishop's finger with the usual kisses; and having taken the towel from the second, each kneeling on one knee, they give the water and towel for the washing of the Bishop's hands, and rise after having received his blessing. (If they are priests, they do not kneel.) After which, the second puts the basin, ewer, and towel on the side-table.

4. The first goes up to the altar, takes the vestments one after the other, and with the assistance of the second, vests the Bishop. Taking first the amice, he presents it to the Bishop to kiss, who puts it around his neck, and, passing the string around the waist, fastens it in front. Then he puts the alb on him; afterwards he girds him with the cincture; Then he presents to him the pectoral cross to kiss, and suspends it from his neck; then the stole is also kissed, and suspended from the neck down on each side and fastened with the cincture; after that, the chasuble is put on him and fastened in front; lastly, the ring is put on his finger with the usual kisses. When the Mass is for the dead, the maniple is put on him after the cincture. If, in vesting, the Bishop wishes to read the prayers, the second chaplain should hold the book and the hand candlestick before him.

5. The Bishop being vested, the first chaplain goes to

his right, and the second to his left; they make a genuflection or a low bow with him (the second having on his arm the maniple). They answer and bow as usual during the confession. After the words *Indulgentiam*, etc., the second rises and presents the maniple to the Bishop to kiss, and fastens it on his arm. When he ascends the steps, they raise the alb a little, go up with him, and remain on each side of him, moving with him to and from the middle of the altar, as may be prescribed; the first, pointing out what is to be read, holds the hand candlestick. They answer, make on themselves the sign of the cross, and bow. When the Bishop makes a genuflection, they do likewise, supporting him by placing each his hand under his elbow.*

6. While the Bishop says *Munda cor meum*, the second chaplain carries the book and the first the hand candlestick to the Gospel side, making the usual genuflections or bows; and the first, stands at the Bishop's left, and holding the hand candlestick, points the text to the the Bishop. (Should a Cardinal be present, the first, as soon as the Bishop has kissed the text, takes another Missal, and observing the usual ceremonies, brings it to be kissed. If there be several high dignitaries, the Gospel is only given to the highest in dignity; if they be equal in rank, it is given to no one.) When the Missal is not to be carried, the first chaplain remains at the left of the Bishop. If the *Credo* be said, they remain by the Bishop during its recital.

7. After the *Dominus vobiscum*, the second goes to the side-table, takes the chalice and carries it up to the altar on the Epistle side, he takes the corporal out of the burse and extends it in the middle of the altar. He gives the paten to the bishop, kissing it and his hand. He then wipes the chalice with a purifier. Having brought the cruets, he pours wine into the chalice; takes the water cruet and holds it up to the Bishop, saying, *Benedicite, Reverendis-*

---

* The first, who holds the hand candlestick, does not genuflect during Epistle, Gospel, *Incarnatus est*, nor during Canon.

sime Pater, and puts some drops of water into the chalice, and having wiped the chalice, presents it to the Bishop with the usual kisses. (In Masses for the dead the water is not blessed.) Then he puts the pall on the chalice, and the paten partly under the corporal, covering the remaining part with the purifier; after which he takes back the cruets to the side-table. When the Bishop says, *In spiritu humilitatus*, the second chaplain takes the basin, ewer, and towel, and goes to minister to the washing of the hands, the first receiving and returning the ring with the usual kisses. The second, having carried the ewer back to the side-table, goes to the right of the Bishop, and the first goes to the book. Whilst the Bishop recites the *Secreta*, the second will have the Canon ready; the *Secreta* being read, the first takes the Missal from the stand, and in its place the second puts the Canon, open at the preface. They answer at the preface, and bow at the *Sanctus*, the second ringing the little bell. Afterwards the second lights two large candles on the side-table, which are put out after the Bishop's Communion, or after he has given Communion. (It would be more conformable to the Ceremonial of Bishops, if two clerks hold two large candles or torches.) Whilst the Bishop is making his memento for the living, the first leaves the hand candlestick on the altar, and both retire a step from the altar, still remaining on the platform: the same is done at the memento for the dead. At the words, *Qui pridie*, they both kneel on the platform; they bow and raise the chasuble as usual, the second giving three strokes of the bell at each elevation. He also uncovers and covers the chalice; afterwards they both rise, make a genuflection on the platform, and stand on each side of the Bishop as before.

8. Towards the end of the *Pater Noster*, the second wipes the paten with the purifier, and gives it to the Bishop with the usual kisses. Then he uncovers and covers the chalice. They incline and strike their breast at the *Agnus Dei*. Should the *Pax* be given, the second chaplain takes the instrument of peace, kneels at the Bishop's right, holding the instrument before him, which

he kisses, saying, *Pax tecum*. Having answered, *Et cum spiritu tuo*, he rises and brings the *Pax* to the dignitary to kiss. In presenting it, he says, *Pax tecum;* and being answered, *Et cum spiritu tuo*, he bows to him. Then he covers the instrument with its veil, carries it back to the side-table, and returns to the Bishop's side.

9. At the *Domine non sum dignus*, they bow and strike their breasts; afterwards the second chaplain uncovers the chalice, and both make a genuflection; then the second goes for the cruets, gives the wine and water with the usual kisses, and puts back the cruets on the side-table. Meanwhile the first puts the Canon in the middle of the altar, and the Missal on the stand, and carries it, together with the hand candlestick, to the Epistle side. The Bishop washes his hands as usual, the second giving the water, and the first attending to the ring and presenting the towel. After which the first assists the Bishop at the book, and the second goes and arranges the chalice, carries it to the side-table, and returns to the left of the Bishop. Should the Bishop give Communion, when he has taken the Sacred Blood, they kneel on the edge of the platform and say the *Confiteor*. They answer and sign themselves with the sign of the cross at the *Indulgentiam*. When the Bishop returns to the altar, they raise his alb while he ascends the steps. The first chaplain takes the paten and holds it below the mouth of the communicants, while they receive; after which he places it on the corporal, on returning to the altar.

10. When the Bishop is about giving the blessing, the chaplains go on the step below the platform, where they kneel, and answer at the blessing. If there be a last Gospel specially prescribed, the first takes the book and the hand candlestick to the Gospel side. If the Gospel of St. John be said, the second chaplain at the Bishop's left, holds the Canon, and the first, at his right, the hand candlestick. After the last Gospel, the first closes the book; all bow to the cross and go down on the floor, where they make a genuflection, or a low bow. Then the first, assisted by the second, disrobes the Bishop, placing the vestments on the altar. Afterwards the first

chaplain puts the cape on the Bishop, and buttons it in front. The Bishop returns to the kneeling-desk, and the chaplains attend him as in the beginning. If he desires to assist at another Mass, they remain kneeling at either side a little behind him. Finally, they accompany him to the door, where they bow to him, and return to take off their surplices. If the Bishop wear a calotte, the first chaplain takes it off at the *Sanctus*, and puts it on him again after the Communion.

Article III.

When there is but one Chaplain.

1. If there be no more than one chaplain, he goes to receive the Bishop at the door, and accompanies him to the kneeling-desk. Then he takes the Canon and the hand candlestick. He opens the book and puts it on the desk, and holds the hand candlestick. The preparation being over, he puts the Canon and the hand candlestick on the altar, and attends to the washing of the Bishop's hands. He vests him in the manner above described. He takes the maniple, goes to the left hand of the Bishop, and answers during the confession as usual. He rises and puts the maniple on the Bishop's arm, after he has said *Indulgentiam*. After the confession he goes to the Missal and assists the Prelate, answering, kneeling, inclining, etc. After the Bishop has done reading, the chaplain carries the book and the hand candlestick to the Gospel side. After the *Dominus vobiscum*, he takes the chalice to the altar, spreads the corporal, and gives the paten to the Bishop with the usual kisses. He takes the cruets and puts wine into the chalice. Then, presenting the water cruet to the Prelate, he says, *Benedicite, Reverendissime Pater*, and puts a few drops of water in the chalice, which he gives to him with the usual kisses. He covers the chalice and prepares for the washing of the Bishop's fingers. He answers at the *Orate fratres*, and assists at the book, pointing out to the Prelate what is to be read. After the Secreta, he puts the Missal aside, and places the Canon on the book-stand. He answers at the

Preface, and rings the bell at the *Sanctus*. At the words *Qui pridie*, he goes to the right of the Bishop and assists him, as marked in the second article. After covering the chalice he makes a genuflection, and goes to the Gospel side, makes a genuflection, and asssists at the book. Towards the end of the *Pater Noster* he makes a genuflection, and goes to the Epistle side, makes a genuflection, again takes the paten and gives it to the Bishop with the usual kisses. He uncovers and covers the chalice. He bows during the *Domine, non sum dignus*, and strikes his breast. He makes a genuflection and uncovers the chalice. He presents the cruets with the usual kisses, and carries them back to the side-table. Then he puts the Canon, open, against the tabernacle, and places the Missal, open, on the stand, and carries it, with the hand candlestick, to the Epistle side. He afterwards attends to the washing of the Bishop's hands. Afterwards he repairs to the Gospel side, arranges the chalice, and takes it to the side-table; after which he returns to the book, and assists the Bishop as usual. He kneels and answers at the Bishop's blessing, and makes the sign of the cross. Then he assists the Bishop during the last Gospel, by holding the Canon and the hand candlestick before him. If there be a special Gospel, he takes the Missal to the Gospel side after the Bishop's blessing. After the Gospel he bows to the cross with the Bishop, and with him he descends the steps, and makes a genuflection or a bow. Then he disrobes the Bishop, and assists him at the thanksgiving in the manner mentioned in the second article.

2. Should there be a boy dressed in surplice, he will generally hold the hand candlestick near the book, attend to the washing of the Bishop's hands, bring the cruets, ring the bell at the *Sanctus*, at the elevation, and at the *Domine, non sum dignus*. He kneels during the confession, at the elevation, during the communion of the people, and when the Bishop gives the blessing.

CHAPTER IX.

MANNER OF CELEBRATING HIGH MASS WITHOUT DEACON OR SUB-DEACON.

THE ASPERGES.*

ARTICLE I.

THINGS TO BE PREPARED.

On the Altar.

1. The chalice, all prepared, should be placed on the extended corporal in the middle of the altar.
2. The burse against the *gradus*.
3. The Missal opened on the book-stand.
4. The altar-cards.
5. If Communion is to be given, the ciborium on the corporal.
6. The antipendium and the veil (if the Blessed Sacrament be there) over the tabernacle, of the color of the day.
7. Six candlesticks with candles.
8. The cross prominently located in the middle of the candlesticks.

On the Side-table.

1. The cruets with wine and water.
2. The finger-towel on the plate.
3. The hand-bell.

The celebrant's bench may be covered with a green cloth, and on it the chasuble and maniple are placed.

---

* The Asperges, or sprinkling of the holy water, takes place every Sunday of the year, except when the Bishop solemnly celebrates. (*Cærem. Epis.*, l. ii, c. xxxi.) The water may be blessed in the church, or in the sacristy. (*Rub. Miss.*) The holy water should be changed, at least, once a week. (*Cærem. Epis.*, l. i, c. vi.)

In the Sacristy.

1. The sacred vestments for the priest, except the maniple and chasuble.
2. A cope.
3. The holy-water vase.
4. The sprinkle.
5. The Missal, or Asperges-card.
6. Surplices for the acolytes.

1. At the appointed time the acolytes put on their surplices, the priest washes his hands, and then puts on the amice, alb, girdle, and stole, assisted by the acolytes. The first acolyte takes the holy-water vase, and the second the Asperges card, placing themselves a little behind the celebrant, who takes off his cap, and all bow to the cross or image in the sacristy. The celebrant, having again put on his cap, goes to the altar, preceded by the acolytes; they bow to the clergy, should they be in the sanctuary.*

2. Having arrived in front of the lowest step of the altar, the first acolyte at the right, and the second at the left, the celebrant gives his cap to the first acolyte, and all make a genuflection on the floor,† rise, and kneel on the lowest step. The priest having received the sprinkle from the acolyte, intones the *Asperges*, or the *Vidi aquam*, according to the season, and then sprinkles the altar three times, first in the middle, then at the Gospel, and lastly, at the Epistle side; in the meantime, the choir continues to sing the *Asperges*. Then the celebrant sprinkles himself, after which, he rises and sprinkles the acolytes, first the one at his right, and then the other, while these remain kneeling.

3. Then turning at their right, they go as far as the railings of the sanctuary, the first acolyte carrying the holy-water vase, at the right of the celebrant, and the second at his left, both raising the borders of the cope.

---

* These bows are not to be made to mere sanctuary boys.
† It is supposed that the Blessed Sacrament is in the tabernacle.

From the railings the priest sprinkles the people three times, first in the middle, then at the Epistle, and lastly, at the Gospel side, or if usual, he passes down the aisles; after which, turning at the right, they go back to the front of the lowest step, and there make a genuflection. During the sprinkling the celebrant recites the *Miserere* or *Confitemini*.

4. When arrived at foot of altar, the first acolyte carries the holy-water vase and sprinkle to sacristy or credence-table, and immediately returns. They stand until the Antiphon *Asperges* is sung and repeated by the choir; after which the celebrant sings in the ferial tone the versicles, and the prayer from the book or card; the choir having answered, *Amen*, all make a genuflection, and go to the bench, where the priest takes off the cope, assisted by the second acolyte, who carries it and the card away; if the Missal has been used for the Asperges, he places it on the book-stand upon the altar. In the meantime, the celebrant, assisted by the first acolyte, puts on the maniple and the chasuble; after which, between the two acolytes, he goes in front of the lowest step, where all make a genuflection, the acolytes kneeling on the floor, a little behind the priest.

5. The celebrant does everything as at Low Mass, except that he sings all that is sung at the solemn High Mass, and also the Gospel. There is no incense used at any time at the High Mass celebrated without deacon and sub-deacon, as it it is only *Missa Cantata*.

6. Towards the end of the confession, at the words *Domini exaudi orationem meam*, both acolytes rise to raise the alb a little, while the priest is ascending to the platform; they then kneel on the last step and answer attentively.

7. After the priest has said the *Kyrie*, if he wishes to sit down, they rise, meet together before the altar, make a genuflection (always on the floor of the sanctuary), and go to the seat, the first at the right, the other at the left; they raise the chasuble, so that he may not sit upon it; the first presents the cap with the usual kisses, and they remain standing, one at each side, nearly face to face, so that their shoulders be not turned to the altar.

8. At the last *Kyrie*, the first gives notice to the celebrant to rise; he takes his cap, lays it on the seat, both accompany the priest before the altar, they make a genuflection on the floor, raise the alb, and then kneel at their places.*

9. When the priest leaves the altar at the *Kyrie*, *Gloria*, or *Credo*, he goes to the bench *per breviorem*. When the priest begins the last prayer, the first, if he be in minor orders, goes to the side-table and takes the Missal, and returns to his place until the concluding words of the prayer, when he goes to the middle, genuflects, and salutes the clergy if any are present in the sanctuary, then returning to his place, sings the Epistle, which being finished, he again goes to the middle, genuflects, bows and replaces the Missal on the credence-table. If neither of the acolytes is in minor orders, the celebrant will read the Epistle.†

10. The second acolyte removes the book at the proper time, going by the lowest step of the altar, and returns to kneel at his place; when the Gospel commences both rise, and at the end answer, *Laus Tibi Christe*, and again kneel down until the end of the *Credo*; then the celebrant goes to sit down.

11. After the *Credo*, while the celebrant is singing the *Dominus vobiscum* and *Oremus*, they rise, make a genuflection together in the middle, and repair to the side-table to put the cruets on the altar. The first hands the cruet with wine, and then that with the water, with the usual kisses, and afterwards the second pours the water on the celebrant's hands; the first presents the towel, and both bow to the priest, before and after.

---

* They should observe the same at the *Gloria* and *Credo*, being punctual to rise as soon as the priest bows, before going to take his seat, after reciting the *Gloria* and *Credo*. When those parts are sung at which the head is bowed, they bow to the cross, and the first gives notice to the celebrant to uncover his head, and to cover it. While the words of the *Credo*, *Et incarnatus est*, are sung, they kneel down with their faces turned towards the altar, and rise after the words, *Et Homo factus est*.

† If there be a *Sequentia*, or long *Tract* after the Epistle, the celebrant, after having read it, sits down, as at the *Kyrie*, and, at the last verse, returns to the altar (by the Epistle side), to say the *Munda cor meum*.

12. After putting away the cruets, they return to the middle of the altar, make a genuflection on the floor, and kneel at their respective places, on each side, fronting the altar.

13. At the elevation, they rise, make a genuflection in the middle, ascend the steps and kneel on the edge of the platform, and both raise the chasuble, and perform everything as in other Masses.

14. When the priest has communicated, and made the genuflection, the first acolyte rises and goes to give the wine and water; which being finished, he returns to the middle and genuflects with the second acolyte, who goes up to the altar and removes the Missal to the Epistle side. Meanwhile the first goes to his place and kneels.

15. At the last Gospel, they both stand up, and the first goes to get the cap. At the *Verbum caro factum est*, they both make a genuflection, and when the priest descends from the altar, they all genuflect, and the first acolyte, presenting the cap with the usual kisses, they return to the sacristy, both going before, as at the beginning.

16. When they arrive at the sacristy, they bow to the cross or image; the first acolyte remains to assist the priest in taking off his vestments; the other goes to put out the candles, and put away the things which are on the altar.

17. If Communion be given, after the priest has communicated and made a genuflection, the first acolyte goes alone to get the communion-cloth, returns to the middle, and kneels down on the floor with his companion. When the celebrant is receiving the Precious Blood, they bow, and recite the *Confiteor*. After the *Indulgentiam*, they rise, make a genuflection at the same time with the celebrant, and kneel on the platform to receive Communion; afterwards they rise, make a genuflection, separate and kneel, holding each end of the communion-cloth, for the communion of the clergy; after which, the first acolyte takes away the cloth. When Communion is over they meet in the middle, make a genuflection together, and go to give the wine and water for the ablution, as said above.

18. Should there be no Asperges, as on holidays, the celebrant puts on all the vestments in the sacristy, then preceded by the acolytes, he goes to the altar. At the foot of the altar the acolytes separate to leave space for the celebrant, the first takes the cap to the bench, both having previously made a genuflection with celebrant. The two acolytes kneel a little behind and at either side of celebrant, and answer as prescribed.

CHAPTER X.

VESPERS SUNG WITHOUT COPE BEARERS.

ARTICLE I.

THINGS TO BE PREPARED.

In the Sanctuary.

1. Six candlesticks on the altar, and the cross in the middle.

2. In the middle of the sanctuary, against the railings, three stools for the two acolytes and the censer-bearer, or a bench sufficiently long to accommodate the three clerks.*

3. Near the bench for the officiating priest, a stool for the master of ceremonies.

4. A book-stand, with the book, in front of the priest's bench, for the officiating clergyman, which may be covered with a cloth of the color of the day.

5. At the altar the antipendium, and if the Blessed Sacrament is there, the veil on the tabernacle, of the color of the day.

---

* If the clerks are to wear caps during vespers, they should be put on the stools beforehand.

In the Sacristy.

1. A surplice and a cope of the color of the day, and if the officiating priest is to give benediction immediately after Vespers without previously returning to the sacristy, a stole of the color of the cope.*

2. Four surplices for the master of ceremonies and the three servers.

3. The censer and incense-boat with incense.

4. Two candlesticks, with candles, for the acolytes.

Article II.

1. The instructions given in the first article of the fourth chapter on solemn vespers, should be observed also during vespers without cope-bearers.

---

* As to the use of the stole, it may be well to remark that the Sacred Congregation of Rites, on the 7th September, 1816, isssued the following decree, which was approved by His Holiness on the 20th of the same month: "Stolam non esse adhibendam præ'erquam in collatione et confectione Sacramentorum; ideoque consuetudinem in contrarium esse abusum, per locorum Ordinarios omnino eliminandum." The stole is less the mark of jurisdiction than of the sacerdotal character; hence it should be used only in performing sacerdotal functions, as is prescribed by the Roman Missal and Ritual. An alb or surplice should always be put on under the stole. Priests should not wear a stole while assisting at High Mass, Vespers, or Benediction; especially as Bishops themselves do not wear it when they assist in cope, the Ceremonial of Bishops not prescribing its use on such occasions. A priest should not use it even in officiating at solemn vespers, though he is to give benediction with the Blessed Sacrament immediately after. He may wear it on the feast of Corpus Christi, when solemn vespers are sung, the Blessed Sacrament being exposed, since the Blessed Sacrament is to be incensed at the *Magnificat*. The Ceremonial does not prescribe that a canon should put on the stole or alb for solemn vespers. "Canonicus hebdomadarius indutus amictu et pluviali supra cottam seu rochetum." According to Gavantus, the priest may put on the stole immediately before going to preach, if such be the established usage, since the Sacred Congregation allows it to be followed. The priest who acts as master of ceremonies at the Benediction of the Blessed Sacrament, should put on the stole when he is to open the tabernacle and touch the Blessed Sacrament and the remonstrance that contains it. He should take it off as soon as these actions are performed, and not wear it during all the time of the ceremony. For a priest to wear a stole while assisting in the sanctuary, even if he be the pastor of the congregation, is improper.

2. A little before the last bell, the master of ceremonies and the three servers put on their surplices. The master of ceremonies helps the officiating priest to vest. The first acolyte lights the candles on the altar, and the two candles in the sacristy. The censer-bearer sees to the fire, that it may be ready when wanted.

3. The censer-bearer in the midst of the two acolytes carrying the candlesticks; the first, being at his right, goes behind the officiating priest. As a general rule, the acolyte at the right will carry the candlestick by holding the foot of it with his left hand, and the middle of the stem with his right; and *vice versa*, the one at the left should hold the foot with his right, and the stem with his left, in such a way that the candlestick be carried straight in front of the bearer, without awkwardness or affectation.

4. At the sign of the master of ceremonies, all bow to the cross, and proceed to the altar in the following order: First walks the censer-bearer with his hands joined, then the two acolytes, carrying the candlesticks, then the master of ceremonies, and lastly, the officiating priest.

5. Having arrived before the lowest step of the altar, the servers place themselves in front, sufficiently distant from the step to leave space for the officiating priest. The priest gives his cap to the master of ceremonies, who receives it with the usual kisses. Then all make a genuflection on the floor. All having risen, the priest and master of ceremonies kneel on the lowest step, and the acolytes go on each side of the altar, and place the candlesticks on the lowest step, one at the Gospel side, the other at the Epistle side, and put out the candles; after which they go in the middle, one on each side of the censer-bearer, where they all make a genuflection and go to their bench.

6. In the meantime, the priest says the *Aperi, Domine*, after which he rises, makes a genuflection and the master of ceremonies accompanies him to the bench.* Being arrived at the bench, the priest says, in a low voice, the

---

* It is customary in Rome for the celebrant to sit down for a brief time before commencing the Vespers.

Pater and *Ave*, after which he intones, *Deus in adjutorium meum intende*, at the same time making the sign of the cross on himself, while the master of ceremonies raises the right border of the cope. All bow at the *Gloria Patri*, towards the altar, and at the commencement of the Psalm all sit. The priest, having received the cap from the master of ceremonies, puts it on, and the master of ceremonies also sits.*

7. Whenever the *Gloria Patri* is sung, the priest takes off his cap, the master of ceremonies giving him notice to that effect each time, by rising and bowing to him. He also raises the border of the cope, and inclines towards the altar during the *Gloria Patri*, or at any similar occurrence, and does not sit till the former replaces the cap on his head. The officiating priest takes off his cap at the names of *Jesus*, *Mary*, and of the saint whose feast is celebrated, and at the words, *Sit nomen Domini benedictum*.

8. Towards the end of the last Psalm, the censer-bearer rises, making a genuflection before the altar, bows to the officiating priest, and goes to the sacristy to prepare the censer. The acolytes also rise, make a genuflection and a bow with the censer-bearer. They light the candles on their candlesticks, and with them they proceed to the middle before the lowest step, make a genuflection, and go to the officiating priest, to whom they bow, and then place themselves one on each side of the book-stand, facing each other, where they stand till the commencement of the hymn, unless it is the *Ave Maris Stella*, or *Veni Creator Spiritus*, in which case they will wait till the end of the first strophe, after which they salute the officiating priest, go to the middle of the altar, make a genuflection, and go to replace the candlesticks in their place, but do not put out the candles; then they return to their seats.

9. The Psalms being ended, the priest rises, after giving his cap to the master of ceremonies, sings the chapter out of the book, before him, during which he remains

---

*The master of ceremonies should not sit on the celebrant's bench, but on a stool near it.

standing. Then, in the same position, the hymn being finished, he intones the antiphon of the *Magnificat*. Whilst the choir sings the said antiphon, the priest sits, and puts on his cap.

10. As soon as the *Magnificat* is commenced, the priest takes off his cap, rises, and, with his hands joined, goes to the altar, accompanied by the master of ceremonies, and makes a genuflection on the floor. (*Cer. Ep.*) Then he goes up to the altar, while the master of ceremonies raises a little the lowest part of his vestments. Having arrived on the platform, the priest bows to the cross, and kisses the altar. At this time the censer-bearer, having made a genuflection on the lowest step at the Epistle side, goes up to the priest, gives the incense-boat to the master of ceremonies, and raises the censer so that the priest may put incense in it. The master of ceremonies presents the little spoon, kissing it first, and then the priest's hand (unless the Blessed Sacrament be exposed), and says, *Benedicite, Pater Reverende*. The priest having put incense into the censer, returns the spoon to the master of ceremonies, and makes a sign of the cross on the censer, saying *Ab illo benedicaris*, etc. Then the censer-bearer lowers the censer's cover, gives it to the master of ceremonies, from whom he receives the incense-boat, and steps down to the floor, where he places the boat on the credence-table, and quickly passes to the Gospel side to raise the border of the cope for the celebrant. The master of ceremonies presents the censer to the officiating priest in the usual manner, and with the usual kisses.

11. The officiating priest incenses the altar in the manner prescribed in No. 6, Art. 7, of the chapter on High Mass. While he incenses the altar he says the *Magnificat;** at the same time, the master of ceremonies and censer-bearer accompany him, supporting the borders of the cope.

12. Having incensed the altar, the priest gives the censer to the master of ceremonies, who receives it with

---

* This recitation of the *Magnificat* is not prescribed, yet it is the custom in Rome.

the usual kisses, and returns it to the censer-bearer. Then he goes to the middle of the altar, where he says the *Gloria Patri*, bowing at the same time; after which he descends the steps from the middle, makes a genuflection on the lowest step, and returns to his bench, where he is incensed with three swings by the master of ceremonies, who, for that purpose, shall have stopped at a convenient distance from the priest's bench, bowing to him before and after incensing, and the priest returning the bow after being incensed.

13. Then the master of ceremonies returns the censer to the censer-bearer, and bowing to the priest, he goes to his place. The censer-bearer from the middle of the sanctuary, incenses the master of ceremonies and the two acolytes, the former with two swings and the others with one, bowing to them, and they to him.

14. Then, having made a genuflection in the middle of the floor, he goes to the railings, and from there he incenses the people, first towards the middle, then at the Gospel side, and lastly, at the Epistle side, bowing before and after the incensing. After which he returns to the sacristy, making a genuflection as he passses before the altar, and bowing to the officiating priest.

15. The priest, being incensed, remains standing at his place till the end of the *Magnificat*, bowing with the rest at the *Gloria Patri*.

16. If the choir sings the antiphon, the priest will sit and cover his head; he rises at the end of it to sing *Dominus vobiscum* and the prayer or prayers out of the book before him, bowing at the *Per Dominum nostrum Jesum*, etc.

17. The two acolytes, after the *Magnificat*, at the *Sicut erat*, take the candlesticks, go to the middle, where they make a genuflection, thence to the officiating priest; they salute him, place themselves as before mentioned, and remain there till after all the prayers are sung. After the *Dominus vobiscum*, they salute the priest, and go to the middle, make a genuflection, and there they remain standing during the anthem of the Blessed Virgin and its prayer. After the *Divinum auxilium*, they

make a genuflection with the priest, and walk before him to the sacristy.

18. The priest, having sung the prayers, sings *Dominus vobiscum.* The *Benedicamus Domino* is sung by one or two members of the choir, after which the priest says, in a lower tone of voice, *Fidelium animæ*, etc., and goes to the altar, accompanied by the master of ceremonies.

19. At the foot of the altar, the priest and master of ceremonies make a genuflection, after which he says, *Pater Noster,* in a low voice; and then intones *Dominus det nobis suam pacem.* Then the anthem of the Blessed Virgin is said or sung by the choir, during which time the priest stands or kneels, according to the season. At the end of the anthem, he says, or sings, in the ferial tone, standing, the prayer, and, after it, *Divinum auxilium.* After which, all make a genuflection, and walk to the sacristy, the priest with his cap on; and there, they bow to the cross, and unvest.

Article III.

Should Benediction of the Blessed Sacrament be given immediately after Vespers, the priest retains the cope he wore at Vespers and, after singing *Divinum auxilium*, he puts on the stole.

The acolytes, having left the celebrant after the *Dominus vobiscum*, which is said after the prayer, go to the middle; there, they genuflect with the thurifer (who will await them if necessary after having incensed the people) and accompany him to the sacristy. During the anthem of the Blessed Virgin they will light the candles on the altar. They return to the sanctuary with the thurifer, and after genuflecting with him, kneel on either side of the altar. The thurifer stands or kneels in the middle, behind the celebrant. If steps are used to place the Blessed Sacrament on the throne, one of the acolytes will attend to this. If there are torch bearers (four or six would do), these accompany the thurifer to the sacristy also, and returning, kneel at either side of him behind the celebrant during Benediction. The humeral-veil, card with prayers, and stole may be placed on the side table before Vespers.

CHAPTER XI.

BENEDICTION OF THE BLESSED SACRAMENT.*

ARTICLE I.

What is to be Prepared.

1. THERE should be, at least, twelve lighted candles on the altar whenever the Blessed Sacrament is exposed in the monstrance, and Benediction given with it.†

2. Likewise a throne, or small canopy, should be placed on the highest step over the altar, between the candlesticks; and in the canopy, a corporal or pall, on which the Blessed Sacrament is to be placed.

3. On the altar, a burse with another corporal, the monstrance covered with a white veil, and the key of the tabernacle.‡

4. On the side-table, a white benediction veil, and the book containing the prayers.

5. In the sacristy, a surplice, white stole, and cope for the officiating priest.§

6. A surplice and white stole, for the priest or deacon, if there be one, who is to expose the Blessed Sacrament.

7. A sufficient number of surplices for the clerks that are to assist the priest, and for the torch-bearers.

8. Two, four, or even eight torches, to be carried by as many clerks.

9. The censer, and the incense-boat.

---

* Benediction with the Blessed Sacrament should not be given without permission from the Ordinary. (*Benedict XIV, Instit. XXX*, n. 9, and *S. R. C.*, 28th April, 1640, 18th Dec., 1647.)

† *Benedict XIV, Instit. XXX*, 22, 24.

‡ The cross, unless it be too difficult to remove, the altar-cards, and reliquaries should be removed from the altar. (*Benedict XIV, ibid.*, n. 17.)

§ According to Merati (Part iv, tit. xii, n. 30), it is commendable for the priest to wear an amice, alb, cincture, stole, and cope.

Article II.

Ceremonies to be Performed when there is but one Priest.

1. The officiating priest[*] having put on his surplice, stole and cope, preceded by the censer-bearer and the acolytes carrying the lighted torches, two by two, goes to the altar, makes a genuflection, rises, and kneels on the lowest step; the acolytes with their torches, forming a line at some distance behind the officiating priest, make a genuflection with him, and then kneel in the same place till the end of the ceremony.[†]

2. The priest rises, goes up to the altar, unfolds the corporal, and extends it in the middle; then he opens the tabernacle, makes a genuflection on one knee, takes the Blessed Sacrament from the tabernacle,[‡] and puts it in the monstrance.[§] By this time, if necessary, one of the servers shall have carried the stool or steps to the platform of the altar, that the priest may reach the place of exposition; the priest makes another genuflection on one knee, and exposes the Blessed Sacrament, then he joins his hands, and makes a low bow, and another genuflection having reached the platform; after which, turning to his right, he descends, kneels on the lowest step, bows, rises, and turns to his right, to put incense in the

---

[*] When Benediction is given immediately after Vespers, the celebrant keeps the same cope which he wore at Vespers. Also, when the Benediction is given immediately after High Mass, the celebrant keeps the stole he had on, and having taken off the chasuble and maniple at his usual seat, he puts on a cope of the color used at Mass. If High Mass be celebrated with deacon and sub-deacon, they take off their maniples only, and assist at the Benediction of the Blessed Sacrament.

[†] The censer-bearer may kneel in the middle, between the torch-bearers.

[‡] At this time, where such is the custom, the choir commences the hymn, *O Salutaris Hostia!*

[§] Should the priest touch the Blessed Sacrament, he ought to purify his fingers in the little vase kept for that purpose near the tabernacle, and wipe them with the purificator.

censer; the censer-bearer goes to the priest with the censer, who puts incense in, without, however, blessing it. If there are clerks assisting the priest, they rise with him: the one at the right receives the incense-boat from the censer-bearer, and presents the spoon to the priest; the other, at the left, supports the border of the cope, as the priest puts incense in the censer.

3. Then the priest kneels on the lowest step, takes the censer, and in the usual manner, incenses the Blessed Sacrament with three swings,* bowing before and after. During the incensing, the censer-bearer, if there are no assisting clerks, kneels at the right of the priest, holding the border of the cope; then he receives back the censer, and goes to his place, where he kneels.

4. In the meantime, the choir may sing such hymns and antiphons as are approved by the Church,† or by ancient usage; nevertheless they should be in the Latin language. The corresponding versicles and responses may be sung also; last of all, the whole hymn, *Pange lingua*, etc., or the two last strophes, *Tantum ergo*, etc., and *Genitori*, etc., should be sung, and after it, the versicle, *Panem de cœlo*, etc., and the prayer, *Deus qui nobis*, etc.

5. During the *Tantum ergo*, at the words, *veneremur cernui*, all make a low bow, without, however, prostrating themselves.‡

6. All remain kneeling, unless the *Te Deum* be sung, during which they stand, except at the verse, *Te ergo quæsumus*, etc., during which verse they kneel; at the commencement of *Genitori*,§ the priest, his assistants, and the censer-bearer bow, rise, and incense is put in the censer, as is said in n. 2, and the Blessed Sacrament is incensed again, as before indicated.‖

---

* The Blessed Sacrament is to be incensed "*triplici ductu*."
† *Alex. VII. constit. Piæ Solicitudinis. Benedict XIV, constit. Inter omnigenas. Gardell.*
‡ Such is the practice in Rome and through all Italy, and it seems very becoming as an expression of deep sentiment of reverence.
§ *Merati*, pars. ix, tit. xii, 31. *Gardell*, § xxxiv, 17.
‖ The officiating priest incenses the Blessed Sacrament only twice, as is indicated. *Rit. Rom., Cærem. Epis.*, and *Instruct., Clem. XI,* n. 2.

7. The hymn being finished, the singers, or the celebrant, intone the versicle, *Panem de cœlo*, etc.; the choir answers, *Omne delectamentum*, etc. During Paschal time and the Octave of Corpus Christi, *Alleluia** is added both to the versicle and response. After this, the priest rises and without making a genuflection or bow, sings, *Oremus*,† *Deus qui nobis sub Sacramento*, etc., out of the book, which, in the absence of sacred ministers, he holds in his hands.

He concludes the prayer with these words, *Qui vivis et regnas in sæculo sæculorum;*‡ neither before nor after this prayer *Dominus vobiscum* is said.

8. After the prayer, the priest kneels, and if there is no one assisting, the censer-bearer goes to the side-table, takes the benediction-veil, and extends it on the priest's shoulders; then, if necessary, he carries the steps to the middle of the platform; then the priest bows, rises, goes to the platform, makes a genuflection on one knee, takes down the Blessed Sacrament from the throne, places it on the corporal, and makes another genuflection. In the meantime the steps are removed.

9. The priest then turns the back of the monstrance to his face; then covering his hands with the extremities of the veil, he takes hold of it at the highest part of its foot with his right hand, and at the lowest with his left; then he turns to his right on the Epistle side towards the people, raises the monstrance as high as his eyes, brings it down lower than his breast, then he raises it in a straight line as high as his breast, afterwards brings it to his left shoulder, and completes the circle, turning himself to the altar to his right, on the Gospel side. At last, he places it on the altar, turns its forepart towards his face, and makes a genuflection.§

---

* *Merati*, pars iv, tit. xii. *Gardell.*, § xxxiv, 17.

† *Gardell*, xxiv, 22.

‡ Other prayers taken from the Missal may be added (especially the collect ordered by the Ordinary), under the same conclusion. (*S. R. C.*, 7th Sept., 1850.)

§ "Sacerdos, ostensorium manibus tenens, vertit se a parte Epistolæ, ita ut in medio Altaris populum respiciat. Tunc illud elevat

10. During Benediction the priest is silent,* but a few strokes of the hand-bell may give notice of Benediction being given; also, the censer-bearer may incense the Blessed Sacrament with three swings.† The organ may play a grave and sweet melody during Benediction, as at the elevation, during Mass.

11. The priest having replaced the monstrance on the altar, makes a genuflection on one knee, and is in the meantime divested of the benediction-veil; having risen, he takes the Blessed Sacrament out of the monstrance, puts It in the tabernacle, makes a genuflection, closes the tabernacle, goes down to the lowest step, makes a genuflection with the clerks, and in the same order as he came to the altar, returns to the sacristy.

12. Whilst the Blessed Sacrament is replaced in the tabernacle, the psalm, *Laudate Dominum omnes gentes*, or anything suitable for the occasion, may be sung.

ARTICLE III.

WHEN THE OFFICIATING PRIEST IS ASSISTED BY ANOTHER PRIEST, OR BY DEACON AND SUB-DEACON.

1. If a priest or deacon assist at the Benediction, he walks from the sacristy before the officiating priest. He carries the stole folded on his left arm. At the altar, he

---

decenti mora, non supra caput, sed tantum usque ad oculos, et eodem modo illud dimittit infra pectus; mox iterum recte illud attollit usque ad pectus; et deinde ad sinistrum humerum ducit, et reducit ad dexterum, nec ante pectus reducit, sed continuo se convertit ad cornu Evangelii; perficiens circulum, nec tamen, dum Crucum efformat, movens pedes." (*Car. Epis.*)

* The Benediction with the Blessed Sacrament is to be given in silence by the celebrant, whether he be a Bishop or a priest, according to the Roman Ritual, the Ceremonial of Bishops, and several decisions of the Sacred Congregation of Rites, 9th Feb., 1763.

† Neither the ringing of the bell, nor the incensing during Benediction is prescribed by the Rubrics, yet, in many well-regulated churches in Europe, the custom prevails of doing either or both. In fact it would seem that, the priest having already incensed the Blessed Sacrament, an inferior should not afterwards incense it; yet, the established custom may be followed. In some places even, the large church bell announces to the people that, at that moment, God, in His mercy, blesses them.

takes his place at the right of the officiating clergyman. After making the genuflection with the others, he puts on the stole,* goes up to the predella, unfolds the corporal in the middle of the altar, opens the door of the tabernacle, and makes a genuflection on one knee. In making a genuflection on the predella, he turns his body a little towards the Epistle side to avoid turning his back to the officiating priest. He exposes the Blessed Sacrament in the manner prescribed in Art. II, n. 2.

2. Having made the genuflection after the exposition, he turns to his left, goes down, kneels on the lowest step, and takes off the stole without kissing it. Then, having bowed with the officiating priest, he rises, moves a little backward so as to allow the censer-bearer to pass at his right in going to the officiating priest with the censer. He receives the incense-boat, and presents the spoon to the officiating priest without kisses. Incense having been put in the censer, the assistant priest receives back the spoon, returns the boat to the censer-bearer, and from him he receives the censer, which he presents to the officiating priest in the usual manner, but without kisses. He bows with the officiating priest, and holds up the border of the cope during the incensing. He bows again with him, takes the censer, and returns it to the censer-bearer.

3. At the *Genitori*, he bows, and rises with the officiating priest for the incense, in which he proceeds as before.

4. After the prayer, *Deus qui nobis sub Sacramento*, etc., he puts on the stole, goes up to the altar, and, with the usual genuflections, he takes the monstrance, places it on the corporal, extended in the middle of the altar, and makes another genuflection. In the meantime, the benediction-veil is extended on the shoulders of the officiating priest by a clerk, or by the censer-bearer. He rises when the celebrant arrives at the predella, hands to him the ostensorium, and assists in adjusting the humeral-veil.

---

* If a deacon assists, he should put on the stole, suspending it from his left shoulder to his right side, under his arm.

5. During the Benediction he kneels on the predella,* and removes the stole. After Benediction he puts on the stole, rises, and takes the ostensorium from the celebrant, places it upon the altar, and genuflects. He remains in that position, having his back a little towards the Epistle corner, until the officiating priest has gone down to the foot of the altar and bowed to the Blessed Sacrament; then having risen he takes the Blessed Sacrament out of the monstrance, and puts it in the tabernacle. Then he makes another genuflection, closes the door of the tabernacle, folds the corporal, places it in the burse, and, having gone down to his place, he takes off the stole and kisses it. Having given the cap to the officiating priest, he makes with him a genuflection on the floor, and all return to the sacristy.

---

* If it is not the custom for the assisting priest to give the monstrance into the hands of the celebrant, this need not be done. The *Form of Exposition and Benediction of the Blessed Sacrament for the Archdiocese of Baltimore* does not prescribe it; hence it is optional with the pastors of churches to observe what we have given above, or adhere to their Diocesan regulations or customs if opposed to it. The custom in Rome is the one we have given.

PART II.

Ceremonies for Holy Week and other Festivals,

According to the small Ritual of Benedict XIII, S. M.

TO BE USED IN CHURCHES WHERE THERE IS BUT ONE PRIEST.

(NOTE.—The acolyte who, throughout all these ceremonies, is instructed to touch the chalice or ciborium, is supposed to be in minor orders.)

CHAPTER I.

BLESSING OF CANDLES ON CANDLEMAS DAY.

ARTICLE I.

OF WHAT IS TO BE PREPARED FOR THE BENEDICTION, PROCESSION, AND MASS.

On the Side-table.

1. THE chalice for Mass, with white ornaments, unless this festival should fall on one of the privileged Sundays; in which case the ornaments must be violet.

2. The chasuble, stole, and maniple, either of white or of violet color, as directed above.*

3. The censer with the incense-boat† filled with incense.

4. The vessel containing holy water, and the sprinkling-brush.‡

---

* The vestments should more properly be placed on the bench.
† The box is so called from its form.
‡ We shall hereafter use the simpler term "sprinkle," as in Worcester's Dictionary.

5. A plate with some bread, and a basin with a pitcher of water, to wash the hands of the priest, after the distribution of the candles.

6. A towel.

7. A plate containing the cruets with wine and water, and a small towel to wipe the fingers.

At the Altar.

1. A violet altar-veil,* that can be easily removed; or, white, if the Mass be of the Blessed Virgin.

2. The Missal on the Epistle side, supported by a violet cushion, or a small bookstand.

At the Epistle Side on the Floor of the Sanctuary.

1. A table covered with white linen; and on it, the candles to be blessed, covered likewise with another white linen cloth.

2. The processional cross.

In the Sacristy.

1. Three surplices for the acolytes.

2. The amice, alb, cincture, with stole and cope of violet color, for the celebrant.

3. A chafing-dish, with fire and tongs.

ARTICLE II.

CEREMONIES TO BE PERFORMED ON CANDLEMAS DAY.

SECTION I.—*Of the Blessing of the Candles.*

1. At the stated time, the acolytes put on their cassocks and surplices, in the sacristy, and prepare everything as in the preceding chapter.

2. The faithful should be called to church by the ringing of the bells.

3. The celebrant, having made his preparation for

---

* The Latin term, "antipendium," is generally used for the veil which covers the front of the altar.

Mass, and washed his hands in the sacristy, being assisted by the second and third acolytes, puts on over his cassock the amice, alb, stole and cope of violet color.*

4. In the meantime, the first acolyte removes from the altar the flower-pots, and lights the candles that are on it.

5. The celebrant, having made a low bow to the cross, or to any other sacred image placed in the sacristy, puts on his cap, and, being preceded by the first acolyte, walks, with his hands joined, to the altar, between the second and third acolytes, who raise the lower part of the cope at each side.

6. When he comes to the middle of the altar, he gives his cap to the first acolyte, who, having placed it on the celebrant's bench, uncovers the candles which are to be blessed.

7. Then the celebrant, still standing on the floor of the sanctuary, makes a low bow to the cross (or a genuflection on the lowest step, if the Blessed Sacrament be in the tabernacle), ascends the altar, and kisses it in the middle. If the holy water is to be given, the celebrant, kneeling on the lowest step, intones the anthem, *Asperges*, and does as is prescribed in the Missal, and afterwards goes up to the altar.

8. The celebrant, having kissed the altar, goes to the Epistle side, having always the two acolytes at his sides, as in No. 5.

9. There, having his face turned towards the altar, and his hands joined, he says in the ferial tone, *Dominus vobiscum, Oremus*, the prayer, *Domine Sancte*, with the four following prayers.

10. In the meantime, the first acolyte puts fire in the censer, holding it and the incense-boat in his hands.

11. While the celebrant is saying the fifth prayer, the third acolyte, who is on his left side, having made a genuflection towards the altar, goes to the side-table, takes from it the holy-water vase, and, with the acolyte who carries the censer, goes to him.

---

* Should this festival fall on Sunday, the celebrant, vested as above, blesses the water for the Asperges, as in the Missal.

12. The celebrant, after the fifth prayer, receiving the incense-spoon from the second acolyte, who is at his right side, and who, as usual kisses first the spoon and then his hand, takes the incense-boat, puts the incense in the censer, and blesses it.

13. Then having received the sprinkle from the second acolyte, he sprinkles the candles thrice, viz., in the middle, at the right, and at the left, saying with a low voice, *Asperges me*, etc., without the *Miserere*.

14. Afterwards he incenses the candles thrice, saying nothing.

15. The blessing being ended, the celebrant bows in the middle of the altar, and retires to the Gospel side, and then explains the institution of this solemnity, the meaning of the ceremonies, and the use of the candles, that the faithful may come and receive them in a proper and respectful manner.

SECTION II.—*Of the Distribution of the Candles.*

1. After the sermon, the first acolyte takes from the table a candle for the celebrant, and, if there is no other priest present, puts it on the middle of the altar.

2. The celebrant, having bowed in the middle of the altar, kneels on the platform, with his face turned towards the cross.

3. Whilst kneeling down, he takes from the altar the candle, kisses it, and hands it to the first acolyte.*

4. Then he goes to the Epistle side, and recites alternately with the acolytes, in a loud and even voice, *Lumen*, etc., and the Canticle, *Nunc dimittis*, etc.

5. The anthem, *Lumen*, etc., having been repeated after *Sicut erat*, the celebrant bows to the cross, turns towards the people, distributes the candles, first to the priests (if any be present), then to the acolytes kneeling on the edge of the platform, who all kiss first the candle, and then his hand.

---

* If there is another priest, he gives the candle to the celebrant, who stands, having his face turned towards the people: the priest kisses the candle only, which is also done by the celebrant on receiving it.

6. The celebrant having bowed to the altar between the acolytes, goes to the chancel, or rails, at the Epistle side.

7. There he begins to distribute the candles, which are brought thither by the second acolyte, and handed to the celebrant by the third.

8. The distribution of the candles being ended, the celebrant washes his hands at the Epistle side; the first acolyte pours the water, and the two others offer the towel.

9. The celebrant, having washed his hands, goes to the middle of the altar, bows to the cross, and then ascends in a straight line with it, until he arrives at the centre of the platform, when he turns to the book at the Epistle side.

10. There he recites with the acolytes the anthem, *Exurge Domine*, etc., with a loud voice.

11. Then standing in the same place, he says, *Oremus*, and if Candlemas day comes after Septuagesima, and not on a Sunday, he subjoins, *Flectamus genua*, kneeling at the same time with all the others; and the second acolyte, first rising, answers, *Levate*.

12. Afterwards the celebrant says the prayer, *Exaudi quæsumus*, etc., keeping always his hands joined.

Section III.—*Of the Procession.*

1. The prayer being ended, the celebrant goes to the middle of the altar, where he receives from the first acolyte a lighted candle, and a copy of this *Ceremonial*, or the Ritual for the anthems, to be recited during the procession.

2. The two other acolytes take likewise lighted candles, and copies of this *Ceremonial*.

3. The celebrant turns towards the people, and says, *Procedamus in pace*, and the acolytes answer, *In nomine Christi. Amen.*

4. The celebrant begins to recite the anthem, *Adorna*, etc., as below, and continues all the anthems with the acolytes alternately.

PROCESSION OF CANDLEMAS DAY.

5. After the acolytes have, as directed above, answered, *In nomine Christi. Amen;* the first acolyte takes the processional cross, and having made a genuflection before the altar, turns towards the people, and leads the procession either out of the church, or within it, as may be customary, and turning to his right, and going round, returns to the altar.

6. The celebrant follows him between the other acolytes, reciting with them the following anthems, which, for greater convenience, are divided into verses:

ANTIPH. *Adorna thalamum tuum, Sion; et suscipe Regem Christum.*
Amplectere Mariam: quæ est cælestis porta.
Ipsa enim regem portat gloriæ, novi luminis.
Subsistit Virgo, adducens manibus Filium ante luciferum genitum: quem accipiens Simeon in ulnas suas, prædicavit populis: Dominum eum esse vitæ et mortis, et Salvatorem Mundi.
Responsum accepit Simeon de Spiritu Sancto: non visurum se mortem, nisi videret Christum Domini:
Et cum inducerent puerum in templum; accepit eum in ulnas suas, et benedixit Deum, et dixit:
Nunc dimittis servum tuum, Domine: secundum verbum tuum in pace.
Cum inducerent puerum Jesum parentes ejus, ut facerent secundum consuetudinem legis pro eo, ipse accepit eum in ulnas suas.

7. As the procession enters the church, if it was made outside; or the·sanctuary, if it did not go out of the church, the following Response is recited:

RESP. *Obtulerunt Domino par turturum, aut duos pullos columbarum:*
Sicut scriptum est, in lege Domini.
Postquam impleti sunt dies purgationis Mariæ: secundum legem Moysis:
Tulerunt Jesum in Jerusalem: ut sisterent eum Domino.
Sicut scriptum est: in lege Domini.
Gloria Patri et Filio: et Spiritui Sancto.
Sicut scriptum est: in lege Domini.

8. The acolyte, who carries the cross, after having made a genuflection before the altar, leaves it at its place.

9. The celebrant ends the Responses before the altar.

SECTION IV.—*Of the Mass after the Procession.*

1. The Responses being ended, the first acolyte receives the candles from the celebrant, and from the other acolytes, and places them on a table.

2. The celebrant goes to the bench, whereon he usually sits in solemn Masses, attended by the second and third acolytes, puts off the cope, and puts on the violet chasuble and the maniple for the Mass of the Sunday.

3. In the meantime, in case the Mass is to be said of the festival, the first acolyte removes from the altar the violet front veil, leaving the white one, and places the flower-pots between the candle-sticks.

4. The celebrant goes to the altar to say Mass, in the course of which, if it be of the festival, the acolytes hold lighted candles during the Gospel, and from the elevation till after the communion.

5. Mass being ended, the celebrant, preceded by the acolytes, returns to the sacristy.

There he makes his thanksgiving as usual.

6. The acolytes take everything from the altar and the table, and carry them to the sacristy, arranging them in their proper places.

CHAPTER II.

OF THE BENEDICTION OF THE ASHES ON ASH-WEDNESDAY.

ARTICLE I.

THINGS TO BE PREPARED FOR THE BENEDICTION AND MASS.

On the Side-table near the Altar.

1. A CHALICE, with a veil of violet color.
2. A violet maniple and chasuble.*

---

* These should be placed on the bench.

ASH-WEDNESDAY. 93

3. The censer and boat, with incense.
4. The holy-water vase, with a sprinkle.
5. A plate, with crumbs of bread; and a basin, with a pitcher of water, to wash the hands of the priest after the distribution of the ashes.
6. A towel.
7. A plate containing the cruets with wine and water, and a small towel to wipe the fingers.

On the Altar.

1. A violet altar-veil, the cross, and candlesticks with candles, but no flower-pots.
2. The Missal on the Epistle side, supported by a bookstand.
3. A vessel containing the ashes, made out of the boughs blessed on Palm Sunday, which should be dry and sifted, covered either with a lid of the same material as the vessel, or with a violet veil, and placed between the Missal and the Epistle side.

In the Sacristy.

1. Three surplices for the acolytes.
2. The amice, alb, cincture, violet stole and cope.
3. A chafing-dish with fire and tongs.

ARTICLE II.

OF THE SACRED RITES TO BE PERFORMED ON ASH-WEDNESDAY.

SECTION I.—*Blessing of the Ashes.*

1. Everything having been prepared, as above, by the acolytes in surplices, the people should be called to church by the usual ringing of the bells.
2. The celebrant, having washed his hands in the sacristy, attended by the second and third acolytes, puts on over the surplice, the amice, alb, cincture, violet stole and cope.
3. The first acolyte lights the candles on the altar, and returns to the sacristy.

4. All having bowed to the cross, or the principal picture in the sacristy, go to the altar.

5. The first acolyte, having his hands joined, walks before, then the celebrant with his head covered, between the second and third acolytes.

6. The celebrant gives his cap to the first acolyte, and bows to the altar.

7. He goes up to the altar, having at his side the second and third acolytes, and kisses it in the middle.

8. In the meantime, the first acolyte, having placed the cap on the celebrant's bench, uncovers the ashes.

9. The celebrant goes to the Epistle side, and says, with the acolytes, the anthem, *Exaudi*.

10. In the meantime, the first acolyte prepares the censer with the fire.

11. The anthem, *Exaudi*, having been repeated, the celebrant, standing in the same place, without turning towards the people, says in a ferial tone, and having his hands joined, *Dominus vobiscum*, and the four prayers, as in the Missal.

12. Whilst the celebrant is saying the fourth prayer, the third acolyte, having made a genuflection before the altar, takes the holy-water vase, and with the censer-bearer, goes to the celebrant.

13. The celebrant, assisted by the second acolyte, puts the incense in the censer, blesses it, and afterwards sprinkles and incenses the ashes, as usual.

14. The blessing being ended, the vessel containing the ashes is placed in the middle of the altar.

15. The celebrant addresses the congregation from the altar, on the ceremony of the ashes.

SECTION II.—*Of the Putting on the Ashes.*

1. The celebrant, if no other priest is present, having made a reverence to the cross, kneels down in the middle of the platform of the altar, and whilst thus kneeling, puts ashes on his own head, saying nothing.

2. But if another priest is present, this priest without stole goes to the altar, and puts ashes on the head of the celebrant, who stands, bowing, and having his face turned

towards the people, the priest saying, *Memento homo, quia pulvis es; et in pulverem reverteris.*

3. The celebrant having received the ashes, goes to the Missal on the Epistle side, and recites, with the acolytes, the anthem, *Immutemur*, with all that follows.

4. Then the celebrant puts the ashes on the clergy (if any are present), who kneel at the edge of the platform of the altar, the first of them in dignity being the nearest to the Epistle side. He says to each one, *Memento*, etc.

5. The celebrant having bowed to the altar, goes between the second and third acolytes, to the railing at the Epistle side, and puts the ashes first on the men, then on the women.

6. After the putting on of the ashes, the celebrant, standing on the floor of the sanctuary at the Epistle side, attended by the acolytes, washes his hands, cleaning them with crumbs of bread, and wipes them.

7. Then he goes up to the altar by the steps that are in front of it, having made a bow in the middle, and goes to the Epistle side.

8. Thus, having his face turned towards the altar, with his hands joined, he says, *Dominus vobiscum*, and the prayer, *Concede nobis, Domine*, and having made a bow to the altar in the same place, descends to the Epistle side.

SECTION III.—*Of the Mass.*

1. The celebrant, going to the Epistle side, near the bench, assisted by the acolytes, takes off the cope, puts on the maniple and chasuble.

2. He goes to the altar for the Mass, in which everything is to be done as in the Missal.

3. After Mass, the celebrant, preceded by the acolytes, returns to the sacristy with his hands joined, puts off the sacred vestments, and makes his thanksgiving.

CHAPTER III.

OF PALM SUNDAY.

Article I.

WHAT IS TO BE PREPARED FOR THE SACRED CEREMONIES OF THIS SUNDAY.

On the Side-table.

1. The chalice, with its ornaments of violet color for Mass.
2. The maniple and chasuble, of violet color.*
3. The censer, with the incense-boat.
4. A basin, with a pitcher of water, and a towel.
5. A plate, with cruets containing wine and water, and a finger-towel.
6. Copies of this *Ceremonial*, for what is to be recited at the procession.

On the Altar.

1. The violet antipendium.
2. The Missal, on the Epistle side, on a cushion, or a small stand.
3. Branches of palms in place of flowers, between the candlesticks.

By the side of the Epistle on the floor.

1. A table, covered with a white linen cloth, and on it the palms to be blessed.
2. The processional cross, covered with a violet veil.

In the Sacristy.

1. Three surplices for the acolytes.
2. The amice, alb, cincture, stole and cope of violet color for the celebrant.
3. A chafing-dish, with fire and tongs.
4. The holy-water vase, with the sprinkle.

---

* As before said, these should more properly be placed on the bench.

Article II.

OF THE CEREMONIES TO BE PERFORMED ON PALM SUNDAY.

SECTION I.—*Of the Blessing of the Palms.*

1. Everything being prepared in its proper place, the people should be called to the church by the ringing of the bells.

2. The celebrant, attended by the second and third acolytes, puts on in the sacristy the amice, alb, cincture, violet stole and cope.

3. He blesses the water, as in the Missal; and in the meantime the first acolyte lights the candles on the altar.

4. The celebrant, preceded by the first acolyte, who carries the holy-water vase, proceeds to the altar, with his head covered, walking between the second and third acolytes, and kneels on the lowest step, for the sprinkling of the holy water.

5. When the sprinkling is done, the first acolyte removes the holy-water vase and card of the Asperges: if the Missal has been used, he replaces it on the small stand, on the Epistle side of the altar.

6. The third acolyte puts the maniple on the celebrant's arm.

7. The celebrant, between the second and third acolytes, goes up to the altar, kisses it in the middle; retires to the Epistle side; and there, in a high and even tone, begins the anthem, *Hosanna*, which is continued by the acolytes.

8. The celebrant standing in the same place, with his hands joined, says *Dominus vobiscum*, and the prayer, *Deus, quem diligere*, etc.

9. Then he recites the lesson, and after it he says, with the acolytes, the Response, *Collegerunt*, etc. *In monte Oliveti*, etc.

10. Having said in the same place, *Munda cor meum*, etc., he reads the Gospel; then kisses the Missal, and takes off the maniple.

11. Then he says, *Dominus vobiscum*, the prayer, and

the preface, keeping his hands joined, whilst he recites the above-mentioned and the following prayers.

12. The acolytes say *Sanctus, Sanctus,* etc.

13. The celebrant having said *Dominus vobiscum,* recites the five other prayers that follow.

14. In the meantime, the first acolyte puts fire in the censer, and takes the incense-boat.

15. Whilst the celebrant says the fifth prayer, the third acolyte, having made a genuflection towards the altar, takes from the side-table the holy-water vase, and with the censer-bearer goes to the celebrant.

16. The celebrant, attended by the second acolyte, puts incense in the censer, and blesses it.

17. Then he sprinkles the palms thrice, saying in a low voice, *Asperges me,* etc., without *Miserere,* and incenses them.

18. The celebrant says again, *Dominus vobiscum,* and then the sixth prayer.

19. The first acolyte carries back to the sacristy the censer, and the second and third acolytes remain with the celebrant.

20. The celebrant addresses to the congregation an appropriate instruction.

Section II.—*Of the Distribution of the Palms.*

1. The first acolyte carries from the side-table the palms for the celebrant and the acolytes, and lays them on the altar.

2. The celebrant, having bowed to the cross, kneels in the middle of the platform before the altar, and takes his palm from the altar; kisses it, and hands it to the first acolyte.*

3. He goes to the Epistle side and recites with the acolytes the anthem, *Pueri Hebræorum,* etc.

4. Then, having bowed to the cross, he turns towards the people, and distributes the palms, first to priests, if

---

* In case another priest is present, the palm should be given by him to the celebrant, as it has been said of the candle, on the feast of the Purification.

any are present, then to the acolytes, who all kneel on the edge of the platform of the altar, beginning from the first in dignity, at the Epistle side; they all kiss, first the palm, then the hand of the celebrant.

5. The celebrant goes down from the altar, bows before it, and goes to the railing of the sanctuary, at the Epistle side.

6. Then the palms are handed to him by the first acolyte, and he distributes them, first to the men, and then to the women.

7. After the distribution, the celebrant, standing on the floor of the sanctuary, attended by two acolytes, washes his hands.

8. He goes by the front steps to the altar, and at the Epistle side says, *Dominus vobiscum*, and the last prayer.

9. In the meantime, the first acolyte ties with a violet ribbon a palm on the top of the processional cross.

10. After the prayer, the first acolyte gives to the celebrant and to the other acolytes the palms, and a copy of this *Ceremonial*, to read what is to be recited at the procession.

SECTION III.—*Of the Procession.*

1. The celebrant, holding the palm in his hands, turns towards the people, and says in the middle of the altar, *Procedamus in pace.* The acolytes answer, *In nomine Christi. Amen.* And the celebrant begins, *Cum appropinquaret*, etc.

2. The acolyte with the cross walks first; then the celebrant, between two acolytes, reciting alternately, in a loud voice, the following anthems divided into verses.

3. The procession goes by the right side out of the principal door; they recite the following

Anthem.

Cum appropinquaret Dominus Jerosolymam: misit duos ex discipulis suis dicens:

Ite in castellum, quod contra vos est: et invenietis pullum asinæ alligatum, super quem nullus hominum sedit:

PALM SUNDAY.

Solvite eum: et adducite mihi.
Si quis vos interrogaverit, dicite: Opus Domino est.
Solventes adduxerunt ad Jesum: et imposuerunt illi vestimenta sua, et sedit super eum.
Alii expanderunt vestimenta sua in via: alii ramos de arboribus sternebant.
Et qui sequebantur, clamabant: Hosanna, benedictus qui venit in nomine Domini.
Benedictum regnum patris nostri David: Hosanna in excelsis: miserere nobis, fili David.

Another Anthem.

Cum audisset populus, quia Jesus venit Jerosolymam: acceperunt ramos palmarum,
Et exierunt ei obviam: et clamabant pueri dicentes:
Hic est, qui venturus est in salutem populi.
Hic est salus nostra, et redemptio Israel.
Quantus est iste: cui Throni et Dominationes occurrunt!
Noli timere, filia Sion, ecce Rex tuus venit tibi sedens super pullum asinæ; sicut scriptum est.
Salve Rex Fabricator mundi: qui venisti redimere nos.

Another Anthem.

Ante sex dies solemnis Paschæ: quando venit Dominus in civitatem Jerusalem,
Occurrerunt ei pueri; et in manibus portabant ramos palmarum.
Et clamabant voce magna dicentes: Hosanna in excelsis.
Benedictus qui venisti in multitudine misericordiæ tuæ: Hosanna in excelsis.

Another Anthem.

Occurrunt turbæ cum floribus et palmis Redemptori obviam: et victori triumphanti digna dant obsequia.
Filium Dei ore gentes prædicant: et in laudem Christi voces tonant per nubila: Hosanna in excelsis.

PALM SUNDAY.

Another Anthem.

Cum Angelis et pueris fideles inveniamur, triumphatori mortis clamantes: Hosanna in excelsis.

Turba multa, quæ convenerat ad diem festum: clamabant Domino:

Benedictus qui venit in nomine Domini: Hosanna in excelsis.

1. The first acolyte, carrying the cross, stops before the principal door, having his face turned towards it.

2. The second and third acolytes go into the church, shut the door, and turning towards the procession, say:

Gloria, laus et honor Tibi sit, Rex Christe Redemptor: Cui puerile decus prompsit Hosanna pium.

3. The celebrant outside of the church, turning towards the door, and having on his cap, repeats:

Gloria, laus et honor, etc.

Clerks. *Israel es Tu Rex, Davidis et inclyta proles, Nomine qui in Domini, Rex benedicte, venis.*

Cel. *Gloria,* etc.

Clerks. *Cœtus in excelsis Te laudat cœlicus omnis, et mortalis homo, et cuncta creata simul.*

Cel. *Gloria,* etc.

Clerks. *Plebs Hebræa Tibi cum palmis obviam venit: cum prece, voto, hymnis adsumus ecce Tibi.*

Cel. *Gloria, laus,* etc.

Clerks. *Hi Tibi passuro solvebant munia laudis: nos Tibi regnanti pangimus ecce melos.*

Cel. *Gloria,* etc.

Clerks. *Hi placuere Tibi; placeat devotio nostra: Rex bone, Rex clemens, cui bona cuncta placent.*

Cel. *Gloria,* etc.

4. The preceding verses being ended, the first acolyte, with the foot of the cross, knocks at the bottom of the door; and the two acolytes within the church open the door, and place themselves at each side of it.

5. The first acolyte, carrying the cross, enters the church, and the celebrant follows him, beginning the Response, *Ingrediente Domino,* etc.

6. The second and third acolytes receive the celebrant, place him in the middle, and with him continue the Response—

Ingrediente Domino in Sanctam Civitatem, Hebræorum pueri resurrectionem vitæ pronunciantes.

Cum ramis palmarum: Hosanna clamabant in excelsis.

Cum audissent quod Jesus veniret Jerosolymam: exierunt obviam ei.

Cum ramis palmarum: Hosanna in excelsis.

7. The procession and Responses are ended before the altar.

8. The first acolyte leaves the cross, takes the palms from the celebrant and the clerks.

9. The celebrant stands on the floor of the sanctuary at the Epistle side, where he is accustomed to sit during Mass; takes off the cope, puts on the maniple and chasuble.

10. The celebrant proceeds to the altar to celebrate Mass. The acolytes hold palms in their hands whilst the Passion is read, and during the Gospel.

11. After Mass, the celebrant, preceded by the acolytes, returns to the sacristy.

12. There he takes off the sacred vestments, and makes his thanksgiving.

13. The acolytes take everything from the altar, and from the side-table, and putting them in their proper places, retire modestly.

CHAPTER IV.

OF MAUNDAY-THURSDAY.

Article I.

WHAT IS TO BE PREPARED FOR THE SACRED CEREMONIES OF MAUNDAY-THURSDAY.

On the Altar.

1. The altar is to be adorned as for solemn festivals; the front veil is to be white.
2. The cross between the candlesticks is to be covered with a white veil.
3. The Missal to be placed on a white cushion, or bookstand, on the Epistle side.

On the Side-table.

1. The chalice for Mass, with white ornaments, and two large particles.
2. Another chalice with a pall, a paten, a white veil, and a white silk ribbon.
3. A pyx with small particles to be consecrated for the communion of the people.
4. A small plate with the wine and water cruets, and a towel for wiping the fingers.
5. The processional cross, covered with a violet veil.
6. The censer with the incense-boat.
7. A white veil for the shoulders.
8. The communion-cloth.
9. The canopy for the procession.
10. The wooden clapper.

In the Sacristy.

1. The surplices for the clerks.
2. The amice, alb, cincture, maniple, stole, and chasuble; all white.

3. A white cope.
4. A violet stole.
5. A chafing-dish, containing fire.
6. Candles for the procession.

In the Repository for the Blessed Sacrament.

1. This repository is to be prepared apart from the principal altar of the church, and hung with precious tapestry, which should by no means be of black color; adorned with flowers and lights, but not with relics or images of saints.
2. The repository or urn, in which the chalice with the Blessed Sacrament is to be placed, should be prepared in the centre of the altar. It should be finely adorned, and secured with lock and key.
3. There should be a corporal in the repository.
4. Another corporal on the altar.
5. Steps to reach to the repository, where the chalice is to be placed.

ARTICLE II.

OF THE SACRED RITES TO BE PERFORMED ON MAUNDAY-THURSDAY.

SECTION I.—*Of the Mass.*

1. The bells, which call the faithful to church, should be rung as on festivals.
2. The acolytes prepare everything as above, in their proper place.
3. Meanwhile the priest hears confessions.
4. At the stated hour the parish priest of the church puts on the sacred vestments for Mass.
5. The first clerk lights the candles on the altar, and the priest places the chalice in the middle of it; and behind it the pyx containing the small particles.
6. The celebrant, with his head covered, preceded by the first acolyte, and then by the second and third, who walk together, each having his hands joined, proceeds to the altar for Mass.

7. Beginning Mass, he does not say the psalm, *Judica me Deus*, nor the *Gloria Patri*.

8. Whilst the *Gloria in excelsis* is said, they ring the bells, which are not rung any more until Holy Saturday.

9. Besides the usual large particle, another large one, and a sufficient number of small ones, are consecrated.

10. The *Agnus Dei* is said, as usual, but the *Pax* is not given.

11. Whilst the celebrant is saying the prayers before the Communion, the first acolyte comes from the side-table to the altar, with the empty chalice, pall and paten.

12. The celebrant having consumed the Sacred Species in both kinds, and covered the chalice out of which he communicated, places the other chalice in the middle of the altar, and uncovers it.

13. He kneels, places the consecrated Host in the chalice, covers it with a pall and paten on the concave side, covers the whole with the veil, and kneels.

14. He takes the pyx, places it before the chalice covered with a veil, uncovers it, kneels, retires to the Gospel side, having his face turned towards the Epistle side.

15. One of the acolytes, kneeling at the Epistle side, recites the *Confiteor*, the other acolyte and the people also kneeling. The celebrant subjoins the *Misereatur* and *Indulgentiam*, as usual.

16. The celebrant going to the middle, kneels, takes the pyx, and turns round towards the people, and says as usual, *Ecce Agnus Dei*, etc.

17. The acolytes receive Communion at the altar, then the people at the rails, holding the communion-cloth before them.

18. After the Communion the celebrant retires to the altar, covers the pyx, and puts it into the tabernacle.

19. Then having said, *Quod ore*, etc., he takes the first ablution; kneels, washes his fingers over the chalice, returns to the middle, kneels, and takes the second ablution.

20. The chalice which has served for Mass, is brought to the side-table; the candles at the repository are lighted,

the canopy is prepared outside the railing, and candles are distributed to some of the people.

21. In the meantime, the celebrant continues Mass, in which the following things are to be observed:

Having purified the chalice, he kneels, goes to the Epistle side, and reads the *Communio;* then goes to the middle, kneels, kisses the altar, withdraws to the side of the Gospel, and says, *Dominus vobiscum.*

He returns to the middle, kneels, goes to the Epistle side, and there reads the *Post Communio.*

He again goes to the middle, kneels, kisses the altar, turns, says, *Dominus vodiscum,* and *Ite missa est.*

Then he turns to the middle, kneels, says, *Placeat,* etc., kisses the altar, and says, *Benedicat vos,* etc., and kneels.

He turns to the Gospel side and gives the blessing, without turning round entirely, but only towards the Gospel side, and he does not return to the middle.

He says the Gospel of St. John, making the sign of the cross, not on the altar, but on the book, or altar-card, out of which he reads it.

At the words *Verbum caro factum est,* he kneels towards the Blessed Sacrament.

22. Mass being ended, the celebrant goes to the middle, kneels and by the shortest way goes down, on the Epistle side, to the floor.

23. There, assisted by the acolytes, he takes off the chasuble and maniple, and puts on the white cope.

Section II.—*Of the Procession with the Blessed Sacrament to the Repository.*

1. The celebrant goes before the altar, and having made a genuflection, he kneels on the lower step, and prays for awhile.

2. The first acolyte takes the censer with fire, and the boat with incense, to the celebrant.

3. The celebrant rises, puts incense into the censer without blessing it, the second acolyte offering the boat, without kissing it or the celebrant's hand.

4. The celebrant goes up to the altar, and, kneeling on the platform, incenses the Blessed Sacrament in the chalice.

5. Then the veil is put over his shoulders, and he rises, goes to the altar, kneels, rises, ties with a white ribbon the veil around the chalice that contains the Sacred Host.

6. He takes the chalice with his left hand covered with the veil, places his right hand on the chalice, and the second acolyte extends over it both corners of the veil.

7. The celebrant, holding the chalice in this manner, turns his back to the altar, and begins the hymn, *Pange lingua*.

8. They proceed to the repository in the following order:

1st. The banner, if there be any.

2dly. Some of the faithful, two by two, carrying candles in their hands.

3dly. The processional cross, carried by the third acolyte.

4thly. The first acolyte with the censer, having incense in it.

5thly. The celebrant under the canopy; having at his right hand the second acolyte, who should take care to raise a little the celebrant's alb in front, when he goes up or down the steps. They say the hymn, *Pange lingua*.

9. When the procession has arrived at the repository, it divides into two lines, one on each side of it, so that the censer-bearer and the celebrant, under the canopy, may pass between them.

10. The cross-bearer stops at one side of the repository.

11. The celebrant goes up to the altar of the repository, places the chalice on it, kneels, goes down one of the steps; kneels on the platform; the veil is taken from his shoulders.

12. In the meantime, those who carried the canopy, leave it in some convenient place.

13. The celebrant arises, puts incense in the censer, without blessing it, and without the usual kisses, and kneeling on the platform, incenses the Blessed Sacrament. The acolytes recite the verse, *Tantum ergo*, etc.

14. The celebrant gives the censer to the censer-bearer, rises, goes up to the altar, kneels, takes the chalice, places it in the repository; the second acolyte placing

the steps near the altar, if it is necessary to reach the repository.

15. The celebrant kneels again, shuts up the repository, kneels, and goes down to the floor of the chapel.

16. Then the celebrant, kneeling on the lower step of the altar, prays for awhile, rises, kneels on both knees on the floor of the chapel, and having covered his head, preceded by the cross, he returns, between the acolytes to the altar.

Section III.—*Of the Removal of the Pyx.*

1. All being come to the altar, the cross is put in its place; the second and third acolytes take lighted candles.

2. The celebrant having made a genuflection, goes up to the altar, takes out of the tabernacle the pyx with the Blessed Sacrament, places it on the corporal, and kneels.

3. Going down, he kneels on the platform, and puts on the veil, assisted by the first acolyte.

4. The celebrant goes up to the altar, kneels, having his hands covered with the veil, takes the pyx, and preceded by the clerks holding lighted candles in their hands, he carries the pyx to the altar of the repository, places it on the corporal, and kneels down.

5. Then going down, he kneels on the platform; there, assisted by the clerks, he takes off the veil; again goes up, kneels, opens the repository, and places in it the pyx behind the chalice.

6. The celebrant kneels, shuts up the repository, and having prayed on the lowest step of the altar, he kneels on the floor of the chapel, and, with his head covered, returns to the sacristy.

7. There, the celebrant takes off the cope and the white stole, and puts on a violet one, crossing it on his breast as usual.

Section IV.—*Of the Stripping of the Altars.*

1. The celebrant vested as above, attended by the acolytes, goes to the altars, with his hands joined.

2. Standing on the floor of the sanctuary at the foot of the altar, he begins with a loud voice the anthem,

Diviserunt sibi, which he continues with the Psalm, *Deus, Deus meus, respice in me,* Ps. xxi; reciting it with the acolytes.

3. In the meantime, the celebrant goes up to the altar, strips it, taking off the altar-cloths.

4. The acolytes receive the cloths, and remove from the altar the flower-pots, the front veil, and the carpet, so that nothing but the cross and six candlesticks, with their candles, but not lighted, is left on the altar.

5. The celebrant, having stripped the principal altar, goes to strip the others, if there be any.

6. The altars being stripped, the celebrant returns to the principal one; there, after the last verse of the Psalm, the anthem *Diviserunt* is repeated, and he waits for the *Angelus Domini.*

7. One of the acolytes gives the sign for it with the usual clapper; and all kneel down.

8. Then the celebrant arises, bows to the cross, and the acolytes kneel; all return to the sacristy.

9. There, the celebrant takes off the sacred vestments, makes the usual thanksgiving, and causes everything to be put in its place.

10. The first acolyte takes from the cross of the high altar the white veil, and covers it with a violet one.

11. The priest should procure some of the faithful to pray before the Blessed Sacrament, whilst It remains in the repository; and he should have a number of candles burning before It.

CHAPTER V.

OF GOOD FRIDAY.

ARTICLE I.

OF WHAT IS TO BE PREPARED FOR THE OFFICE OF GOOD FRIDAY.

At the High Altar

1. On the altar, which is to be altogether bare, six candlesticks, with candles of brown wax, not lighted.
2. A wooden cross, covered with a black veil, fixed in such a manner as to be easily removed.
3. A violet cushion on the second step of the altar.

On the Side-table.

1. A towel, covering the side-table, without hanging down.
2. An altar-cloth, folded, large enough to cover the altar, without hanging down.
3. A book-stand with a Missal.
4. A black burse containing a corporal, pall, and purifier.
5. The censer, with the box containing incense.
6. A black veil for the chalice, to be used at the end of the office.
7. A little plate with the cruets and finger-towel.

Near the Table.

1. A carpet with a cushion of violet color, and a white veil, adorned with golden and violet silk fringe.
2. The processional cross, covered with a violet veil.
3. The wooden clapper.

At the Repository.

1. A white veil for the shoulders.
2. The canopy. On the altar a corporal.
3. Torches and candles for the procession.

In the Sacristy.

1. Three surplices for the acolytes.
2. The amice, alb, cincture, black maniple, stole, and chasuble.
3. A chafing-dish with fire and tongs.

ARTICLE II.

OF THE SACRED RITES TO BE PERFORMED ON GOOD FRIDAY.

SECTION I.—*From the Beginning of the Office to the Uncovering of the Cross.*

1. At the stated hour, the signal being given, the acolytes put on their surplices in the sacristy, and everything is prepared as above.
2. The celebrant washes his hands, puts on the amice, alb, cincture, black maniple, stole, and chasuble.
3. Preceded by the acolytes, with his hands joined, he goes to the altar with his head covered.
4. He takes off his cap, kneels on the floor of the sanctuary before the altar, and prostrates himself, laying his hands on the cushion placed on the second step, and prays for the space of a minute.
5. The first acolyte takes the altar-cloth, unfolds it over the altar, assisted by the second acolyte, but they do not unfold it in its width, as they must leave the foremost part of the altar uncovered.
6. The third acolyte places the bookstand with the Missal on the Epistle side of the altar.
7. The celebrant rises, and the cushion being removed by one of the acolytes, he goes up to the altar and kisses it in the middle.
8. He goes to the Epistle side, and reads the first lesson, with the *Tract*.
9. He says, *Oremus*, and, kneeling down with all the clergy and people, says, *Flectamus genua;* the second acolyte, who rises first, answers, *Levate;* and the celebrant says the prayer, *Deus a quo*, etc.

10. Then he reads the second lesson and Tract, and immediately the Passion.

11. Having said in the same place, *Munda cor meum*, he continues to read that part of the Passion which is sung as the Gospel.

12. At the end he does not kiss the book, but immediately (in case there be no sermon) he reads the prayer, as in the Missal.

13. Before every prayer, with the exception of the eighth, the celebrant says, *Flectamus genua*, on which all the clergy and people kneel; and the second acolyte, rising up before the other, says, *Levate*.

14. About the end of the prayers, the first acolyte, assisted by the third, extends before the steps of the altar, or of the sanctuary, a carpet, and on the first steps, a violet cushion, and over all, the white veil.

SECTION II.—*Of the uncovering and Veneration of the Cross.*

1. The prayers being ended, the celebrant goes down at the Epistle side, and takes off the chasuble only.

2. Then he kneels at the middle of the altar, takes the cross from it, and the first acolyte takes the Missal.

3. The celebrant goes to the Epistle side, at foot of the steps, and having his face turned towards the people, the clerk holding the Missal before him.

4. The celebrant, with his right hand, uncovers the top of the cross, as far as the transverse piece, and raising the cross a little with both his hands, he says or sings with a solemn voice, *Ecce Lignum Crucis;* and the acolytes, in the same tone of voice continue, *In quo Salus mundi pependit;* and all but the celebrant kneel down, and the acolytes say, *Venite, adoremus;* after which words, all arise.

5. The celebrant, in front of the altar, at the side of the Epistle, uncovering the right arm of the cross, and the head of the crucifix, raising his voice and the cross higher, says again, *Ecce Lignum Crucis.*

6. The clerks continue, *In quo salus*, etc.; then all kneeling, they say, *Venite, adoremus*, as before.

GOOD FRIDAY.

7. The celebrant, finally, in the middle of the altar, uncovering the whole cross, and raising his hands and his voice still higher, says the third time, *Ecce Lignum Crucis*, etc.

8. The acolytes also answer, and kneel as before.

9. The first acolyte uncovers the processional cross, and all other crosses in the church are now uncovered, and the second acolyte replaces the book on the bookstand on the altar.

10. The celebrant, going down from the altar by the Gospel side, carries the cross devoutly, holding it raised up with both his hands, to the place prepared for it.

11. There, kneeling down, he places it on the cushion covered with the white veil, and, if necessary, he fastens it with some strings.

12. The celebrant rises, kneels, goes to the bench, takes off the maniple, sits down, and, with the assistance of the acolytes, takes off his shoes.

13. The celebrant, thus without shoes, goes to venerate the cross, to which, at suitable distances, he bows, kneeling on both knees, the first, second, and third time, and then he kisses it.

14. The celebrant rises, and having knelt to the cross, returns to his seat at the Epistle side, and puts on the maniple and his shoes.

15. The clerks also take off their shoes, and after the celebrant, and before the people, venerate the cross in the same manner as the celebrant, then return to their places, and put on their shoes.

16. After the acolytes, the people venerate the cross, first the men, and then the women.

17. The first acolyte remains by the cross whilst it is venerated by the people, and the second and third acolytes go to the celebrant, and with a loud and distinct voice, recite with him the verses and responses called the *Improperia*.

The *Improperia* to be recited by the celebrant, with the second and third acolytes, are as follows:

GOOD FRIDAY.

Part 1st.

Celebrant. *Popule meus quid feci, tibi, aut in quo contristavi te? Responde mihi.*
V. *Quia eduxi te de terrâ Ægypti: parasti crucem Salvatori tuo.*
Clerk 2. R. *Agios o Theos.*
Cl. 3. *Sanctus Deus.*
Cl. 2. R. *Agios ischyros.*
Cl. 3. V. *Sanctus fortis.*
Cl. 2. *Agios athanatos, eleison imas.*
Cl. 3. *Sanctus immortalis, miserere nobis.*
Cel. *Quia eduxi te per desertum quadraginta annis; et mannâ cibavi te, introduxi te in terram satis bonam: parasti crucem Salvatori tuo.*
Cl. 3. *Agios o Theos.*
Cl. 2. *Sanctus Deus.*
Cl. 2. *Agios ischyros.*
Cl. 3. *Sanctus fortis.*
Cl. 2. *Agios athanatos, eleison imas.*
Sanctus immortalis, miserere nobis.
Cel. *Quid ultra debui facere tibi et non feci? Ego quidem plantavi te vineam meam speciosissimam; et tu facta es mihi nimis amara; aceto namque sitim meam potasti, et lanceâ perforasti latus Salvatori tuo.*
Cl. 2. *Agios o Theos.*
Cl. 3. *Sanctus Deus.*
Cl. 2. *Agios ischyros.*
Cl. 3. *Sanctus fortis.*
Cl. 2. *Agios athanatos, eleison imas.*
Sanctus immortalis, miserere nobis.

Part 2d.

Cel. V. *Ego propter te flagellavi Ægpptum cum primogenitis suis; et tu me flagellatum tradidisti.*
Cl. 2 and 3. R. *Popule meus quid feci tibi? aut in quo contristavi te? Responde mihi.*
Cel. *Ego eduxi te de Ægypto, demerso Pharaone in mare rubrum; et tu me tradidisti principibus sacerdotum.*

Cl. 2 and 3. *Popule meus quid feci tibi? aut in quo contristavi te? Responde mihi.*
Cel. *Ego ante te aperui mare; et tu aperuisti lanceá latus meum.*
Cl. 2 and 3. *Popule meus quid feci tibi? aut in quo contristavi te? Responde mihi.*
Cel. *Ego ante te præivi in columna nubis; et tu me duxisti ad prætorium Pilati.*
Cl. 2 and 3. *Popule meus quid feci tibi? aut in quo contristavi te? Responde mihi.*
Cel. *Ego te pavi manná per desertum; et tu me cecidisti alapis et flagellis.*
Cl. 2 and 3. *Popule meus quid feci tibi? aut in quo contristavi te? Responde mihi.*
Cel. *Ego te potavi aquá salutis de petrá: et tu me potasti felle et aceto.*
Cl. 2 and 3. *Popule meus quid feci tibi? aut in quo contristavi te? Responde mihi.*
Cel. *Ego propter te Chananæorum reges percussi: et tu percussisti arundine caput meum.*
Cl. 2 and 3. *Popule meus quid feci tibi? aut in quo contristavi te? Responde mihi.*
Cel. *Ego dedi tibi sceptrum regale: et tu dedisti capiti meo spineam coronam.*
Cl. 2 and 3. *Popule meus quid feci tibi? aut in quo contristavi te? Responde mihi.*
Cel. *Ego te exaltavi magná virtute; et tu me suspendisti in patibulo crucis.*
Cl. 2 and 3. *Popule meus quid feci tibi? aut in quo contristavi te? Responde mihi.*

Part 3d.

Cel. *Crucem tuam adoramus Domine; et sanctam resurrectionem tuam laudamus et glorificamus: ecce enim propter lignum venit gaudium in universum mundum.*
Psal. *Deus misereatur nostri et benedicat nobis.*
Cl. 2 and 3. *Illuminet vultum suum super nos: et misereatur nostri.*
Cel. *Crucem tuam adoramus Domine: et sanctam res-*

GOOD FRIDAY.

urrectionem tuam laudamus et glorificamus; ecce enim propter lignum venit gaudium in universum mundum.

Cl. 2 and 3. *Crux fidelis inter omnes, arbor una nobilis; nulla sylva talem profert, fronde, flore, germine. Dulce lignum, dulces clavos, dulce pondus sustinet.*

Cel. *Pange lingua gloriosi lauream certaminis, et super crucis trophaeo dic triumphum nobilem; qualiter Redemptor orbis immolatus vicerit.*

Cl. 2 and 3. *Crux fidelis inter omnes arbor una nobilis: nulla sylva talem profert, fronde, flore, germine.*

Cel. *De parentis protoplasti fraude factor condolens; quando pomi noxialis in necem morsu ruit; ipse lignum tunc notavit, damna ligni ut solveret.*

Cl. 2 and 3. *Dulce lignum, dulces clavos, dulce pondus sustinet.*

Cel. *Hoc opus nostræ salutis ordo depoposcerat, multiformis proditoris ars ut artem falleret: et medelam ferret inde, hostis unde læserat.*

Cl. 2 and 3. *Crux fidelis inter omnes, arbor una nobilis; nulla sylva talem profert, fronde, flore, germine.*

Cel. *Quando venit ergo sacri plenitudo temporis: missus est ab arce Patris, natus orbis Conditor: atque ventre virginali, carne amictus prodiit.*

Cl. 2 and 3. R. *Dulce lignum, dulces clavos, dulce pondus sustinet.*

Cel. V. *Vagit infans inter arcta, conditus præsepia, membra pannis involuta Virgo mater alligat, et Dei manus pedesque stricta cingit fascia.*

Cl. 2 and 3. R. *Crux fidelis inter omnes, arbor una nobilis; nulla sylva talem profert, fronde, flore, germine.*

Cel. V. *Lustra sex qui jam peregit, tempus implens corporis: sponte libera Redemptor passioni deditus; Agnus in Crucis levatur immolandus stipite.*

Cl. 2 and 3. *Dulce lignum, dulces clavos, dulce pondus sustinet.*

Cel. *Felle potus ecce languet; spina, clavi, lanceâ, mite corpus perforarunt, undâ manat et cruor; terra pontus, astra, mundus, quo lavantur flumine.*

Cl. 2 and 3. *Crux fidelis inter omnes, arbor una nobilis: nulla sylva talem profert, fronde, flore, germine.*

Cel. *Flecte ramos arbor alta, tensa laxa viscera: et rigor lentescat ille, quem dedit nativitas; et superni membra regis tende miti stipite.*

Cl. 2 and 3. *Dulce lignum, dulces clavos, dulce pondus sustinet.*

Cel. *Sola digna tu fuisti ferre mundi victimam; atque portum præparare arca mundo naufrago, quem sacer cruor perunxit, fusus Agni corpore.*

Cl. 2 and 3. *Crux fidelis inter omnes, arbor una nobilis; nulla sylva talem profert, fronde, flore, germine.*

Cel. *Sempiterna sit Beatæ Trinitati gloria: æqua Patri, Filioque par decus Paraclito; Unius Trinique nomen laudet universitas. Amen. Dulce lignum,* is repeated.

18. Towards the end of the veneration of the cross, the first acolyte lights the candles on the altar, and the third takes from the altar the book-stand, with the Missal.

19. Then the second and third acolytes go, one to the Epistle side, and the other to the Gospel side, and unfold the altar-cloths.

20. This being done, the second acolyte, if in orders, brings to the altar the burse with the corporal, and the purifier over it; he takes the corporal out of the burse, unfolds it, and places the purifier near it, on the Epistle side.

21. The third acolyte places on the altar, at the Epistle side, the book-stand, with the Missal opened.

22. The veneration being over, the celebrant brings the cross back to the altar, places it between the candlesticks, and makes a genuflection.

23. The acolyte removes the cushion and the veil from the place where the cross lay, and one of them puts fire in the censer.

24. The celebrant again puts on the chasuble at the bench, on the Epistle side, and goes up to the altar, with his head uncovered.

SECTION III.—*Of the Procession to the Repository, and the return to the Altar with the Blessed Sacrament.*

1. The celebrant, standing before the altar, puts the incense in the censer, without the usual blessing.

2. The procession goes to the repository in the following order:
The banner.
Some pious men of the congregation.
The censer-bearer.
The cross, uncovered, carried by the third acolyte.
The celebrant, with the second acolyte at his left hand.

3. At the repository, the banner and the cross top on one side of the altar, the others who compose the procession divide themselves into two lines, one on each side of the altar.

4. The celebrant, having made a genuflection before the repository, kneels down on the lowest step of the altar, and, with others, prays awhile.

5. Then he arises, opens the repository, kneels, goes down the first step, and, standing, puts incense in the censer without blessing it, and without the usual kiss. The candles for the procession are lighted, and the canopy is prepared.

6. The celebrant, kneeling on the platform of the altar, incenses the Blessed Sacrament in the repository, arises, makes a genuflection, takes out of the repository the chalice, and places it on the altar.

7. The celebrant makes a genuflection, shuts the repository, in which he leaves the pyx with the consecrated Hosts; makes another genuflection, and then goes down the first step.

8. There kneeling, he puts on the veil, rises, makes a genuflection, and takes the chalice as he did the day before, which the second acolyte covers with the veil.

9. The celebrant, turning his back to the altar, and his face to the procession, with a loud voice, begins the hymn, *Vexilla Regis,* which he continues with the second clerk, as follows:

Vexilla regis prodeunt,
Fulget Crucis mysterium :
Quo vita mortem pertulit,
Et morte vitam protulit.

Quæ vulnerata lanceæ
Mucrone diro, criminum
Ut nos lavaret sordibus,
Manavit undâ et sanguine.

Impleta sunt quæ concinit.
David fideli carmine,
Dicendo nationibus,
Regnavit a ligno Deus

Arbor decora et fulgida,
Ornata regis purpura,
Electa digno stipite
Tam sancta membra tangere.

Beata, cujus brachiis
Pretium pependit sæculi,
Statera facta corporis,
Tulitque prædam tartari.

O Crux, ave, spes unica !
Hoc passionis tempore,
Piis adauge gratiam,
Reisque dele crimina. .

Te fons salutis, Trinitas !
Collaudet omnis spiritus :
Quibus crucis victoriam
Largiris, adde præmium.   Amen.

10. The procession returns to the altar in the following order:
The banner.
Some pious men with candles.

The processional cross.
The censer-bearer with the censer.
The celebrant under the canopy, and the second acolyte at his left.

11. Four candles should be left burning at the repository.

12. The banner and the canopy are left outside the railing; the processional cross is put near the side-table.

13. The men of the congregation carrying candles, stop outside the railing in regular order, holding the candles in their hands to the end of the office.

14. The celebrant goes up to the altar, and places the chalice on the corporal; he then kneels, rises, and goes down the first step of the altar.

15. There he takes off the veil, and standing, puts incense in the censer without blessing or kissing; then kneeling down on the platform, he incenses the Blessed Sacrament.

SECTION IV.—*Of the last part of the Ceremony.*

1. The celebrant arising, goes to the altar, makes a genuflection, takes off the veil from the chalice, and places the paten on the corporal.

2. Then he takes the chalice, lays the consecrated Host on the paten, takes the paten with both his hands, and places the Host on the corporal, not saying anything; and not making the sign of the cross, he places the paten on the corporal at his right hand.

3. The celebrant, having made a genuflection, takes the chalice, goes to the Epistle side, and holding the chalice in his left hand, puts in it wine and water, without blessing, and without saying anything.

4. The chalice is not wiped, but is placed on the side of the corporal.

5. The celebrant goes to the middle, and having made a genuflection, replaces the chalice in the usual place, without making the sign of the cross, and covers it with the pall.

6. Remaining in the same place, the celebrant puts incense in the censer, without blessing.

GOOD FRIDAY.

7. Then taking the censer, he kneels, incenses the offering, saying, as usual, *Incensum istud*, etc.

8. Having incensed the offerings, he kneels again, and incenses the cross (*ex Decr.S. R. C.* 14 *Maii*, 1707), saying *Dirigatur Domine*, etc., and having again knelt to the cross, continues, as usual, the incensing of the altar, kneeling every time he passes by the middle of the altar.

9. The celebrant then gives the censer to the censer-bearer; saying, *Accendat in nobis*, etc.; he is not incensed.

10. Immediately, taking care not to turn his back to the Blessed Sacrament, he goes from the platform down to the second step, a little back of the altar on the Epistle side, having his face turned towards the people, and washes his hands, saying nothing.

11. He returns to the middle of the altar, kneels, rises, and placing his hands joined on the altar, bowing, says with a low, but intelligible voice, *In spiritu humilitatis*, etc.

12. He kisses the altar, kneels, and turning towards the people on the Gospel side, he says, *Orate fratres;* and returns by the same way to the middle, without completing the circle, and kneels again.

13. The words, *Suscipiat*, are not answered.

14. The celebrant, with his hands joined before his breast, in a ferial tone says, *Oremus. Præceptis*, etc.; and whilst he says, *Pater Noster*, he extends his hands.

15. The clerks answer, *Sed libera nos a malo*, and the celebrant, *Amen;* with a low voice, still holding his hands extended, he continues in the ferial tone as before, *Libera nos*, etc., and at the end, the acolytes answer, *Amen.*

16. The celebrant kneels, arises, uncovers the chalice, puts the paten under the Host, and holding with his left hand the paten on the altar, with the right he raises the Host, so that it may be seen by the people.

17. Immediately after, he raises the Host over the chalice already uncovered, and forthwith divides it into three parts, as usual, saying nothing; the last part he

puts into the chalice, in silence, and without making the sign of the cross.

18. The chalice being covered, he kneels, rises, and with his hands joined over the altar, his body inclined, he says secretly, *Perceptio Corporis*, omitting the two other prayers.

19. He again kneels, then taking the paten with the Host, says, as usual, *Panem Cœlestem*, etc., and also the *Domine, non sum dignus*, etc., striking his breast.

20. He signs himself with the Host, saying, *Corpus Domini nostri*, etc., and communicates.

21. Having meditated a little, he uncovers the chalice, and kneels.

22. He rises, and having gathered, as usual, the fragments, he takes the chalice with both his hands, not saying anything, and without making the sign of the cross, he reverently takes the particle of the Host with the wine.

23. Omitting the usual ablution of the chalice, he washes his fingers, as customary, over the chalice, with wine and water.

24. Meanwhile, all rise, and the candles are put out.

25. Having taken the ablution in the middle of the altar, the celebrant wipes the chalice, covers it with the small black veil, arranges it, and bowing, with his hands joined before his breast, he says secretly, *Quod ore sumpsimus*, etc.

26. The first acolyte, if in holy orders, carries the chalice to the side-table.

27. The celebrant, going down, makes with the clerk a genuflection to the cross, and having covered his head, he returns to the sacristy.

28. There he takes off the sacred vestments, and puts on a white stole over his surplice.

SECTION V.—*Of the bringing back the Pyx to the Altar.*

1. The celebrant, preceded by the first acolyte, with the veil, and the other two with candles, goes to the repository.

2. Having made a genuflection on the floor of the chapel, he kneels on the lowest step, and prays for awhile.

3. Then he rises, goes up to the altar, opens the repository, kneels, takes the pyx, and places it on the corporal, and kneels again.

4. Going down the first step, he kneels on the platform, and receives the veil from the first acolyte.

5. He goes up to the altar, kneels, and with his hands covered with the veil, takes the pyx, and preceded by the clerks with lighted candles, brings back the pyx, which should be kept in a tabernacle, in some remote chapel within the church, or in the sacristy, placing it there with the accustomed genuflections.

6. When the pyx is shut up in the tabernacle, all kneel down, and the sign for the *Angelus Domini* is given with the usual wooden instrument.

7. Lastly, the candles of the altar are put out, and everything is put in its proper place.

8. Should there be no chapel or sacristy, the pyx must be left in the repository, with a lamp burning before it.

CHAPTER VI.

OF HOLY SATURDAY.

ARTICLE I.

WHAT IS TO BE PREPARED FOR THE SACRED RITES TO BE PERFORMED ON THIS DAY.

Outside the Door of the Church.

1. A TABLE covered with a white cloth, and on it,
2. A small book-stand with a Missal.
3. A plate with five grains of incense.
4. The censer, with the box, containing incense.

5. A vessel with holy-water and the sprinkle.
6. A white maniple, stole, and dalmatic.
7. A lantern with a candle.
8. Also, near the table, a chafing-dish with coals, or wood to be lighted for the new fire.
9. Tongs.
10. A long ornamented rod, with the triple candle fastened on the top. This has but one common stock, from which three candles, of equal length, rise.

At the High Altar.

1. The altar is to have on it the candlesticks and cross, as on solemn festivals.
2. Its front is to be covered with two altar-veils, a white one under another of violet color.
3. A stand on the Gospel side, to fix in it the rod with the triple candle.
4. On the same side, a high book-stand for the *Exultet*.
5. The paschal candle on a large candlestick, the wick of which should be so prepared as to be easily lighted; five holes in the form of a cross should be made in the candle.
6. The lamps prepared at proper and convenient places.

On the Side-table.

1. The side-table should be covered with a white cloth.
2. A Missal for the *Exultet* and for Mass.
3. The chalice covered with a white burse and veil.
4. A plate with the cruets of wine and water, and a small linen towel.

In the Sacristy.

1. Four surplices for the acolytes; the amice, alb, cincture, violet stole and cope; also, a violet maniple, stole and chasuble.
2. A white maniple, stole and chasuble.
3. A white veil.
4. Candles, to accompany the ciborium, when the priest brings it back to the altar.

HOLY SATURDAY.

At the Baptismal Font.

1. A table covered with a white cloth.
2. The towels.
3. The holy-water vase, with the sprinkle.
4. Vessels to fill water from the font.
5. The vessels containing the oil of the catechumens and the holy chrism.
6. A pitcher of water, with a basin for washing the hands, and a few slices of bread without crust on a small plate, for the same purpose.
7. Some clean cotton on a plate, for wiping the fingers.

If baptism be administered, besides what is above-mentioned, the following things ought to be prepared:

1. The Roman Ritual.
2. A small plate with salt.
3. The vessels with the oil of the catechumens, and the holy chrism.
4. A white stole and cope.
5. A towel to wipe the head of the baptized person.
6. Another piece of linen for the white garment.
7. A candle, to be lighted.

ARTICLE II.

OF THE SACRED RITES TO BE PERFORMED ON HOLY SATURDAY.

SECTION I.—*From the beginning of the Office to the blessing of the Paschal Candle.*

1. Outside the church, fire is struck from a flint, and with it the charcoals in the pan are kindled.
2. At a proper hour, four clerks put on their surplices in the sacristy, and prepare everything at their proper places.
3. The sign being given with the clapper, the celebrant washes his hands, puts on the amice, alb, cincture, violet stole and cope.
4. They proceed to the principal door in the following order:

The first acolyte with his hands joined.

The third acolyte with the processional cross.
The celebrant between the second and fourth acolytes.

5. When outside, the acolyte with the cross stops, turning and holding the crucifix turned towards the celebrant.

6. The celebrant places himself before the table, which is between him and the cross.

7. There, standing, he reads out of the Missal, placed on the book-stand on the table, the three prayers for the blessing of the fire, and then the prayer for the blessing of the incense.

8. Whilst the celebrant blesses the incense, the first acolyte takes, with the tongs, some of the new blessed fire, and puts it in the censer.

9. The celebrant, with the usual blessing and kiss, puts the incense in the censer, then he sprinkles the fire, and the grains of incense, saying the anthem *Asperges me*, and incenses them.

10. The censer-bearer, having received the censer, puts some more new fire into it.

11. The celebrant takes off the cope and stole, puts on a maniple, and a stole on his left shoulder, as deacons wear it, and a dalmatic of white color.

12. Meanwhile the second acolyte lights a candle with the new fire, and places it in a lantern, and the fourth acolyte takes the plate with the grains of incense.

13. The celebrant again puts incense in the censer with the usual blessing and kisses, and takes the rod with the triple candle.

14. They go to bless the paschal candle in the following order:

The acolyte, carrying the grains of incense on the right hand, and the censer-bearer on the left.

The third acolyte with the cross.

The celebrant, holding the rod with the triple candle, and the second acolyte, with the lighted taper, at the left.

15. The acolytes, carrying the grains of incense, the censer, and the cross, go into the church, and stop when the celebrant has entered the door.

16. The celebrant having entered the church, lights

one of the three candles with the lighted taper, and kneels with the rest of the clergy and the people, the cross-bearer excepted.

17. Thus kneeling, the celebrant says with a distinct voice, *Lumen Christi;* then he rises, and the acolytes also arising, answer, *Deo gratias.*

18. They go as far as the middle of the church, where again the second candle being lighted, everything is done as before, except that the celebrant raises his voice higher.

19. At last they go as far as the steps of the altar, and the third candle being lighted, everything is done the third time, as before, but they raise their voice still higher.

SECTION II.—*Of the blessing of the Paschal Candle.*

1. The acolytes having answered for the third time, *Deo gratias,* all rise, and form a straight line, with the celebrant in the middle, before the altar.

2. The second acolyte retiring, lays the taper on the table, takes the Missal for the *Exultet,* gives it to the celebrant, who gives him the rod with the triple candle.

3. The celebrant, holding the Missal in his hands, kneels on the lowest step of the altar, and without saying *Munda cor meum,* says only, *Jube, Domine, Benedicere. Dominus sit in corde meo, et in labiis meis, ut digne et competenter annuntiem suum paschale præconium. Amen.*

4. Then rising, and having made with the others a genuflection to the altar, they go to the book-stand, which is covered with a white veil, and placed at the Gospel side, in the following order:

The censer-bearer, having at his right the fourth acolyte, with the grains of incense.

The third acolyte, with the cross, having at his left the second acolyte, with the triple candle.

The celebrant with the Missal.

5. Being arrived at the book-stand, they range themselves by it in the following order, in a straight line, with their faces turned towards it:

The celebrant lays the Missal on the book-stand.

The cross-bearer at the right of the celebrant.

The censer-bearer at the right of the cross-bearer.

The acolytes, holding the triple candle, at the left of the celebrant.

The acolytes, with the grains of incense, at the left of the triple candle.

6. The celebrant, receiving the censer from the censer-bearer, incenses the Missal open on the book-stand, and with a clear and joyful voice begins the *Exultet*.

7. At the words, *Curvat imperia,* he puts the grains of incense in the side of the paschal candle, in the following order:

    1
4 2 5
    3

8. The fourth acolyte leaves on the side-table the plate, in which the grains were, and takes a rod, with a wax taper fastened at the top, and returns to his former place, at the left of the triple candle.

9. At the words, *Rutilans ignis accendit,* the celebrant lights the candle from the triple candle.

10. At the words, *Apis mater eduxit,* the celebrant stops, until the fourth acolyte has lighted a taper to light the lamps of the church.

11. The *Exultet* being ended, the celebrant shuts the Missal, and the second acolyte puts the triple candle in the stand prepared for it at the Gospel side. The third acolyte leaves the cross at the Epistle side.

12. Then, preceded by the censer-bearer, with the acolyte that carried the grains of incense, at his left, and also by the second and third acolyte, he kneels before the altar with them all, and returns to the sacristy.

13. There, having taken off the white vestments, he puts on the violet maniple, stole, and chasuble.

Section III.—*Of the Prophecies.*

1. The celebrant thus vested, preceded by the acolytes, goes to the altar.

2. Having bowed to the cross, he goes up to the altar, kisses it in the middle, and goes to the Epistle side.

3. There, with a loud voice, he reads the twelve prophecies, with the prayers and tracts; he kneels with all the clergy and the people, whilst he says, *Flectamus genua,* before every prayer, the last one excepted; and the clerk, arising, says, *Levate.*

HOLY SATURDAY.

4. After the last prayer, the celebrant, having made, from the place where he stands, a bow to the cross, goes down to his seat at the Epistle side, and takes off the chasuble and maniple.

5. If the church has a baptismal font, the celebrant puts on a violet cope, and sits down. Otherwise he goes before the altar for the litany, as below.

Section IV.—*Of the Blessing of the Font.*

1. The celebrant being seated as above, the first acolyte takes from its stand the paschal candle, lighted, and goes before the altar.

2. The third acolyte takes the cross, and likewise goes before the altar.

3. The two other acolytes go to the celebrant.

4. The celebrant, arising, begins with a loud voice the tract, *Sicut cervus*, as here below, which he continues slowly with the acolytes.

5. When the tract is begun, the procession moves to the front, bowing to the altar, in the following order:

The acolyte with the paschal candle.   The cross-bearer. The celebrant, between the two other acolytes, with his head covered, reciting the tract:

"*Sicus cervus desiderat ad fontes aquarum: ita desiderat anima mea ad te Deus.*

"*Sitivit anima mea ad Deum vivum: quando veniam, et apparebo ante faciem Dei?*

"*Fuerunt mihi lacrymæ panes die ac nocte, dum dicitur mihi per singulos dies, ubi est Deus tuus?*"

6. All stop before the railing of the font, and the celebrant having his face turned to the cross, after the tract is over, says, *Dominus vobiscum*, and the prayer, *Omnipotens sempiterne Deus*, etc., the fourth acolyte holding the Missal before him.

7. The acolyte carrying the paschal candle, and the cross-bearer, go within the railing, if the place is spacious enough; they, however, stand opposite the celebrant.

8. The celebrant goes near the font, and says the second prayer and the preface, as in the Missal, holding always his hands joined.

9. During the preface, at the proper places, as pointed out by the Rubrics, he performs the following rites:

1. At these words, *Gratiam de Spiritu Sancto*, with his right hand he divides the water in the form of a cross, and immediately after wipes his hand.

2. After the words, *Non inficiendo corrumpat*, he touches the water with his hand and wipes it.

3. After the words, *Indulgentiam consequatur*, with his right hand he makes three crosses over the font.

4. After the words, *Super te ferebatur* he divides the water with his right hand, and sprinkles it towards the four parts of the world, east, west, north, and south, in the following manner:

      1
 3   4
      2

5. After the words, *In nomine Patris*, etc., he changes his voice in the tone of a lesson.

6. After the words, *Tu benignus aspira*, the celebrant breathes thrice over the water in the form of a cross.

7. After the words, *Purificandis mentibus efficaces*, he dips the paschal candle a little into the water, saying, *Descendat in hanc plenitudinem fontis*, etc., and draws it forth. He dips it deeper the second time, saying louder, *Descendat*, etc., and takes it out again. Lastly, he dips the paschal candle to the bottom of the font, and says still louder, *Descendat*, etc.

8. The celebrant breathes three times over the water, in the form marked in the Missal, and continues, *Totamque hujus aquæ*, etc.

9. At the words, *Fœcundet effectu*, he takes the paschal candle out of the font, and it is wiped.

10. He continues the preface, and in a lower tone concludes it, saying, *Per Dominum nostrum*, etc., and the assistant acolytes answer, *Amen*.

11. The second acolyte takes the holy-water vase, and with it takes some water out of the font.

12. The celebrant having received the sprinkle, already dipped into the water of the font, sprinkles both himself and the bystanders; then, accompanied by two clerks, he sprinkles the people in the church and returns to the font.

13. Holy water is also taken out of the font for the vessels that are by the doors of the church.

14. The celebrant, having returned to the font, puts in the water the oil of the catechumens in the form of a cross, saying, *Sanctificeteur*, etc.*

15. Then he puts in the chrism, saying, *Infusio chrismatis*, etc.

16. Lastly, he puts in both oils together, in the form of a cross, saying, *Commixtio chrismatis*, etc.

17. He mixes with his hands in the font the oils with the water, spreading them all over the font.

18. He wipes his hands with some cotton, and cleanses them with some crumbs of bread.

Section V.—*Baptism of Infants.*

"*Duo potissimum* (these words are from the Roman Ritual) *ex antiquissimo Ecclesiæ ritu, sacri sunt dies, in quibus solemni cæremonia hoc Sacramentum administrare maxime convenit, nempe Sabbatum Sanctum Paschæ, et Sabbatum Pentecostes, quibus diebus Baptismatis fontis aqua rite consecratur.*"

The celebrant, having finished the blessing of the font, proceeds to the baptism of the infants, if any are to be baptized.

1. After the blessing of the font, the children to be baptized should be with their sponsors outside the door of the church.

2. The celebrant, having washed his hands, preceded by an acolyte with the cross, another acolyte remaining by the font with the paschal candle, goes between the two other acolytes, to the door of the church.

3. There the celebrant performs all that is prescribed by the Ritual, as far as the introducing of the child into the church.

4. Then he lays on the infant the extremity of the stole which hangs from his left shoulder, and introduces it into the church, saying, *N. Ingredere in Templum Dei*, etc.

5. Then having said the *Credo* and *Pater*, with his

---

* As, generally, the font is not sufficiently large, the water is blessed in a more capacious vessel; in which case the font is filled with blessed water by means of vases prepared for that purpose.

back turned to the railing of the font, he says the *Exorcism;* touches the ears and nostrils of the infant, and anoints it with the oil of catechumens on the breast, and between the shoulders.

6. Remaining still outside the railing, the celebrant takes off the violet cope and stole, and puts on the white.

7. Preceded by the cross, and followed by the infants to be baptized, with the godfathers and godmothers, he goes inside the railing of the font.

8. The celebrant makes the usual questions before the font, *N. Credis?* etc., *N. Vis baptizari?* etc.

9. The godfather having answered, *Volo,* he administers baptism in the manner prescribed in the Ritual, etc.

10. After the baptism, the celebrant washes his hands, and having put off the white cope and stole, puts on the violet.

SECTION VI.—*Of the Litany, Mass, and Vespers.*

1. The celebrant, preceded by the cross and paschal-candle bearers, and attended by the other acolytes, returns before the altar.

2. The paschal candle is placed on its stand, and the cross laid against the wall on the Epistle side.

3. The celebrant, standing before the altar, takes off the cope only.

4. Then kneeling down with the clergy and people he recites or sings the Litany from the Missal, which is placed on a stool before him.

5. The acolytes repeat all that is said by the celebrant.

6. At the verse, *Peccatores,* the violet front veil is removed from the altar, the candles are lighted, and flower-pots are placed between the candlesticks.

7. The celebrant continues the Litany, as far as *Christe exaudi nos,* inclusively.

8. Then he rises, and, preceded by the acolytes, goes to the sacristy; where, having taken off the violet stole, he puts on a white maniple, stole and chasuble.

9. Accompanied by the acolytes, as above, he returns to the altar, before the step of which he makes his confession as usual, saying the Psalm, *Judica me, Deus,* and the *Gloria Patri.*

10. He goes up to the altar, and having said the prayer, *Aufer a nobis*, in the middle of it, he says immediately, *Kyrie eleison*, there being no *Introit*.

11. At the *Gloria in excelsis*, the bells are rung.

12. After the Epistle, the celebrant says thrice, *Alleluia*, raising his voice gradually each time; and the acolytes repeat it in the same tone of voice as the celebrant, who continues the verse and the tract.

13. *Credo* is not said, neither the *Offertorium* after the *Dominus vobiscum*, nor the *Agnus Dei;* the *Pax* is not given.

14. In place of the *Communio*, vespers are said as in the Missal, viz.:

15. The celebrant, at the Epistle side, says the anthem *Alleluia*, and with the acolytes continues the Psalm, *Laudate*, after which he repeats, *Alleluia*.

16. Then he says the antiphon, *Vespere autem*, etc., with the canticle, *Magnificat*.

17. The antiphon, *Vespere*, etc., having been repeated, the celebrant goes to the middle of the altar, kisses it, and, turned towards the people says, *Dominus vobiscum*, and then the prayer, as usual, at the Epistle side.

18. At the *Ite, Missa est*, is added, *Alleluia, Alleluia*.

19. After the Gospel of St. John, the celebrant returns to the sacristy, and puts off the sacred vestments.

SECTION VII.—*Of bringing back the Pyx to the Altar.*

1. The celebrant puts on a white stole over his surplice, and, preceded by two acolytes with candles, and by another with the burse and veil, he goes to the place where the pyx with the Blessed Sacrament is kept.

2. There with the usual genuflections, he takes the pyx with his hands covered with the veil, and brings it back to the usual tabernacle.

3. He returns to the sacristy, in which he puts off the sacred vestments, and reads the anthem, *Trium puerorum*, with *Alleluia* and the Canticle, Psalm, prayers of thanksgiving, as in the Missal.

4. Meanwhile the candles of the altar are put out.

5. Likewise the triple candle, which is not lighted any more; and the rod is removed.

6. Also the paschal candle is extinguished, but it is left in its stand. It is to be lighted on all Sundays and festivals of obligation at Mass and Vespers, until the Gospel of Ascension-day, inclusively; after which it is put out, and after Mass removed from its stand. Afterwards, it is lighted only on the eve of Pentecost, for the blessing of the font.

PART III.

Ceremonies of High Mass.

CHAPTER I.

RULES TO BE OBSERVED BY THE CLERGY IN CHOIR.

ARTICLE I.

The Order of going to the Choir.

1. THE clergy, dressed in their cassocks and surplices,* go out of the sacristy, two by two, so close together that the right shoulder of the one may almost touch the left shoulder of the other; and they proceed gravely, with regular step, holding their caps with both hands below their breasts, each pair keeping at equal distance from the other.

2. When they arrive at the altar, they make a genuflection to the cross, both taking care to make it at the same time, and to rise slowly, and with gravity; in this, the uniformity and decorum of the ceremonies consist. Each pair make their genuflection in the same place that the first made theirs; it will, therefore, be necessary that those who are behind should advance slowly, so as to allow those before them time to make the genuflection

---

* It is difficult to give any precise rule regarding the size and shape of the surplice. It would, however, seem more fitting that lace surplices should not be used except by Prelates. The surplice might very properly have a narrow edging of lace.

with decorum. After the genuflection, they turn and salute each other, and then proceed to their place,* one on one side of the choir, the other on the other, and remain standing.

ARTICLE II.

The Order to be observed in Choir.

1. There are three different postures to be observed in choir, viz., to stand, sit, or kneel. When it is time to stand, all must stand, and no one must sit down or kneel; so all must be uniform, when it is time to sit or kneel.

The clergy should remember not to kneel down during the elevation at Low Masses that may be celebrated whilst they are in the choir. (*Sac. Con. Rit.*, 5th Mar., 1667.) And they should conform to the directions of the master of ceremonies, in whatever regards divine worship. (*Sac. Con. Rit.*, 4th June, 1817.)

2. During High Mass, the clergy remain standing, from the end of the confession, until the celebrant has said the *Kyrie eleison*, whilst he is singing the *Gloria in excelsis*, and until he is seated after reciting it; whilst he is singing the prayers; whilst the deacon is singing the Gospel; whilst the celebrant is singing the *Dominus vobiscum*, and the *Oremus*, at the *Offertory;* during the incensing of the choir; during the preface, until the *Sanctus* is recited; after the elevation, until after Communion; at the prayer, or prayers, after Communion, and at the last Gospel.

---

* There should be no chairs in the sanctuary, except that of the Bishop, or some very distinguished personage. Priests, even Canons, and others belonging to the clergy, should sit on benches. These should be neatly made, with high backs, especially when attached to the walls. The bench for the celebrant should be near the altar on the Epistle side, and should be sufficiently large to accommodate the celebrant, deacon and sub-deacon. It may be richly ornamented with carved work, but should never look like a throne.

"Sacerdos, Diaconus, et Subdiaconus, celebrantes solemniter, possunt et debent sedere in banco, dum canitur Gloria, Credo, etc.; non obstante qualibet consuetudine." (*S. R. C.*, 15th Jan., 1611.)

"Canonici Missam celebrantes coram Episcopo, non debent sedere in sede cum postergali, sed in aliquo scamno oblongo, tapete, vel panno cooperto in latere Epistolæ." (*S. R. C.*, 19th Maii, 1614.)

3. The clergy kneel from the beginning of Mass until the end of the confession; whilst the deacon sings the *Flectamus genua*, rising again when the sub-deacon sings *Levate;* whilst the sub-deacon sings in the Epistle, *In nomine Jesu omne genu flectatur*, etc., to the word *infernorum*, inclusively; in time of Lent, at the verse, *Adjuva nos;* at Pentecost, at the verse, *Veni Sanctus Spiritus;* at the *Verbum caro factum est*, and at the *Incarnatus est* of the Credo in the Masses of Christmas and of the Annunciation of the Blessed Virgin; from the *Sanctus*, till after the consecration; at the Communion of the clergy, after the celebrant has said *Indulgentiam;** in the ferial Masses of Advent, Lent, ember days and vigils, which are fast days; and in Masses for the dead, at the prayers, at the *Sanctus*, till the *Pax Domini*, inclusive; at the *Post Communio*, except the vigils of Easter, Pentecost, Christmas, and the ember days of Pentecost. (*Rub. Miss.*, part 1.) The clergy remain seated with their caps on, at all times when it is not prescribed above for them to stand or kneel unless the Blessed Sacrament be exposed.

4. The clergy take off their caps whenever they stand up; when they are saluted by the officiating clergy, or by others, who come to and from the choir, to return the salutation; whenever they have to bow their heads. In the above cases, it is understood that the cap only should be taken off. Should any wear the calotte,† it is taken off also when a genuflection is made; when the deacon sings the Gospel; at the *Incarnatus est;* when the choir is incensed; at the consecration; in giving and receiving the *Pax;* at the Communion of the clergy; when the celebrant gives the blessing.

5. They bow the head during Mass at the following times: at the *Gloria Patri*, till the *Sicut erat* exclusively; whilst it is sung by the choir; when the name of Jesus or

---

* Only those of the clergy kneel who are to receive Holy Communion, the rest stand, even when Holy Communion is being given.

† This is a small cap, used for covering the crown of the head, where the clerical tonsure is made.

Mary, or of the saint whose office is recited, or of whom a commemoration is made, is pronounced; and at the name of the Pope; during the *Gloria in excelsis*, at the words, *Adoramus te, Gratias agimus tibi, Jesu Christe, Suscipe deprecationem nostram;* during the *Credo*, at the words, *Jesum Christum, Et incarnatus est,** etc., *adoratur.*

6. During the time of singing, all should sing in a uniform manner, not elevating or lowering the voice more than the rest, and if any be unable to keep tune, it is better to be silent. They should also be attentive not to be faster, or slower than the others, but all should utter at the same time, the same syllable and note, and each one should be attentive not to get out of tune.

7. When the sub-deacon goes to give the *Pax*, the first of the choir should, on his approach, bow to him, and lean his head towards his left cheek, placing at the same time his hands under his elbows, and the sub-deacon, laying his hands on the shoulders of the others, says, *Pax tecum;* to which he answers, *Et cum spiritu tuo*, and again bows to the sub-deacon, then turning to the one next, he gives the *Pax* in the same way that the sub-deacon gave it to him, and so on, each one to the one next to him.

8. The clergy in choir should always observe silence, with modesty and recollection, shunning anything that might have an air of levity or irreverence.

Article III.

The Internal Dispositions required of those who attend the Choir.

1. A right intention to worship God purely for His glory, and not for interest or vanity.

2. Reflection on what is to be done, in order that no mistakes may be made, which are the cause of many

---

* Liturgical writers are divided on the question as to what position should be assumed by the clergy whilst the choir sings *Et incarnatus est*. The *Cer. Ep.* prescribes that all, except prelates and canons in their own church, should kneel. However, from various decrees of the S. C. R. it would seem that the clergy who are seated need not genuflect while these words are being sung. Of course this does not apply to the Masses of Christmas and the Annunciation, when all kneel.

defects. This preparation should be made before going to the choir, by reading the instructions for the ceremonies, and impressing them upon the mind by serious recollection, and, even in time of choir, at leisure moments, by reflecting on what ceremony comes next, and how it is to be performed. Thus nothing will be unforeseen, and all will be done well.

3. Attention to what is doing; not giving way to thoughts, even good in themselves, foreign to the present occupation, as such thoughts do not come from God, but proceed from some evil cause, to divert us from the good we are doing. The presence of God will aid us to have proper attention, that we may apply our mind to what is done, or said, attending to the signification; exciting sentiments corresponding to those, which the words express, as St. Augustin beautifully recommends in his commentary on the tenth Psalm: *Si orat psalmus, orate; et si gemit, gemite; et si timet, timete; omnia enim quæ hic conscripta sunt, speculum nostrum sunt.* What St. Augustin recommends in singing the Psalms, we should do in regard to whatever is recited or sung in Mass, or any other sacred function.

4. Devotion is required, making us delight in those sacred duties, lest we be as those who perform them reluctantly and with tepidity, to whom that sentence is applicable: *Maledictus homo, qui facit opus Domini fraudulenter.*

ARTICLE IV.

The Order to be observed in receiving Holy Communion.

1. After all have received the *Pax*, all who go to Communion meet together in the middle, two by two, with their caps and calotte off, with their hands joined, bowing at the *Confiteor*, and striking their breast, etc. The officiating clergy, who assist at Mass, communicate first; as also the priests (if any wish to communicate), with their stoles of the color of the day. Whilst the acolytes, after their Communion, are descending the side-steps on each side, the two first of the clergy, who are yet to communicate, approach, making their usual genuflection, on the

floor, before they ascend the steps, and after descending, they separate in coming down the steps, so as to leave space for the two who follow them to communicate; and so on, throughout. All kneel on the edge of the platform to receive Communion; and, afterwards, with gravity and devotion, return to their places in the choir, and conform themselves to the rest of the clergy. If any of the laity communicate, they do it at the railings of the choir, or on the floor, at the foot of the altar; and the celebrant descends to the lowest step to give them Communion, beginning always at the Epistle side.

2. The same order is likewise observed in going to receive candles from the celebrant, ashes, or blessed palms, or in going to kiss sacred relics, and in similar ceremonies; each one holding in his hand his cap and calotte, and kissing first the candle, or blessed palm, and then the celebrant's hand.

ARTICLE V.

The Order in going from the Choir.

1. No one should leave the choir without necessity; in which case, he goes to the middle, makes a genuflection, salutes the choir, first on the Gospel side, then at the Epistle side. If the celebrant is sitting at the Epistle side, he should bow first to that side, then to the other. The same is done when any one enters the choir after the functions have commenced; he should, however, remain some time kneeling, saying some prayers, then make a genuflection, and bow to the choir, as mentioned above. No one should go out of the choir or enter it, whilst the celebrant is reciting the Confession, during the singing of the prayers, the *Gloria Patri, Incarnatus est, Veni Sancte Spiritus, Adjuva nos,* etc. Should any one enter the choir at these times, he must stop, and kneel, or stand, conforming himself to the rest of the choir; during the Confession, at the beginning of Mass, he must remain kneeling till it is finished.

2. After the service, the acolytes go out of the sanctuary, and after them the members of the choir; those

who are last on the Gospel side, and the last on the Epistle side, advance in a straight line, and meet together in the middle, make a genuflection, and turning, follow the acolytes; the others do the same, and proceed to the sacristy, in the same order as they left it. When they arrive at the sacristy, they separate; one going on one side, and the other on the other, forming two lines: when the celebrant arrives, he bows to them, and they return a similar bow, and then with modesty, gravity, and in silence, unvest.

CHAPTER II.

INSTRUCTIONS FOR THE OFFICERS.

ARTICLE I.

THINGS TO BE PREPARED.

At the Altar.

1. THE altar should be decorated according to the solemnity of the festival.
2. Six candlesticks with candles, and the cross with image of the Crucified, in the middle, prominently located.
3. Relic-cases with relics, or flowers, between the candlesticks.
4. The *Antipendium* and the veil of the Tabernacle of the color of the vestments.
5. The altar-cards.
6. The book-stand, with the Missal opened at the proper place.

On the Side-table.

1. The table is to be covered with a linen cloth.
2. A plate with the cruets containing wine and water, the finger-towel, and the hand-bell.
3. The chalice with the purificator, paten, host, pall, covered with the chalice-veil, on which is placed the burse having in it the corporal.

4. The Book for Epistle and Gospel, or Missal, with marks in the right place.

5. The veil for the sub-deacon should cover the chalice, and hang down on each side of the side-table.

In the Sanctuary.

1. A carpet on the steps, and platform of the altar.
2. A carpet on the platform of the celebrant's bench.
3. The celebrant's bench may be covered with a green cloth. (*Merati.*) On the bench, the chasuble and maniple of the celebrant, and the maniples of the sacred ministers.

In the Sacristy.

1. On the sacristy altar the sacred vestments for the celebrant, viz.: the amice, alb, cincture, stole and cope, of the color of the day.

2. On one side of the chasuble the dalmatics for the deacon and sub-deacon, the stole for the deacon, two cinctures, two albs, and two amices.

3. In a convenient place, the surplices for the master of ceremonies and for the three clerks; also as many surplices as there are clergymen to assist.

4. Two candlesticks with candles, for the acolytes.
5. The censer and the incense-boat.
6. The fire ready for the censer.
7. A number of torches for the elevation, if they are to be used.
8. The holy-water vase and sprinkle.

Article II.

Instruction for the Censer-Bearer.

1. The censer-bearer goes to the sacristy a quarter of an hour before Mass, puts on his surplice, and, if no acolytes be present, assists the deacon and sub-deacon to vest.*

---

* Should the clergy proceed to the altar in solemn procession, preceded by the cross, the censer-bearer will have incense blessed by the celebrant (or by the Bishop if present) before leaving the sacristy; and then, with smoking censer, will walk immediately before the cross-bearer. (*Cærem. Epis.*, lib., ii, ch. viii.)

2. Before Mass, he prepares the fire in the censer; and, at the signal from the master of ceremonies, he goes to the sacristy before the acolytes, and carries the holy-water vase and sprinkle; he goes to the deacon's right and presents to him the sprinkle; he accompanies the celebrant and sacred ministers during the sprinkling of the people, always remaining at the right of the deacon. When the deacon hands him the sprinkle, on returning to the altar, he genuflects, and goes back to the sacristy and puts away the holy-water vessel and sprinkle; and, having prepared the thurible, he re-enters the sanctuary, and may so time his entry as to arrive during the *Confiteor;* and, at the end of the Confession, he approaches the altar, and goes up to the platform at the Epistle side, hands the incense-boat to the master of ceremonies, and when the incense is put in, and blessed, he adjusts the cover of the censer, and hands it to the deacon; he takes the boat in his left hand, and goes down holding his right hand on his breast.*

---

* As the censer-bearer moves either alone or with the clergy, he carries the censer in his right hand, holding it at the top just under the chain-holder, having previously pulled the cover chain sufficiently high that the fire may burn. Unless there is another clerk for the incense-boat, he carries it in his left hand, otherwise he keeps his left hand extended on his breast, as he moves along modestly and gravely. Should there be two censer-bearers, the one at the left carries the censer in his left hand. In making a genuflection, while holding the censer, he will so raise his hand that the censer will not touch the floor. When his hands are not employed, they should be joined. When incense is to be put in the censer, with his left hand he will present the boat to whom he should; then, with the same hand, he takes from his right the top of the censer's chains, and brings it to his breast, and with his right he takes the censer's chains near the top of the cover, and raises the censer sufficiently high that he who is to put incense in it may easily do so. After the blessing, if a blessing is to be given, he lowers the censer, and takes it in his right hand at the top. When the censer-bearer puts incense in it, he will hold the chains at the top, and also near the cover with his left hand, and with his right will put in incense. If he presents the censer to one of the ministers who is to give it to some one else, he will present it with his right hand. If to the officiating priest, or to a minister who is to incense, he will present the top with his right hand, and the middle of the chains near the cover with his left. If to the celebrant or officiating priest, and the Rubrics require it, he will kiss first the top of the chain, and then the right hand of the receiver. When he re-

3. He stands near the deacon, whilst he is incensing the celebrant, and bows to the priest both before and after; then takes the censer in his right hand (he should make a genuflection, if he is obliged to pass before the altar, to put away the censer, and the Blessed Sacrament is present), puts it in its proper place, and returns to the choir, or waits in the sacristy.

4. When all the prayers are sung, he goes to prepare the censer; and as soon as the priest has finished the Gospel (unless there be a long tract), he goes to the altar, to have incense put in and blessed; then, holding the censer in his right hand, and the boat in his left, he descends to the floor, and goes before the acolytes, in the middle of the choir, before the altar at some distance from the steps, and stands between the acolytes. If there be a second master of ceremonies the thurifer stands on his left, in front of the acolytes. When the master of ceremonies gives the sign, he makes a genuflection, then bows to the clergy,* together with the officiating ministers; passes before the first acolyte, and goes on the left of the deacon, a little in the rear, so that he may be opposite the first acolyte.

5. At the proper time he gives the censer to the master of ceremonies, and takes it again in the same manner; he raises the lid of it a little, in order to keep the coals alive, having to use it to incense the priest.

6. At the end of the Gospel, he approaches the deacon, and presents him the censer, making with him the usual bows before incensing the celebrant and after. He then

---

ceives back the censer, he does so with his right hand. To incense in a proper manner, having lowered the cover of the censer, he takes the top of the chains in his left hand, and brings it to his breast; with the fingers of his right hand he takes the chains close to the cover, and brings it as high as his eyes; then he lowers it, and stretches his arm, while he raises it again towards the one whom he is incensing, causing the censer to swing forward, and then lowers it again towards himself. He will repeat the same as often as he is to give throws, or swings. He bows before and after incensing. This manner of incensing is the same practiced in Rome and throughout Italy, in well-regulated churches.

* Such bows, as we have before stated, are not to be made to mere sanctuary boys.

goes slowly before the altar, behind the sub-deacon, and remains there while the celebrant intones the *Credo*, if it is to be said, bowing at the word *Deum*, and, having made a genuflection, he goes to the sacristy; if the *Credo* is not said, after receiving the thurible from the deacon he goes to the Epistle side.

7. Towards the end of the *Credo*, he goes to prepare the censer, and is ready at the altar after the oblation of the chalice. The incense is put in as usual; he takes the incense-boat and places it upon the credence-table, and remains there at the Epistle side, with his hands joined before the breast. He attends the deacon whilst he is incensing the celebrant, the choir and sub-deacon; and he stands at his left hand, a little in the rear, making the bows and genuflections at the same time with him. He receives the censer from the deacon, and when he arrives at his place behind the celebrant, incenses him twice; then he incenses the master of ceremonies, and the acolytes once each; he goes then to the entrance of the sanctuary, and incenses the people thrice, once in the middle, then on the left, and last on the right, making the usual bows both before and after, and the genuflections to the altar, passing and repassing. He then goes to the credence-table, takes the incense-boat, and places himself just behind the sub-deacon, where he awaits the torch-bearers, with whom he goes to the sacristy, having saluted the clergy as usual.

8. He again returns with the torch-bearers, and genuflecting with them, not omitting the usual bows to the clergy, he approaches the altar at the Epistle side, to the right of the master of ceremonies, to have the incense put into the censer; when that is done, he kneels on the floor, and, at the elevation of the sacred Host, incenses it three times, making a low bow, both before and after. He does the same at the elevation of the chalice. (*Rub. Miss.*, part ii.) After this, he goes to the middle, genuflects with the torch-bearers, and goes, without saluting the clergy, to the sacristy.

9. Here his duty ends, but he may accompany the sub-deacon when he gives the *Pax*.

10. If the clergy communicate, and the torch-bearers remain after the elevation, he should receive the humeral veil from the sub-deacon at the end of the *Pater noster*, and, after the celebrant's Communion, attend to the wine and water.*

Should there be no *Asperges*, as on holidays, the thurifer may enter the sanctuary before the acolytes, and, having genuflected with them, he may go at once and prepare the thurible; or he may carry the thurible when entering, and remain at the Epistle side until after the Confession.

The censer-bearer makes a genuflection on one knee, when he goes from the choir, or returns to it; when he leaves or approaches the altar, after the consecration only, not before it; in passing from one side of the altar to the other.

When the incense is not blessed, the censer is held in the left hand; otherwise in the right, and the boat in the left. When it is carried for any particular function, viz., when the Gospel is sung, or in processions, the censer-bearer puts his little finger in the ring of the small cover, and the thumb through that of the large cover. On other occasions—for instance, when he goes to have incense put into it, etc.—it is usual to hold it by the chains below the small cover, with the large cover a little raised, except in the act of incensing.

ARTICLE III.

Instruction for the Acolytes.

1. The acolytes, who should be of equal size (*Cœrem. Episc., lib.* i), put on their surplices a quarter of an hour before Mass, and prepare, and take to the altar whatever is necessary; they assist the deacon and sub-deacon in vesting, after they have lighted the candles on the altar (unless some other person do this), one on one side, the other on the other, beginning from the candle nearest to the cross; and in putting them out, they begin with the furthest. If there be only one to light them, he will begin on the Epistle side,

---

* It is supposed that the acolytes are acting as torch-bearers.

and end with those on the Gospel side; and *vice versa*, in extinguishing them.

2. They must take care not to let the wax fall upon the altar-cloth.

3. The second acolyte lights the candles in the sacristy.

4. At a signal given by the master of ceremonies, they take their candles, and, meeting together, make a bow to the cross, or to the chief picture in the sacristy, then with their eyes modestly cast down, with a moderate pace, they go before the clergy to the altar. (*Rub. Miss.*, part ii.)

5. The first acolyte, at the right of his companion, holds the knob of the candlestick with his right hand, and the foot with his left; the second with his left holds the knob, and the foot with his right. (*Cærem Episc., ib.*)

6. When they arrive at the altar, they make a genuflection on the floor; they then separate, and go to the corners of the steps, and stand facing each other.

7. When the sacred ministers have arrived, they turn towards the altar, make with them a genuflection, and then go to place their candles on the table and kneel down; and as soon as the celebrant and sacred ministers go to the bench after the *Asperges*, they assist the deacon and sub-deacon to put on their maniples. Then the first may take the cope from the sub-deacon or master of ceremonies and carry it to the sacristy. They answer in a low voice to the priest; at the end of the Confession they rise, and stand near the table.

Whenever the sacred ministers go to sit down, the acolytes raise the dalmatic and chasuble over the back of the seat, so that they may not sit upon them; this, however, depends upon its situation; should it be necessary to pass before the celebrant, they bow to him. If the celebrant makes a genuflection during the Epistle, they do the same; and they make the usual signs of the cross at the *Sequentia Sancti Evangelii*, while the celebrant reads the Gospel, but not when it is sung by the deacon.

If the deacon and sub-deacon use the folded chasuble, the second acolyte, during the singing of the prayer, takes off the sub deacon's chasuble, and puts it on again, after he has kissed the celebrant's hand. In like manner he takes off that of the deacon, while the priest is reading the Gospel; the first acolyte puts on him the large stole, and takes it off after removing the book for the *Post Communio;* and then the second acolyte puts on him the folded chasuble.

8. Whilst the celebrant is putting incense into the censer for the Gospel, they take their candlesticks, and the censer-bearer having descended from the altar, they follow him to the middle of the choir; he then goes between them (if there is no second master of ceremonies), they make a genuflection to the altar, and salute the clergy, together with the sacred ministers. In these, and in similar actions, uniformity as to manner and time is requisite, that they may appear as one person moving and bowing. Then they go to the place where the Gospel is to be sung.

9. When the sub-deacon arrives at the place where the Gospel is usually sung (*Rub. Miss.*, part ii), the first acolyte places himself at his right, and the second at his left, in a straight line, facing the left part of the choir. During this time, they never kneel down (*Rub. Miss.*, part i), neither do they make the sign of the cross, but remain motionless.

10. At the end of the Gospel, they go to the middle of the choir, three or four steps from the lowest front step of the altar, according as the space will allow, and make there a genuflection, and then return to the side-table. Having placed the candlesticks there, they remain standing, and kneel at the *Incarnatus,* on one knee, when it is repeated by the priest; and on both, when it is sung.

11. While the celebrant sings *Oremus* at the *Offertory,* the second acolyte takes the humeral-veil and puts it on the sub-deacon, who has come for the chalice; the first follows the sub-deacon with the cruets and towel,* (*Rub. Miss.*, part ii), places all upon the altar, and

---

* This towel is used in Rome for the purpose of protecting the altar-cloth, and is spread on the altar and the cruets are placed on it.

presents the cruets to the sub-deacon. When the wine and water are put into the chalice, he takes them back, and remains standing at his place.

12. Whilst the deacon is incensing the celebrant, they prepare the water to wash his hands. The first acolyte takes the towel; the other the cruet and basin. When the deacon has done incensing, they attend to the washing of the celebrant's hands (*Rub., ibid.*), bowing to him both before and after. They then put everything on the side-table, and remain there standing.

13. They bow to the censer-bearer both before and after being incensed; and the first acolyte bows to his companion before being incensed.

14. At the commencement of the Preface, they go to the sacristy to light the torches, and return at the *Sanctus* (*Rub., ib.*, tit. vii); and both enter together in the middle of the choir before the altar; they make a genuflection, then bow to the clergy, and to each other, and kneel at some distance apart, in a straight line.*

15. After the elevation, if there be no one to go to Communion (*Rub.*), and it is not a privileged feast, according to the Rubrics, they meet together, make a genuflection, and take away the torches. Otherwise, they remain with the torches, kneeling until after Communion. (*Rub., ib.*)

16. The first acolyte takes the veil off the sub-deacon at the proper time, and folds it, and lays it on the table. They bow when the celebrant is communicating.

17. The first acolyte takes the cruets to the altar at the proper time for the ablutions, taking care to genuflect before ascending the steps at Epistle side; and, in the meantime, the second takes the veil of the chalice to the other side of the altar, making a genuflection in passing and repassing. If they hold the torches till after Communion, the censer-bearer supplies their place.

18. During the blessing, at the end of Mass they kneel down on both knees; at the beginning of the Gospel, they rise and make the sign of the cross on themselves, as usual, at the *Initium Sancti Evangelii*.

---

* It would be better to have four others to act as torch-bearers, in which case the acolytes would remain at their places.

If the clergy remain in choir after the Gospel, the acolytes take the candles, go together to the middle, make a genuflection, and, with the sacred ministers, bow to the choir.

19. Towards the end of the Gospel, they take the candlesticks and go to the middle; they make a genuflection at the words, *Et Verbum caro,* or at the end of any other Gospel, and move towards the sacristy; there they bow to the cross, and with the candlesticks in their hands wait until the sacred ministers arrive, and then make a bow together. They put out their candles afterwards, and assist the deacon and sub-deacon in unvesting, and then go to put out the candles on the altar, unless some other person do it.

The acolytes remain always standing by the side-table, except when they are engaged, as on the occasions mentioned above. Whilst the celebrant is singing, or reading, they keep their hands joined before their breast; at other times they keep them folded. In the choir the bow is generally made, first on the Gospel side, then on the Epistle side, beginning always with the greater dignitary. In holding the torches, or carrying them, they should hold them always as follows: the first acolyte being always on the right hand of the other, holds the torch in his right hand, and his companion holds his torch in his left. When one hand only is occupied, the other is held open upon his breast. When they present anything to the celebrant, they kiss it before they present it; and also when they receive it from him (except in Masses for the dead). If they pass before the altar in going for the torches, they make a genuflection. Should they communicate in time of Mass, after the deacon and sub-deacon, and the priests, if any communicate, they make a genuflection on one knee, before and after Communion. During their Communion, they hand their torches to others.

ARTICLE IV.
Duty of the Master of Ceremonies.

1. The Master of Ceremonies should be acquainted with the duties of all the clergy, and be attentive to

their performance, making signs to them, but not pulling or pushing them; and in case some mistake be not of much importance, it is better to let it pass.

2. He should go to the sacristy, a quarter of an hour beforehand, and after a short prayer, put on his surplice, and prepare the chalice,* together with the pyx (in case the clergy communicate), and put in as many particles as there are persons to communicate. He prepares two Missals with the marks at their proper places, and takes all to the side-table, which should be covered with a white cloth (*Rub. Miss.*, part ii), and there, aided by the acolytes, he arranges everything: he should see that the cruets are prepared, together with the towel, and that a humeral-veil of the color of the vestments of the day covers the chalice, etc., and hangs down on each side of the table. He should also see that the holy water vase and sprinkle, the thurible and boat, torches, etc., are prepared. He leaves one Missal on the table; the other he places on the bookstand at the Epistle side, and opens it at the Mass of the day.

3. He gives notice in time to the clergy that are to officiate, and with the acolytes assist them in vesting.

4. When it is time, he gives notice to the acolytes to move towards the sanctuary; when the clergy have passed on, he makes a sign to the officiating clergy to proceed; they bow to the cross, and he precedes them, without either cap, or calotte, on his head; which is to be observed in all other functions. (*Cong. Rit.*, 17th Jul., 1734.)

5. He takes the deacon's and celebrant's caps from the former, and passing to the other side, takes also the sub-deacon's, all of which he places on the bench. He then kneels at the Epistle side. During the *Asperges* he may remain there, or, if the people are sprinkled only from the railing, he may accompany the thurifer who carries the holy water vase. When the celebrant has returned to the foot of the altar, he will have the card for the prayer ready and will hand it to the deacon.

---

* If he be a cleric.

When the prayer is finished he goes to the bench and assists the celebrant, and returning with him and sacred ministers to the altar, he kneels down at the Epistle side, with his face turned to the Gospel side, and answers the celebrant in a low voice, making the usual signs of the cross, and bows.

6. At the end of the Confession, he goes up to the altar with the ministers, to have the incense put in; and comes down again to the Epistle side. When the celebrant is incensing that side, he takes off the Missal, and afterwards replaces it, without making any genuflection.

7. If in time, after the incensing of the altar and the celebrant, he points out the beginning of the *Introit*, as he should do, whenever he attends to the book, raising or lowering it as may be necessary, and pointing out what is to be read or sung, turning the leaves, etc.

8. When the celebrant has said the *Kyrie Eleison*, if the singing is to continue for any length of time, the master of ceremonies makes him the signal to go and sit down on the bench (*Cærem. Episc*, lib. i), as is expressly ordered by the *Sac. Cong. Rit.* 17th Sept., 1822. He descends to the floor, and with his hands modestly folded before his breast, stands at the right hand of the deacon; he should observe the same at the *Gloria* and *Credo*, whilst the clergy are sitting.

9. When the choir is singing the last *Kyrie*, he makes a moderate bow, to invite the ministers to the altar, and he goes to the Epistle side. When the ministers do not sit, during the singing of the *Kyrie*, he gives them notice to go to the middle of the altar, and to stand in a line, one after the other; when the *Gloria in Excelsis Deo* is intoned, he directs them to go on each side of the celebrant to recite it with him.

10. When they have said the *Gloria in Excelsis*, he gives them notice to sit down; but not whilst the choir is singing, *Adoramus te, Gratias agimus tibi*. When they are seated, by a moderate bow, he gives them notice to take off their caps, whilst the choir is singing the above-mentioned words, *Adoramus te, Gratias*

agimus tibi; Jesu, etc., *Suscipe*, etc., during which time he bows to the altar.

11. At the *Cum Sancto Spiritu*, he makes them a sign to go to the altar, and he goes to the Missal to find the prayers which are to be sung, pointing them out to the celebrant, and turning the leaves of the Missal.

12. At the beginning of the last prayer, he goes to the side-table, takes the Missal in both hands, so as to turn the opening of it to his right, and presents it to the sub-deacon, bowing both before and after. He then places himself at his left, standing a little in the rear, and at the conclusion of the last prayer, at the words *Jesum Christum*, he bows, and goes to the middle of the altar with the sub-deacon, makes a genuflection, salutes the clergy, returns to the same place, and points out the Epistle, supporting his left whilst he is singing. He makes a genuflection at the words *In nomine Jesu*, etc., and bows at the names of Jesus and Mary, and of the saint whose feast is celebrated; giving notice to the clergy, immediately before, to kneel down, or take off their caps.

13. When the Epistle is finished, he accompanies the sub-deacon to the middle of the altar, makes a genuflection and bows to the clergy, then goes with him to the Epistle side, to receive the celebrant's blessing. He receives the Missal from the sub-deacon, and gives it to the deacon, at the beginning of the Gospel. When the celebrant has recited the Gospel, he goes up to the platform, or to the highest step at the Epistle side, to have incense put in, and he hands the incense-boat, open, to the deacon.

Should the choir sing a *Sequentia*, or long *Tract*, he makes a sign to the ministers to sit down, and he stands near the bench, as at the *Gloria*. At the end of it he makes a sign to rise, and goes to the Epistle side to have incense put in.

During the Ferial days in Lent, the ministers kneel on the edge of the platform, at the words *Adjuva nos Deus*, so that it is well to have the incense put in before, to give time to the deacon to say the *Munda cor meum*. And as the organ is not played on those days, he can request the choir to prolong their chant, so as to have time to perform these ceremonies without confusion.

14. Whilst the deacon is receiving the celebrant's blessing, the master of ceremonies stands at the Epistle side, with his face towards the altar. He then places himself at the right hand of the deacon, and makes a genuflection with all the other ministers, and goes to the Epistle side, always at the right hand of the deacon, a little in the rear; he presents him the censer after the *Sequentia Sancti Evangelii*, he takes it again after the Missal is incensed, gives it to the censer-bearer, and remains at the side of the deacon to turn the leaves of the Missal.

If it be necessary to make a genuflection, or bow, during the singing of the Gospel, he makes it towards the altar, which will serve as a notice to the celebrant.

15. At the end of the Gospel, he goes to the Epistle side, and there makes a genuflection with the others. He receives the Missal from the sub-deacon, with the usual bows, and places it on the side-table, then returns to the Epistle side, and remains there until the *Credo* is recited, he bows at the same time with the celebrant, and also makes the sign of the cross with him.

16. When the celebrant says, *Et incarnatus est*, the master of ceremonies makes a genuflection on one knee only, and at the end of the *Credo*, makes a sign to sit down; he stands in order to give notice when they are to take off their caps. When the *Incarnatus est* is sung by the choir, he kneels on both knees, together with the acolytes and censer-bearer; the sacred ministers take off their caps. In the Masses of Christmas and the feast of the Annunciation, all kneel down at those words; he, therefore, should prepare cushions for the occasion.

17. After *Et homo factus est*, he makes a sign to the deacon to come for the burse, and after giving it to him, he returns to the bench of the sacred ministers. At the words, *Et vitam venturi*, etc., or a little before, he gives notice to the celebrant and others to go to the altar, and goes to the Epistle side.

18. When the celebrant has said the *Oremus*, at the *Offertory*, he makes a sign to the sub-deacon to make a genuflection, and go to the side-table. When there, he puts the veil upon him, letting it hang down somewhat lower on the right than on the left. He accompanies him to the altar, taking the pyx with him from the side-table; he assists in uncovering the chalice, and when the sub-deacon has taken the paten, he should have the incense put in as usual.

19. He afterwards goes to the Epistle side, and when the celebrant is incensing the cross or the Epistle side, he passes to the Gospel side, making a genuflection in the middle, and removing the Missal, goes down to the floor. After the celebrant has incensed that side, he replaces it and remains there to attend to the book, pointing to the prayers, and turning the leaves.

20. At the end of the Preface, he gives notice to the deacon to go up on the platform to the right of the celebrant to recite the *Sanctus*.* At the *Te igitur*, the deacon goes to the left of the celebrant, and the master of ceremonies to the Epistle side, both making a genuflection in the middle, as they pass. The master of ceremonies remains there until the words, *Qui pridie quam pateretur;* when after putting incense in the censer, he kneels down with the censer-bearer, and, at the elevation, rings the bell three distinct times. He makes a low bow with the censer-bearer, both before and after each elevation.

21. After this he rises, and remains there until the *Nobis quoque peccatoribus* and then passes to the other side, making a genuflection in the middle, always behind the sub-deacon.

22. When the deacon goes from the left side of the celebrant, the master of ceremonies takes his place, makes a genuflection with the celebrant and deacon, who should be at the right hand of the celebrant. The master of

---

* Should the sub-deacon go up to recite the *Sanctus*, the master of ceremonies will retire, and, at the commencement of the *Canon*, take his place as above.

ceremonies remains at the left, attending to the Missal, until the *Agnus Dei*, making the genuflections with him, and turning the leaves, etc.

23. Before the *Pater Noster* is commenced, he makes a sign to the deacon to make a genuflection and go behind the priest, on the usual step; and at the words, *Dimitte nobis*, he again gives notice to the deacon and sub-deacon to make a genuflection, and go up to the altar at the Epistle side; the sub-deacon leaves there the paten, and takes off the veil; the master of ceremonies makes him a sign to make a genuflection there, and return to his place on the floor. The deacon remains at the right of the celebrant, and he at the left until the *Pax Domini* is sung, at which time he gives the sub-deacon notice to make a genuflection at his place, and come up to the left of the celebrant, where he makes again a genuflection, and says the *Agnus Dei*. (*Rub., Miss.*, part ii.) The master of ceremonies makes a genuflection at the same time, goes down to the floor, and waits to accompany the sub-deacon when he goes to give the *Pax* to the choir, beginning at the Gospel side, giving it to the first in dignity, and then passing to the Epistle side, making a genuflection in the middle.

24. When this ceremony is over, he returns to the altar, makes a genuflection on the floor with the sub-deacon, and receives the *Pax* from him, bowing both before and after. He then gives it to the first acolyte, or to the censer-bearer, when he assists at the side-table in place of the acolytes, who are occupied in holding the torches. He remains after this in his usual place, at the Epistle side, until the celebrant has communicated.

If the clergy communicate, the sub-deacon covers the chalice, after the celebrant has received the Precious Blood. The two sacred ministers make a genuflection and change places. The deacon uncovers the pyx, and they both again make a genuflection with the celebrant. After this, the deacon stands upon the highest step at the Epistle side, facing the Gospel side, and bowing low, he sings the *Confiteor*, and the celebrant, turning on the platform, towards the deacon, says the *Misereatur* and *Indulgentiam*, making the sign of the cross over those who are to communicate, and holding his left hand on his breast. When the deacon is about to sing the *Confiteor*, the sub-deacon retires to the highest step on the Gospel side, with his face turned towards the deacon, and with his hands joined; he remains there till after the *Indulgentiam;* both of them then change places, making a genuflection as they pass the middle of the altar, one behind the other, at the same time with the celebrant, and place themselves by the side of the celebrant, the deacon at the Gospel side, the sub-deacon at the Epistle side.

If the sacred ministers communicate, after the *Indulgentiam*, they kneel upon the edge of the platform in front of the celebrant; after Communion, they make a genuflection in the same place, and place themselves by the side of the celebrant as mentioned above, taking the communion cloth from those who hold it, as they pass, and giving it back when they have passed. The deacon takes the paten, and holds it at a just distance below the Sacred Particle, and accompanies the priest's hand in giving Communion. The sub-deacon stands near the priest, with his hands joined, and face turned towards the people, during the Communion; at the end of which, the censer-bearer takes the communion cloth, and places it on the side-table, and the master of ceremonies assists at the ablution on the Epistle side.

25. When the celebrant returns to the Epistle side, the master of ceremonies stands by him at the Missal, which he closes after the last prayer, if there be not a particular Gospel at the end of Mass. In case there be, after the deacon sings the *Ite, missa est*, the master of ceremonies hands the Missal to the sub-deacon for greater convenience, to take to the other side.

26. In time of the blessing, he and all the ministers kneel down, and rise after it is given. Towards the end of the last Gospel, he makes a sign to the acolytes to take the candlesticks, and go to the middle of the altar. They make a genuflection there at *Verbum caro factum est*, or at the end of any other Gospel, and move

towards the sacristy, followed by the clergy. He takes the caps of the sacred ministers, with whom, at the proper time, he makes a genuflection, and gives them their caps, presenting first to the deacon that of the celebrant.

27. They return to the sacristy in the same order as they came; he salutes the clergy at the same time with the sacred ministers, and having bowed to the cross, or picture, in the sacristy, he assists in disrobing the celebrant, and then removes the things from the side-table.

If the clergy remain in choir, the acolytes take the candlesticks at the end of the Gospel, and go to the middle. When the sacred ministers descend, all make a genuflection together, and salute the choir; the master of ceremonies presents the caps, and they proceed in the above mentioned order to the sacristy.

The sacred ministers make a genuflection on the floor, when they first come to the altar before Mass, and at the end before they leave the sanctuary; at other times they make it on the step, as far as practicable.

Article V.

Instruction for the Sub-deacon.

1. The sub-deacon should repair to the sacristy a quarter of an hour before Mass; and, after a short prayer, wash his hands, and put on the vestments, except the maniple, which he puts on at the bench after the celebrant is vested. After assisting the celebrant to vest, he puts on his cap.

2. On a sign made by the master of ceremonies, he bows before the picture in the sacristy, holding his cap in his hand; he makes also a moderate bow to the celebrant, and then puts on his cap, and holding the edge of the celebrant's cope, goes at his left to the sanctuary or choir.

3. When he enters the choir, he goes to the left of the celebrant, gives his cap to the master of ceremonies, and proceeds with the other ministers.

4. He kneels with the celebrant while the *Asperges* is being intoned, and then accompanies him during the sprinkling of holy water. The prayer being ended, he goes to the bench, where he puts on the maniple. He may hold the cope while the celebrant puts on the maniple and chasuble, and then give it to the acolyte. Then he goes to the foot of the altar.

He makes a genuflection with the deacon before the altar, and answers with him during the Confession, making the sign of the cross, and bowing with the celebrant. He stands erect when the celebrant says the *Confiteor;* bows moderately when he says *Misereatur vestri;* and bows profoundly when he recites the *Confiteor;* turning a little towards the celebrant at the words, *Et tibi Pater,* and *Et te Pater.* (*Rub. Miss.*, part ii.) He stands upright when the celebrant says, *Indulgentiam;* and again bows moderately at the *Deus, tu conversus,* until the *Oremus.*

He holds his hands joined before his breast, except when he sits down, or is engaged, when he performs some sacred rite with his right hand, he keeps his left open upon his breast; and when the priest makes a low bow, or a genuflection, he also bows, or makes a genuflection, and supports the priest's arm as he rises.

5. When the celebrant has said the *Oremus,* he goes up to the altar with him, raising a little the extremity of his alb. When the celebrant incenses the altar, he raises the chasuble with his hand, and makes a genuflection every time he passes before the cross. (*Rub., ib.,* iv.) When the celebrant returns the censer to the deacon, he goes down to the Epistle side, and stands at the left of the deacon facing the celebrant, and makes with him a a low bow, both before and after incensing.

6. After that, he goes to the Epistle side, and stands on the step below that on which the deacon stands at his right, so that, with the celebrant and deacon, who stands at his right, an imperfect semi-circle may be formed.

7. He makes the sign of the cross at the beginning of the *Introit,* and answers to the *Kyrie,* and remains there, or goes to sit down (*Rub. Miss.*, part i), accord-

ing to the directions of the master of ceremonies, making a moderate bow to the altar.

8. On notice given by the master of ceremonies, when the choir is at the last *Kyrie*, he goes with the deacon to the altar, the celebrant being between them; they bow to the choir. When they arrive before the altar, he makes a genuflection at the same time with the deacon, on the lowest step, and then he stands behind the deacon. (*Rub. Miss.*, part ii.)

9. He bows at the word *Deo*, when the celebrant sings the *Gloria;* then he goes up to the platform, to the left of the celebrant, and says the remainder of the *Gloria* with him. (*Rub., ib.*) He should take care not to say it faster than the celebrant. He ought also to bow and make the sign of the cross with him.

10. At the end of the *Gloria*, he makes a genuflection with the deacon, and, turning on his left, goes down the steps with the celebrant, whose arm he apparently supports, to the bench. He takes his cap, makes a moderate bow with the deacon to the celebrant, and then sits down at his left; puts on his cap, keeps his hands open on his lap, and takes off his cap, when directed by the master of ceremonies.

If the choir is singing a verse, at which it is necessary to bow, whilst he is going to the bench, he stops, and bows towards the altar.

11. At the sign made by the master of ceremonies, he rises, takes off his cap, places it on the bench, and, after two or three steps, salutes the clergy, together with the deacon and celebrant; first on the Epistle side, then on the Gospel side.

12. When he arrives at the altar, he makes a genuflection with the others, raises the celebrant's alb, as he goes up to the altar, and then stops at his place behind the deacon.

13. After the *Dominus vobiscum*, he goes behind the deacon at the Epistle side. (*Rub., ib.*) He bows with the celebrant during the prayers; but does not answer *Amen*, which he should observe whenever the choir responds.

When *Flectamus genua* is to be said, the deacon sings it in the act of bending the knee, and the sub-deacon sings *Levate;* and rises before the rest. All kneel down except the celebrant. (*Rub., ib.,* lib. v.) If the sub-deacon has on the folded chasuble, he will take it off to sing the Epistle and put it on after receiving the celebrant's blessing.

14. He takes the book, when it is presented by the master of ceremonies, bowing a little in the act of receiving it. He rests the upper part of the Missal on his breast, holding it below with both hands (*Rub., ib.,* lib. vi, n. 4), with the edge to his left, and turning towards the altar, he waits until the celebrant has said the words, *Jesum Christum;* when they occur in the conclusion, he bows at them, and then goes to the middle of the altar, makes a genuflection on the lowest step, bows to the clergy at the Gospel side, and at the Epistle side; he returns behind the celebrant, opens the book, and sings the Epistle (*Rub. ib.*), and when these words occur, *In nomine Jesu omne genu flectatur*, etc., he makes a genuflection, on one knee only, upon the step.

15. When the Epistle is ended, he shuts the book, and holding it, as was mentioned above, he returns to the middle of the altar, makes a genuflection, salutes the clergy as he did before the Epistle, goes to the Epistle side, kneels upon the upper step, and kisses the celebrant's hand placed on the Missal. (*Rub., ibid.*)

16. After receiving his blessing, he rises, gives the book to the master of ceremonies, then puts on the folded chasuble if he has worn it, and removes the Missal to the Gospel side (*Rub., ibid.,* n. 5), making a genuflection in passing before the altar.

17. After placing the book upon the altar, he remains on the upper step with his face turned towards the Epistle side, and there answers to the priest, making the sign of the cross, and bowing with him, and turning the leaves, if necessary. He answers, *Laus tibi, Christe*, at the end, and goes upon the platform, and turns the book for the convenience of the celebrant, leaving room to spread the corporal.

If the choir sings the *Adjuva nos*, the *Veni, Sancte Spiritus*, etc., he kneels on the edge of the platform at the celebrant's left until it be finished. (*Rub. Miss.*, part i.)

18. When the incense is put into the censer, and blessed, he goes down to the floor, and waits for the deacon. He makes a genuflection with the other ministers, salutes the clergy, and proceeds before, or if the space will allow, at the left of the deacon, to the place where the Gospel is to be sung, and there stands between the acolytes, holding the book open (*Rub. Miss.*, part ii), and leaning it upon his forehead or upon his breast, as may be more convenient for the deacon. Being occupied in holding the book, he does not bow, nor make a genuflection, when the name of Jesus occurs, although the others do. (*Rub. Miss.*, part i.)

19. At the end of the Gospel, he takes the book open to the celebrant (*Rub., ibid.*), by the shortest way (he does not make a genuflection, even if he pass before the Blessed Sacrament), and presents it to him to kiss, pointing out with his right hand, the beginning of the Gospel, which was sung. He shuts the book after the priest has kissed it, withdraws a little, salutes the celebrant, and then goes down to the floor in front of the Epistle side, where, without making a genuflection, he gives the Missal to the master of ceremonies, and remains there a little turned towards the deacon whilst the latter incenses the celebrant.

20. At the intoning of the *Credo*, he stands behind the deacon, and having made a genuflection with him on arriving at the middle of the altar, he bows at the word *Deum*, and goes up to the celebrant's left, observing the same that was prescribed for the *Gloria*. (*Rub., ibid.*)

21. At the *Incarnatus est*, he makes a genuflection, and at the end of the Creed goes to sit down, as he did at the *Gloria*. When the *Incarnatus est* is sung, he takes off his cap, and bows moderately till *Homo factus est* is finished.

In the three Masses of Christmas, and on the feast of the Annunciation, even if the office is not said on this festival, on account of its occurring on some privileged day, he kneels down with the other ministers, whilst the words *Et incarnatus*, etc., are sung.

22. When the deacon goes for the burse, the sub-deacon rises, and stands with his cap in his hand until the deacon has passed with the burse, and bowed to the celebrant; then sits down, and puts on his cap. When the deacon returns to sit down, the sub-deacon rises a little before, bows with him to the celebrant, and sits down again with him. He takes off his cap whenever the master of ceremonies gives notice.

23. At the end of the *Credo*, when the sign is made, he returns with the other ministers to the altar, observing what was prescribed at the end of the *Gloria*.

24. When the celebrant says *Oremus* at the *Offertory*, he bows, then makes a genuflection, and goes to the table, receives the veil upon his shoulders, takes the veil off the chalice, and gives it to the second acolyte; he takes hold of the chalice at the knob with his left hand, covers it with the right end of the veil, places his right hand over it, goes upon the platform to the deacon's right, and there places the chalice upon the altar. (*Rub., ibid.*)

When there is no *Credo*, he takes the burse upon the chalice. (*Rub., ibid.*)

25. After the deacon has taken off the pall and paten, he wipes the chalice with the purifier, and presents it to the deacon. He receives the cruets from the acolyte, presents wine to the deacon, and receives back the cruet in his left hand. When the deacon has poured the wine into the chalice, he presents the cruet of water to the celebrant, and bowing a little toward him, says, *Benedicite Pater Reverende* (*Rub. Miss., ibid.*); but if he is a prelate, he says, *Benedicite Reverendissime Pater*. After the celebrant has blessed it, he pours a few drops into the chalice, and gives back the cruets to the acolyte. (*Rub., ibid.*)

26. He does not cover his hands with the veil before he receives the paten from the deacon; after receiving it in his right hand, he covers it with the end of the veil,

which is at his right, and then rests it against his breast, as he should do whenever he moves from one place to another, when he is incensed, while he is kneeling, and when he responds to the *Orate Fratres*. He goes in front of the altar, makes a genuflection on the lowest step, and then remains standing until the words of the Pater Noster, *Dimitte nobis debitta nostra ;* holding the paten on a level with his eyes, with his left hand under his right elbow. The end of the veil at his left hangs down at his side.*

27. When the deacon kneels at the elevation, he also kneels at his place, on the lowest step, until it is over. (*Rub., ibid.*)

28. At the words *Dimitte nobis*, he makes a genuflection at his place, and goes up to the altar at the Epistle side, near the deacon, and presents him the paten. When the acolyte or censer-bearer has taken off the veil, he makes a genuflection there, and returns to the floor behind the celebrant, and without making another genuflection, stands there with his hands joined. (*Rub., ibid.*)

29. When the celebrant says *Pax Domini*, he makes a genuflection, and goes up to his left, makes there a genuflection with the others, and then bowing towards the Blessed Sacrament, says, *Agnus Dei*, etc., striking his breast at the *Miserere nobis*, and at the end of the third he makes a genuflection, and returns where he was at first. (*Rub., ib.*)

30. When the deacon comes to give him the *Pax*, he salutes him both before and after, then makes a genuflection at his place (at the same time that the deacon makes it on the platform), and accompanied by the master of ceremonies, he proceeds to give the *Pax* to the clergy, beginning with the first one on the more worthy side, and then on the other. (*Rub., ibid.*) Laying his hands on the shoulders of the one to whom he gives it, he says, *Pax tecum*, bowing to each of them after having given it, but not before. If there be several rows of

---

*S. R. C., Nov. 12, 1831, has decreed that the sub-deacon should proceed to say the *Sanctus* with the celebrant in churches where the custom exists; otherwise, he remains in his place.

clergymen, he gives it to the first in each row, and makes his genuflection before the Blessed Sacrament when he passes in the middle of the choir.

Should he have to give the *Pax* to prelates, he puts his hands under their elbows.

31. After giving the *Pax* to the clergy, he returns to the middle of the altar, makes a genuflection on the step, and gives it to the master of ceremonies; then goes up to the right of the celebrant, and there makes again a genuflection. (*Rub., ibid.*)

32. At the *Domine non sum dignus*, he strikes his breast, and bows moderately to the Blessed Sacrament. He bows profoundly to the Blessed Sacrament whilst the celebrant is receiving both species. (*Rub., ibid.*)

33. He uncovers the chalice at the proper time, makes a genuflection, and presents wine and water for both ablutions, observing the usual ceremonies. (*Rub., ibid.*) After giving the water, he lays the purifier on the celebrant's fingers.

34. He gives back the cruets to the acolyte, and changes place with the deacon, making a genuflection only in the middle of the altar behind the deacon. When he comes to the Gospel side, he wipes the chalice, and adjusts it in the usual manner, putting the purifier upon it, the paten with the pall, the veil, and lastly the burse, with the corporal in it; then holding the chalice with his left hand, and placing his right upon the burse, he takes it to the table, makes a genuflection in the middle of the altar, and returns behind the deacon. (*Rub., ibid.*)

35. After the *Ite, missa est*, or *Benedicamus Domino*, whilst the celebrant is saying the *Placeat*, he goes up to the second step, and he kneels on the edge of the platform, at the words *Benedicat vos*, and bowing, receives the blessing.

36. He rises and goes to the Gospel side, and there holds the card for the celebrant, or attends to the book, if necessary. (*Rub., ib.*) He does not make a genuflection towards the altar, at the *Verbum caro*, being obliged to hold the Gospel-card with both hands for the con-

venience of the celebrant, and for the same reason he does not make the sign of the cross at *Initium Sancti Evangelii*, etc.

If any other Gospel is read, after the *Ite, missa est*, or *Benedicamus Domino*, he receives the Missal from the master of ceremonies, makes a genuflection, and takes it to the Gospel side, and kneels down as was said, at the left of the deacon, upon the edge of the platform, to receive the blessing. He rises, and attends at the celebrant's left, making the sign of the cross, genuflection, etc.; at the end, he shuts the Missal, and leaves it there.

37. At the end of the Gospel, he goes upon the platform at the celebrant's left, and, on notice given by the master of ceremonies, bows to the cross, goes down to the floor with the other ministers, makes a genuflection with them, puts on his cap, and proceeds immediately after the clergy towards the sacristy.

38. When in the sacristy, he stands at the left of the celebrant; he salutes the clergy, bows to the picture or cross in the sacristy, and to the celebrant, then takes off his maniple, and the folded vestment when it is used, and assists the celebrant to disrobe.

If the clergy remain in the choir, he bows to them after having bowed towards the altar, then puts on his cap, and proceeds as above.

39. Should there be no *Asperges*, as on holidays, the sub-deacon puts on the maniple in the sacristy, and goes to the sanctuary before the deacon, and does as directed above after the *Asperges* at the foot of the altar.

Article VI.

Instruction for the Deacon.

1. The deacon goes to the sacristy a quarter of an hour before Mass, makes a short prayer, and looks over the Gospel, and *Ite, missa est*, or *Benedicamus Domino*, which he has to sing; he then washes his hands, and puts on all the vestments, except the maniple (and the folded vestment when it is used), which he puts on after the *Asperges*. He assists the celebrant in vesting,

handing him the sacred vestments, by turns with the sub-deacon.

2. When the celebrant is vested, and has put on his cap, he also puts on his, and remains standing at the celebrant's right, with his hands joined, until the master of ceremonies gives the signal, he then descends, bows to the cross or image, with his cap in his hand, and again bows moderately to the celebrant, and, with his cap on and hands joined, and sustaining the edge of the cope, he goes to the sanctuary.

3. He gives his cap to the master of ceremonies, then receives the celebrant's cap with both hands, with the usual kisses (except in Masses for the dead), and hands it to the master of ceremonies.

4. He kneels down with the celebrant, and having received the sprinkle, hands it to him. He accompanies him during the sprinkling of holy water, holding the border of the cope. On their return to the foot of the altar, he receives back the sprinkle, and hands it to the thurifer. The prayer being concluded, he goes to the bench and puts on the maniple.

5. He goes to the altar at the celebrant's right, makes a genuflection, answers with the sub-deacon, and makes the sign of the cross on himself, with the priest, etc. He bows moderately towards him when he says the *Misereatur*, and makes a low bow towards the altar when he says the *Confiteor*, turning a little towards the celebrant at the words, *Et tibi, Pater*, and *Et te, Pater*. (*Rub. Miss.*, part ii.)

He rises at the *Indulgentiam*, and bows again at *Deus, tu conversus*, continuing in this posture to the *Oremus*, inclusively.

He generally holds his hands joined before his breast, except when he is sitting, or enaged. When he uses his right hand, he keeps his left upon his breast. When the celebrant makes a genuflection, if he be by his side, he makes it with him, and with one hand supports his arm whilst he is rising.

6. After the *Oremus*, he goes up to the altar at the

celebrant's right, raising the alb a little in front. He receives the incense-boat from the master of ceremonies, takes the spoon, kisses it, and presents it to the celebrant, kissing his hand, and says, *Benedicite, Reverende Pater.* If he be a Prelate, *Benedicite, Reverendissime Pater.* (*Rub., ib.*)

7. After the incense is put in, he receives the spoon from the celebrant, and kisses it, after kissing his hand. (*Rub., ib.*) He should observe this on similar occasions. When the incense is blessed, he takes the censer, holding with his right hand the top of the chain, with his left the other extremity, and presents it to the celebrant, kissing first the upper part of the chain, then the right hand of the celebrant, which is placed between his own hands. (*Rub., ib.*)

8. Whilst the celebrant is incensing the altar, the deacon stands a little in the rear at his right, and with his left hand holds up the back of the chasuble. He makes a genuflection every time he passes before the cross. (*Rub., ib.*)

9. At the end of the incensing, he receives the censer from the celebrant, kissing his right hand and the upper part of the chain, as above; then with the top in his left, and with his right holding the botttom of the chain near the cover, he descends to the floor at the Epistle side, and incenses the celebrant thrice, making a low bow both before and after; he gives the censer to the censer-bearer, and goes up to the step, near the platform, to the celebrant's right. (*Rub., ib.*) He points out the *Introit*,* makes the sign of the cross with the celebrant, and answers at the *Kyrie*, etc. He remains in the same place, or, if the master of ceremonies gives notice, he goes to sit down with the other sacred ministers, making first a bow towards the altar, from whatever place he is standing. (*Rub. Miss.*)

10. At the last *Kyrie*, if he is sitting, he returns to the altar in the same manner as at the end of the *Gloria* and *Credo*. If he is not seated, at the sign made by the

---

* Unless the master of ceremonies attends to this.

master of ceremonies, he goes behind the celebrant (*Rub. Miss.*, part ii), in the middle, on the step next to the platform, and at the word *Deo* in the *Gloria*, he bows, and goes up to the celebrant's right, and continues the *Gloria* with him (*Rub. Miss., ib.*), making the bows together, and at the end the sign of the cross; he makes a genuflection with the rest; he goes with the sub-deacon, the celebrant being between them, to the seat.

11. On arriving at the bench, he takes the celebrant's cap, and presents it with the usual kisses, he then takes his own cap, and bows to the celebrant at the same time with the sub-deacon, sits down, and puts on his cap. He keeps his hands open on his knees, and when the master of ceremonies gives notice, he takes off his cap and rests it on his right knee.

12. Towards the end of the hymn, at the words, *Cum Sancto Spiritu*, etc., he takes off his cap and rises, places his cap on the bench, receives the celebrant's, first kissing his hand, then the cap, and lays it on the bench. Going to the altar, he salutes the clergy at the same time with the other ministers, first on the Epistle side, then, after a few steps, on the Gospel side, and at the celebrant's right.

13. When he comes before the altar, he makes a genuflection on the first step, and raises the celebrant's alb; he remains behind on the upper step, and after the *Dominus vobiscum*, goes behind him to the Epistle side, (*Rub., ibid.*), without making a genuflection, or bow; and remains there whilst the celebrant is singing the prayers, bowing when he bows.

If the *Flectamus genua* is to be sung after the *Oremus*, the deacon sings it in the act of bending the knee, and rises, after the sub-deacon has sung *Levate*. (*Rub., ib.*)

14. As soon as the celebrant terminates the last prayer, the deacon goes to his right on the upper step, and at the end of the Epistle, which the celebrant reads in a low voice, he answers, *Deo gratias*, and remains there until the celebrant begins the Gospel. (*Rub., ib.*)

15. On notice from the master of ceremonies he goes down to the floor, and receives from him the Missal, and

holds it nearly on a level with his eyes, the edge of the book being at his left; he salutes the clergy first on the Epistle side, then on the Gospel side, and goes to the middle of the altar, makes a genuflection on the lower step, then goes up and places upon the altar the closed book (*Rub.*, *ib.*), with the edge towards the Gospel side; and he remains there without repeating the genuflection.

If the deacon has on a folded vestment, at a signal from the master of ceremonies, whilst the celebrant is reading the Gospel, he comes down, takes it off, assisted by an acolyte, and puts on the large stole, which he keeps on until he removes the Missal, at the *Post Communio;* and then he puts the vestment on again. After putting on the large stole, he receives the Missal from the master of ceremonies, and proceeds as above.

16. When the master of ceremonies directs, the incense is blessed, at which he assists as before; then the deacon goes upon the upper step, kneels on the edge of the platform, and bowing profoundly, says: "*Munda cor meum, ac labia mea, Omnipotens Deus, qui labia Isaiæ Prophetæ calculo mundasti ignito: ita me tua grata miseratione dignare mundare, ut Sanctum Evangelium tuum digne valeam nuntiare. Per Christum Dominum nostrum. Amen.*" After this prayer he rises, takes the book, and turning towards the celebrant (who also turns towards the deacon), kneels on the platform and says, *Jube, Domne, benedicere.* (*Rub.*, *ib.*)

17. He kisses the celebrant's hand placed on the book, after receiving his blessing; then he rises, bows to the celebrant, and goes down to the floor; he makes a genuflection at the sub-deacon's right, bows to the clergy, and proceeds abreast with, or after the sub-deacon, to the place where the Gospel is to be sung; then he gives the sub-deacon the Missal open, and with his hands joined, he intones the *Dominus vobiscum.* After *Sequentia Sancti Evangelii,* placing his left hand open on the book, with his right thumb he makes the sign of the cross on the beginning of the Gospel, and then on his forehead, lips and breast, putting his left hand on his breast. After this, he takes the censer, and incenses

the book, first in the middle, then at his right, and lastly at his left; he returns the censer to the master of ceremonies, and sings the Gospel with his hands joined. (*Rub., ib.*) He bows and genuflects wherever it is prescribed. (*Rub. Miss.*, part i.)

18. Having finished the Gospel, he points out the text to the sub-deacon, and incenses the celebrant thrice, as usual, from the Gospel side, making a low bow, both before and after. (*Rub., ib.*)

19. He then gives the censer to the censer-bearer, and goes up to the second step, or to the top one, behind the celebrant, and makes a genuflection there, at the same time with the sub-deacon and censer-bearer. When the celebrant intones the *Credo*, he bows at the word *Deum*, and goes up to the celebrant's right, and observes all the ceremonies prescribed for the *Gloria in excelsis*; then he goes to his seat. (*Rub. Miss.*, part ii.)

20. After the choir has sung *Et homo factus est*, he rises, leaves his cap upon the bench, with his hands joined, bows to the celebrant, and goes to the table, takes the burse, holding it up with both hands, and keeping the open part of it towards his eyes. He bows to the celebrant as he passes him by, then to the clergy, first at the Epistle side, next at the Gospel side; after which he makes a genuflection on the lowest step, and goes up to the altar.

21. After taking out the corporal, he places the burse at the Gospel side, and spreads the corporal; then adjusts the Missal for the convenience of the celebrant. (*Rub., ib.*) He makes a genuflection there, without putting his hands upon the altar, and goes *per breviorem* to his seat, bowing to the celebrant before he sits down. Towards the end of the *Credo*, at the words *Et vitam*, or a little before, he returns to the altar with the others, as at the end of the *Gloria*.

In the three Masses on Christmas day, and on the day of the Annunciation, even if this festival be not then celebrated, all kneel when the *Incarnatus est* is sung.

22. He bows when the celebrant says *Oremus*; then goes up to his right; and when the sub-deacon brings the

chalice, he uncovers it (if it be a Mass in which there is no *Credo*, he takes the burse, and spreads the corporal, takes off the pall, and places it near the corporal,) then takes the paten with the particle, and presents it, kissing first the paten and then the celebrant's hand. (*Rub.*, *ib.*)

23. If it is necessary to consecrate particles for the Communion of the clergy, he uncovers the pyx, and during the oblation of the particle, he raises it up a little in his right hand, and with his left supports the celebrant's arm; he then covers it, and places it upon the corporal, behind the foot of the chalice. When the sub-deacon has purified the chalice, he takes it in his left hand, and pours in the wine, and the sub-deacon pours the water. (*Rub.*, *ib.*)

24. After having wiped off the drops of wine and water from the side of the chalice, he takes it, holding it below the cup with his right hand, and the foot with his left, and presents it to the priest, with the usual kisses. He supports with his right hand the foot of the chalice, or the celebrant's arm (*Rub.*, *ib.*), and with his left on his breast, he says with him, "*Offerimus tibi, Domine, calicem salutaris, tuam deprecantes clementiam, ut in conspectu devinæ majestatis tuæ, pro nostra et totius mundi salute cum odore suavitatis ascendat. Amen.*" At the end, he covers the chalice with the pall, and puts the paten in the sub-deacon's right hand, and covers it with the right extremity of the veil. (*Rub.*, *ibid.*)

25. The incense is put in and blessed, as was explained above. When the celebrant incenses the offerings, the deacon raises the chasuble with his left hand, and places his right hand on the foot of the chalice. After the genuflection, he removes it from the middle towards the Epistle side, but not outside of the corporal; after the incensing of the cross he puts it back in its place. (*Rub.*, *ib.*) He makes a genuflection with the celebran', and proceeds as at the *Introit*.

26. After having incensed the celebrant, he incenses the clergy, beginning at the Gospel side, and ending at the Epistle side; he makes a genuflection in the middle of the choir, in passing from one side to the other.

27. In incensing, he makes a moderate bow to those he is going to incense; and then incenses each one once; he bows to them when he is done. After incensing the clergy at the Epistle side, he incenses the sub-deacon twice; he then gives the censer to the censer-bearer, and goes up behind the celebrant, on the highest step, makes a genuflection, and turns, that he may be incensed by the censer-bearer. (*Rub., ib.*)

If there be Prelates in the choir, they are incensed with a double swing of the censer, as the sub-deacon, and a bow is made both before and after.

28. Whilst the Preface is sung, the deacon remains behind the celebrant; at the words *Supplici confessione dicentes*, he goes up to the platform at his right, says with him the *Sanctus*, makes on himself the sign of the cross at the *Benedictus*, passes to the left to turn the leaves of the Missal, and as he passes across he makes a genuflection on the edge of the platform.

29. At the words, *Quam oblationem*, the deacon goes to the celebrant's right, making a genuflection, as he crosses to the other side; if the pyx be there, he places it before the celebrant, uncovers it, kneels on the platform during the elevation of the Sacred Host, raises the celebrant's chasuble with his left hand, and rises with him, after he has adored the Blessed Sacrament, covers the pyx, replaces it behind the chalice, uncovers the chalice, kneels down again, and raises the celebrant's chasuble.

30. When the celebrant is about to place the chalice on the altar, the deacon rises, covers it, makes a genuflection with him, and returns to his left. He does not make the genuflection as he recrosses, but only after he has arrived at the celebrant's left, where he attends him at the Missal.

31. At the words, *Per quem hæc omnia*, the deacon makes a genuflection, and goes to the right of the celebrant; at the words, *Præstas nobis*, he uncovers the chalice, and makes a genuflection with the celebrant. After the words, *Omnis honor et gloria*, he covers it, makes a genuflection with the celebrant, and remains

there till he begins the *Pater*. Then, having made a genuflection, he retires behind the celebrant, on the highest step.

32. At the words, *Et dimitte nobis*, the deacon makes a genuflection with the sub-deacon, and goes to the right of the celebrant, where, having received from the sub-deacon the paten, he wipes it with the purifier, kisses and presents it to the celebrant, kissing his hand. He then uncovers the chalice, makes a genuflection, covers the chalice again as soon as the celebrant has put into it the small particle of the consecrated Host, makes again a genuflection, bowing together with the celebrant, and says the *Agnus Dei*, striking his breast, after which he kneels at the right of the celebrant.

33. After the celebrant has finished the first prayer, the deacon rises at the same time with the celebrant, kisses the altar outside of the corporal; receives from him the *Pax*, supporting meanwhile the celebrant's elbows and making to him a bow before and after, and answers, *Et cum spiritu tuo*. Then, having made a genuflection, the deacon goes down as far as the last step, and standing on it, gives to the sub-deacon the *Pax*, makes to him a bow, goes up to the left of the celebrant, makes a genuflection, and remains there till after the last ablution. Whilst the celebrant communicates under both species, the deacon bows profoundly.

34. After the last ablution, the deacon carries the Missal to the Epistle side, making a genuflection at the same time with the sub-deacon as they pass before the middle. And when he uses the large stole, takes it off and puts on the folded chasuble. Then he goes on the highest step behind the celebrant, follows him when he goes to the middle, and returns to the Epistle side.

35. When the celebrant has said *Dominus vobiscum*, after the last prayer, the deacon turns to the people, and sings, *Ite, missa est*.

When the *Benedicamus Domino* or *Requiescant in pace* is sung, the deacon does not turn round to the people. In Lent, when *Humiliate capita vestra Deo* is to be sung, after the third prayer of the *Post Communio*, the celebrant having sung *Oremus*, the deacon turns round to the people by his left hand, sings *Humiliate*, and turns again to the altar by the same side.

36. Whilst the celebrant says the *Placeat*, the deacon, retiring towards the Epistle side, turns to the altar. When the celebrant says *Benedicat vos*, the deacon, kneeling on the edge of the platform, receives the blessing, making on himself the sign of the cross; he then rises, makes with his thumb the usual crosses on his forehead, lips and breast, at the beginning of the Gospel, and makes a genuflection at the words, *Et Verbum caro*.

37. After the Gospel, the deacon goes up to the right of the celebrant; at the sign made by the master of ceremonies, he bows to the cross, descends with the rest below the steps, makes a genuflection, salutes the clergy, if they remain in the sanctuary, presents the cap to the celebrant with the usual kisses, first of the cap, and secondly of the hand, receives from the master of ceremonies his cap, puts it on, and walks to the sacristy behind the sub-deacon.

38. When arrived at the sacristy, the deacon takes off his cap, salutes the clergy, if they have also left the sanctuary, makes a bow to the crucifix and to the celebrant, takes off his maniple (also the folded chasuble when used), helps the celebrant to disrobe, salutes him, and takes off his sacred vestments. Should there be no *Asperges*, the deacon puts on the maniple in the sacristy and goes to the altar just behind the sub-deacon, and at the door he gives holy water to the celebrant, having first taken off his cap. Having arrived at the foot of the altar, he gives his cap to the master of ceremonies, takes the celebrant's, and commences Mass as directed above.

When the sacred ministers have to pass from one side of the altar to the other, before the consecration, they make the genuflection in the middle; but after the consecration, they make it on each side near the celebrant, both before and after, without placing their hands, which they hold joined, upon the altar. Only at the *Dimitte nobis* they make the genuflection in the middle, before they go up to the altar. The first and last genuflection is to be made on the floor, below the lowest step; all the others on the lowest step.

Article VII.

Instruction for the Celebrant.

1. The priest who is to celebrate High Mass should foresee everything that is to be sung, especially the *Gloria*, the prayers, the Preface, and the manner of singing them, according to the quality of the Mass, and the festival which is celebrated.

2. At the proper hour, the celebrant, having spent some time in prayer, and washed his hands, puts on the sacred vestments, attended by the ministers, who should have previously put on their own.

3. The celebrant, after he has put on the stole, blesses the water, then, having received the cope, he puts on his cap, and on notice given by the master of ceremonies, takes it off, goes below the steps, makes a bow to the crucifix, or to the principal image of the sacristy, salutes the sacred ministers at his right and at his left, covers his head, and, with his hands joined and his eyes modestly cast down, walks towards the sanctuary.

If, on their way to the altar, where High Mass is to be celebrated, the celebrant pass before the high altar, he should make a profound bow to it, and in case the Blessed Sacrament be kept there, he should make a genuflection. If he pass before an altar whilst Mass is celebrated, and in time of the elevation, as the bell rings, the celebrant, with ministers on each side of him, should stop, and kneel on both knees, till after the elevation.

4. As the celebrant enters the sanctuary, he takes off his cap, gives it to the deacon, and kneels down. He intones the *Asperges* or *Vidi Aquam*, and having received the sprinkle from the deacon, sprinkles the altar, first in the middle, then at the Gospel, and lastly at the Epistle side. He signs himself with the sprinkle, and rising, he sprinkles the sacred ministers. Then he

goes, accompanied by them, to sprinkle the clergy, and afterward the people. Returning to the altar, he hands the sprinkle to the deacon, and having sung the versicles and prayers, he genuflects and goes to the bench, where he puts off the cope and receives the maniple and chasuble. He returns to the foot of the altar (making the usual bows), and there makes a profound bow to the cross, or a genuflection, if the Blessed Sacrament be kept there, and begins the *Confession*, having the deacon at his right and the sub-deacon at his left.

If the clergy are already in the sanctuary, the celebrant should salute them as he enters it.

5. At the words, *Vobis, fratres—Et vos, fratres*, the celebrant turns towards the deacon and sub-deacon. After the *Confession*, he goes up to the platform, kisses the altar, puts incense thrice into the censer, saying, *Ab illo benedicaris in cujus honore cremaberis. Amen*, and makes the sign of the cross on the censer with his right hand, holding the left on his breast.

6. The celebrant, having received the censer from the deacon, makes a profound bow to the cross, or a genuflection to the Blessed Sacrament (if it is on the altar), in the latter case, laying his left hand on the altar; he then incenses the cross with three swings* (as directed in the plates,† n. 2, 3); after this, he again makes a bow to the cross, or a genuflection to the Blessed Sacrament, and, remaining in the same place, incenses the relics (if there be any) with two swings, between the candlesticks at the side of the Gospel (as in n. 4, 5), makes again a bow or genuflection, and with two other swings, incenses the relics at the Epistle side (as in n. 7.) If there are more or less than two cases of relics on each side, the celebrant incenses them all with two swings. If the relic of the saint whose festival is celebrated is placed in the middle of the altar, the celebrant, after having incensed the cross, incenses it with two swings,

---

* The Rubrics and Ceremonial prescribe the incensing of the Cross, etc., to be done *triplici ductu*.

† See frontispiece.

bowing to it before and after. Having incensed the relics, the celebrant proceeds to incense the altar; he incenses the table of it, at the Epistle side, with three swings, corresponding to the places where the three candlesticks stand (as in n. 8, 9, 10), walking one step at each swing. On arriving at the Epistle side, the celebrant lowers his hand, and incenses with one swing, the lower part of that side of the altar, and with another the upper part (as in n. 11, 12). Then, turning to the altar and raising his hand, he incenses the table of the altar with three swings as far as the middle (as in n. 13, 14, 15), advancing in like manner, one step at each swing; when he is arrived at the middle, he makes the bow or genuflection, and incenses the other side of the altar with three swings (as in n. 16, 17, 18), then he incenses the lower and the upper part of the Gospel side with two swings (as in n. 19, 20); without moving from that corner, he raises the censer, and incenses with three swings the table of the altar towards the middle (as in n. 21, 22, 23); then lowering his hand, he incenses with three swings the front of the altar on the Gospel side (as in n. 24, 25, 26), advancing one step at each swing; having arrived at the middle, he makes a bow or genuflection, and continues to incense the front of the altar with three other swings (as in n. 27, 28, 29), advancing likewise one step at each swing; when he is arrived at the Epistle side, he stops, gives the censer to the deacon, and, standing with his face turned towards him, is incensed by him.

7. After the incensing, the celebrant reads the *Introit*, says the *Kyrie*, and if the music is long, makes a bow to the cross, and goes *per breviorem* to sit down. He should be sitting when he receives his cap from the deacon, as also when he gives it back to him. Whilst sitting, the celebrant holds his hands spread on his lap, and when he returns to the altar, he salutes the clergy, first at the Epistle side, then the Gospel side, before he arrives at the middle.

8. When he is arrived before the lowest step, the cele-

brant makes a profound bow or a genuflection, goes up to the platform, and there, in the middle, intones the *Gloria in excelsis Deo*, and continues it with the ministers in a low voice. Having finished it, at the signal from the master of ceremonies, the celebrant makes a bow, and by the nearest way goes to the bench as before. At the end of the *Gloria* he takes off his cap and returns to the altar, as directed above, he kisses it in the middle, turns to the people, sings *Dominus vobiscum*. Then he goes to the Missal and sings the prayers.

9. If the altar is fixed in such a manner that the priest is always turned to the people, the celebrant, saying, *Dominus vobiscum, Orate fratres, Ite, missa est*, and giving the blessing, ought not to turn.

10. After the sub-deacon has sung the Epistle, the celebrant places his hand on the Missal, to be kissed by the sub-deacon, and then gives him the blessing; afterwards he goes to the middle, says, *Munda cor meum*, goes to the Missal, reads the Gospel, but after reading it he does not kiss the book, nor does he say *Per evangelica dicta;* then he returns to the middle of the altar to put the incense into the censer, and to bless it.

If there is in the Gradual any verse at which the clergy kneel, when the choir sing it, the celebrant kneels on the edge of the platform, with the ministers at his side, till the verse is sung.

11. When the deacon, having said *Munda cor meum*, kneels before the celebrant, and says, *Jube Domne benedicere*, the celebrant turned towards him, with his hands joined, says, "*Dominus sit in corde tuo, et in labiis tuis, ut digne et competenter annunties Evangelium suum: In nomine Patris, et Filii, et Spiritus Sancti. Amen.*" In saying *In nomine*, etc., he makes on him the sign of the cross, then he places his right hand on the book, to be kissed by the deacon.

12. When the deacon goes down below the steps, the celebrant retires to the Epistle side, and remains turned to the altar, with his hands joined, till the deacon begins to sing the Gospel; then he turns round towards the deacon, makes the usual signs of the cross at the words,

Sequentia, etc., bows to the cross at the name of Jesus, bows also towards the book, at the name of Mary, and of the saint whose feast is celebrated.

13. When the sub-deacon offers him the Missal, the celebrant kisses it, saying, *Per evangelica dicta*, etc., remains in the same place till he is incensed by the deacon, goes to the middle, intones the *Credo*, if it is to be said, and continues it in a low voice with his ministers.

14. Having said the *Credo*, the celebrant goes to sit, as said above; at the *Incarnatus* he takes off his cap, and bows towards the cross, till the verse is finished; he takes it off also at the words, *Simul adoratur*, and at the end of the *Credo* returns to the altar, kisses it in the middle, and sings *Dominus vobiscum* and *Oremus*.

15. After having said the *Offertory*, the celebrant receives from the deacon the paten with the particle, offers it, saying the usual prayer, blesses the water, saying *Deus, qui humanæ substantiæ;* receives from him the chalice, offers it, saying, *Offerimus*, etc.

16. The celebrant having said, *In spiritu humilitatis* and *Veni sanctificator*, puts incense into the censer, saying the prayer, "*Per intercessionem Beati Michaelis Archangeli, stantis a dextris altaris incensi, et omnium Electorum suorum incensum istud dignetur Dominus benedicere, et in odorem suavitatus accipere. Per Christum Dominum nostrum. Amen.*" At the word *benedicere*, the celebrant makes the sign of the cross on the incense, then he receives the censer, and without making any reverence, he incenses the sacred offerings, forming with the censer three crosses on both chalice and particle, saying at the first, *Incensum istud;* at the second, *a te benedictum;* at the third, *ascendat ad te, Domine;* and afterwards making three circles round the chalice and particle, beginning the first two from the right to the left, and the third from the left to the right (see the plate), and saying at the first, *et descendat super nos;* at the second, *misericordia;* and at the third, *tua*.

17. After the incensing of the sacred offerings, the celebrant makes a profound bow, or a genuflection, and

incenses the cross and the altar, as directed above, but with this difference, that at each swing he says the prayer, distributed as follows: at n. 1 (see the plate), *Dirigatur;* 2, *Domine;* 3, *Oratio mea;* 8, *Sicut;* 9, *Incensum;* 10, *In conspectu tuo;* 11, *Elevatio;* 12, *Manuum;* 13, *Mearum;* 14, *Sacrificium;* 15, *Vespertinum;* 16, *Pone;* 17, *Domine;* 18, *Custodiam;* 19, *Ori;* 20, *Meo;* 21, *Et ostium;* 22, *Circumstantiæ;* 23, *Labiis meis;* 24, *Ut non declinet;* 25, *Cor meum;* 26, *In verba malitiæ;* 27, *Ad excusandas;* 28, *Excusationes;* 29, *In peccatis.**

18. When the celebrant gives back the censer to the deacon, he says, *Accendat in nobis Dominus ignem sui amoris et flammam æternæ charitatis. Amen.* Afterwards he is incensed, he washes his hands, and continues Mass; he sings the Preface, the *Pater,* etc. After the *Agnus Dei,* having said the first of the three prayers before the Communion, he kisses the altar, gives the *Pax* to the deacon, saying, *Pax tecum,* and goes on as usual.

19. After having received the Precious Blood, if Communion is to be given, the celebrant, after the deacon has uncovered the pyx, makes a genuflection with him; then turns towards the deacon whilst he says the *Confiteor;* after which, he says, *Misereatur* and *Indulgentiam,* etc. As usual, he turns to the altar, makes a genuflection, takes the pyx in his left hand, and one of the small Hosts in his right, and, turned to the people, says, *Ecce Agnus Dei,* etc. Then he gives the Communion, first to the deacon, afterwards to the sub-deacon; and likewise he gives the Communion to the others, first to him who kneels at the Epistle side, then to the other who kneels at the Gospel side.

For the Communion of the people, the celebrant goes to the railing of the sanctuary, and there gives the Communion, beginning from the Epistle side.

20. After Communion, the celebrant either consumes

---

* This distribution of the words is neither prescribed by the Rubrics nor by the Ceremonial, yet it is well to do as recommended here.

the Hosts that are left, or, if the Blessed Sacrament is kept at that altar, he puts them in the pyx with the others in the tabernacle. When requisite, he removes from the pyx into the chalice the small particles that may be there, takes the purification and ablution as usual, wipes the chalice with the purifier, leaves it to the sub-deacon, and goes to the Epistle side, to read the *Communio*.

21. When the choir has sung the *Communio*, the celebrant sings, *Dominus vobiscum, Oremus*, and the prayers; then he sings again, *Dominus vobiscum*, and remains turned towards the people, whilst the deacon sings *Ite, missa est*, or he turns to the altar, if the *Benedicamus Domino* be said, and he says it in a low voice. (*Decr. S. R. C.*, 7th Sept., 1816.)

22. The celebrant then says, *Placeat*, gives the blessing, and reads the last Gospel, as usual; after which he goes to the middle, makes a bow to the cross, goes down below the lowest step, makes a profound bow or a genuflection. If the clergy remain in the sanctuary, the celebrant salutes them on each side, receives from the deacon the cap, puts it on, and walks to the sacristy, after the deacon.

23. At the door of the sacristy, if the clergy have returned thither, the celebrant takes off his cap, having his ministers at his side, salutes them, first at the right, then at the left; makes a bow to the cross, salutes the ministers, and, assisted by them, takes off the sacred vestments, salutes them again, and retires to make his thanksgiving.

24. Should there be no *Asperges*, the celebrant puts on all the vestments for Mass in the sacristy. Then, having bowed to the cross, he goes after the deacon to the sanctuary. He receives holy water from the deacon at the door. At the foot of the altar he bows or genuflects and commences Mass, having first given his cap to the deacon.

CHAPTER III.

HIGH MASS FOR THE DEAD.*

ARTICLE I.

THINGS TO BE PREPARED.

1. In the sacristy, black vestments.
2. The bench of the ministers should be bare.
3. Antipendium of black; a carpet of purple color, covering the platform only.
4. The side-table is to be covered with a cloth, hanging down a little on each side; besides everything necessary for the celebration of Mass, the candles to be distributed to the clergy should be prepared on it. The chalice is not to be covered with the long veil, which is not used by the sub-deacon at this Mass.

ARTICLE II.

What is to be particularly observed at High Mass for the Dead.

1. During the *Confiteor*, the master of ceremonies kneels below the steps at the Epistle side; after the *Confiteor*, the deacon and sub-deacon, going up to the middle of the altar, pass at once to the Epistle side, to attend, as usual, the celebrant for the *Introit*. There is no incensing at the beginning of this Mass. The clergy and the minor ministers kneel down, while the celebrant sings the prayers.

2. The sub-deacon, after having sung the Epistle, does

---

* Solemn Mass for the Dead *præsente cadavere* is permitted every day, except on great festivals of precept of first class, on the last three days in Holy Week, and on the feast of the titular saint. (*S. R. C.*, 29 Jan., 1752.)

not carry the Missal to the celebrant, but immediately gives it to the master of ceremonies, and does not kiss the celebrant's hand nor receive his blessing.

3. While the *Sequentia* is sung, the celebrant having read it, goes with the ministers to sit on the bench; then candles are distributed to the clergy, who keep them lighted in their hands whilst the Gospel is sung, and from the *Sanctus* till after the communion of the celebrant.

4. Five or six strophes before the end of the *Sequentia*, the ministers and the celebrant go to the middle, bow or genuflect, and the celebrant ascends the steps, and says, *Munda cor meum*, etc.; the sub-deacon removes the book with the stand from the Epistle side to the Gospel, and the celebrant reads the Gospel. The deacon, at the proper time, carries, as usual, the Missal to the altar, lays it in the middle, kneels on the edge of the platform, and says, *Munda cor meum*, but does not ask the blessing of the celebrant nor kiss his hand.

5. After the celebrant has read the Gospel, the deacon and sub-deacon go down below the steps. The acolytes, without candlesticks, go behind the deacon and sub-deacon. All make a genuflection, and go to the usual place, where the deacon sings the Gospel. Incense is not used at the Gospel.

6. After the Gospel, the sub-deacon does not carry the book to the celebrant to kiss, but gives it back at once to the master of ceremonies.

7. After the celebrant has said *Oremus*, at the *Offertory*, the sub-deacon goes to the side-table, and carries from thence to the Epistle side the chalice, with its veil and burse.

8. The deacon takes the corporal out of the burse, and spreads it on the altar, as usual; the sub-deacon takes the veil off the chalice, and gives it to the acolyte; when he presents the water, he does not offer it to the celebrant to be blessed.

9. At the Mass for the Dead, neither the celebrant's hand nor anything given to or received from him is to be kissed.

10. While the celebrant is making the oblation of the chalice, the sub-deacon goes to the left of the celebrant, making a genuflection in the middle. The sub-deacon does not hold the paten, as at the other Masses.

11. After the oblation of the chalice, the deacon places the paten partly under the corporal, and covers the rest of it with the purifier; at the proper time he presents the censer for the incense, and both ministers attend the celebrant at the incensing, which is done in the usual manner; the celebrant only is incensed by the deacon, after the incensing of the altar.

12. The celebrant being incensed, the sub-deacon receives from one of the acolytes the water-cruet and the basin; the deacon having given the censer to the censer-bearer, receives from the other acolyte the towel, and both assist the Lavabo; afterwards they go to the middle, as usual, behind the celebrant. The deacon at the proper time answers, *Suscipiat*, etc.

13. At the end of the Preface, the deacon goes up to the right of the celebrant, and the sub-deacon to the left, and say with him the *Sanctus;* then the sub-deacon returns to his place below the steps, and the deacon goes to the left of the celebrant to attend to the book.

14. At the words, *Quam oblationem*, the deacon goes to the right of the celebrant, and the sub-deacon to the Epistle side, where he kneels on the second step. He receives the thurible from the censer-bearer, and incenses the Blessed Sacrament thrice, at each elevation; afterwards he gives back the censer to the censer-bearer, returns to his place in the middle, makes a genuflection, and remains there till *Pax Domini*.

The acolytes remain kneeling on each side of the altar, holding their candles until after the celebrant's communion.

15. At the words, *Dimitte nobis*, the deacon only makes a genuflection, and goes up to the right of the celebrant, to give him the paten.

16. A little before the celebrant says *Agnus Dei*, the sub-deacon makes a genuflection, and goes to the left of the celebrant; there he makes a genuflection with the

others, who profoundly bowing towards the Blessed Sacrament, say the *Agnus Dei*, without striking their breast.

17. After the *Agnus Dei*, the deacon and sub-deacon exchange places, making a genuflection both before and after; the *Pax* is not given; the rest goes on as usual.

18. After the last *Dominus vobiscum*, the deacon, without turning himself to the people, sings, *Requiescant in pace* (always in the plural number). The celebrant, turned likewise to the altar, says the same in a low voice. (*Decr. S. R. C.*, Sept. 7th, 1816.) The blessing is not given; the rest is as usual.

CHAPTER IV.

SOLEMN VESPERS.

Article I.

THINGS TO BE PREPARED.

In the Sanctuary.

1. Six candlesticks on the altar, and the cross in the middle.

2. In the middle of the sanctuary, at a proper distance, two or four stools for the cope-bearers.

3. Against the railings in the middle, three stools, or a bench sufficiently long to accommodate the censer-bearer and the two acolytes.

4. Near the bench for the officiating priest, a stool for the master of ceremonies.*

---

* If the servers are to wear caps, they should be put on the bench beforehand.

5. A book-stand with the book, in front of the priest's bench, for the officiating priest, which may be covered with a veil of the color of the day.

6. The celebrant's bench, covered with a green cloth.

7. On the side-table may be placed the humeral-veil and stole, if Benediction of the Blessed Sacrament immediately follows.

8. At the altar the antipendium; and if the Blessed Sacrament is there, on the tabernacle the veil, of the color of the day.

In the Sacristy.

1. A surplice and a cope of the color of the day.

2. Two or four surplices and copes of the same color for the cope-bearers.

3. Four surplices for the master of ceremonies and the three servers; and surplices for the clergy.

4. The censer and incense-boat.

5. Two candlesticks with candles for the acolytes.

ARTICLE II.

General Rules to be observed by the Clergy in the Sanctuary for Solemn Vespers and Compline.

1. Besides what has already been said concerning High Mass, clergymen should observe what follows, in Solemn Vespers: They should not enter the sanctuary whilst *Deus in adjutorium, Gloria Patri,* prayers, *Capitulum,* the first verse, and the last strophe of any hymn, the first strophe of the *Ave Maris Stella,* and *Veni, Creator Spiritus,* and the last two strophes of the hymns, *Pange Lingua, Vexilla Regis prodeunt,* are sung.

2. At Compline, they should not go into the sanctuary whilst the *Confession* is being made; should, however, any one enter the sanctuary at the above-mentioned times, he should kneel, or bow, or stand, during the singing of the aforesaid verses or strophes, in conformity with the clergy already in the sanctuary.

3. As soon as the officiating clergyman arrives at the altar, the clergy kneel to say, each in particular, the prayer, *Aperi;* they should kneel likewise during the first strophe of the hymns, *Ave Maris Stella,* and *Veni Creator;* during the hymn, *Tantum ergo;* when the Blessed Sacrament is exposed; while they sing the strophe, *O Crux ave, spes unica,* even if it be said during the Paschal time; at the ferial prayers; at the anthem of the Blessed Virgin, said at the end of the office, and at the *Pater, Ave,* and *Credo,* recited after said anthem, except all Saturdays after Vespers, and all Sundays and the Paschal time, in which the clergy kneel only at the prayer *Sacrosanctæ.*

4. The clergy should stand while the *Pater* and *Ave* are said; and from the beginning of Vespers till the first Psalm is intoned. When the antiphon is intoned, all the clergy who are on the same side with the clergyman that intones it, rise as soon as the chanters in cope come to give the tone: the clergy should stand also during the chapter, the hymn, and from the hymn till the end of Vespers, only except whilst the choir sing and repeat the antiphon of the *Magnificat;* at which time they sit, if the incensing be over. They should likewise stand during the prayer and commemorations, and till the end of Vespers.

5. At Compline, the clergy stand from the beginning till the intonation of the first Psalm; from the intoning of the hymn till the end of Compline.

6. The clergy bow, and take off their caps at the *Gloria Patri,* at the names of Jesus and Mary, at the last strophe of the hymns, when it contains the doxology; at the words, *Sit nomen Domini benedictum,* of the Psalm, *Laudate pueri Dominum,* and whilst the *Confiteor* is said at Compline.

Article III.

Instruction for the Acolytes.

1. Before the beginning of Vespers, the acolytes go to the sanctuary, and put their caps at their places. Having lighted the candles on the altar, they afterwards light

those of their own candlesticks, and go to the sanctuary, as when High Mass is to be celebrated.

2. When the officiating clergyman has arrived at the altar, the acolytes turn themselves to the altar, make with the others a genuflection, and immediately after go to place the candlesticks on the steps near the altar, each on his own side; they put out the candles of their candlesticks, and go to their place.

3. Towards the end of the last Psalm, the acolytes, leaving their caps at their places, go to light the candles of their candlesticks, and with them go to the middle before the lowest step, make a genuflection with the cope-bearers, if there be any, and go with them to the officiating clergyman, unless the celebrant intones the antiphon of the *Magnificat*, in which case they remain by their candles, and at the conclusion of the hymn return to the celebrant's bench as before; and, the antiphon being intoned, they place their candles where they formerly were, and remain by them during the incensing of the altar.

4. Having made a bow to him, the acolytes, turned towards each other, stop on each side of the book-stand which is before him, till he has intoned the hymn, and when the *Ave Maris Stella* or the *Veni Creator Spiritus* is said, they stand during the first strophe; then they go, after having saluted the celebrant; they should take care to turn in such a manner that each one remains on his own side; that is, the first acolyte at the right, and the second acolyte at the left; then they return to the altar, where, having made a genuflection, they carry the candlesticks to their place, and leave them lighted; afterwards they go to their seats.

5. After the *Gloria Patri* of the *Magnificat*, the acolytes take the candlesticks, and go, as before, to the celebrant, salute him, place themselves as before, and remain there till after all the prayers are sung; after which, when the celebrant has said *Dominus vobiscum*, having saluted him, they go to the middle; and when he has arrived at the same place, they make a genuflection together with him, salute the clergy, and walk to the sacristy.

If the clergy also immediately after Vespers return to the sacristy, when the celebrant has arrived before the altar, they remain standing during the anthem of the Blessed Virgin, and its prayer; after the celebrant has said *Divinum auxilium*, they make a genuflection, and walk to the sacristy, as directed.

6. Should Benediction follow, the acolytes light the candles on the altar whilst the choir is singing the anthem of the Blessed Virgin, and then kneel near their candles during Benediction.

Should the steps be needed, one of them will attend to this.

Article IV.

Instruction for the Censer-Bearer.

1. The censer-bearer prepares everything as directed for High Mass.

2. He goes to the sanctuary with the clergy, and sits in such a place of the sanctuary as may be most convenient, that he may go to the sacristy when required. The hymn being intoned, or if there be no hymn, as in Easter-week, about the end of the fifth Psalm, he takes off his cap, leaves it at his place, and having made a genuflection to the altar, goes to the sacristy to prepare the censer.

3. When the celebrant, after intoning the antiphon of the *Magnificat*, arrives at the altar, the censer-bearer also goes thither, making a genuflection below the steps; the incense having been put into the censer, and blessed as usual, the censer-bearer gives the censer to the master of ceremonies, from whom he receives the incense-boat; then, without making a genuflection in the middle, he goes immediately to the left of the celebrant, having first placed the boat on the side-table; there he makes a genuflection, keeps the celebrant's cope raised on his side during the incensing, and follows him, making a genuflection at the same time with the master of ceremonies, whenever the celebrant makes it; or if the Blessed Sacrament be not on the altar, whenever he makes a bow in the middle.

4. After the incensing of the altar, the censer-bearer goes to the Epistle side, receives the censer from the master of ceremonies, gives back the censer to the master of ceremonies when the celebrant has arrived at the bench; remains at his left, makes with him a profound bow to the celebrant before and after he is incensed; receives the censer, and incenses the clergy, as directed in the instruction for the deacon.

5. The censer-bearer having incensed the clergy, incenses the master of ceremonies, and then incenses the people, as directed for High Mass; he then goes for the boat, and returning, genuflects in the middle and carries the censer to the sacristy, and returns to the sanctuary, making the usual genuflections.

If there be chanters in cope, the censer-bearer hands the boat to the first of them when he goes up to the altar at the *Magnificat;* he then receives back the boat, and going down, stands at the Epistle side during the incensing. The incensing being finished, he places the boat on the credence-table and receives the censer; he goes to the bench and hands the censer to the first cope-bearer, who incenses the celebrant; then if there are more than two cope-bearers the thurifer accompanies one during the incensing of the clergy and holds the border of his cope; otherwise the thurifer incenses the clergy; the thurifer, however, in any case incenses the people, and then returns to the sacristy.

If, besides the high altar, any other altar is to be incensed, the censer-bearer will follow the directions of the master of ceremonies.

This ends his duties, and he returns to the sacristy and puts away the censer and boat. Should Benediction follow, the thurifer is accompanied to the sacristy by the torch bearers, who return with him when the *Divinum auxilium* has been sung; he kneels behind the celebrant between the torch-bearers and assists as usual.

Article V.

Instruction for the Master of Ceremonies.

1. The master of ceremonies having prepared everything, and placed the marks in the book of the celebrant, which is to be placed on a stand covered with a long veil of the same color of the vestments, and which should be sufficiently light to be easily removed, goes to the sacristy, helps the celebrant to put on the surplice and cope; and everything being ready, gives the signal to the acolytes to walk to the sanctuary, having first, in an audible voice, announced to the clergy the Vespers, the commemorations to be made, and other particulars.

2. As the clergy walk out of the sacristy, the master of ceremonies bows to the celebrant to follow them, and walks with him to the altar; at the door of the sacristy he gives him the holy water; when they arrive at the altar, he makes a genuflection at the right of the celebrant below the steps, kneels during the *Aperi*, and rises with the celebrant.

3. When the celebrant bows to the altar, the master of ceremonies makes a genuflection, salutes the clergy at the Gospel side and at the Epistle side; accompanies the celebrant to his seat, stops there at his left, receiving from him and giving him at the proper times his cap, with the usual kisses, turning the leaves of the book when necessary, pointing out to him everything that he has to read or sing, and raising his cope whenever he has to make the sign of the cross.

4. The master of ceremonies sits on a stool near the celebrant, whilst he is not employed in attending him particularly, and whilst the Psalms are sung; he rises and bows to him at the *Gloria Patri* as a signal for him to remove his cap; he likewise makes the same signs to the clergy in the sanctuary, unless another be appointed for this purpose, which is desirable.

5. Towards the last Psalm, the master of ceremonies makes a sign to the acolytes to light their candles, and to come before the celebrant, whilst the antiphon is

repeated; likewise he makes them a sign when they should go.

6. When the *Magnificat* is intoned, the master of ceremonies receives the celebrant's cap, accompanies him to the altar, having, with him, saluted the clergy, first on the Epistle side, then on the Gospel side.

7. When arrived at the altar, the master of ceremonies makes a genuflection below the steps at the right of the celebrant, raises his cassock a little in front, and the lower extremity of the cope, whilst with him he ascends to the platform, presents the incense-boat and the spoon, as usual, with the customary kisses, for the benediction of the incense, saying, *Benedicite, Pater Reverende*.

8. The incense being blessed, the master of ceremonies gives the boat to the censer-bearer, receives from him the censer, and gives it to the celebrant; whilst the latter incenses the altar, the master of ceremonies raises his cope on his side, and with the censer-bearer makes a genuflection whenever the celebrant makes a bow, or a genuflection.

9. After the incensing, the master of ceremonies receives the censer from the celebrant, gives it to the censer-bearer, goes again by the celebrant on the platform, makes with him a bow to the cross, goes down below the steps, makes a genuflection, salutes the clergy, accompanies the celebrant to the bench, and there incenses him with three swings, gives the censer to the censer-bearer, goes near the celebrant, and points to him whatever he has to read or sing. The master of ceremonies is incensed after the clergy on each side of the sanctuary.

10. When the celebrant has said *Fidelium animæ*, the master of ceremonies gives him the cap, and goes with him to the altar, after having saluted the clergy.

11. If Compline is not said after Vespers, the master of ceremonies, having made a genuflection before the altar, presents to the celebrant the book, to intone the anthem of the Blessed Virgin, either kneeling or standing, as required by the particular time; then, at the left of the celebrant, he returns to the sacristy, salutes the

clergy, makes a bow to the cross, and assists the celebrant to take off the sacred vestments.

12. If there be chanters in cope, they attend the celebrant at the altar for the incensing, and the first of them incenses the celebrant and the clergy.

13. If, besides the high altar, any other be incensed, as for instance that of the Blessed Sacrament, which ought to be incensed first, the master of ceremonies should observe what follows: whilst the hymn is sung, he should invite two or four of the clergymen in the sanctuary, who are the first in dignity, to assist at the incensing.

14. The *Magnificat* having been intoned, the acolytes will be ready with their candlesticks in the middle of the sanctuary, and the censer-bearer between them, and the two or four clergymen behind the acolytes, all turned to the altar.

15. The master of ceremonies accompanies the celebrant to the altar between the two chanters in cope; whither being arrived, they make the genuflection, salute the clergy, and walk out of the sanctuary in the following order:

16. The censer-bearer walks first, then the acolytes, the chanters in cope, having the celebrant in the midst, and raising his cope on each side. They put on their caps before they move forward.

17. If there be four cope-bearers, the two chanters walk first, and the two others after them, at the side of the celebrant. The four clergymen follow the celebrant, two by two.

18. Having arrived at the altar of the Blessed Sacrament, they make a genuflection. The acolytes and the cope-bearers, with the celebrant in their midst, place themselves in a row before the lowest step. The celebrant, with the two cope-bearers next to him, ascends to the altar to incense it, and the others remain standing below.

19. After the incensing, having made a genuflection, they return to the high altar as they came. The acolytes having arrived at the sanctuary, divide and retire,

the first with the censer-bearer at his right towards the Epistle side, the second towards the Gospel side, so also the chanters in cope; and the celebrant between the two assistant cope-bearers, having arrived, and all forming one line, they salute the clergy on each side, walk to the altar, and make a genuflection below the steps.

20. The acolytes immediately put the candlesticks at their places on each side of the altar; the others remain as before till after the incensing of the high altar, for which the incense is not again put into the censer.

21. After the incensing, they all make the genuflection (the celebrant only makes an inclination, if the Blessed Sacrament be not at the high altar), salute the clergy, and the four clergymen return to their places, after having bowed to each other.

22. When Benediction follows after Vespers, the master of ceremonies will bring the stole from the side-table; he will assist when the incense is put in, and during the incensing he will raise the border of the cope. After the prayer he will put the humeral-veil on the celebrant's shoulders; whilst the priest is giving the Benediction, he bows profoundly; at the close he returns to the sacristy with the celebrant as prescribed above.

Article VI.

Instruction for the Cope-Bearers.

On some festivals, Vespers are sung with the assistance of two or four clerics, according to the greater or less degree of solemnity of the festival, dressed in surplice and cope. When there are four, two of them, who are inferior in dignity, should perform the office of chanters, and go to the celebrant and clergy to pre-intone the antiphon and intone the Psalms in the middle of the sanctuary. The two others attend immediately the celebrant; when there are only two, these perform the office of assistants and chanters.

1. The cope-bearers having put on their surplices, assist the celebrant to put on his surplice and cope; then, attended by the acolytes, they put on their own copes,

which should be of the proper color and uniform, as also their caps.

2. At a sign made by the master of ceremonies, they come down, bow to the cross, and with their caps on, walk after the clergy, at the side of the celebrant, raising his cope on each side; if there be four cope-bearers, the two chanters walk together first.

3. As they enter the sanctuary, they take off their caps, and when arrived at the altar, all in one line make a genuflection below the lowest step (the celebrant bowing, if the Blessed Sacrament be not at the altar); they kneel on the lowest step; at a sign made by the master of ceremonies they rise, make a genuflection, salute the clergy, accompanying the celebrant to the bench, they stop before him, being turned towards him, without turning entirely their back to the altar, until the first cope-bearer chanter has pre-intoned to him the first antiphon.

4. Then they all go to the middle to intone the Psalm, taking care always to make a genuflection to the altar, in going to and from it, and a bow to the celebrant every time they pass before him. Having intoned the first Psalm, they make a genuflection, salute each other, and go to sit down on the stools prepared for them in the middle of the sanctuary, before the altar.

5. The cope-bearers put on their caps only after having seated themselves, and sing together with the rest of the clergy.

6. After the first Psalm, both chanters go to pre-intone the antiphon to the clergyman who occupies the first place on the Gospel side; and when having intoned it, they go to the middle to intone the Psalm, and thus successively and alternately on each side of the sanctuary; the two assistants remain sitting during all this time.

7. All the Psalms being sung and the last antiphon repeated, the four cope-bearers go to the celebrant, and remain before him, whilst he sings the chapter; then the first chanter pre-intones to him the hymn; which being done, they return to their places, after having made a

bow to the celebrant and a genuflection to the altar. They remain there standing, with their heads uncovered.

When the *Ave Maris Stella,* or *Veni Creator,* is sung, the cope-bearers go to the middle, and kneel during the first strophe.

8. After the hymn, the cope-bearers go to the middle, and sing the verse; then they go to pre-intone the antiphon to the celebrant, return to the middle, intone the *Magnificat,* make a genuflection, and go to the celebrant.

9. As they accompany him to the altar, he being between them (in case no other altar is to be incensed), they salute the clergy, and make together a genuflection to the altar; the two assistant cope-bearers, with the celebrant, go up to the altar, and the others, if there be any, remain below the steps; the first assistant cope-bearer presents the incense-boat for the benediction of the incense, and the second raises the celebrant's cope a little on his right.

10. During the incensing, they hold the celebrant's cope raised a little on each side; after which they return to the middle, make a bow to the cross, go below the steps, make a genuflection to the altar, salute the clergy and accompany the celebrant to the bench; the first assistant cope-bearer incenses the celebrant, then the clergy, beginning at the Gospel side; and the others go to their places.

11. After having incensed the clergy, who are on the first or highest row of benches, or stools, on each side, the first assistant cope-bearer incenses the cope-bearers, each with two swings; then he continues to incense those who are in the inferior rows; then, having returned to his place, he is incensed by the censer-bearer.

12. When the celebrant is about to say the prayer, all the cope-bearers rise, go to attend him at the conclusion, bowing at the name of Jesus, and having bowed to the celebrant, they go to the middle to sing the *Benedicamus Domino;* or if there be any commemorations, after the first prayer, they go to the middle to sing the verses; they remain there, and sing the *Benedicamus Domino.*

13. Having sung the *Benedicamus,* the cope-bearers

go again to the celebrant, make with him a bow to the clergy, go to the altar, make a genuflection to the cross, go to the sacristy in the same order as they had come from it, or assist to recite the usual anthem.

14. The cope-bearers go to the sacristy, and if the clergy also have left the sanctuary, and are already in the sacristy, they salute them, and take off their copes, after having assisted the celebrant to disrobe.

If, besides the high altar, any other is to be incensed, they follow the directions of the master of ceremonies.

ARTICLE VII.

Instruction for the Celebrant.

1. The officiating priest, having made an inclination to the cross, walks with his cap on, to the altar, attended by the master of ceremonies; when arrived there, he takes off his cap, makes a profound bow to the cross, or if the Blessed Sacrament be at the high altar, makes a genuflection below the steps, and kneels down to say the *Aperi Domine*, which he, as well as each of the clergy, say *submissd voce*.

What has been said about the profound bow or genuflection, is to be observed whenever we say that the celebrant makes a profound bow; for if the Blessed Sacrament is kept at the high altar, the celebrant should make a genuflection.

2. After the *Aperi*, the celebrant rises, makes a profound bow, salutes the clergy at each side of the sanctuary, and goes to the bench, which is the same where he sits with the ministers at High Mass, and should be placed at the Epistle side near the wall, facing the Gospel side, and near the altar. There, standing, he says, *Pater et Ave;* * intones *Deus in adjutorium;* bows at the *Gloria Patri*, towards the altar; sits when the first Psalm is begun, and, having received the cap from the master of ceremonies, he puts it on.

3. Every time the *Gloria Patri* is sung, he takes off

---

* See note, page 74.

his cap, and bows during that verse, then he puts on his cap; likewise he takes it off, and bows at the names of Jesus, Mary, and of the saint whose feast is celebrated.

4. After the Psalms have been sung, the celebrant rises, sings the chapter, intones the hymn, during which he remains standing, and intones the antiphon of the *Magnificat*.

5. Whilst the choir sings the antiphon of the *Magnificat*, the celebrant sits down; when the *Magnificat* is begun, he rises, goes to the altar with his hands joined, and salutes the clergy as usual; when he has arrived at the altar, he makes a profound bow to the cross, goes up, kisses the altar, and makes the incensing as directed for High Mass. After it, he gives the censer to the master of ceremonies (if there be no cope-bearers), goes to the middle, bows to the cross, goes below the steps, makes a profound bow, and goes to his place, where he is incensed with three swings.

6. After the *Magnificat* is sung, the celebrant sits down, with his cap on, whilst they sing or repeat the antiphon of the *Magnificat;* then he rises, sings the prayers, and the *Dominus vobiscum;* the *Benedicamus* is to be sung either by the cope-bearers or the choir; and having said *Fidelium animæ*, etc., he goes to the altar in the usual manner.

7. The celebrant when arrived at the altar, if Compline is not to be sung, after having said the *Pater noster*, secretly, says, *Dominus det nobis suam pacem;* then the anthem of the Blessed Virgin is said or sung, either standing or kneeling, according to the different prescriptions of the Rubrics for the different times; the celebrant standing, says or sings, in the ferial tone, the prayer, and after it, *Divinum auxilium.*

8. If the clergy leave the sanctuary, the celebrant waits till the last couple have made the genuflection, then at the sign made by the master of ceremonies, having made a profound bow to the altar, he walks, with his cap on, to the sacristy, and on his entering it, he takes it off, salutes the clergy, and disrobes, as usual.

9. If Compline is to be sung after Vespers, then the

celebrant leaves the sanctuary after having said *Fidelium animæ*, etc., and returns to the sacristy preceded by the acolytes, and attended by the master of ceremonies and cope-bearers, if there be any.

At the hymn, *Ave Maris Stella*, or *Veni Creator Spiritus*, the celebrant, after having intoned them, kneels at his place before his seat, during the first strophe. He kneels also there on similar occasions. For the incensing of another altar besides the principal one, he follows the directions of the master of ceremonies.

The celebrant should never put on his cope in the sanctuary during Vespers; but he must do it in the sacristy, before he goes to the sanctuary for Vespers. Neither should he incense the bishop, or any other superior prelate; but after having incensed the altar, he must be incensed at his place, with three throws, but if the bishop be present, only with two throws, after which the bishop is incensed with three throws.

If Benediction follows immediately after Vespers (which is the general custom in this country), the celebrant, after having sung *Divinum Auxilium*, etc., will put on the stole; then he proceeds as directed in Part I, Chap. XI, Art. II, No. 2, page 80. In case he is assisted by another priest or by a deacon, he will follow what is prescribed in Art. III of same chapter, page 83.

CHAPTER V.

OF SOLEMN BENEDICTION, WHEN THE CELEBRANT IS ASSISTED BY DEACON AND SUB-DEACON.

1. WHEN the celebrant is assisted by a deacon and sub-deacon in giving Benediction of the Blessed Sacrament, besides what is prescribed in the first part of this ceremonial, page 79, in the sacristy are prepared a cope and stole, dalmatic and stole, dalmatic for sub-deacon, three cinctures, three albs, and three amices.

2. The celebrant and sacred ministers having vested, and having, together with the clerics, made a bow to the cross or image of the sacristy, they proceed to the altar in the following order: The thurifer carrying the censer and boat; four or six torch-bearers with torches; the celebrant between the deacon and sub-deacon, who raise the borders of his cope.

3. The deacon exposes the Blessed Sacrament and assists the celebrant when he puts incense in the censer, the sub-deacon meanwhile holding the edge of the celebrant's cope. During the incensing both of them hold the edge of the cope.

4. The deacon and sub-deacon, still kneeling, hold the book or card from which the celebrant sings the prayer, and this being concluded, the deacon, having received the humeral-veil from the master of ceremonies, rises and puts it on the celebrant's shoulders, and the sub-deacon fastens it. Then the deacon goes up to the altar, genuflects, and having risen, ascends the steps which one of the attendants shall have brought; he takes the monstrance and places it on the corporal and kneels down, his face a little turned towards the Gospel side. Meanwhile the steps are removed.

5. The celebrant and sub-deacon ascend the platform, and the sub-deacon remains kneeling at the Gospel side. The celebrant and deacon rise, and the deacon hands the monstrance to the celebrant and arranges the veil and then genuflects, and both he and the sub-deacon remain kneeling during the Benediction. This being over, the deacon rises and takes the monstrance from the celebrant and places it on the altar, and makes a genuflection with the celebrant.

6. The celebrant rises and goes down the steps with the sub-deacon, and with him kneels on the lowest step and bows profoundly. The sub-deacon takes off the humeral-veil and gives it to the master of ceremonies.

7. The deacon rises as soon as the celebrant and sub-deacon have knelt down, and takes out the Blessed Sacrament and replaces It in the tabernacle, taking care when genuflecting not to turn his back to the celebrant.

8. When the deacon goes down the steps the celebrant and sub-deacon rise, and all having made a genuflection, they return to the sacristy.

CHAPTER VI.

OF SOLEMN VESPERS, AND OF THE PROCESSION ON CORPUS CHRISTI, AND DURING THE OCTAVE OF THIS FEAST.

ARTICLE I.

Of Solemn Vespers, the Blessed Sacrament being exposed.

1. THE master of ceremonies should see that everything necessary for this solemnity be prepared; and besides what is required for Solemn Vespers, a stole for the clergyman who is to expose the Blessed Sacrament.

2. If the Blessed Sacrament be not kept at the high altar, but at another, the master of ceremonies should have the ombrellino,* long veil and candles ready to carry It to the high altar.

3. On the altar he should prepare a corporal, the key of the tabernacle, and monstrance.

4. On the side-table, the long veil, and the Missal with a mark in it, at the place where the prayer of the Blessed Sacrament may be found.

5. The cope-bearers and the celebrant, having put on their copes—the celebrant, besides the cope, should have on a stole—the clergy walk to the sanctuary preceded by the acolyte, and the censer-bearer with his censer and boat before them.

6. Arrived before the altar, they make a genuflection; the acolytes carry their candlesticks to the usual place; the celebrant, with the cope-bearers, kneels on the lowest step; the priest who is to expose the Blessed Sacrament

---

* A small ornamented canopy, somewhat in the shape of an umbrella, which is carried over the Blessed Sacrament.

puts on the stole, goes up to the altar, extends the corporal in the middle of it, opens the tabernacle, makes a genuflection turning towards the Gospel side, takes the Blessed Sacrament, puts It in the monstrance and places it in the middle, makes a genuflection, and places it on the throne; then he goes below the steps at the Gospel side, takes off the stole, and remains there kneeling.

7. The celebrant, with his two assistants, having made a profound bow, rises; he then puts incense into the censer, the first assistant holding the incense-boat and presenting the spoon, without kissing it, and the second holding the cope at his right, kneels down again; receives the censer from the first assistant, makes a profound bow, incenses thrice the Blessed Sacrament, the two assistants raising in the meantime his cope on each side; makes again a profound bow, gives back the censer to the first assistant, who gives it to the master of ceremonies; and having said the *Aperi Domine*, they rise, make a genuflection below the steps on both knees, and a profound bow, and go as usual to the bench.

8. But if the Blessed Sacrament be kept at another altar, a little before Vespers, a priest in surplice and stole, with his cap on, carrying the burse with a corporal in it, and the key of the tabernacle before his breast, preceded by some acolytes with candles, and attended by the master of ceremonies, carrying the long veil and the ombrellino, goes from the sacristy to the altar where the Blessed Sacrament is kept.

9. When they have arrived at the altar, they all make a genuflection; the priest gives his cap to the master of ceremonies, goes up to the altar, extends the corporal on it, opens the tabernacle, and having made a genuflection, takes out the Blessed Sacrament, kneels, receives the veil, which the master of ceremonies puts on his shoulders, rises, covers his right hand with the veil, takes the Blessed Sacrament, covers it with the other extremity of the veil, and carries It with both his hands before his breast, reciting some Psalms, to the high altar preceded by the acolytes with lighted candles, who alternately with the priests say the Psalms; and followed by the

master of ceremonies, who carries the ombrellino opened over him.

10. Having arrived at the altar, the acolytes kneel below the steps at a short distance from them; the priest goes up, places the Blessed Sacrament on the corporal, kneels, and in the meanwhile takes off the veil, which the master of ceremonies carries to the side-table, leaving the ombrellino in some convenient place.

11. The priest rising, places the Blessed Sacrament in the monstrance, makes a genuflection, places it on its throne, goes below the steps, makes a genuflection on both knees on the lowest step, rises, puts incense into the censer, but does not bless it; kneels again, makes a profound bow, incenses the Blessed Sacrament with three throws; after a short prayer, rises, and all make a genuflection on both knees, and go to the sacristy.

12. After the exposition of the Blessed Sacrament, at a sign made by the master of ceremonies, the clergy go into the sanctuary, and make a genuflection on both knees in the middle; they go to their places without bowing to each other; there they stand, and wait till the celebrant, with the cope-bearers, have arrived before the altar; then they kneel on the lowest step. The latter, as soon as they arrive within sight of the Blessed Sacrament, take off their caps and carry them in their hands; they make a genuflection on both knees below the lowest step.

13. After having made a profound bow, while kneeling, the celebrant and his assistants rise with the master of ceremonies, and the acolytes; the acolytes carry their candlesticks, each to his side of the altar, and place them on the highest step near it; the celebrant with his assistants kneels on the lowest step; and at the same time all the clergy in the sanctuary kneel at their places; say the *Aperi;* at the sign made by the master of ceremonies, all rise, and the celebrant with the cope-bearers goes to the bench. It is to be remarked, that when the Blessed Sacrament is exposed, no bow is made to any one in the sanctuary.

14. Vespers are sung as usual as far as the *Magnificat*,

except that no one should put on his cap, and the singers and cope-bearers do not bow to each other.

15. At the *Magnificat*, the celebrant with the cope-bearers goes to the altar, where, having made a genuflection on both knees, he goes up with his assistants, kisses the altar, puts in the incense, kneels on the edge of the platform, incenses the Blessed Sacrament, rises, makes a genuflection, and incenses the altar as usual.

16. After the incensing of the altar, the celebrant and his assistants go to the middle, make a genuflection, bending one knee, go below the steps, the celebrant with the second assistant by the Gospel side, and the first assistant by the Epistle side; make a genuflection, bending both knees on the floor below the steps, and return to the bench. No other altar is incensed; but the celebrant, clergy and people are incensed as usual; the censer-bearer incenses the people, not from the middle, but from one side, taking care not to turn his back to the Blessed Sacrament.

17. After the prayers, the acolytes carry the candlesticks to their place, and after the *Benedicamus Domino*, the celebrant does not say *Fidelium animæ*, but goes with the cope-bearers immediately to the altar, makes a genuflection on both knees below the steps, and a profound bow, rises, and kneels with them on the lowest step.

18. In the meanwhile the acolytes come to the sanctuary with lighted candles, and kneel on each side; the singers intone the *Tantum ergo;* the celebrant incenses the Blessed Sacrament as usual, and after the verse, *Panem de cœlo*, etc., says the prayer, *Deus qui nobis*, etc, with the short conclusion, *Qui vivis et regnas in sæcula*, etc.; then a priest in surplice puts on the stole, goes up to the altar, and with the usual genuflection places the Blessed Sacrament on the corporal, in the middle of the altar, and assists as at page 84.

19. The celebrant receives the long veil, makes a profound bow, goes up to the altar, makes a genuflection, rises, receives with both his hands, covered with the veil, the Blessed Sacrament, and turning by his left to the people, gives the Benediction as usual.

20. After the Benediction, the celebrant makes a genuflection, goes down, kneels on the lowest step, makes a profound bow and takes off the humeral-veil. Then the assistant priest makes a genuflection, puts the Blessed Sacrament in the tabernacle, makes again a genuflection, and shuts it.

If there be no tabernacle at the high altar, the priest above mentioned, having taken the sacred Host from the monstrance, and put It into a pyx, covers It with a veil, and after the clergy have left the sanctuary, he carries It to the altar where the Blessed Sacrament is kept, in the manner described above.

21. At a sign made by the master of ceremonies, the acolytes with the candles go back, or, if necessary, leave them in a convenient place, take their candlesticks, go to the middle, make a genuflection, and walk to the sacristy, as usual.

Article II.

Of the Procession on Corpus Christi* and its Octave.

1. The master of ceremonies should take care to have prepared in the sacristy, the cope, stole, cincture, alb, and amice for the celebrant; dalmatic, etc., for the deacon; tunic, etc., for the sub-deacon, but without maniples; the candlesticks for the acolytes, the processional cross, and, according to custom, the sacred vestments for the priests and other clergymen who attend— such as copes, chasubles, dalmatics, tunics, etc., but without stoles and maniples.

2. The canopy should be prepared in a convenient place, and the ombrellino, two censers with their boats, and at least four lanterns, with candles within.

3. The Blessed Sacrament being exposed, when everything is ready, at the sign made by the master of ceremo-

---

* This ceremony should more regularly take place immediately after Mass, in which case the celebrant and ministers will go down to the bench at the end of Mass and take off the maniples; the celebrant will also take off the chasuble and put on the cope. Then he will proceed as directed in No. 5.

nies, the acolytes, preceded by the censer-bearers, walk from the sacristy to the sanctuary, followed by the clergy, two by two, according to their order and dignity, and the celebrant walking between the deacon and subdeacon, who raise his cope on each side.

4. When they arrive within sight of the Blessed Sacrament, they take off their caps, and, when they have arrived before the altar, they make a genuflection on both knees; the clergy go to their places, and the celebrant and ministers kneel on the lowest step.

5. At a sign made by the master of ceremonies, the ministers rise, the celebrant puts incense in the two censers, and incenses the Blessed Sacrament. The deacon takes from the throne the Blessed Sacrament, puts It on the corporal in the middle of the altar, makes a genuflection, and goes down.

6. The celebrant, having put the long veil on his shoulders goes up with the ministers, and kneels on the edge of the platform; there he receives the Ostensorium from the deacon, rises, turns to the people, having the ministers at his side, who raise the extremities of his cope; and the chanters intone the *Pange Lingua*, and the procession moves, and makes the usual tour.

7. If there is a repository with an altar, where the procession is to stop, when the ministers arrive before it, the deacon kneeling receives the Blessed Sacrament from the celebrant, rises, puts it on the altar, or on the throne, if there is any, makes a genuflection, returns to the right of the celebrant, who takes off his veil; the choir sings the *Tantum ergo*, and the Blessed Sacrament is incensed as usual.

8. After the *Panem de cœlo*, etc., the celebrant sings the prayer with the short conclusion, puts on the veil, but does not give the Benediction, and the procession is continued.*

---

* The Benediction is to be given at the end of the procession, as a reading of the *Cæremoniale Episcoporum* (Lib. II, Cap. XXXIII, ¿ 22) will show; and it is permitted, in case the route is long, to stop once or twice; the S. C. R. has declared, May 11, 1652, that Benediction shall be given "*in fine Processionis.*" Afterwards the Sacred

9. The procession having returned to the church, and the sacred ministers having arrived at the altar, the deacon receives the Ostensorium, etc. The *Tantum ergo*, etc., the verses, and the prayers are sung, and the Benediction given as usual.

CHAPTER VII.

VESPERS FOR THE DEAD ON THE FIRST DAY OF NOVEMBER.

Article I.

Things to be Prepared.

1. In the church, a cenotaph,* or representation of a tomb, covered with a black cloth, with candlesticks and candles of unbleached wax around it.
2. At the altar, the black antipendium under the white one, if possible, otherwise it should be kept ready in the sacristy; also, if the tabernacle with the Blessed Sacrament is on the altar, the violet veil under the white one.
3. On the side-table, a black cope for the celebrant.
4. A book-stand, or desk, in a convenient place.

Congregation, not wishing to disturb any very ancient customs, merely *permitted* that where such a condition (Vetustissima consuetudo) was verified, the Benediction might, with many restrictions, be given once, or even twice. As no such condition can exist here, we have thought it right to observe what is prescribed above.

* This should not be placed in church until after the Vespers of All Saints, and, strictly speaking, the cenotaph need only be erected in time for the Mass of All Souls, when the absolution takes place. It would seem better and more convenient to use a black cloth covered during the Vespers of All Saints, and at the proper time the cover might be removed; or the black cloth might be kept in the sacristy and brought out when needed.

Article II.

Ceremonies peculiar to these Vespers.

1. Whilst the *Magnificat* of the Vespers of *All Saints* is sung, the candles around the tomb are lighted, and whilst the cope-bearers sing the *Benedicamus Domino*, the acolytes go from the celebrant's bench, place their candlesticks as usual at each side of the altar, put out their candles, go behind the cope-bearers, make together a genuflection to the altar, and bow to the clergy, and go before them with their hands joined, to the sacristy, where the cope-bearers take off their copes.

2. After the *Benedicamus Domino*, the celebrant does not say *Fidelium animæ;* he takes off his white cope, and puts on the black; the acolytes take the carpet from the steps of the altar, and remove the white antipendium and the white veil.

3. The celebrant having put on the black cope, all rise, and the choir begin *Placebo Domino*, and sing it entirely, the Vespers being of double rite; and when they begin the Psalm, all the clergy sit, till the beginning of the *Magnificat*.

4. At the beginning of the *Magnificat*, they all rise, and the acolytes light their candles. After the *Magnificat*, they all sit down whilst the antiphon is repeated; the acolytes take their candlesticks, make a genuflection in the middle, and go before the celebrant.*

5. The antiphon being repeated, all the clergy kneel, except the acolytes, the celebrant intones *Pater Noster*, which is continued in a low voice; then the celebrant says, *Et ne nos inducas*, with the other verses, and the choir answers them. After the *Dominus vobiscum*, the

---

* Mgr. Martinucci directs that the acolytes shall not assist with candles, since the *Cæremoniale Episcoporum* only prescribes this when the Bishop is present in his seat in the choir. "*Ad preces et orationem non assistent Acolythi candelabra gestantes, quoniam Cæremoniale Episcoporum nequaquam hoc præscribit pro Ebdomadario, sed tantummodo pro Episcopo quum aderit in primo chori stallo.*" (Martinucci, Lib. II, Cap. IX, No. 21.)

celebrant rises and says the prayer, *Fidelium Deus*, and after it *Requiem æternam*, etc.

6. The acolytes make the usual bow to the celebrant, go to the middle, make a genuflection, put the candlesticks in the proper place, return to the middle, and when the singers have sung *Requiescant in pace*, they make a genuflection, and with their hands joined, go to to the sacristy, followed by the clergy and the celebrant.

PART IV.

Ceremonies for the Principal Festivals

THROUGHOUT THE YEAR.

CHAPTER I.

FEAST OF THE PURIFICATION.

ARTICLE I.

Necessary Preparations.

1. IN the sacristy, a cope, stole, cincture, alb, and amice for the officiating clergyman; a folded chasuble, stole, cincture, alb, and amice for the deacon; likewise a folded chasuble, cincture, alb, and amice for the sub-deacons. The sacred vestments should be violet.

2. On the altar, six candlesticks and the cross as usual, and a violet altar-veil over a white one.

3. A small table covered with a white cloth should be placed near the altar, at the Epistle side; and on the table the candles to be blessed, covered also with a white linen cloth.

4. On the small table, a vessel with holy water, a sprinkle, and a basin, ewer, and towel; also the chalice with everything else necessary for Mass; the whole covered during the blessing of the candles with a violet veil.

5. In any convenient place, the processional cross, the censer with the incense-boat, and a chafing-dish with fire and tongs.

6. At the bench of the officiating clergyman, a white chasuble, stole, and maniple for him; on those of the ministers, a white dalmatic, stole and maniple for the deacon; and also a white tunic and maniple for the sub-deacon.

7. If the Mass be not of the Blessed Virgin, but of the Sunday, the sacred vestments ought to be such as are required for the Sunday.

Article II.

From the vesting of the Ministers to the distribution of the Candles.

1. At a stated hour, the ministers put on the amice, alb, and cincture; then the officiating clergyman, attended by them, puts on the amice, alb, cincture, violet stole, and cope; lastly, the ministers put on the folded chasubles without maniples. The signal being given by the master of ceremonies, the ministers, with the officiating clergyman between them, bow to the cross, put on their caps, and go to the sanctuary; the deacon at the right of the officiating clergyman, and the sub-deacon at the left. Both sacred ministers raise the cope of the officiating clergyman.

2. Having arrived at the sanctuary, the celebrant gives his cap to the deacon, and the deacon and sub-deacon give theirs to the master of ceremonies, and, having knelt on the floor of the sanctuary, they go up to the altar; the celebrant kisses it, and the ministers at the same time make a genuflection, and all go to the Epistle side, where the deacon stands on the first step, at the right of the celebrant, and the sub-deacon at the left, on the platform. Then the master of ceremonies uncovers the candles.

If the Blessed Sacrament be not kept on the great altar, the celebrant bows profoundly to the cross, and the ministers and the other clergymen make a genuflection.

3. The celebrant thus between the ministers, with his hands joined, sings in a ferial tone, *Dominus vobiscum, Oremus,* and the prayer *Domine Sancte,* with the other

four that follow. When he blesses the candles, he lays his left hand on the altar; the deacon in the meantime raising the hem of his cope; as also when the celebrant uses the censer and the sprinkle.

4. At the beginning of the prayers, the censer-bearer puts fire into the censer, and at the end he goes to the Epistle side, having at his right hand the first acolyte, carrying the vessel with holy water and the sprinkle.

5. The fifth prayer being ended, the censer-bearer makes a genuflection, goes up to the highest step of the altar, to have incense put into the censer and blessed as usual by the celebrant, and goes down with the censer and the incense-boat; then the first acolyte makes likewise a genuflection, goes up to the highest step, gives the sprinkle to the deacon, who, taking it in the middle, with the usual kisses, gives it to the celebrant, who sprinkles the candles thrice, first in the middle, then at the right, and lastly at the left of the candles, saying the anthem, *Asperges me*, etc., without the Psalm. The deacon, having received the sprinkle from the celebrant, gives it back to the first acolyte; then takes the censer from the censer-bearer, gives it with the usual kisses to the celebrant, who incenses the candles thrice, in the same manner as he sprinkled them, but without saying anything.

6. Afterwards the censer-bearer takes back the censer, and with the first acolyte makes a genuflection to the altar, and they carry the censer and the vessel with holy water to their proper places.

Article III.

From the distribution of the Candles to the Procession.

1. After the blessing of the candles, the celebrant and ministers go to the middle of the altar, and having bowed to the cross, turn to the people; the first acolyte at the Epistle side hands the candles to the deacon, who stands at the left of the celebrant.

2. Before the celebrant turns towards the people, the second master of ceremonies calls the clergyman first in

dignity amongst those who are present in the sanctuary, who, without stole, goes to the highest step of the altar; where, standing, he receives from the deacon a candle, kisses it, and gives it to the celebrant, without kissing his hand; the celebrant also kisses the candle, but not the hand of the clergyman from whom he receives it; and gives the candle to the sub-deacon, who, having received it with the usual kisses, lays it on the altar. The celebrant having received another candle from the deacon, gives it to the clergyman highest in dignity, who receives it kneeling with the usual kisses, and having made a genuflection to the cross, and bowed to the celebrant, retires, accompanied by the second master of ceremonies. The latter should direct the clergy to go in proper order to receive the candles.

If there be not a priest to offer the candle to the celebrant, the deacon, having received it from the acolyte, places it on the middle of the altar; then the celebrant, having bowed to the cross, kneels on the platform towards the cross, and thus takes the candle from the altar, kisses it, and gives it to the sub-deacon; then, rising, he continues the distribution as is hereafter directed.

3. At the beginning of the distribution of the candles, the choir sings the anthem, *Lumen ad revelationem*, and the canticle, *Nunc dimittis*.

4. If the distribution be not finished at the end of the canticle *Nunc dimittis*, the canticle ought to be repeated, and the *Gloria Patri* sung at the end of the distribution.

5. The clergyman highest in dignity having retired, the deacon and sub-deacon go on the highest step, kneel on the platform, receive with the usual kisses their candles from the celebrant; rise, and return to their former places, that is, the deacon to the left, to hand the candles to the celebrant, and the sub-deacon to the right, to hold up the border of his cope. The ministers give their candles to the acolytes, and then the celebrant distributes the candles, first to the priests, then to the clergy in inferior orders, who go up to the altar, two by two, kneel on the platform, kiss first the candle, then the celebrant's hand.

6. Towards the end of the distribution, at a signal given by the master of ceremonies, the acolytes light the candles of the clergy for the procession.

7. The distribution being ended, the celebrant and the ministers turn towards the altar, bow to the cross, go back in the same order as before, to the Epistle side, where the celebrant washes his hands, and in the meantime the choir sings the anthem, *Exurge*, etc., which is repeated.

8. After the anthem, the celebrant, standing at the Epistle side, without saying *Dominus vobiscum*, sings *Oremus*, and the prayer, *Exaudi*.

After Septuagesima, provided it be not on Sunday, before the celebrant says *Oremus*, the ministers place themselves behind the celebrant, the deacon sings *Flectamus genua*, immediately after the *Oremus* has been sung; he and all in the church kneel; the sub-deacon sings *Levate*, and they all arise, and stand till the prayer is finished. Where it is customary that the candles should be distributed to the people by the celebrant, he shall do it at the railing; the men first kiss the candle, then the hand of the celebrant; but the women kiss only the candle. After the distribution, the ministers go back to the altar, make genuflections on the lowest step, and the celebrant bows to the cross. They then go to the Epistle side, where the celebrant washes his hands at the small table. In case the number of people be great, another priest, in surplice and violet stole, may distribute the candles with the celebrant.

Article IV.

The Procession.

1. Whilst the celebrant sings the last prayer, the censer-bearer puts fire into the censer; when the prayer is finished, he goes to the Epistle side, the incense is put into the censer, and blessed by the celebrant as usual. Then the sub-deacon bows to the altar, and goes by the shortest way, to take the cross, which he receives from the second master of ceremonies, and walks between the

acolytes to the middle of the sanctuary, where he stands turned towards the altar.

2. In the meanwhile, the deacon receives from the master of ceremonies the celebrant's candle, gives it to him, kissing it and the celebrant's hand, and having received his own candle, at the signal given by the master of ceremonies, turned towards the people, he sings with a loud voice, *Procedamus in pace.* The clergy answer, *In nomine Christi, Amen.*

3. The procession then moves in the following order: first, the censer-bearer, who makes a genuflection; then the cross bearer between the acolytes, none of whom make a genuflection; then follow the singers, and the rest of the clergy, who make genuflections, two by two, and carry their candles lighted; then the deacon and the celebrant, who likewise carry their candles lighted, and, when notified by the master of ceremonies, descend the steps, and bow to the altar; the deacon then gives the cap to the celebrant, kissing it first, then the celebrant's hand. He afterwards places himself at the left of the officiating clergyman, raising the border of his cope. The singers sing the anthems as in the Missal.

If, during the procession, a Low Mass is said in the church, the bell should not be rung at the elevation; but if the bell should be inadvertently rung, the procession passing before that altar should kneel till the end of the elevation. (*Decr. R. S. C.*, 1 Mar., 1681.)

4. When they are out of the door of the church, they all put on their caps, the censer-bearer, cross-bearer, acolytes and master of ceremonies excepted; but as soon as they re-enter the church, they uncover their heads, the celebrant and deacon only excepted.

5. Coming into the church, the singers chant the response, *Obtulerunt,* even if the anthems be not yet finished.

6. The censer-bearer makes a genuflection in the middle of the sanctuary, and carries the censer back to its place. The cross-bearer and the acolytes do not kneel; they go to the side-table, on which the acolytes place their candlesticks, and the cross-bearer the cross;

the latter goes to the minister's bench, where he waits for the celebrant and the deacon.

7. The clergy having made a genuflection in the middle of the sanctuary, go to their places, and extinguish their candles. The celebrant and deacon, as they come into the sanctuary, take off their caps, go to the middle of the sanctuary, put out the candles, give them to the master of ceremonies, make the usual bows, go to the ministers' bench, turn towards the altar, and the ministers take the cope from the celebrant, help him to put on the chasuble, put on their own vestments, accompany him to the altar, and having made the usual bows, begin Mass, which is said as usual, and is to be sung by the priest that officiated at the distribution of the candles. (*Decr. S. C. R.*, 12 Jun., 1627.) If a Bishop bless the candles, a priest may say the Mass.

When the Mass of the Feast of the Purification is to be celebrated, an acolyte should remove from the side-table and the altar all the violet ornaments.

Also, when the Mass of said festival is celebrated, the celebrant and the clergy hold lighted candles in their hands during the Gospel; the clergy, moreover, hold them from the *Sanctus* till after the Communion.

CHAPTER II.

ASH-WEDNESDAY.

Article I.

Necessary Preparations.

1. In the sacristy, the violet cope and stole, also the cincture, alb, and amice for the celebrant; the folded chasuble and stole of violet color, with the cincture, alb, and amice for the deacon; the same things (the stole ex-

cepted) are to be prepared in the usual place for the sub-deacon.

2. On the altar, six candlesticks, with the cross and the violet altar-veil. At the Epistle side, a vessel containing ashes, and covered either with a violet veil or with its own cover.

3. On the side-table, besides the things that are necessary for High Mass, the holy-water vase with the sprinkle; a small plate with some bread; a ewer and basin with a towel.

4. On the ministers' bench, the chasuble and maniple for the celebrant; two other maniples for the ministers, who put them on, after having assisted the celebrant to put on his vestments.

5. In any convenient place, the censer with the incense-boat, and a chafing-dish, with fire and tongs.

Article II.

Of the Blessing and Distribution of the Ashes.

1. The deacon and sub-deacon, having put on, as usual, all their vestments (the maniples and folded chasubles excepted), help to vest the celebrant with the amice, alb, cincture, stole, and cope; then they put on their folded chasubles. The signal being given by the master of ceremonies, they all bow to the cross, put on their caps, go out of the sacristy, having the celebrant in the middle, and raising his cope on each side.

2. Having arrived at the altar, they give their caps to the master of ceremonies, kneel, go up to the platform, the celebrant kisses the altar in the middle, and the ministers make a genuflection; then they go to the Epistle side, the celebrant having the sub-deacon at his left, and the deacon at his right; the master of ceremonies uncovers the ashes.

3. There the celebrant, with his hands joined, reads the anthem, *Exaudi*, while it is sung by the choir.

4. After the anthem has been repeated by the singers, the celebrant, in the same place, without turning to the people, sings, in a ferial tone, with his hands joined,

DISTRIBUTION OF THE ASHES.

Dominus vobiscum, Oremus, bowing as usual to the cross, and then the four following prayers; when he blesses the ashes, he places his left hand on the altar, and the deacon raises his cope, which is also to be observed whenever the celebrant uses the sprinkle or the censer.

5. At the beginning of these prayers the censer-bearer prepares the censer, and at the end of them he goes to the Epistle side, having on his right the first acolyte, who carries the holy-water vase and the sprinkle; they both kneel, and the censer-bearer goes up to the highest step, that the incense may be put into the censer, and blessed; he then descends, and gives his place to the acolyte, who presents to the deacon the sprinkle, which is presented by him to the celebrant, whose hand, as well as the sprinkle, is kissed by the deacon. The celebrant sprinkles the ashes thrice, first in the middle, then on the right, and lastly on the left, saying with a low voice, *Asperges me,* etc., but not the Psalm, *Miserere.* The deacon returns the sprinkle, and having received the censer from the censer-bearer, gives it to the celebrant, who incenses the ashes thrice.

6. The censer-bearer, having received the censer, makes a genuflection to the altar with the acolyte, and they carry the censer and the holy-water vase to their proper places.

7. The celebrant and the ministers proceed to the middle of the altar without their caps; the deacon, on the left, holds the vessels with the blessed ashes, and the sub-deacon, turned towards the people, stands at the celebrant's right.

8. The signal being given by the master of ceremonies, the clergyman who is first in dignity amongst those that are present, goes, without stole, to the highest step, when, forming as usual the sign of the cross, and saying, *Memento homo,* etc., he places the ashes on the forehead of the celebrant, who stands with his hands joined.

9. The celebrant then forming the sign of the cross, and saying, *Memento homo,* places the ashes on the head of the same clergyman, who kneels to receive them, and

after having made the usual bows and genuflection, returns to his place, accompanied by the master of ceremonies, who directs the clergy in what order they are to proceed to the altar.

If there be no priest present dressed in surplice, the celebrant kneeling on the platform of the altar makes the sign of the cross on his own head, with the ashes, without saying anything; which must be observed even if the ministers be priests.

10. At the beginning of the distribution of the ashes, the singers chant the anthem, *Immutemur habitu,* etc., which they repeat, if necessary, during the distribution.

11. The priest who is first in dignity having retired, the deacon gives the vessel containing the ashes to the master of ceremonies, or lays it on the altar. He then kneels on the highest step at the right of the sub-deacon, where they both receive the ashes; then the deacon goes to the right side of the celebrant, where he holds the vessel with the ashes, and the sub-deacon proceeds to the left. The celebrant puts the ashes on the foreheads of the clergymen, who go to the altar, two by two, according to their respective dignity and order.

12. After the distribution of the ashes, the deacon returns the vessel in which they are contained to the master of ceremonies, who places it on the table; the celebrant, attended by the ministers, goes to the Epistle side, where he washes his hands, rubbing them also with bread prepared for that purpose, one of the acolytes pouring the water, and a minister holding the towel.

Where it is customary, the celebrant may distribute the ashes to the people at the railing.

13. Then, the ministers standing at the side of the celebrant, he sings, *Dominus vobiscum,* and the prayer, *Concede nobis,* in a ferial tone. The prayer being ended, and the singers having answered, *Amen,* they bow to the cross, and go by the shortest way to their seats, where the celebrant, assisted by the ministers, takes off the cope, and puts on the maniple and the chasuble. The ministers also put on their maniples. They then go to the altar to sing Mass, which must be sung by the

same priest who has blessed the ashes. (*Decr. S. C. R.,* 12 Jun., 1627.)

Article III.

Of the Mass.

1. The ministers having left their seats, bow, as usual, to the clergy, and on arriving at the steps of the altar, kneel before the cross. Mass is celebrated as usual, with the following exceptions: at the *Confession,* and at the prayers, the clergy, as well as the acolytes, who serve at the altar, remain kneeling; the same is to be observed from the *Sanctus* to the *Agnus Dei.*

2. Whilst the celebrant sings the prayer before the last previously to his reading the Epistle, the second acolyte takes off the sub-deacon his chasuble, and lays it on the bench, and assists him in putting it on again after he has sung the Epistle, and kissed the hand of the celebrant. Whilst the celebrant is reading the Gospel, the same acolyte helps the deacon to take off the chasuble and put on the large stole; taking care to assist him again in taking off the large stole and resuming the chasuble, after he has removed the Missal from the Gospel side to the Epistle side, after the Communion.

3. The celebrant should not kneel whilst he reads the *Adjuva nos,* etc., but after having read the Gospel, he goes as usual to the middle of the altar, where he remains till the *Adjuva nos,* etc., then he and the ministers kneel on the platform; when the *Adjuva nos,* etc., is ended, they all arise, incense is then put into the censer, and the rest proceeds as usual.

4. The acolytes holding their candles, remain kneeling from the *Sanctus* to the communion of the celebrant.

5. At the prayer, *Super populum,* the celebrant having sung *Oremus,* the deacon at his right side, turned towards the people, sings, *Humiliate capita.*

CHAPTER III.

Sundays Lætare *and* Gaudete.

On these Sundays three things are particularly to be observed:

1. The organ, which is silent during Lent, is played at High Mass and Vespers.
2. The sacred vestments should be of rose color.
3. The deacon and sub-deacon, instead of folded chasubles, make use of the dalmatic and tunic.

CHAPTER IV.

PALM-SUNDAY.

Article I.

Preparations.

1. In the sacristy, for the celebrant, the violet cope and stole, the cincture, alb, and amice; for the deacon, the folded chasuble, stole, and maniple of violet color, the cincture, alb, and amice; for the sub-deacon, the violet folded chasuble and maniple, the cincture, alb, and amice. Also, three amices, albs, and cinctures, and three violet maniples and stoles; besides three books for the three deacons who sing the Passion.
2. On the altar, the cross and six candlesticks, without any ornaments; where the custom prevails, branches of olive or palm trees may be placed between the candlesticks.
3. Near the altar, on the Epistle side, a small table

for the palms, covered with a linen cloth; on the Gospel side, in any convenient place, three bookstands for the Passion.

4. On the table, the holy-water pot with the sprinkle, the chalice in the middle, covered as usual with the veil, the cruets, bell, the Missal for the Epistle and Gospel, the large stole for the deacon, a basin with a pitcher of water, and a towel.

5. In any convenient place, the processional cross, covered with a violet veil, a chafing-dish, with fire and tongs.

6. On the minister's bench, the violet chasuble and maniple, for the celebrant.

ARTICLE II.

From the beginning of the Ceremony to the Distribution of the Palms.

1. The ministers dressed as usual, with amice, alb, and cincture, and the deacon having put on his stole, assists the celebrant in putting on the amice, alb, cincture, stole, and cope; they then put on their folded chasubles. The master of ceremonies having given the signal, they bow to the cross; and proceed to the altar, having their heads covered, walking at each side of the celebrant, and raising the border of his cope.

2. Having arrived at the altar, and given their caps to the master of ceremonies, they kneel, and the Asperges having taken place as usual, they go up to the platform, where the celebrant kisses the middle of the altar, and the sacred ministers make a genuflection; they immediately go to the Epistle side, where they remain; the sub-deacon standing at the left hand of the celebrant, and the deacon on the highest step at his right. The palms are then uncovered by the master of ceremonies.

3. The celebrant, with his hands joined, and without making the sign of the cross, reads from the Missal the anthem, *Hosanna,* which is sung by the chanters.

4. The anthem being sung, the celebrant remaining

turned towards the Missal, and with his hands joined, sings in a ferial tone, *Dominus vobiscum*, and the prayer that follows; during this, the ministers at each side raise the celebrant's cope. At the beginning of the prayer, the sub-deacon, bowing to the cross, descends to the floor, and standing below the steps, behind the celebrant, with his face turned towards the altar, with the assistance of the second acolyte he takes off the chasuble, and receives the Missal from the second master of ceremonies.

5. At the end of the prayer, having made the usual bows to the clergy, he sings the lesson that follows it in the tone of the Epistle; then, bowing as before the lesson, he goes to the celebrant, and kneeling kisses his hand, and receives his blessing. Having put on the chasuble, he goes by the shortest way to the left of the celebrant, and remains there.

6. After the lesson, the singers chant one of the two responses with its verses, and in the meantime the deacon having bowed to the cross, goes down, and taking off his chasuble, puts on the large stole, receives from the second master of ceremonies the Missal, which he places on the middle of the altar; then making a genuflection, he returns by the shortest way to the right of the celebrant, to hold the incense-boat whilst he puts the incense into the censer; in the same time the sub-deacon raises the border of the celebrant's cope.

7. The incense being blessed, the sub-deacon goes down the steps, and the deacon goes by the shortest way to the middle of the altar; there, kneeling on both knees, he says, *Munda cor meum;* then takes the Missal, and saying, *Jube Domne*, etc., asks the blessing of the celebrant, who, turning himself to the Gospel side, gives it in the usual words, *Dominus sit*, etc. The Gospel is sung, as usual in High Masses; at the end of which the sub-deacon carries the book to the celebrant, who kisses it, and the deacon incenses him as customary; he then takes off the large stole, puts on the folded chasuble, and returns to the right of the celebrant, the sub-deacon being on his left.

8. After the celebrant has been incensed, he turns towards the altar, and sings in a ferial tone the prayer that follows; after which he sings the *Præfatio*. After this, standing at the Epistle side with the ministers, and bowing at the same time, he says in a low voice the *Sanctus*, which is sung by the choir.

9. The celebrant, with his hands joined, sings in a ferial tone, *Dominus vobiscum*, and the prayers for the blessing; when he makes the sign of the cross on the palms, he lays his left hand on the altar, and the deacon raises the border of his cope; the same is to be observed when he makes use of the sprinkle or the censer.

10. At the beginning of the prayers, the censer-bearer prepares the censer, and when they are ended, he goes to the Epistle side, having at his right the first acolyte, who carries the vessel with holy water. Both bow at the lowest step, and the censer-bearer goes up to the highest step; and after the celebrant has put the incense into the censer, and blessed it, he retires; the acolyte then takes his place, gives the sprinkle to the deacon, who, holding it in the middle of its handle, kisses it and presents it to the celebrant, whose hand he also kisses. The celebrant sprinkles the palms three times, first in the middle, afterwards at the right, and lastly at the left, saying, at the same time, *Asperges me;* the deacon returns the sprinkle to the acolyte, and receives the censer from the censer-bearer, kisses and gives it to the celebrant, whose hand he also kisses; the celebrant incenses the palms also three times, in the same manner as has been said for the sprinkling, but without saying any words.

11. The censer-bearer receives the censer from the deacon, makes a genuflection with the acolyte, and both retire to place the censer and the vessel in their proper places.

12. After incensing the palms, the celebrant sings *Dominus vobiscum*, and the prayer that follows.

Article III.

Of the Distribution of the Palms.

1. After the prayer, the ministers and the celebrant proceed to the middle of the altar, bow to the cross, and turn towards the people; the first acolyte, at the Epistle side, holds the palms, which he gives to the deacon.

2. The clergyman who is first in dignity amongst those who are present at the ceremony, when invited by the second master of ceremonies, goes in his usual choir-dress, without stole, to the highest step of the altar; there, standing, he receives from the deacon the palm, which he kisses and gives to the celebrant, without kissing his hand; the celebrant also kisses the palm only, and gives it to the sub-deacon, who, having kissed the celebrant's hand and the palm, lays it on the altar. The celebrant having received from the deacon another palm, gives it to the clergyman who is first in dignity. He kneels on the platform to receive it, and kisses both the celebrant's hand and the palm. (*Decr. S. R. C.*, 14th Feb., 1703.) After which, bowing and making a genuflection, he returns to his place, attended by the second master of ceremonies, who invites the clergy to go to the altar in proper order.

3. When the distribution of the palms commences, the anthem *Pueri Hebræorum* is sung by the chanters, and repeated, if necessary, during the distribution.

4. The deacon and sub-deacon then go to the highest step, and, kneeling on the platform, receive the palm from the celebrant, and kiss his hand and the palm; afterwards they arise, and make a genuflection; the sub-deacon returns to the right, and the deacon to the left of the celebrant, to give him the palms that are to be distributed, having previously placed their own on the altar, or given them to the acolytes. The celebrant distributes the palms to the clergy, beginning with the priests and ending with the inferior clergy, who must come, two by two, and kiss first the palm, then the hand of the celebrant.

5. After the distribution, the celebrant and the ministers turn towards the altar, bow to the cross, and go in the same order as before to the Epistle side, where the celebrant washes his hands, and sings the prayer, *Omnipotens sempiterne Deus*, etc.

The celebrant, where it is customary, may go to the railing to distribute the palms to the people; the men kiss the palm and the celebrant's hand, but the women kiss only the palm. After the distribution, the ministers return to the altar, make a genuflection on the lowest step, but the celebrant merely bows, if the Blessed Sacrament is not present, after which they all go to the Epistle side, as in the preceding number.

Should the congregation be large, another priest, dressed in surplice, and having on a violet stole, may assist the celebrant in distributing the palms; the same is to be observed with respect to the distribution of the candles and of the ashes.

Article IV.

Of the Procession.

1. When the ministers go to the Epistle side, the censer-bearer prepares the censer; after the prayer, he goes to the Epistle side, where the incense is put into the censer, and blessed by the celebrant. Then the sub-deacon goes to the side-table, where, taking off his maniple, he takes the processional cross, and, preceded by the censer-bearer, walks between the acolytes to the middle of the sanctuary, where he remains with his face turned towards the altar.

2. In the meantime, the deacon, having taken off his maniple, gives the palm to the celebrant, at the same time kissing it, and also the hand of the priest; then he takes his own palm, and withdraws to the highest step behind the celebrant; and at a signal given by the master of ceremonies, he turns towards the people, and sings, *Procedamus in pace*, to which the clergy answer, *In nomine Christi. Amen.*

3. They then walk in procession out of the door of the church in the following order: the censer-bearer, having made a genuflection, proceeds first; then come the acolytes, (on each side of the cross-bearer),* who also genuflect; after them the chanters and the rest of the clergy, two by two, who all make a genuflection in the middle of the sanctuary, and carry their palms in their right or left hand, according to their position; if they are on the left, they must carry them in the left hand; but if on the right, they must bear them in their right. Last of all, the deacon and the celebrant, who at the signal given by the master of ceremonies, go down the steps, the celebrant bows, and the deacon kneels before the cross; he then gives the cap to the celebrant, kissing it and the celebrant's hand; and having received his cap from the master of ceremonies, he goes to the left of the celebrant, whose cope he raises with his right hand, holding in his left his own palm. They follow the procession with their caps on.

4. As the procession goes out of the door of the church, all the clergy, except the cross-bearer, the acolytes, the censer-bearer, and the master of ceremonies, put on their caps. The procession is made through the usual places round the church, and the chanters sing either all or only a part of the anthems that are in the Missal, according to the length of the way.

5. On their return to the door of the church, some of the singers enter the church, and shut the door; the censer-bearer goes to the right of the first acolyte, the cross-bearer stops between the acolytes near the door, and turns the crucifix towards the people. The clergy, as they arrive, keep their respective rows, but draw near the acolytes, and form a circle, which is completed by the celebrant, with the ministers at his side, who remain turned towards the door; all may wear their caps.

6. The singers within the church, turned towards the door, sing *Gloria, laus,* which is repeated by the clergy,

---

* The cross-bearer does not genuflect.

who are without; then the other strophes are sung by those within, the clergy alternately repeating *Gloria, laus.*

7. When all the verses have been sung, the sub-deacon, turning the crucifix, knocks at the door with the foot of the cross; the door is immediately opened, the procession enters the church, and the anthem *Ingrediente Domino* is sung.

If the procession cannot be made out of the church, it should be made within; and should stop at the door of the sanctuary.

8. As the clergy enter the church, all, with the exception of the celebrant and ministers, uncover their heads, and proceed to the sanctuary. The censer-bearer arriving at the middle of it, makes a genuflection together with the acolytes, and carries the censer to its place. The cross-bearer and acolytes go to the side-table, the acolytes place their candlesticks on it, the sub-deacon leaves the cross near it and goes to the bench, waiting there for the celebrant and deacon. The clergy having made a genuflection in the middle of the sanctuary, go to their respective places, carrying the palms in their hands.

9. The celebrant and deacon, as they enter the sanctuary, uncover their heads, go to the middle, make a genuflection, and go to the bench of the ministers; there the deacon receives from the celebrant his palm, kissing it and the celebrant's hand, and gives it with his own to the master of ceremonies; then, having turned towards the altar, the ministers take off the cope from the celebrant, and put on his maniple and chasuble; after which, they put on their own maniples, and having bowed to the clergy as usual, go to the altar, and begin Mass, which ought to be celebrated by the same one who blessed the palms, unless they were blessed by the Bishop.

Article V.

Of the Mass and Passion.

1. Mass is celebrated as on other Sundays during Lent, with the following exceptions: the Psalm *Judica* is not said, nor the *Gloria Patri* at the *Introit* and *Lavabo*.

2 Only one prayer is said. Whilst the sub-deacon sings the Epistle, the clergy, deacon and celebrant, unless the latter should actually be reading the *Gradual* or *Tract*, kneel at the words, *In nomine Jesu omne genu flectatur*, till the words, *Et infernorum* are sung.

3. After the Epistle, the sub-deacon waits till the celebrant has read the *Tract*, he then receives his blessing, descends the steps, puts on his chasuble, and goes to the right of the deacon, as observed for the *Introit*. The celebrant and ministers sit at their seats, whilst the *Tract* is sung.

4. During the Passion and Gospel, the celebrant and all the others, except the deacons who sing the Passion, the acolytes and the master of ceremonies, hold palms in their hands; the same is to be observed by all, except the sacred ministers, when they return to the sacristy.

5. The Gospel of St. John is read at the end of the High Mass.

6. Whilst the Epistle is sung, the deacons, who are to sing the Passion, put on the amice, alb, cincture, violet maniple, and stole. The acolytes place in a straight line, at a little distance from each other, the three book-stands, in the place where the Gospel is usually sung.

7. Towards the end of the *Tract*, the three deacons appointed for the Passion, each holding in both hands his book, which he lays against his breast, accompanied by the second master of ceremonies, bow to the cross, put on their caps, and go out of the sacristy in the following order: first, the master of ceremonies, with his hands joined; next the deacon, who sings the words of the Evangelist; then he who sings the words of the multitude; and, lastly, the one who sings the words of our Saviour.

8. When they enter the sanctuary, they uncover their heads, and give their caps to the master of ceremonies; then the deacon, who sings the words of our Saviour, is placed in the middle; he who sings the part of the Evangelist, at the right; and he who sings the words of the multitude, at the left; they make a genuflection before the altar, bow to the celebrant, and the clergy go to the book-stands, place their books upon them, so that he who personates the Evangelist, be in the middle; he who sings the words of our Saviour at the right; and the one who represents the multitude at the left. Then the Evangelist begins, *Passio Domini*, etc.; during the Passion, they stand with their hands joined, and near them the second master of ceremonies.

9. When he who is in the middle begins the Passion, the clergy take off their caps, rise, and stand during it; the celebrant and the ministers rise, and go by the shortest way to the Epistle side, place themselves as for the *Introit;* the deacon gives, as usual, the palm to the celebrant; the ministers receive it from the master of ceremonies, and all hold them in their hands; then the celebrant, turning a little towards the singers, reads the Passion at the Epistle side (*Decr. S. R. C.*, 4 Aug., 1663), turning a little, as far as that part which is sung like the Gospel, exclusively; but when he arrives at the words *Emisit Spiritum*, he makes no genuflection.

10. When the celebrant has read the Passion, the ministers place themselves behind each other, and, with the celebrant, turn towards the singers. In their right hands they hold their palms, and place their left on their breast; at the name of Jesus they bow to the cross; at the words *Emisit Spiritum* they all kneel, where they are, but turned towards the altar; the deacons, however, who sing the Passion, kneel towards their books; they all rise at the signal given by the master of ceremonies.

11. At the end of the Passion, the clergy sit down, the deacons, by whom it was sung, go to the middle of the altar in the same order in which they came, kneel to the cross, bow to the clergy, receive their caps from the second master of ceremonies, and leaving the sanctuary,

they cover their heads, go to the sacristy as they came out, and the acolytes remove the bookstands from the place where the Passion was sung.

12. In the meantime, the sub-deacon gives his palm to the first master of ceremonies, and carries the Missal to the Gospel side. The celebrant gives his palm to the deacon, who gives it and his own to the master of ceremonies, goes to the middle of the altar, and says, *Munda cor meum, Jube Domne Benedicere*, as usual; he then reads the Gospel, as in the Missal, without saying *Dominus vobiscum*, or making the sign of the cross either on himself or on the book; at the end, the sub-deacon anwers, *Laus tibi Christe*. In the meantime, the deacon having taken off his chasuble, puts on the large stole, and carries the book to the altar.

13. The celebrant having read the Gospel, everything is performed as usual, except that the acolytes do not carry the candlesticks, but they go, either with their hands joined, or, if it be customary, holding the palm in their hands; the deacon does not say, *Dominus vobiscum*, neither does he make the sign of the cross on himself or on the book, but having incensed it, he begins by singing, *Altera autem*, etc., in the usual tone of the Gospel. In the meantime, the celebrant holds the palm in his right hand; and at the end of the Gospel he kisses the Missal, which the sub-deacon presents at these words, *Altera die*, and Mass is continued as usual.

CHAPTER V.

OFFICE OF THE TENEBRÆ,

ON WEDNESDAY, THURSDAY, AND FRIDAY, IN HOLY-WEEK.

ARTICLE I.

Preparations.

1. At the altar, the carpet, violet altar-veil, six candle sticks with brown wax candles; the Blessed Sacrament is to be removed to another altar, in case it is usually kept at the principal altar. The altar-cards also should be removed.

2. In the place where the Epistle is sung, a triangular candlestick, with fifteen candles of unbleached wax, and a rod with the proper instrument to extinguish them.

3. In the middle of the sanctuary, a book-stand, for the lessons that are to be sung.

ARTICLE II.

From the Commencement to the End of the Office.

1. At the stated hour, the candles of the altar and those of the triangular candlesticks being lighted, at the signal given by the master of ceremonies, the clergy leave the sacristy. When they are arrived at their places in the sanctuary, they all kneel down for awhile, to say in secret the *Aperi Domine;* then they arise, and say in secret, *Pater, Ave,* and *Credo.*

2. At the signal from the presiding clergyman, the chanters sing the anthem, *Zelus domus;* after which they begin the Psalm, and all sit down.

At the end of every Psalm, *Gloria Patri* is not said, but the anthem is immediately repeated.

3. At the end of the first Psalm, the acolyte appointed to put out the candles, puts out the last candle of the triangle at the Gospel side; at the end of the second, he extinguishes that on the Epistle side, and so on at the end of each Psalm alternately, leaving lighted only the candle at the top of the triangle.

4. After the verses at the end of the third Psalm and anthem of each nocturn, the clergy rise, and say, *Pater noster;* at the end of which, they sit down, and put on their caps.

5. In the meanwhile, the second master of ceremonies invites the clergyman who is to sing the first lamentation, by bowing to him; he then places himself at his left, accompanies him to the bookstand, where both make a genuflection, and bow to the clergy. Then the lamentation is sung, without asking the blessing, and ended without saying *Tu autem Domine.* Afterwards they make a genuflection, bow to the clergy, and the master of ceremonies accompanies the singer back to his place, and bows to him. The same is to be done for each lesson.

6. Whilst the singers begin the *Benedictus,* all rise, and stand till they begin to sing *Christus,* etc.; at the verse *Ut sine timore,* the same acolyte extinguishes the last candle of the altar at the Gospel side; at the verse *In sanctitate* that at the Epistle side, and so at each of the following verses alternately.

Whilst the *Benedictus* is sung, all the lights in the church are put out, except the lamps before the Blessed Sacrament.

7. When the anthem of the *Benedictus* is repeated, the top candle is taken from the triangular candlestick by the acolyte, who carries it to the Epistle side, and holds it lighted at the corner of the altar. When they begin *Christus factus est,* he hides it behind the altar.

8. At the beginning of *Christus,* etc., all kneel and say in secret, *Pater noster;* then the Psalm *Miserere* is either said or sung, at the end of which the presiding clergyman recites, without *Oremus,* the prayer *Respice quæsumus,* but says, in a low and inaudible voice, *Qui tecum vivit,* etc.

9. At the end of the prayer, the celebrant taps his book with his hand, as the others also do; then the lighted candle is brought from under the altar, and all rise and depart in silence, after the usual genuflection.

10. The same is to be observed on the two following days, except that the altar is without a cloth, altar-veil, or carpet; having only the cross and six candlesticks on it.

CHAPTER VI.

MAUNDAY-THURSDAY.

ARTICLE I.

Preparations.

1. IN the sacristy, white vestments for High Mass; besides two violet stoles to be used when the priest strips the altars; also a third white tunic, with amice, alb, and cincture, but without maniple for the cross-bearer. The candlesticks for the acolytes, two censers, with their incense-boat, and a sufficient number of candles for the procession; also torches for the elevation.

2. The principal altar is to be decorated with the most precious ornaments, with a white altar-veil, and if it has a tabernacle with the Blessed Sacrament, it is to be covered with a veil of the same color; the cross on the altar is to be covered with a white veil. (*Decr. S. R. C.*, 20 Dec., 1783.)

3. On the table, besides everything necessary for High Mass, a chalice for the repository, with pall, paten, and a white veil and ribbon; on the paten used for the Mass, two hosts, one of which should be of such a size that it may be put in the chalice prepared for the repository; as many white stoles as will be sufficient for the

priests who are to go to Communion; a pyx with small particles; the communion-cloth, and a white cope for the celebrant; near the table, a clapper, used instead of a bell.

4. In any convenient place, the canopy and the processional cross, covered with a violet veil.

5. A proper place, or repository, should be prepared in some chapel, or on some altar of the church, and decently adorned with hangings, flowers and lights. Above the altar, in the most conspicuous and elevated part, should be placed an urn, or tabernacle, that may be locked, with a corporal in it, where the Blessed Sacrament may be kept for the following day. On the altar, an unfolded corporal, with the burse and the key of the urn. Near the altar, steps, or a stool, that the deacon may reach the door of the tabernacle.

ARTICLE II.

Of the Mass.

1. This day, at Mass, the Psalm *Judica me* is not said; nor the *Gloria Patri* at the *Introit* and *Lavabo*.

2. The celebrant having sung the words, *Gloria in excelsis Deo*, one of the acolytes rings the small bell till the celebrant has finished it; all the large bells of the church are rung, and the organ is played till the singers have chanted the whole of the *Gloria in excelsis*.

3. At the *Sanctus*, and at the elevation, the bells are not rung. Neither the rubrics of the Missal nor those of the *Ceremonial* prescribe that the clapper should be used instead.

4. The *Pax* is not given; consequently, after the *Agnus Dei* the sacred ministers change places, the deacon goes to the left of the celebrant, near the Missal, and the subdeacon to the right, to uncover and cover the chalice at the proper time, making the usual genuflections.

5. Whilst the celebrant says the last of the three prayers that precede the Communion, the master of ceremonies carries from the table to the altar the chalice, in

which the consecrated Host is to be kept; also the paten, pall, veil, and ribbon, prepared for that purpose.

6. After the celebrant has received the Sacred Blood of our Lord, the ministers make a genuflection, change places, make another genuflection together with the celebrant; who, rising, takes the Host with reverence on the paten, and places It horizontally in the chalice, which is presented to him by the deacon, who covers It with the pall, over which he places the paten, with the inside part turned down, and covers it with the veil, fastening it with the ribbon near the knot of the chalice.

7. Then the deacon places it in the middle of the corporal, and uncovers the pyx; here all make a genuflection; the ministers then retire to the two corners of the altar, bowing, and with their faces turned towards each other; the celebrant turns towards the clergy; the deacon sings the *Confiteor*; after which the celebrant says, *Misereatur*, etc., *Indulgentiam*, etc., and then turns towards the altar, and makes a genuflection, whilst the deacon and sub-deacon kneel on the platform before him.

8. Whilst the deacon sings the *Confiteor*, the second master of ceremonies and the censer-bearer go to each side of the altar, and make a genuflection there; they kneel, turned towards one another, and wait till the ministers have knelt before the celebrant; they then extend the communion-cloth, which the censer-bearer must have carried from the table, and hold it with both their hands.

9. The celebrant, holding in his left hand the pyx, and in his right one of the small Hosts, turns towards the people, and having said *Agnus Dei*, etc., gives the Communion to the ministers, who, having received it, make a genuflection, go to the side of the celebrant, at the same time changing their places—viz., the deacon goes to the right, and the sub-deacon to the left; the censer-bearer withdraws the communion-cloth, that they may have room to pass. Then the clergy receive the Communion as usual; the priests, however, having on their stoles, which must be given them by an acolyte, receive it before the others in inferior orders.

10. After the Communion, the celebrant and the ministers turn towards the altar, and make a genuflection. Should any Hosts remain, they are received by the celebrant. The acolytes, who held the communion-cloth, make a genuflection, leave the cloth on the table, and retire to their places.

11. The acolytes return to the sacristy with their torches, and distribute the candles to the clergy, who light them immediately. The censer-bearers prepare their censers, and the cross-bearer puts on the amice, alb, cincture, and white tunic. One of the acolytes carries the caps of the celebrant and ministers to the chapel of the repository.

12. The celebrant receives both ablutions without leaving the middle of the altar. The ministers change places, and make a genuflection at each side of the celebrant, both before and after they change places. When they minister to the celebrant, they no longer kiss his hand, nor anything they present to him, or receive from him. The sub-deacon wipes the chalice, and covers it; leaves room for the celebrant when he says *Dominus vobiscum;* makes a genuflection on the platform, and also on the lowest step, when he passes before the Blessed Sacrament; carries the chalice to the table, and goes behind the deacon.

13. The celebrant, having given the chalice to the sub-deacon, makes a genuflection, and goes to read the communion. He then returns to the middle, kisses the altar, makes a genuflection with the deacon, turns towards the people from the Gospel side, so as not to turn his back to the Blessed Sacrament, and sings *Dominus vobiscum.* Afterwards the celebrant makes a genuflection with the ministers, goes to sing the prayer, then returns to the middle, kisses the altar, genuflects, and turns towards the people, as before, and sings *Dominus vobiscum.* In the meantime the deacon makes another genuflection, turns towards the people, as the celebrant also turns: he sings, *Ite, missa est,* after which they all make a genuflection. The celebrant says, *Placeat,* etc., and the ministers go to each side of the platform, and kneel down to receive the blessing.

14. The celebrant, after the *Placeat*, kisses the altar, and having said *Benedicat vos omnipotens Deus* instead of bowing, makes a genuflection, and turns in the same manner as for the *Dominus vobiscum*, and then without completing the circle, or repeating the genuflection, he turns on his left to the Gospel side, to read the Gospel of St. John, without making the usual sign of the cross on the altar; he makes it, however, upon himself; when he pronounces the words, *Et Verbum caro*, he makes a genuflection to the Blessed Sacrament.

15. The Gospel of St. John being ended, the ministers go up the platform to each side of the celebrant, and having made a genuflection, go to the bench by the shortest way.

Article III.

Of the Procession.

1. When the ministers arrive at the bench, they assist the celebrant in taking off the maniple and chasuble, and putting on the cope; they also take off their own maniples; after which they go to the lowest step before the altar, kneel on both knees on the floor of the sanctuary, rise, and kneel on the lowest step, where they adore the Blessed Sacrament for a short time; at a signal given by the master of ceremonies, they rise. Incense is then put into the censer by the celebrant, but not blessed. The celebrant, whilst the ministers raise his cope, incenses the Blessed Sacrament. Everything is prepared for the procession, which is to be made in the church, and not out of doors. (*Decr. S. R. C.*, 6 Aug., 1591.)

2. Whilst the celebrant incenses the Blessed Sacrament, the master of ceremonies brings the veil from the table, which he puts on the shoulders of the celebrant, as soon as he has returned the censer to the deacon. The censer-bearers go to each side of the altar, and the acolytes, appointed for the purpose, give the canopy to the priests dressed in surplices, or to others, according to custom.

3. The celebrant, having put on the veil, goes up to the second step, with the ministers at his side; there the celebrant and the sub-deacon kneel down, and the deacon goes upon the platform to the altar, makes a genuflection, takes the chalice, holding it with his right hand at the knob, and with his left at the foot, gives it to the celebrant, who takes it with his left at the knob, and places his right hand over it; then the deacon covers it with both extremities of the veil; and having made a genuflection, goes to the right of the celebrant, who rises with the ministers, and goes up with them to the platform; there they turn towards the people, the deacon standing at the right, and the sub-deacon at the left of the celebrant, and holding up the border of his cope. The singers begin the *Pange lingua*.

4. The following order is to be observed in the procession: first, the cross-bearer, sub-deacon dressed in tunic, between the acolytes. All three should go to the middle of the sanctuary, near the rails, whilst the celebrant incenses the Blessed Sacrament, and remain standing with their faces towards the altar. When the *Pange lingua* is intoned, they turn towards the people, and walk with gravity towards the chapel of the repository. Next to them, the rest of the clergy, having made a genuflection on both knees before the Blessed Sacrament, walk two by two, carrying lighted candles in their hands.

5. Lastly, the sacred ministers descend the steps, place themselves under the canopy, and are preceded immediately by the censer-bearers, who keep their censers in continual and regular motion, and walk after the clergy.

6. During the procession, the celebrant recites, alternately with the ministers, psalms and hymns, without saying *Gloria Patri* at the end, whilst the chanters continue to sing the *Pange lingua*.

7. When the cross-bearer and the acolytes arrive at the door of the chapel, they retire a little aside, in order that the procession may pass, and they remain there standing, with their faces turned towards the procession.

Those of the clergy who walked next to the cross-bearer stop, the first on each side of the chapel, and those who follow stop next to them, so that the clergymen who walked the last are nearest to the altar of the repository; having divided into two lines, the celebrant, with the sacred ministers, passes between them. The censer-bearers, on entering the chapel, keep their censers still.

8. The celebrant and ministers having arrived at the altar, ascend the steps; the deacon, kneeling on the platform, receives the Blessed Sacrament, rises, and after the celebrant has adored It, places It on the altar, makes a genuflection, and kneels at the right of the celebrant; then the singers begin the *Tantum ergo*. After the *Veneremur cernui* has been sung, incense is put into the censer, as usual; the deacon, or a priest in surplice and stole, places the Blessed Sacrament in the urn, which he shuts at the end of the hymn.

It is prescribed by the Ceremonial of the Bishops (lib. 2, c. 23, n. 13), that the deacon, on receiving the chalice, as has been said above, should not place it on the altar, but in the urn, which he should leave open till the Sacrament is incensed, etc.

Article IV.

Of Vespers, and of the Stripping of the Altars.

1. When the urn or tabernacle, is shut, some acolytes take the candles from the clergy, who, having prayed for a short time, at a signal from the master of ceremonies make a genuflection on both knees, and return to the sanctuary, the first in dignity walking first, and so on.

2. When they have come to the sanctuary, they make a genuflection in the middle, and return to their places; where, standing, they say in secret the *Pater* and *Ave;* then the clergyman first in dignity, begins in a moderate tone of voice, the first antiphon of Vespers, and at the proper time, the *Magnificat* and the *Miserere;* after which he recites the prayer, *Respice*, etc.

3. The clergy having left the chapel of the repository, the ministers and the censer-bearers make a genuflection

on both knees on the floor of the chapel, and, having received their caps, go to the sacristy, preceded by the censer-bearers and the cross-bearer, with the acolytes carrying the candlesticks with lighted candles. The ministers, on each side of the celebrant, raise his cope. After they have entered the sacristy, they make a profound bow to the cross, take off their white vestments, and the celebrant and deacon put on violet stoles.

4. Towards the end of the Psalm, *Miserere,* the celebrant, with the ministers walking after each other, and having their caps on, go out of the sacristy, preceded by the acolytes, and attended by the master of ceremonies. On entering the sanctuary, the ministers walk on each side of the celebrant, and, having given their caps to the master of ceremonies, bow to the clergy, make a genuflection to the cross, with the exception of the celebrant, who merely bows; they then go up the platform, and the prayer, *Respice,* being ended, the celebrant begins in a moderate tone, *Diviserunt sibi,* which is continued by the clergy, together with the Psalm, *Deus, Deus, meus,* etc., which they should recite slowly so as to finish them when the celebrant comes back to the sanctuary, after having stripped all the altars.

5. The celebrant alternately with the ministers recites in a low voice the same Psalm, whilst they strip the altars. They first take off the upper cloth, then the others; and the acolytes remove the front veil, the altar cards, the carpet, and all the other ornaments, leaving only the cross and six candlesticks. Afterwards, the ministers descend the steps, and having made a genuflection with the acolytes, the celebrant only bowing, they bow to the clergy, put on their caps, and walk one after the other, preceded by the acolytes, and proceed to strip the other altars; when they pass before the chapel of the repository, they make a genuflection on both knees.

In churches that have many altars, whilst the celebrant strips the high altar, other priests in surplice and stole may strip the others, reciting the same Psalm.

6. After the stripping of the altars, the celebrant having returned to the high altar, waits there till the antiphon, *Diviserunt*, is repeated by the clergy; then, after the usual genuflection, they go the sacristy.

CHAPTER VII.

GOOD FRIDAY.

ARTICLE I.

Preparations.

1. IN the sacristy, the black vestments, viz.: two folded chasubles for the deacon and sub-deacon; a chasuble for the celebrant, two stoles, three maniples, albs, cinctures, and amices.

2. Also three albs, with cinctures and amices, as many black maniples, and stoles, and three Missals for the deacons, who sing the Passion. Besides, two censers and incense-boat, a chafing-dish, with fire and tongs; the torches and candles for the procession.

3. The altar must be undressed, having, however, six candlesticks, and candles of unbleached wax, and the cross covered with a black veil, fastened in such a manner as to be easily and gradually taken off.*

4. On the edge of the platform of the altar, three violet cushions, one on each side, and one in the middle, at a proper distance.

5. On the side-table, a plain linen cloth, projecting only a little on each side; and on it the cruets in their plate, and the finger towel; a bookstand with the Missal for the celebrant; another Missal for the ministers; a folded altar-cloth, and a large black stole for the deacon; a small vessel with water, covered with a purifier for the ablution of the fingers in case the priest should touch the Blessed Sacrament; a black burse, con-

---

* A small cross may be substituted, if the other cannot be readily used.

taining a corporal, and a purifier on it; a black veil for the chalice, two candlesticks with brown wax candles for the acolytes. The candles should not be lighted.

6. In any convenient place, the processional cross, covered with a violet veil, and the wooden clapper.

7. At the Epistle side, in the sanctuary, a violet carpet, with a long white veil, and a violet cushion, on which the cross may be placed for the adoration. Also three bookstands for the Passion. The minister's bench must be without ornaments.

8. At the chapel of the repository, besides the canopy, the white veil on the side-table. On the altar, the key of the urn, or tabernacle; and near the altar, the steps, etc.

Article II.

From the Vesting of the Ministers to the Uncovering of the Cross.

1. After the ministers are dressed, they proceed with the clergy to the sanctuary, as usual, except that the acolytes, without candlesticks, and with their hands joined, walk before the clergy. When they arrive at the altar, they make a genuflection and retire to their usual places. The ministers at the foot of the altar give their caps to the master of ceremonies, and make a genuflection with the celebrant, without bowing to the clergy; they prostrate themselves, and lay their hands and faces on the cushions.

2. At the same time the clergy kneel down, and bow their heads; the acolytes having knelt and made a short prayer, rise, and with the assistance of the second master of ceremonies, extend on the altar a cloth, which should hang down only very little on each side; then the acolytes go to their places; and the master of ceremonies places on the Epistle side of the altar the bookstand, with the Missal open.

3. After a few minutes, the signal being given by the master of ceremonies, the sacred ministers and all the clergy rise. Immediately, the acolytes remove the

cushions; and the celebrant, with the deacon and sub-deacon, goes up to the altar; the celebrant kisses it; the deacon and sub-deacon make a genuflection, and they all go to the Epistle side, as for the *Introit.**

4. At the same time, one of the acolytes receives the Missal from the second master of ceremonies, goes, accompanied by him, to the middle of the altar, makes a genuflection, bows to the clergy, goes to the place where the Epistle is usually sung, and there sings the lesson in the tone of the prophecies. At the beginning of it the clergy sit down, and the celebrant reads it with a low voice; the ministers do not answer, *Deo gratias*, at the end, but the celebrant immediately reads the *Tract*.

5. The acolyte having sung the prophecy, makes a genuflection before the altar, bows to the clergy, and returns to his place. The singers chant the *Tract*, during which the celebrant and ministers may sit down.

6. When the choir sing the words, *Operuit cœlos*, the deacon and sub-deacon go, one after the other, behind the celebrant. In case they be sitting, they should first return to the altar by the shortest way.

7. After the *Tract*, the celebrant sings *Oremus*, and the deacon immediately subjoins, *Flectamus genua*, kneeling, with all the clergy, the celebrant excepted; then the sub-deacon answers, *Levate*, and all rise.

8. Whilst the celebrant sings the prayer, with his hands extended, the second acolyte helps the sub-deacon to take off his chasuble. The latter, having received the Missal from the second master of ceremonies, kneels before the altar, bows to the clergy, and sings the lesson, without the title, in the usual tone of the Epistle.

9. The lesson being ended, the sub-deacon kneels to the altar, bows to the clergy, and without asking the blessing from the celebrant, returns the Missal to the second master of ceremonies, puts on his chasuble, and returns to his place, as at the *Introit*. The celebrant

---

* Mgr. Martinucci says that the deacon and sub-deacon do not genuflect. He prescribes the same for the ceremonies of the Purification, Ash-Wednesday, Palm Sunday, and generally during Holy Week. The majority of authors, however, prescribe a genuflection.

having read the lesson with the *Tract*, goes with the ministers to sit down.

10. Whilst the *Tract* is sung, three book-stands are prepared for the Passion, and everything is done as directed in the fourth chapter, with the following exceptions: the celebrant reads all the Passion at the Epistle side, even that part which is sung in the tone of the Gospel; saying before it, *Munda cor meum*, in the same place, but profoundly inclined, and omitting *Jube Domne*, etc.

11. After the Passion, those who sang it having returned to the sacristy, the sub-deacon goes down the step before the altar, and the deacon to the Epistle side; the latter takes off his chasuble, puts on the large stole, and carries the Missal to the altar, making the usual bows and genuflection. Then, kneeling on the platform, he says, *Munda cor meum*, without asking the blessing; he rises, takes the Missal, goes down the steps at the right of the sub-deacon, and after the usual genuflection and bows, goes to sing the Gospel, at which neither the censer nor the candlesticks are used.

12. The Gospel being sung, the sub-deacon does not carry the Missal to the celebrant, but shuts it, and gives it to the second master of ceremonies; and all having made a genuflection in the middle, the acolytes go to their place; the master of ceremonies lays the Missal on the table, and the ministers go, one after the other, behind the celebrant at the Epistle side.

13. Then the celebrant begins to sing the first preamble, with his hands joined; at the end of it, he extends and joins them, bowing to the cross, and sings, *Oremus;* then the deacon adds, *Flectamus genua*, and the sub-deacon, *Levate*, as in n. 7.

The celebrant immediately sings the prayer in the ferial tone, with his hands extended. All the following preambles and prayers are sung in the same manner.

14. At the prayer which begins with the words, *Omnipotens sempiterne Deus, qui salvas, omnes*, etc., the acolytes go to spread the violet carpet, covering the lowest step of the altar with one end of it, and extend-

ing the other on the floor of the sanctuary; they also lay the cushion on the lowest step, and cover the whole with the white veil.

15. All the prayers being ended, the ministers go by the shortest way to the bench, where the celebrant and the sub-deacon take off their chasubles, go to the Epistle side and stop before the lowest step, turned towards the people.

16. Then the master of ceremonies and the deacon go up to the altar, having first made a genuflection on the lowest step. The master of ceremonies takes the cross, and gives it to the deacon, who, having received it, reverently carries it by the shortest way to the celebrant, having the image of the crucifix turned towards himself; the celebrant receives it with great respect, holding the crucifix turned towards the people.

Article III.

From the Uncovering of the Cross to the Procession.

1. The celebrant, standing on the lowest step at the Epistle side, having the sub-deacon at his left, and the deacon at his right, turned towards the people, holds the cross in his left hand, and with the right uncovers the top of it, as far as the cross-piece, assisted, if necessary, by the ministers, raises it to the height of his eyes, and, with a grave and moderate voice, sings, *Ecce lignum Crucis*, from the book, which one of the acolytes holds open before him.

2. At these words, the clergy, having uncovered their heads, rise; the celebrant, with the ministers and the acolytes, continues to sing the whole anthem. At the end of it, the choir and the clergy all kneel down and answer, *Venite adoremus*. The ministers also and all the others, the celebrant excepted, kneel at the same time.

3. The words *Venite adoremus* being sung, the celebrant and the ministers ascend in the same order as before to the platform, and stop at the Epistle side. The celebrant uncovers the right arm and the head of the

crucifix, and, raising his voice one tone higher than the first time, sings, *Ecce lignum,* and everything is done as before.

4. Then the celebrant and the ministers go to the middle of the altar, in the same order; there he uncovers the whole cross, giving the veil to the sub-deacon, who gives it to one of the acolytes, by whom it is placed on the side-table; afterwards, raising his voice one tone higher, he sings, *Ecce lignum,* and the rest is done as above.

5. The clergy having risen, the celebrant, accompanied by the master of ceremonies, who raises his vestments as he goes up or down, carries the cross, without making any bow, to the place prepared for it, and kneeling, puts it on the cushion and veil; then rises, makes a genuflection, and goes to the bench.

6. Whilst the celebrant kneels, the clergy rise, and the ministers, making a genuflection on the platform towards the cross, go by the shortest way to the bench. The second acolyte uncovers the processional cross, and another acolyte uncovers the other crosses that are in the church and in the sacristy, but not the images.

7. When the celebrant and ministers arrive at the bench, they take off their maniples and their shoes. The ministers remain at the bench, and the celebrant, attended by the master of ceremonies, goes to venerate* the cross.

8. Towards the extremity of the sanctuary, the celebrant kneels before the cross, and makes a short prayer; then rises, and about the middle of the sanctuary kneels again, and prays in the same manner; he does the same for the third time at the foot of the cross, which he humbly kisses. Lastly, he rises, makes a genuflection to the cross, returns by the shortest way to the bench, puts on his shoes, with the assistance of the acolytes, and, assisted by the ministers, puts on his chasuble and maniple; then he sits down, and puts on his cap.

9. The ministers bow to the celebrant, and, attended

---

* The technical term is adoration; but to prevent misconception, we use the one less likely to be misinterpreted.

UNCOVERING OF THE CROSS.

by the second master of ceremonies, go to venerate the cross, observing what has been said in regard to the celebrant, n. 8. The deacon kisses the cross before the sub-deacon.

10. After the ministers, the clergy go, two by two, first the priests, then those in inferior orders; and lastly, the laymen, if custom allows them to enter the sanctuary.

Otherwise, a priest, with a surplice and a black stole, carries another crucifix to some other place for the veneration of the people, laying it on the cushion, as above, and the same priest removes it, if it be in the way of the procession.

Another method might be followed where the congregation is very numerous, viz., that one or two clergymen, in surplice and stole, should present the crucifix to be kissed at the railing.

11. During the whole time of the veneration of the cross, the choir sings the *Improperia*. It is not necessary to continue them after it, nor to sing them all.

12. The ministers having returned to the bench, put on their shoes and maniples; the sub-deacon resumes also his chasuble, and both sit down at the side of the celebrant. Then one of the acolytes brings the Missal from the table, bows to the celebrant, opens it at the place where the *Improperia* are found, and holds it so that the celebrant and the ministers may read them alternately.

13. When the acolytes have venerated the cross, the first of them lights the candles on the table and on the altar, and the second goes to hold the Missal before the ministers in the place of the censer-bearer, till they have finished the *Improperia;* then he shuts it, bows to the celebrant, puts it on the table, and returns to his place. The censer-bearers having venerated the cross, the second of them goes to assist the cross-bearer to put on the amice, alb, cincture, and chasuble, and the first prepares the censers.

If there be no sub-deacon besides the one that ministers to the celebrant, any acolyte dressed in surplice may carry the cross.

14. Towards the end of the veneration, the deacon rises, bows to the celebrant, and carries to the altar the burse with the corporal and purifier. When he has reached the platform he kneels to the cross, unfolds the corporal as usual, and places the purifier near it, at the Epistle side. At the same time the master of ceremonies carries the Missal with its stand to the Gospel side, kneeling to the cross. The deacon having unfolded the corporal, makes a genuflection to the cross, and returns by the shortest way to the right of the celebrant, sits down and covers his head.

15. After the veneration, the deacon, invited by the master of ceremonies, takes off his cap, rises, and attended by the master of ceremonies, goes to the place in which the cross was laid, makes a genuflection, takes it up with both his hands, and assisted by the master of ceremonies, carries it to the altar, and places it between the candlesticks, makes a genuflection, and returns to the side of the celebrant. At the same time the celebrant, the sub deacon, and all the clergy kneel down at their places.

16. Then the celebrant, ministers, and clergy rise, and sit down. In the meanwhile an acolyte removes the veil, cushion, and carpet. From this time until None, of the following days, the usual bows are omitted. (*S. R. C.*, 12 Sept., 1857.)

Article IV.

Of the Procession.

1. The cross being placed on the altar by the deacon, the censer-bearers go to the middle of the sanctuary, followed by the cross-bearer, who walks between the acolytes with the candlesticks; then they all proceed to the repository by the shortest way; the clergy follow them, first those in inferior orders, then the priests, lastly the ministers, one after the other, with their hands joined and their caps on, all making a genuflection before the cross.

2. On arriving at the repository, the censer-bearers

make a genuflection in the middle on both knees, and retire to the Epistle side; the cross-bearer and the acolytes, having first genuflected, stop at the entrance of the chapel on the Epistle side, as on preceding day; all the others, after making a genuflection on both knees, place themselves as on preceding day.

3. The sacred ministers, at the entrance of the repository, give their caps to the master of ceremonies, who gives them to an acolyte to carry to the sanctuary, and place them on the bench of the ministers. Then the deacon passes to the right, and the sub-deacon to the left of the celebrant. When they arrive before the altar, they make a genuflection on both knees, rise, kneel on the lowest step of the altar, and pray for a few moments; in the meantime candles are distributed to the clergy, who light them.

4. The signal being given by the master of ceremonies, the deacon rises, makes a genuflection, and goes to open the urn, or tabernacle, and having made another genuflection, returns to the right of the celebrant, who puts incense in both censers without blessing, and kneeling with the ministers, incenses the Blessed Sacrament. The canopy is given to be carried either to priests dressed in surplice, or to other persons, according to custom.

5. After the incensing of the Blessed Sacrament, the master of ceremonies puts the veil on the shoulders of the celebrant; the deacon takes the Blessed Sacrament from the urn, and gives it to the celebrant, as on the day before, who, having covered it with the lower parts of the veil, turns towards the people, having the deacon on his right and the sub-deacon on his left hand. The singers, still kneeling, intone *Vexilla Regis*, etc. The procession moves off; first the cross-bearer with the acolytes, then the others, who make a genuflection as the day before. When they are arrived at the sanctuary, the cross-bearer leaves the cross at the Epistle side, makes a genuflection, and goes to the sacristy to take off the sacred vestments. The clergy, on arriving at the sanctuary, go to their place, and remain there kneeling.

6. The sacred ministers having arrived at the high

altar, the deacon receives the Blessed Sacrament from the celebrant, and having placed it on the corporal, unties the ribbon, and extends the veil, as at the beginning of Mass; then he makes a genuflection, and returns to the right of the celebrant, from whose shoulders the veil should have been removed in the meantime by the sub deacon. Incense is put into the censer, and the Blessed Sacrament should be incensed as usual.

7. The clergyman who carried the canopy leave it aside, take candles, and kneel down before the altar, forming a semi-circle, till after the Communion. If the canopy is carried by laymen, they remain kneeling at the rails, holding lighted candles in their hands.

8. The censer bearers, after the incensing, make a genuflection on both knees in the middle, and the second of them goes to the sacristy; the first remains at the Epistle side.

Article V.

Of the remaining part of the Office.

1. When the celebrant has incensed the Blessed Sacrament, he goes up to the altar with the ministers. They make a genuflection, bending one knee; the deacon takes the veil from the chalice, and gives it to the master of ceremonies; he removes also the paten and the pall from the chalice. Then he takes the paten with his right hand, raises it a little from the corporal, and the celebrant, taking the chalice, lets the consecrated Host fall gently on the paten, taking care not to touch It; but should he happen to do so, he washes his fingers in the small vase prepared for this purpose, and the deacon presents to him the purifier. Then the celebrant receives with both his hands the paten from the deacon who kisses neither it nor the celebrant's hand; and without making any cross, or saying anything, the celebrant places the Host on the corporal, laying the paten also on the corporal at the Epistle side.

2. The Host being placed on the corporal, the subdeacon makes a genuflection, goes to the right of the

deacon, makes another genuflection, and, receiving the cruets from an acolyte, takes that which contains wine, and gives it to the deacon, who puts some of the wine into the chalice, taking care not to place it on the altar, nor to wipe it with the purifier. Then the sub-deacon puts a little water into the chalice, without asking the blessing of the celebrant, who does not give it, nor say the prayer, *Deus qui humanæ*, etc. This done, the acolyte carries back the cruets to the side-table; the sub-deacon goes to the left of the celebrant, making the usual genuflections, and the deacon presents the chalice, without kissing it, to the celebrant, who, without making any cross, or saying any prayer, places it on the corporal, and it is covered with the pall by the deacon.

3. Then the censer-bearer, having made a genuflection below the steps, goes to the platform, and the incense is put into the censer as usual, but without blessing or kissing the censer, or the hand of the celebrant. The sacred oblations are incensed as usual, with the words, *Incensum istud;* likewise, the cross and the altar, with the customary genuflections, and with the words, *Dirigatur Domine*, etc., *Accendat*, etc. At the Epistle corner the deacon receives the censer from the celebrant, and gives it to the censer-bearer, who carries it to the sacristy, as it is not used again.*

4. The celebrant, having given the censer to the deacon, descends one step on the Epistle side, turned towards the people, and washes his hands, the sub-deacon pouring the water, and the deacon presenting him the towel; the psalm, *Lavabo*, is not said; the celebrant and the ministers go to the middle of the altar, and the acolytes carry everything back to the side-table.

5. The celebrant and ministers arriving at the middle, make a genuflection; the deacon goes to the left of the celebrant, near the Missal, and the celebrant, placing his hands joined on the altar, and bowing, says with a low but audible voice the prayer, *In spiritu humilitatis*, etc. He then kisses the altar, makes a genuflection, and turn-

---

* The deacon does not incense the celebrant.

GOOD FRIDAY.

ing his face towards the people, and his back to the Gospel side, says, *Orate fratres ;* he continues what follows in a low voice, and without going round, returns to the middle. The ministers do not answer, *Suscipiat,* etc.

6. The celebrant having said the *Orate fratres,* etc., sings, in a ferial tone, *Oremus : Præceptis, salutaribus moniti,* with his hands joined, and the *Pater noster* with his hands extended. At the beginning of the *Pater,* the deacon makes a genuflection, and goes behind the celebrant. The master of ceremonies takes his place by the Missal.

7. At the end of the *Pater noster,* the choir answers, *Sed libera nos a malo,* and the celebrant says, in a low voice, *Amen,* continuing to hold his hands extended, and not signing himself with the paten. Then he subjoins in the same tone of voice, *Libera nos quæsumus Domine,* etc. After which, the choir answers, *Amen.*

8. The celebrant makes a genuflection, places the paten under the Host, and holding with his left hand the paten on the altar, with his right raises the Host, so that it may be seen by all; without, however, taking it out of the limits of the corporal. In the meanwhile the ministers kneel on the platform; they do not raise the lower part of the celebrant's chasuble; the Blessed Sacrament is not incensed. The clapper is not sounded.*

9. Whilst the celebrant lays the Host on the paten, the ministers rise, go to his side, and with him make a genuflection. Then the deacon uncovers the chalice, the celebrant takes the Host, divides It as usual into three parts, without making the sign of the cross, or saying anything, and places the smallest part in the chalice.

10. The deacon having covered the chalice, the celebrant, with the ministers, makes a genuflection. The ministers change places, and make another genuflection. Then the celebrant, omitting the *Agnus Dei* and the first two prayers before the Communion, says only the third, which begins, *Perceptio Corporis,* etc., holding his

---

* See *Maunday-Thursday, Art. II, No.* 3, p. 236.

hands joined on the altar; when he has finished the prayer, he makes a genuflection, with the ministers, and rising says, *Panem cælestem*, then takes the paten and Host, and communicates, having previously said, as usual, *Domine, non sum dignus*.

11. After the Communion of the Sacred Body, the sub-deacon uncovers the chalice, the celebrant and ministers make a genuflection, the fragments are collected and put into the chalice by the celebrant, who, without saying anything, or making the sign of the cross, consumes the wine with the consecrated Particle, the ministers in the meantime bowing profoundly.

12. One of the acolytes carries the cruets to the altar; the sub-deacon gives the wine and water to the celebrant, who takes the usual ablutions without saying anything. In the meantime the clergy sit down, and put out their candles.

13. After the ablution, the ministers change places, making a genuflection as they pass by the middle; the sub-deacon goes to the Missal, and the deacon to the side-table; where, having taken off the large stole, and put on the folded chasuble, he returns to the platform at the right of the celebrant; who, having taken the last ablution, says in the middle, with a low voice, with his head inclined, and with his hands joined before his breast, the prayer, *Quod ore sumpsimus*. The sub-deacon, as usual, wipes the chalice, and covers it with the veil, which one of the acolytes must have brought to the altar, and carries it to the side-table, making a genuflection to the cross as he passes by the middle; then he returns to the left of the celebrant, and closes the Missal.

14. The signal being given by the master of ceremonies, the celebrant and the ministers bow to the cross, go down to the foot of the altar, make a genuflection, together with the master of ceremonies, and the acolytes, who do not carry the candlesticks; and, having put on their caps, they go to the sacristy, where they take off the sacred vestments.

15. The sacred ministers having left the sanctuary,

Vespers are recited as yesterday. In the meantime, the censer-bearers remove from the altar the book-stand with the Missal, and the covering, so that it be left quite bare, with no other ornament than the cross and the six candlesticks. They carry everything to the sacristy.

16. After Vespers, the clergy make a genuflection to the cross, and return to the sacristy. Then the candles on the altar are extinguished.

CHAPTER VIII.

HOLY SATURDAY.

ARTICLE I.

Things to be Prepared.

1. AT a convenient and proper time, the church is adorned with white and precious ornaments. The high altar is prepared as on the greatest solemnities. The relic-cases may be placed between the candlesticks, when the ministers put on white vestments. A white altar-veil should be under another of violet color, which is to be removed only before the beginning of Mass; at that time, also, the carpet should be placed on the platform and steps of the altar, which, during the first part of the sacred office, should be left bare.

2. The lamps of the church should be so prepared as to be easily lighted at the proper time. The images of the church should be covered. The tabernacle should have a white veil under another of violet color, which latter ought to be removed when the violet antipendium is taken away from the front of the altar.

3. In the sacristy, the sacred vestments of violet color for the ministers, viz., a cope, stole, cincture, alb, and amice for the celebrant; two folded chasubles, with two

maniples, a stole, two cinctures, albs, and amices for the ministers. Under the same, or in any other place, the usual white vestments for the celebrant and the ministers. The censer with the incense-boat, the vase for the holy water with the sprinkle, a plate with five large grains of incense, the processional cross, the candlesticks, with white candles for the acolytes.

4. At the baptismal font, everything should be cleaned; any water remaining there ought to be put into the piscina. A table is to be placed near it, and covered with a linen cloth; on it the vessels containing the oil of catechumens, and the sacred chrism in a plate; a vessel with water, and a basin; a towel on a plate; some slices of bread and lemon, likewise on a plate; some cotton on another plate; an empty vessel for holy water, with the sprinkle.

If it is customary to distribute among the people the water blessed on this day, a large vessel might be prepared before the baptismal font, and filled with water, which is, in that case, blessed; before the oils are mixed with the water, the baptismal font is filled with part of the water blessed in the large vessel, and then the oils are put into the water contained in the baptismal font, not into that contained in the large vessel. Some small vessels ought to be prepared to take the water from the large vessel, to put it into the font.

5. The bench of the ministers must be adorned as on the greatest solemnities, and covered with a violet cloth, which is removed when the ministers change their vestments. On this second cloth is to be placed the violet chasuble and maniple for the celebrant, also another violet maniple for the deacon, and a cap for the subdeacon.

6. At the Gospel side, a book-stand must be prepared, covered with a white veil, and a cushion placed on it for the *Exultet*. On the same side should be a large candlestick for the Paschal candle, and on it the Paschal candle* itself; also a stand for the triple candle, and,

---

* See *Cær. Ep. lib. II, Cap. 27, No.* 1.

on the Epistle side, a book-stand, uncovered, for the prophecies.

7. On the side-table, everything necessary for High Mass; the burse and veil of the chalice, and over them the white veil, which must be covered with another violet veil. Near the table, three violet cushions for the ministers during the litany.

8. In the porch, or if the church have none, in any other convenient place, a table covered with a white linen cloth, and on it a white dalmatic, stole, and maniple for the deacon, a violet maniple for the sub-deacon, a Missal, a plate containing a small candle, and matches to light it.

9. A large chafing-pan, with pieces of dry wood so arranged that fire may be easily lighted, which must be done before the ceremony, and be struck from a flint; near it, tongs to put the new fire into the censer.

10. Near the table, the triple candle on its rod, adorned with flowers, at the place the stock of the candle is connected with the rod. The candle is to be made so as to have one common stock, out of which proceed three branches at the same distance from each other.

Article II.

From the Benediction of the New Fire to the Exultet.

1. The sacred ministers being vested as in chap. iv, with this difference only, that they do not wear their maniples, and the signal being given by the master of ceremonies, the sub-deacon takes the processional cross, and the procession for the benediction of the new fire is arranged in the following order: first, three acolytes; the one who is in the middle carries the vessel with holy water, and the sprinkle; the one at the right carries the plate with the five grains of incense, and the one at the left carries the censer without fire, and the boat with incense, and the small spoon within it. The sub-deacon follows, carrying the cross; after him the clergy, two by two; lastly, the celebrant, with the deacon at his left. The latter, with all the clergy, must

have their heads uncovered. As they pass before the cross of the high altar, they all make a genuflection, with the exception of the cross-bearer and the celebrant; the latter only bows to the cross.

2. When the procession arrives at the porch, the sub-deacon places himself by the table, turning his back to the door, or to the walls of the church, holding the cross, with the image of the crucifix turned towards the celebrant. The clergy divide into two lines, on each side of the sub-deacon, so that the highest in dignity amongst them may be nearest to the celebrant, who places himself opposite the cross, with the deacon at his right. The deacon receives the cap from the celebrant, and assists him in raising the border of his cope when he makes the sign of the cross, or uses the sprinkle or the censer, and turning the leaves of the book.

3. The first acolyte having placed on the table the vase with holy water, takes the Missal, and holds it open before the celebrant. The two other acolytes stand at the right of the deacon, but a little behind him, and the master of ceremonies at the left of the celebrant.

4. All being so arranged, the celebrant, with his hands joined, says, in a ferial tone, *Dominus vobiscum*, and the three prayers that follow, for the benediction of the new fire, which is to be made before any other. (*Decr. S. R. C.*, 12th April, 1755.) At the end of each prayer the clergy answer, *Amen.*

5. Then the acolyte who holds the plate with the grains of incense comes before the celebrant, who says the fourth prayer for the blessing of the five grains of incense; and in the meanwhile the censer-bearer puts some of the new fire into the censer, and returns to his place.

6. After the fourth prayer, the first acolyte shuts the book, and having placed it on the table, takes the vase with holy water, and joins the other acolytes. The celebrant puts incense as usual into the censer, and blesses it, saying, *Ab ilo benedicaris*, etc. Then the deacon, having received from the first acolyte the

sprinkle, gives it to the celebrant; the celebrant thrice sprinkles, first the five grains of incense, then the fire, saying, *Asperges me*, without the Psalm and *Gloria Patri*, and having received the censer, incenses likewise, first the five grains, then the fire.

7. After the incensing, the first acolyte leaves the holy-water vase on the table, and with one of the matches prepared for that purpose lights the small candle from the new fire; the second acolyte, laying the plate with the five grains of incense on the table, together with the second master of ceremonies, assists the deacon to take off his violet vestments, and put on the white, and carries the maniple to the sub-deacon, who puts it on. Then he takes again the plate with the five grains, and returns to the right of the censer-bearer.

8. The deacon having put on the white vestments, goes to the right of the celebrant, to assist at the blessing of the incense for the procession and the *Exultet*, which is performed as usual. Then he takes the triple candle with both his hands, and at a signal given by the master of ceremonies, the procession advances in the following order:

9. First the censer-bearer, slowly moving his censer, and at his right the second acolyte, who carries the five grains of incense; the sub-deacon follows with the cross; then the clergy, two by two; after them the deacon, carrying the triple candle, having at his left the first acolyte, with the lighted candle; last of all, the celebrant, with his hands joined, and near him the master of ceremonies; all walk with their heads uncovered, the celebrant alone excepted.

10. During the procession, an acolyte carries the cap and the violet vestments of the deacon to the bench of the ministers, and the other things to the sacristy.

11. As the celebrant enters the church, the second master of ceremonies gives a signal to the clergy to stop; and the deacon bends the rod of the triple candle towards the first acolyte, who lights one of the three candles; then the deacon raises the rod, and bends one

knee, and all the clergy do the same, the cross-bearer excepted; the celebrant uncovers his head before he makes a genuflection. The deacon sings *Lumen Christi*, in such a tone of voice that it may be raised a tone higher twice, and the clergy answer, *Deo gratias*. Then they all rise, and the procession continues to advance. When they reach the middle of the church, the same ceremony is again performed; and it is repeated the third time before the steps of the altar.

12. After the *Deo gratias* has been answered for the third time by the clergy, they all go to their places. On arriving before the altar, the censer-bearer stops at the Gospel side, the acolyte, with the grains of incense, at the Epistle side, and the cross-bearer at the right of the censer-bearer. The first acolyte, having extinguished the small candle, receives the triple candle from the deacon, and places himself at the left of the second acolyte; and the deacon, retiring a little towards the Gospel side, and turning from his right side, makes room for the celebrant, who goes up to the platform, and stands at the Epistle corner.

Article III.

From the Exultet to the Prophecies.

1. The celebrant, on arriving at the Epistle side, turns towards the altar; the second master of ceremonies gives the Missal to the deacon, who, kneeling on the platform, without saying *Munda cor meum*, asks as usual the blessing of the celebrant, who gives it, saying as usual, *Domine sit in corde tuo*, etc., but instead of saying *Evangelium suum*, says, *Suum paschale præconium*, making the usual sign of the cross, but without giving his hand to be kissed.

2. The deacon having received the blessing, goes down to the foot of the altar, between the cross-bearer and the acolyte who carries the triple candle, where, having made a genuflection with the acolytes (the cross-bearer should not make it), and bowed to the clergy, they go, one after the other, to the place prepared at

the Gospel side, and place themselves in the following order: the deacon in the middle, having at his right the sub-deacon, who turns the image of the crucifix towards the celebrant, and the censer-bearer; and at his left hand having the acolyte with the triple candle, and the acolyte with the grains of incense. The master of ceremonies places himself behind the deacon, who, with all the others, are turned towards the book.

3. When they have arrived at the book-stand, and placed themselves in the order already mentioned, the deacon lays the book upon it, and opens it; then, without making the sign of the cross on himself, and without saying *Dominus vobiscum*, he incenses it as for the Gospel, and, with his hands joined, he sings the *Exultet;* during which the clergy remain standing, as also the celebrant, who turns towards the deacon.

4. The deacon having said the words, *Curvat imperia*, stops, the clergy sit down, but not the celebrant, and the acolyte who holds the plate with the five grains approaches the deacon, who, assisted by the master of ceremonies, goes with them to place the five grains in the Paschal candle, in the form of a cross, in this order, 1 which being done, they return to their place, and 4 2 5 the clergy rise. The acolyte places the plate in 3 which were the five grains on the side-table, and takes a small candle not lighted.

5. The deacon having returned to the Missal, continues the *Exultet*, and having sung the words *Rutilans ignis accendit*, the clergy sit down; he goes with the acolyte that carries the triple candle, to light the Paschal candle with one of them, and returns to continue the *Exultet*. The clergy rise.

6. The acolyte places the triple candle on the stand prepared for it near the altar.

7. The deacon having sung the words, *Apis mater eduxit*, stops awhile, and the first acolyte lights his small candle, either from the Paschal candle or from the triple candle, and lights the lamps of the sanctuary; the deacon continues the *Exultet*, and bows at the name of the Pope.

8. After the *Exultet*, the clergy sit down; the sub-

deacon leaves the cross at its place, the deacon immediately shuts the Missal, and leaves it on the stand, and both, with their hands joined, make a genuflection in the middle, and go to the bench—the celebrant also going thither at the same time; the latter, assisted by the subdeacon, takes off his cope, and puts on the violet maniple and chasuble.

9. The deacon, assisted by the first acolyte, takes off his white vestments, and puts on violet; then the celebrant and the ministers go by the shortest way to the Epistle side, as for the *Introit*. The second master of ceremonies prepares, in the middle of the sanctuary, a book-stand without any covering, and a Missal on it for the prophecies.

Article IV.

From the Prophecies to the Benediction of the Baptismal Font.

1. When the ministers have arrived at the Epistle side, the second master of ceremonies invites the clergyman who is to sing the first prophecy, as in chapter v, except that, before he leaves the book stand with the clergyman, he waits till the deacon has said, *Flectamus genua*, (when there is no *Tract*), then they make a genuflection, with all the clergy, and rise at the word *Levate*. Whilst the celebrant sings the prayer, the second master of ceremonies invites him who is to sing the second prophecy, doing as has been already said; and so likewise for all the other prophecies.

2. The clergy sit down whilst the prophecies are sung, rise at the prayers; the celebrant reads the prophecies in a low voice, and sings the prayers in a ferial tone, with his hands extended, the ministers standing behind him, one after the other; and the deacon, immediately after the celebrant has said, *Oremus*, sings, *Flectamus genua*, and the sub-deacon, *Levate*. After the prayers, the ministers go up near the celebrant, as for the *Introit*.

3. After the last prophecy and prayer, the second master of ceremonies removes from the middle of the

sanctuary the book-stand with the Missal, and the celebrant, with the ministers, goes by the shortest way to the bench, where the celebrant, assisted by the ministers, takes off his maniple and chasuble, and puts on the cope; and the ministers take off their maniples.

Article V.

*From the Benediction of the Baptismal Font to the beginning of Mass.**

1. The first acolyte, after the celebrant has put on his cope, takes the Paschal candle from its candlestick, and goes with it to the middle of the sanctuary; likewise the sub-deacon takes the cross, and places himself immediately before the first acolyte; the celebrant, with the deacon on his left, goes before the steps of the altar, in the middle. At a signal given by the master of ceremonies, the first acolyte makes a genuflection, turns towards the people, and walks slowly to the baptismal font; the sub-deacon carrying the cross, without making the genuflection, follows him; then the singers; and the rest of the clergy make a genuflection in the middle, and follow them; last of all, the celebrant, with his head covered, and the deacon at his left, accompanied by the master of ceremonies. On the way, the tract, *Sicut cervus*, is sung by the choir. Arrived at the font, the cross-bearer stops at one side, near the door or entry, the first acolyte at his left; the clergy divide into two lines, those in inferior orders remaining near the door, and those in higher dignity near the font. Before the celebrant enters, he stops, takes off his cap, and the second acolyte bringing and holding before him the Missal, he says in a ferial tone, *Dominus vobiscum*, etc., and the following prayer. Then he goes, with the deacon at his left, to the font, and places himself so as to be turned towards the cross, and the clergy. The second acolyte follows him with the Missal, and having opened it, the celebrant begins

---

* This article has been added by the translator.

BENEDICTION OF THE BAPTISMAL FONT.

the blessing of the font, saying, in a ferial tone, *Dominus vobiscum*, with the following prayers; in concluding it, he sings, *Per omnia sæcula*, in the tone of the ferial preface, with what follows; after the words, *Gratiam de Spiritu Sancto*, the celebrant divides the water in form of a cross, the deacon holding up the side of his cope, and offering him the towel, which one of the acolytes should have brought on a plate.

2. After the words, *Inficiendo corrumpat*, the celebrant touches the water with his right hand, which he afterwards wipes, as before. At the words *Per Deum ✠ vivum, Per Deum ✠ verum, Per Deum ✠ sanctum*, he makes the sign of the cross three times on the water. After the words *Super te ferebatur*, he divides the water with his hand, and throws some of it out, towards the four parts of the world, in this form, 1 after the words *Benignus adspira*, he breathes thrice 3 4 upon the water, in the form of a cross. At the 2 words *Mentibus efficaces*, the first acolyte carries the Paschal candle to the deacon, that he may give it to the celebrant, who dips it into the water at three different times, but each successive time he dips it deeper, and sings, one tone higher, the words *Descendat in hanc*. Then breathing thrice upon the water in this form ✠ he goes on with the Preface. After the words *Fœcundet effectu*, the Paschal candle is taken out of the water, wiped, and given back to the first acolyte, who goes to his place near the cross-bearer. The celebrant continues what follows in the tone of the Preface, as far as the words *Per Dominum*, exclusively, which, with the following words, he only recites; the minister answers, *Amen*. Then the clergyman who is first in dignity, having first put on a violet stole, takes the sprinkle which has been dipped in the blessed water and hands it to the celebrant, who first sprinkles himself, then the clergyman from whom he received the sprinkle, and lastly the deacon and sub-deacon; then he hands the sprinkle to the clergyman, who afterwards goes and sprinkles the people; whilst this is being done the celebrant and min-

isters may sit down. If the water is blessed in another vessel, the font is filled with it; but if it is blessed in the font, some of it is taken out to satisfy the devotion of the people, and to bless their houses and other places.

3. After this, the celebrant receives from the deacon the oil of the catechumens, and pours some of it into the baptismal font, in form of a cross, saying, *Sanctificetur*, etc. The ministers answer, *Amen*. Then he pours the chrism into it, in the same manner, saying, *Infusio*, etc.; the ministers answering also, *Amen*. Lastly, he pours the oil and chrism both together into the water, in the form of a cross, saying, *Commixtio*, etc.; and the ministers answer, *Amen*. Then he mingles the oil with the water, and with his hand spreads it all over the font. This done, two acolytes bring everything necessary to wash the hands, also the slices of bread and lemon prepared on a plate; the celebrant, assisted by the deacon, washes and wipes his hands.

4. If any are to be baptized, they are solemnly baptized by the celebrant, as in the ritual. After the blessing of the font, they return to the high altar in the same order in which they came. Arrived there, the first acolyte makes a genuflection, replaces the Paschal candle on its candle-stick, and goes to the side-table, near which the cross-bearer leaves the cross, and goes to the bench. The clergy, having made a genuflection in the middle, go to their places and sit down. The celebrant having bowed, and the deacon having made a genuflection, go to the bench, where the celebrant, assisted by the ministers, takes off his cope, who also take off their chasubles, and, having bowed to the clergy, go to the altar. In the meanwhile, the acolytes should place on the border of the platform three violet cushions at equal distance; the celebrant and the ministers, having made the usual reverence to the cross, prostrate themselves, laying their hands and their heads on them. The clergy kneel down. The acolytes carry the chasubles to the sacristy.

5. Two chanters, kneeling before two stools, behind the ministers, in the middle of the choir, begin to sing

the Litany of the Saints, and the clergy repeat the same words sung by the chanters. The master of ceremonies and acolytes kneel by the steps of the altar.

6. Whilst the chanters sing *Peccatores*, which, with the rest of the Litany, ought to be sung very slowly, to give time to prepare what is necessary, the celebrant, the ministers, and the acolytes, at a signal given by the master of ceremonies, rise; the ministers receive their caps from him, and having made a genuflection (the celebrant bowing) to the cross, and bowed to the clergy, go to the sacristy; the acolytes walking first, then the ministers, and lastly the celebrant, one after another, with their heads covered; there they take off their violet stoles, and put on the white vestments.

7. After the ministers have left the sanctuary, the acolytes appointed for it remove the cushions and the violet veil and antipendium from the altar, the violet veil from the side-table, and the violet cloth from the bench of the ministers; they also spread the carpet on the platform and steps of the altar, light the candles on the altar, and put the altar-cards on. In the sacristy, the acolytes light their candles, and the censer-bearer puts fire into the censer.

ARTICLE VI.

The Mass.

1. When the chanters have come to the *Agnus Dei*, or thereabouts according to the greater or less distance of the sacristy from the altar, the celebrant and ministers, preceded by the acolytes with their candles lighted, walk towards the altar, so as to be in the sanctuary at the end of *Exaudi nos;* which being repeated by the choir, the clergy rise, the chanters go to the desk, to sing the *Kyrie* in a slow and solemn manner, as the procession enters the sanctuary (because to-day the *Kyrie* takes the place of the *Introit*, which the singers should not begin to sing before the ministers have arrived at the sanctuary). (*Decr. S. R. C.*, 14 Apr., 1753.) The ministers bow, as usual, to the clergy, make a genuflection (the celebrant profoundly bowing) to the cross, and Mass is begun.

2. Mass to-day goes on as usual, till the end of the celebrant's Communion inclusively, with the following exceptions: the psalm, *Judica me*, with the *Gloria Patri*, is resumed. After the incensing there is no *Introit*, but the sacred ministers say, as usual, *Kyrie eleison*.

3. The celebrant having sung the words, *Gloria in excelsis Deo*, the first acolyte rings the bell by the side-table, the second rings another in the sacristy, and the large bells of the church are also rung, whilst the sacred ministers continue the *Gloria* to its end, during which the picture or statue of the main altar and those of the other altars are uncovered. (*S. R. C.*, 22 *Jul.*, 1848, *in Florent*, ad. 3, 4965). At the same time the organ is played, as usual.

4. The celebrant having given the blessing to the sub-deacon after the Epistle, sings thrice, *Alleluia*, raising every time his voice one tone higher; and the choir repeats it after each time in the same tone, the ministers standing by the celebrant, as for the *Introit*, who, having read the *Tract*, goes to read the Gospel, as usual.

5. The acolytes, at the Gospel, go as usual with the ministers, but do not carry their candlesticks. The *Credo* is not said, neither the *Offertory*, nor the *Agnus Dei*; the *Pax* is not given.

6. The deacon, having covered the chalice after the celebrant has put into it the small particle of the consecrated Host, immediately changes places with the sub-deacon.

7. According to the decree of the *S. C. R.*, 22 Mar., 1806, Communion may be given to the faithful at this Mass, by which, in parochial churches, they fulfill the paschal precept. If it be given, the deacon and sub-deacon do not exchange places, and everything for the Communion should be done as on Holy Thursday.

8. After the Communion of the celebrant, the censer-bearer goes to prepare the censer, puts fire into it, and the choir, instead of the *Communio*, sing *Alleluia*, and the psalm, *Laudate Dominum*, etc.

9. The celebrant, having taken the last ablution, goes to the Epistle side, where he recites in a low voice the

Alleluia, and the psalm, *Laudate Dominum*, alternately with the ministers who are near him, placed in the same position as at the *Introit*. The choir having repeated the anthem *Alleluia*, the celebrant intones *Vespere autem Sabbati*, and, with the ministers, continues it to the end, in a low voice, whilst the choir sing it.

10. When the chanters begin the *Magnificat*, the celebrant and the ministers make the sign of the cross, and go to the middle of the altar, the sub-deacon at the left and the deacon at the right of the celebrant, where he presents the incense. Then the altar is incensed, as usual at Vespers.

11. The deacon having incensed the celebrant, goes to incense the clergy, as usual. In the meantime, the celebrant and the sub-deacon remain at the Epistle side, as at the *Introit*. After the clergy, the sub-deacon is incensed by the deacon, for which purpose the sub-deacon turns towards him, without, however, turning his back to the celebrant. Then the deacon goes to the place where he usually stands at the *Introit*, and turns to the censer-bearer, who incenses him; he also incenses the acolytes and the people. Afterwards he takes the censer to the sacristy, and returns to the altar.

12. The antiphon, *Vespere autem*, etc., being repeated by the choir, the celebrant goes to the middle, the ministers following him, one after the other, kisses the altar, says *Dominus vobiscum*, and finishes the Mass as usual. The deacon sings, *Ite, Missa est, Alleluia, Alleluia.*

PART V.

Ceremonies for Mass and Vespers

SOLEMNLY CELEBRATED BY THE BISHOP,

OR IN HIS PRESENCE.

CHAPTER I.

SOLEMN PONTIFICAL VESPERS.

ARTICLE I.

Things to be Prepared.

1. THE altar is to be covered with a long veil, which should not hang down before it, but only on the two sides. In the middle of the altar are placed the sacred vestments for the Bishop, viz., the amice, alb, cincture, stole, and cope; on the Epistle side the ornamented mitre; on that of the Gospel, the golden mitre; on the highest step near the Epistle corner, the crosier, and near the vestments, on the Gospel side, on a small plate, the pectoral cross and the ring.

2. On the side-table, the two candlesticks for the acolytes, the Missal for the prayers to be sung by the Bishop, and the hand-candlestick.

3. In the middle of the sanctuary, two or four stools for the cope-bearers, according to their number.

4. In the sacristy, a cope for the assistant priest; two dalmatics, stoles, albs, cinctures, and amices for the assist-

ant deacons; two or four copes for the chanters, according to their number; and a sufficient number of copes, chasubles, and dalmatics, with amices, albs, cinctures, etc., for the clergy who assist at Vespers, dressed according to their order.

5. In a convenient place, the censer with the incense-boat, a chafing-dish, with fire and tongs.

ARTICLE II.

From the entrance of the Bishop and Clergy into the Church, to the Beginning of Vespers.

1. The Bishop, preceded by the clergy, two by two, goes from the sacristy to the church, the assistant priest walking immediately before him, and the two deacons at his side; having adored the Blessed Sacrament, he goes up to his seat. There he sits for a short time; then rising, he takes off his cape,* and puts on the amice, alb, cincture, pectoral cross, stole, and cope; he sits down, the first deacon puts the mitre on his head, and the assistant priest the ring on his finger.

2. Being thus vested, and having sat for awhile, his mitre is taken off by the second deacon. The Bishop then rises, and with him all the clergy; he turns towards the altar, and says, secretly, *Pater* and *Ave;* then, making the sign of the cross on himself, he sings, *Deus in adjutorium meum intende.* Whilst the choir sings *Gloria Patri*, the Bishop and all the clergy bow towards the altar.

---

*The technical name is *mozetta*. It is regarded as a mark of jurisdiction, and is therefore only to be worn by the diocesan, unless in Councils.

Article III.

From the Beginning to the End of Vespers.

1. In the meanwhile, two or four chanters in copes, accompanied by the second master of ceremonies, make the usual genuflection and bows, go to the Bishop's seat, and the first among them gives the tone of the first antiphon to the Bishop, who repeats the same words aloud; then having made the accustomed bows and genuflection, they all return to their places. At the beginning of the first psalm, the Bishop and the clergy sit down, and the first deacon puts the plain mitre on the Bishop.

2. At the *Gloria Patri,* the Bishop, with his mitre on, bows towards the altar, and the clergy do the same, taking off their caps.

3. Two of the singers, in copes, attended by the master of ceremonies, go to give the tone of the antiphons as follows: the second antiphon to the first assistant deacon, the third to the assistant priest, the fourth to the clergyman who occupies the first place in the sanctuary, and the fifth to the second assistant deacon. Those to whom the tone is given, stand, and with them, if they be assistants at the Bishop's seat, all the other assistants; but if not, all the clergy who are in the sanctuary.

4. All the psalms and antiphons being ended, the first chanter, in cope, or the sub-deacon, attended by the master of ceremonies, goes to the place where the epistle is usually sung, and turning towards the Bishop, sings the chapter; the Bishop, with his mitre on, and all the clergy, with their heads uncovered, stand whilst it is sung. The choir having answered *Deo gratias,* the same one who intoned the antiphon, accompanied by the master of ceremonies, goes to the Bishop, who is still standing with his mitre on, to intone the hymn; immediately after, the mitre is taken from the Bishop, who repeats the same words of the hymn, and the hymn is continued by the choir.

At the hymns *Veni Creator,* or *Ave Maris Stella,* all

the clergy kneel whilst the Bishop intones them; and the Bishop himself, after the intonation, kneels either at the faldstool before the middle of the altar, or on a cushion near his seat. All rise after the first strophe.

5. After the hymn, the verses having been sung by the four singers in copes, and answered by the choir, the antiphon of the *Magnificat* is intoned in the same manner, as the hymn, to the Bishop, who is still standing; having repeated the first words, he sits down, receives the precious mitre, attended by the assistant priest, puts the incense into the censer, and blesses it. In the meanwhile, two acolytes go to each side of the altar, and fold in the middle the veil that covers it, so as to leave the half of it near the front uncovered.

6. As the choir begins the *Magnificat*, the Bishop rises, with his mitre on; all the assistants likewise rise; the Bishop makes the sign of the cross, receives in his left hand the crosier from the assistant priest, and walks to the altar, between the deacons, who raise his cope on each side; when arrived before the lowest step, he gives the crosier to the assistant priest; the second deacon takes off his mitre, he bows to the cross (the others making a genuflection), and all go up to the altar, where the Bishop, having received the censer from the assistant priest, incenses the cross and the altar; the deacons who are at his side, raising the border of his cope, and reciting the *Magnificat* alternately with him.

7. The Bishop, having incensed the altar, goes to the middle, says the *Gloria Patri*, bowing to the cross, goes below the lowest step, makes a reverence to the altar, receives the mitre and crosier, and returns to his seat, where he is incensed by the assistant priest; then the deacon takes off his mitre, and the Bishop, holding the crosier with both his hands, remains standing till the end of *Sicut erat in principio*, after the *Magnificat*.

8. As soon as the Bishop leaves the altar, the acolytes spread the veil over the altar.

9. After the Bishop has been incensed by the assistant priest, the clergy are incensed by the first of the four

singers in copes, and the singer, the master of ceremonies, the acolytes, and the people, by the censer-bearer, as it has been said elsewhere.

The *Magnificat* is to be sung, so as to give time for the incensing.

10. Whilst the choir repeats the antiphon of the *Magnificat*, the Bishop gives up his crosier, sits down and receives the mitre. In the meantime, the master of ceremonies accompanies the acolytes, carrying the candlesticks with lighted candles, and the four chanters in copes, to the Bishop's seat. After the antiphon, the Bishop takes off the mitre, rises, and the assistant priest, holding the book before him, he sings *Dominus vobiscum*, and the prayer, with his hands joined, during which all the clergy stand. While the Bishop says *Dominus vobiscum*, after the prayer, the four chanters in copes, the acolytes, and master of ceremonies bow to him, and go to the middle of the sanctuary; where, having made a genuflection, the acolytes go to the side-table and the chanters sing the *Benedicamus Domino*.

11. Whilst the choir answer, *Deo gratias*, the Bishop sits down, receives the mitre, rises, sings *Sit nomen Domini*, etc., and gives the benediction, as usual, from his seat, if he can be seen thence by the people; otherwise he gives it from the altar.

If the celebrant be an Archbishop, the cross is brought before him, he bows profoundly to it, and gives the benediction without mitre.

Indulgences are never published at Vespers.

12. After Vespers, the Bishop puts off the sacred vestments as usual.

13. The pontifical Vespers are sung in the manner heretofore described, when the Bishop is to celebrate a pontifical Mass the next day, or on the great solemnities of the year, such at least, as Easter, Christmas, the Feast of the Patron Saint of the Diocese, the Titular of the Church, etc.

14. On other occasions, Vespers are celebrated with less solemnity; then all the clergy do not put on the sacred vestments; four of them only are dressed in copes;

the antiphons are intoned, first to the Bishop, then to the other clergymen in the sanctuary, according to their dignity and order.

Article IV.

Benediction of the Blessed Sacrament given by the Bishop.

1. Besides the preparations mentioned in Chap. XI, Art. I, p. 79, the following things are to be prepared: The cope, stole, pectoral cross, cincture, alb, amice, mitre, and, if the Bishop is in his diocese, the crosier.* Also, the hand-candlestick with a candle in. (These articles are prepared instead of the vestments for the priest.) On the lowest step of the altar a cushion.

2. The same ceremonies are observed as when a priest gives Benediction with the following particulars: The Bishop, having put on the amice, alb, cincture, pectoral cross, stole, cope, and mitre, takes the crosier, if he be in his diocese, to the sanctuary, preceded by the censer-bearer, torch-bearers, master of ceremonies, deacon and sub-deacon dressed with dalmatics, holding up the borders of the cope. Then follow the crosier-bearer and mitre-bearer.

3. On arriving at the foot of the altar, the Bishop gives the crosier to the sub-deacon, and the mitre is taken off by the deacon, then he makes a genuflection on the floor,† for which purpose the master of ceremonies will put the cushion, and replace it on the lowest step, on which the Bishop kneels.

4. The Benediction veil having been put on the Bishop's shoulder, he bows profoundly, rises, with the deacon and sub-deacon, and with them ascends the steps, while they raise his alb in front. Then he genuflects on the platform, rises with the deacon who first arranges the humeral-veil on the Bishop's hands, and then gives him

---

* Should the Bishop wash his hands, the pitcher, basin with water, and a towel, are prepared.

† *Cærem. Episc.* lib. i, ch. xv, and *S. R. C.*, 12th Nov., 1831.

the Ostensorium. The Bishop blesses the people with three signs of the cross,* *i. e.*, the first on the Epistle side, the next in the middle of the altar, and the third on the Gospel side.

During the Benediction, the deacon and sub-deacon, kneeling on the edge of the platform, raise the cope on each side. While standing, the Bishop gives the monstrance to the deacon or priest at his right, and goes down the steps, having first genuflected on the platform, and the humeral-veil is taken off.

5. The deacon or the priest, having placed the monstrance on the corporal, takes the Blessed Sacrament out of it, and places It in the tabernacle, with the usual genuflections.

6. After this, the Bishop takes his mitre and crosier, if he use it, makes a genuflection on the floor,† and returns to the sacristy.

If there be no sacred ministers to assist the Bishop at the Benediction with the Blessed Sacrament, he will conform to the directions found in Art. I, p. 79, for the Benediction given by a priest in a similar case; however, in blessing the people, he will make three signs of the cross, as explained above, n. 4.

CHAPTER II.

SOLEMN VESPERS IN PRESENCE OF THE BISHOP.

1. WHEN the Bishop does not officiate at Vespers, he is vested as usual, with his rochet and cappa: he sits at his seat, having two clergymen in surplices at his side; he puts incense into the censer and blesses it; he is incensed, immediately after the celebrant, by the assist-

---

* *Cærem. Episc.* lib. ii, ch. xxxiii.
† Ib., lib. i, ch. xv, *S. R. C.*, 12th Nov., 1831.

ant priest; and after the *Benedicamus Domino* and *Deo gratias*, the Bishop gives the solemn blessing from his seat, if he can be seen thence by the people, otherwise from the altar.

2. The officiating priest is dressed in cope, and sits in the usual place on the Epistle side. Before he begins *Deus in adjutorium*, he asks the Bishop's leave by bowing to him; every time he goes from the altar to his seat, or from it to the altar, he bows to the Bishop; he does not bless the incense, or put it into the censer; he is incensed only with two swings, and not at his seat, but at the Epistle corner near the altar.

3. There may be four, or two chanters, in copes, who sit on their stools as usual, in the middle of the sanctuary; two give the tone of the first antiphon, and that of the *Magnificat*, to the officiating priest; the others to the other clergymen, according to their dignity and order; and sing the verses, *Benedicamus Domino*, etc. The two first amongst them accompany the celebrant to the altar for the incensing of it, raising his cope on each side; and the first of them incenses the celebrant and the clergy, including the three other singers.

4. The acolytes carry their candlesticks as usual in other Vespers.

5. The officiating priest, with the two or four chanters in cope, the acolytes, and master of ceremonies, must go to the sanctuary before the Bishop, sit at their places till he enters it, as he enters, preceded by the rest of the clergy, they rise, and whilst he kneels, they kneel also.

CHAPTER III.

COMPLINE, WHEN THE BISHOP OFFICIATES.

1. For Compline, the Bishop is dressed in rochet and cappa; he sits in his usual place.

2. When the chanter says, *Jube Domne*, etc., he stands and answers, *Noctem quietam;* after the Lesson, he says,

Adjutorium nostrum; then the *Pater,* the confession, and absolution, etc., *Deus in Adjutorium;* all of which are to be said standing. At the beginning of the psalms, he takes his seat.

3. All the rest is said by the choir and by the priest who should have officiated if the Bishop were not present, with the exception of the prayer and of the *Benedicat et custodiat nos,* etc., which are to be sung by the Bishop.

4. When the Bishop, although present at Compline, does not officiate, nothing is to observed in particular, except that the officiating priest, at the words *Indulgentiam, absolutionem,* and at the *Benedicat et custodiat,* bows profoundly to the Bishop.

CHAPTER IV

MATINS, WHEN THE BISHOP OFFICIATES.

1. THE Bishop is dressed in rochet and cappa. He is seated at his usual place; no clergymen sit by him. He is attended by the master of ceremonies.

2. Whilst the *Pater, Ave,* and *Credo* are said, all stand; the *Credo* being ended, the Bishop, making with his thumb the sign of the cross on his lips, sings, *Domine labia,* and making the sign of the cross on himself as usual, he sings, *Deus in adjutorium.* He remains standing during the *Invitatorium,* and the Psalm, *Venite exultemus;* at the words, *Venite adoremus et procidamus,* he kneels, then rises, and remains standing during the hymn, (which he intones only in case he is to celebrate Mass,) one of the chanters having intoned it. As the psalm begins, the Bishop and all the clergy take their seats.

3. The antiphons, are intoned by the chanters in surplices to the clergy, beginning with those who are first in dignity and order. At the *Gloria Patri,* all take off their caps and bow.

4. At the versicles, which are sung by two of the chanters, after the third antiphon of each nocturn, all rise. The Bishop says, in a loud voice, the words, *Pater noster;* the rest is said secretly, as far as the words, *et ne nos,* which are sung by the Bishop, who also sings the absolution, and the words of the blessing, after the *Jube Domne benedicere.* The Bishop does not rise to give the second and third blessing at each nocturn, but remains sitting.

5. After the verses of each nocturn, the second master of ceremonies goes to invite, with a bow, the clergyman who is to sing the Lesson, beginning by those who are inferior in order or dignity. He accompanies him to the middle of the sanctuary before the desk prepared for the purpose; there they make a genuflection to the altar, bow first to the Bishop, then to the clergy on each side of the sanctuary; after the absolution for the first Lesson of each nocturn, or the response for the two others, the clergyman who is to sing the Lesson bows profoundly towards the Bishop, and sings, *Jube Domne benedicere.* After the words of the blessing, he sings the Lesson, at the end of which he kneels to the altar, on one knee, saying, *Tu autem Domine,* then bows profoundly to the Bishop, who makes the sign of the cross towards him, and after having bowed to the clergy as before, he returns to his place. The same is done for all the other Lessons. The seventh and eighth Lessons are sung by those who are to officiate at Mass as assistant deacons, at the side of the Bishop. Whilst the text of the Gospel is sung, at the seventh Lesson, the Bishop and all the clergy should stand.

6. The ninth Lesson is sung by the Bishop at his seat, standing with his face turned towards the altar. Before he begins it, the two assistant deacons, and one of the acolytes with the hand-candlestick, and another with the book, go to him; the two former place themselves at his side, and the latter before him. The Bishop, bowing profoundly towards the altar, sings, *Jube Domine,* not *Jube Domne;* all the clergy rise, and answer, *Amen.* Then the Bishop sings the Lesson, during which the

clergy remain standing. At the end of it, the Bishop, bowing profoundly towards the altar, says, *Tu autem Domine*, etc. The choir having answered, *Deo gratias*, the tone of *Te Deum* is given to the Bishop, who repeats the same words, and the choir continue the hymn. At the words, *Te ergo quæsumus*, the Bishop and all the clergy kneel down.

CHAPTER V.

LAUDS, WHEN THE BISHOP OFFICIATES.

1. When the Bishop has officiated at Matins, it is proper that he should officiate at Lauds also. Everything is to be done as directed for Vespers, when the Bishop is not to celebrate Mass the next day. Soon after the *Te Deum*, the Bishop, at his seat, puts on all the sacred vestments, as for Vespers, and four or six clergymen put on copes.

2. The Bishop begins, *Deus in adjutorium*, making the sign of the cross on himself. The antiphons are intoned as for Vespers, and everything else is done as directed for the same.

3. At the *Benedictus*, everything is done as at the *Magnificat;* and after the *Benedicamus* and *Deo gratias*, the solemn blessing is likewise given by the Bishop.

CHAPTER VI.

SOLEMN PONTIFICAL MASS.

ARTICLE I.

Things to be Prepared.

THERE should be in Cathedral churches a place or chapel to answer the purpose of that which was formerly called the *Secretarium*. It should have an altar, the Bishop's seat, seats for all the clergy, and a side-table.

On the altar of this chapel, all the pontifical vestments should be prepared; and the copes, chasubles, dalmatics, and tunics for the clergy, at their own seats. On the side-table, the Bishop's sandals and stockings, the candlesticks for the acolytes, the incense-boat and censer, the book, and hand-candlesticks, etc., should be placed; to this chapel the Bishop and all the clergy ought to go, immediately after having adored the Blessed Sacrament. There, the Bishop, having begun Tierce, should make his preparation for Mass; the clergy should put on the vestments suitable to their order and dignity; the Bishop should put on his sacred vestments, finish Tierce, and, after having taken off the cope, put on the tunicella and chasuble; and lastly, being preceded by the clergy, he should go in procession from this place to the high altar.

Wherever there is not such a convenient place, everything is to be done in the sanctuary; we shall, therefore, in the present chapter, adapt the instructions to the ordinary construction of our churches.

1. The altar is to be prepared with the best and richest ornaments; three large candlesticks with candles on each side of the cross, and a seventh one behind it. This seventh candlestick with candle is to be placed behind the cross only when the Bishop of the diosese celebrates a solemn Pontifical Mass. Between the candlesticks, relic-cases of a suitable size may be placed.

2. On the altar, the pontifical vestments, of suitable color should be placed, one over the other, viz., immediately on the altar-cloth in the middle, the chasuble, then the dalmatic, tunic, cope, stole, cincture, alb, and over all the others the amice. On the Epistle side, near the vestments, the pectoral cross and the ring should be on a plate; on the Gospel side, the gloves on another plate. On the Gospel side the precious mitre, and the golden mitre on the Epistle side, standing against the candlesticks, and the crosier at the same corner, against the angle formed by the altar and the pilaster near it.

3. The Bishop's seat is to be on the Gospel side, against the side-walls of the sanctuary; it should be on a platform, raised by three steps above the floor of the sanctuary; the platform should be large enough to admit two wooden stools without backs, decently painted, for the two assistant deacons, on each side of the Bishop's chair, which should have a high back and convenient arms, and be covered with silk cloth; there should be a third stool, of the same form with the others, near that of the second assistant deacon, but projecting more towards the front of the platform, for the assistant priest. Over the Bishop's chair there should be a canopy, with hangings all around; the walls behind the chair, and the assistants' stools, should likewise be covered with hangings, which ought to be of a color suitable to the festival.

4. The side-table ought to be placed on the Epistle side of the altar, and covered all around and on the top with white linen cloth. It should be sufficiently large.

On this table there should be two candlesticks with candles for the acolytes, the chalice with its purifier, paten, host, pall, and burse, containing the corporal; the Missal, for the Epistle and Gospel; behind the chalice, standing against the wall, the cruets on a plate, the basin and ewer for washing the Bishop's hands, two or three fine towels on a plate, the book containing the canon, the Missal for the Bishop, with his maniple in it, the hand-candlestick, the Bishop's sandals and stockings on a plate, covered with a veil. Over the chalice, the long veil, the two extremities of which ought to hang down on each side of the table.

5. The bench of the ministers should be on the Epistle side, below the table, and against the side-walls of the sanctuary. It should be covered with baize. On it the maniples of the deacon and sub-deacon should be placed.

6. A sufficient number of seats for the clergy should be placed on each side of the sanctuary; they ought not to be the usual chairs, but benches with a back, covered with drapery.

7. There should be a number of acolytes in surplices, no fewer than eight. The first of them carries the book, and holds it when the Bishop reads out of it; but when he sings, the book must be held by the assistant priest. The second holds the hand-candlestick whenever the Bishop reads or sings anything, either at his seat or at the altar. The third acolyte, who, besides the surplice, wears a cope, is to carry the crosier. The fourth, if he is not dressed in cope, wears on his surplice a long veil, hanging from his neck before him, in order to cover his hands with it when he holds the mitre. The fifth is the censer-bearer. The sixth and the seventh are to carry the candlesticks. The eighth carries the apron, which is a rich cloth that is spread on the lap of the Bishop, when seated.

8. The faldstool is a kind of folding seat, sufficiently large, the four corners of which project about a foot above the cushion, when laid on it; these corners are connected together only on the two sides, six inches above the cushion, with two cross-pieces, which, as well as the projecting corners, should be of gilt metal. Thus it remains open behind and before. It is covered with a silk cloth of the color of the vestments, which hangs down to the ground on the four sides. It is used as a praying desk for the Bishop, and as a chair, when, for ordinations or other ceremonies, he is to sit at the altar. Two cushions covered with the same cloth are to be prepared; one on the seat and another before it, to kneel on. It is to be placed in the middle of the sanctuary, whenever the Bishop is to kneel.

9. We suppose in the following instructions that the Cathedral church has no *Secretarium* or chapel, as men-

tioned in the beginning of the chapter; but in case it should have one, the Bishop and clergy vest and sing Tierce in it.

10. In the sacristy, the following things are to be prepared: a cope for the assistant priest, who puts it on over his surplice, without stole; two amices, albs, cinctures, and dalmatics for the two assistant deacons. They wear neither stoles nor maniples. Also two amices, albs, and cinctures for the deacon and sub-deacon; also a stole for the deacon. Their maniples are to be placed on their seats in the sanctuary. The clergy are to be in sacred vestments. Some of them, the first in dignity, wear copes over their surplices; some, chasubles over their albs; no maniples or stoles are to be used by them. The clergymen who are not priests are to be dressed in dalmatics over their albs, but without stoles and maniples. A sufficient number of these vestments ought to be prepared in the sacristy. In order to have a sufficient number of clergymen in towns and cities, where there are several congregations besides that of the Cathedral, the service ought to be performed in those earlier than usual, so that all the clergy may go to the Cathedral. This custom is observed in other countries, and it is conformable to what was practiced in remote antiquity. The Bishops can and ought to introduce it into this country.

Article II.

Of the vesting of the Clergy and of the Bishop.

1. The clergy put on their vestments in the sacristy, before the Bishop arrives. Those who are to officiate as assistant priest and assistant deacons, preceded by the inferior clergy, who wear no sacred vestments, all in surplices, accompany the Bishop from his house to the sacristy, if there be no street between it and the church; otherwise, from the room where he has put on the rochet and cappa magna, and two by two, walk before him; lastly, the deacon and sub-deacon; the assistant priest walks alone immediately before the Bishop, and the two assistant deacons at each side of him.

VESTING OF THE CLERGY AND BISHOP.

2. The Bishop having arrived at the sacristy, and bowed to the cross, the clergy go to the sanctuary, first those in surplices, then those in dalmatics, chasubles, and copes. The assistant priest goes immediately before the Bishop, and the two assistant deacons on each side of him. As the clergy arrive at the middle of the sanctuary, they make a genuflection, bow to one another, and go to their places on each side of the sanctuary; the inferior clergy towards the railing, and those in superior grades towards the altar. The deacon and sub-deacon go to their bench. The Bishop bows to the cross, and kneels for awhile at the faldstool. All the clergy kneel and rise with him. After a short prayer he goes to his seat, having at his side the assistant deacons in surplices.

3. The Bishop, standing with his head uncovered, turning towards the altar, says secretly, *Pater* and *Ave*. Then making the sign of the cross on himself, he sings, *Deus in adjutorium*, etc.; then the hymn, *Nunc Sancte* etc. is intoned; one of the singers intones the antiphon, then the Psalm, *Legem pone;* which having been begun, the Bishop and the clergy sit down and put on their caps; the assistant priest and deacons alone remaining standing by the Bishop.

4. The acolytes bring the book and the hand-candlestick to the Bishop; the book-bearer kneels down. The Bishop reads the anthem *Ne reminiscaris*, and the Psalms for the preparation of Mass. The sub-deacon, accompanied by the second master of ceremonies, brings from the table the plate with the sandals and stockings covered with the veil; six acolytes follow him and surround the Bishop's seat; the sub-deacon, assisted by the second master of ceremonies, takes off the Bishop's shoes and puts on him the stockings and sandals; afterwards the sub-deacon and acolytes retire to their places.

5. The Psalms having been read, and the anthem, *Ne reminiscaris*, repeated by the Bishop, he rises, with his head uncovered, and turning towards the altar, says, *Kyrie eleison*, with the verse and prayers that follow. Then he takes off the cappa, saying the appropriate prayer. The acolytes bring the basin, ewer, and towels,

and the Bishop washes his hands, saying the prayer, *Da Domine.* The assistant priest takes off the Bishop's ring before he washes his hands, and puts it on after he has washed them, and presents him the towel to wipe them.

6. When the Bishop rises, after having read the Psalms, the second master of ceremonies goes up to the altar, followed by the acolytes, who, one after another, make first a genuflection before the lower step, go up, receive severally one of the vestments, make another genuflection on the platform, go down and place themselves in a line, beginning at the Gospel side. When all have received the vestments, that is, the amice, alb, cincture, pectoral cross, stole, cope, and mitre, at a signal given by the master of ceremonies, they make a genuflection, and walk one after another in a line to the Bishop's seat. When the first who carries the amice is arrived before the last step of the Bishop's seat, he and all the others stop one behind another. The second master of ceremonies stops at the left hand of the first acolyte, who, having given the amice, gives his place to the next, goes to his right hand; they both bow to the Bishop, and the first acolyte returns to his place; the others do in like manner.

7. Whilst the Bishop is washing his hands, the deacon and sub-deacon go to the throne, and as soon as he has washed his hands, the assistant deacon and priest go down, where, having with the deacon and sub-deacon bowed to the Bishop, the assistant priest and deacons go to put on their vestments in the sacristy; the deacon goes to the Bishop's right, and the sub-deacon to the left. The deacon receives from the acolytes all the vestments, with the assistance of the sub-deacon, that is, the amice, alb, cincture, pectoral cross, stole, cope, and mitre. After which the Bishop takes his seat. The deacon and sub-deacon go down, and having made a bow to the Bishop, together with the assistant priest and deacons, retire to their bench; the assistant priest and deacons go up to their usual places, and seat themselves.

8. When all the Psalms, with the anthem, have been sung, which ought to be done slowly, to give sufficient

time for the vesting of the Bishop, the second master of ceremonies accompanies the sub-deacon to the place where the Epistle is sung, and the latter turning towards the Bishop, sings the chapter. The Bishop, before the sub-deacon begins it, rises with his mitre on; the clergy likewise rise with their heads uncovered. The sub-deacon having sung the chapter, returns to his place. The chanters chant the responses and verses; which being ended, the acolytes with the candlestick, and those with the book and hand-candlestick, go to the Bishop's seat; the second assistant deacon takes off the mitre, and the Bishop sings the *Dominus vobiscum*, and the prayer from the book, which the assistant priest holds before him.

9. The singers having sung *Benedicamus Domino*, and the choir answered *Deo gratias*, the deacon and sub-deacon return to the Bishop's side, exchanging places with the two assistant deacons; they take off the cope from the Bishop, and give it to an acolyte, who carries it to the sacristy. In the meanwhile, the second master of ceremonies gives to the acolytes, in the same manner as in n. 6, the tunic, dalmatic, the plate with the gloves, the chasuble, and the crosier, and the plate with the ring. The acolytes with the book and the candle, go to the Bishop's seat, and the acolytes with the vestments also go at a signal given by the master of ceremonies.

10. The deacon and sub-deacon vest the Bishop, who reads the prayers appointed for each vestment.

If he be an Archbishop, after he has put on the chasuble, a sub-deacon brings from the altar the pallium, gives it to the deacon, who, assisted by the sub-deacon, puts it on him.

Then the Bishop sits, and the deacon puts on him the mitre, and the assistant priest the ring on his finger.

11. The Bishop having thus put on all the sacred vestments, the deacon and sub-deacon retire to their bench, and give their places to the two assistant deacons.

If Tierce has been sung in the chapel, or *Secretarium*, the censer-bearer comes to the Bishop with the censer and boat, gives it to the assistant priest, and the Bishop puts the incense into the censer and blesses it. Then they go to the high altar in procession, in the following order: the censer-bearer first, the cross-bearer in sub-deacon's dress, between the acolytes carrying the candlesticks, the clergy in surplices, those in dalmatics, the priests in chasuble, those in cope, all two by two. Then the sub-deacon, who is to officiate at Mass, carrying before his breast the Missal closed, with the Bishop's maniple in it; after him the deacon, at the left of the assistant priest, in cope; last, the Bishop, between the two assistant deacons, with the crosier in his left, and blessing the people with his right hand. After the Bishop follow the acolytes, who carry the cross, mitre, book, hand-candlestick, etc., two by two.

As the clergy arrive in the sanctuary, they make a genuflection in the middle, bow to one another, and go to their places. The Bishop goes to the altar and begins Mass, as will be said hereafter.

If the pontiff be an Archbishop, the archiepiscopal cross is carried by the cross-bearer, in sub-deacon's dress, immediately before the clergy in sacred vestments.

Article III.

The Pontifical Mass.

1. The Bishop rises, takes the crosier in his left hand, and with his right blesses the clergy (who arise and bow to him) and the people as he goes to the altar between the two assistant deacons. The deacon and sub-deacon put on their maniples. The second master of ceremonies gives the Missal with the Bishop's maniple in it to the sub-deacon, and all go to the altar.

2. The Bishop having arrived before the lower step, in the middle, the two assistant deacons give place to the assistant priest, who goes to the Bishop's right, and to the deacon, who goes to the left, and place themselves at a little distance behind them; the sub-deacon goes to the left of the deacon, and remains a little behind him, giving the book to the master of ceremonies. The acolytes who carry the crosier and the mitre place themselves a little behind the two assistant deacons. The

Bishop, after his mitre has been taken off by the deacon, makes a profound bow to the cross, and all the others make a genuflection. Then the Bishop begins Mass, *In nomine Patris*, etc.; at the words *Et vos fratres*, he turns himself towards the ministers, and they, at the words *Tibi, pater*, etc., bow to the Bishop.

3. After the prayer, *Indulgentiam, absolutionem*, etc., the sub-deacon, taking the maniple out of the Missal, gives it to the Bishop to kiss, and puts it on his arm.

4. Whilst the Bishop makes the confession, all the clergy in sacred vestments standing, make it alternately, two by two. The inferior clergy kneel down during the confession. After it, the Bishop goes up to the altar as usual, but the assistant priest passes to his left, and the deacon to his right hand. The sub-deacon at the Gospel side goes up with the Missal, which he with the assistant priest present open to the Bishop, who, after having kissed the altar, touching it with both his hands, kisses it at the beginning of the Gospel to be read on that day.

5. The incense is then put into the censer and blessed, the deacon offering the boat, and presenting the censer to the Bishop, who incenses the altar, as usual; and after it, standing with his mitre on, by the corner of the altar, at the Epistle side, he is incensed by the deacon; then, having received the crosier, and made from the same place a reverence to the cross, he goes, between the two assistant deacons, to his seat. The deacon and sub-deacon go to their bench on the Epistle side. The Bishop, standing, without mitre, making the sign of the cross on himself, reads the *Introit*, from the book which the acolyte holds open before him; another acolyte holding near him the hand-candlestick, and the assistant deacons turning the leaves of the book when necessary. Then he says, alternately with them, *Kyrie eleison*. The same is said likewise by the deacon and sub-deacon, and by all the clergy, two by two, alternately. Afterwards the Bishop sits down, and the first deacon puts on him the lighter mitre and the apron. All the clergy also sit at their places.

6. After the *Kyrie* is sung by the choir, all rise, and

the mitre and apron being taken off, the Bishop turned towards the altar, sings, *Gloria in excelsis Deo*, the assistant priest holding the book before him, whilst he sings those words; but whilst he reads the rest, the book is held by the acolyte. The same is to be observed on all other occasions, viz.: when the Bishop sings, the assistant priest holds the book; but when he reads, the acolyte holds it, and the assistant deacons point out what is to be read, and turn the leaves of the book. The assistants say with the Bishop, in a low voice, the rest of the Angelical Hymn, likewise the deacon and sub-deacon, and all the clergy.

The hymn having been recited, the Bishop and the clergy sit down, and the deacon puts the plain mitre on the Bishop, and the apron on his lap. The choir having sung the *Gloria*, the deacon takes off the Bishop's mitre and the apron; all rise; and the Bishop, turned towards the people, sings, *Pax vobis*, and the prayer; after which all sit down, and the deacon puts on the Bishop the mitre, and the apron on his lap.

7. The sub-deacon, having received the Missal from the second master of ceremonies and holding it on his breast, goes, attended by the same, to the middle, makes a genuflection to the altar, bows to the Bishop and to the clergy, goes to the Epistle side, and turned towards the Bishop, sings the Epistle; after it, he makes the usual genuflection and bow, goes to the Bishop, kneels before him, lays the book on his knees, and kisses the Bishop's hand, placed on the book, and having received his blessing, returns to his place, where he gives the book to the master of ceremonies.

8. After the sub-deacon has kissed the Bishop's hand, the acolytes, with the book and the hand-candlestick, go before him, and the Bishop sitting, with his mitre on, reads the Epistle, Tract, and says the *Munda cor meum*, etc., and reads the Gospel, with his hands joined, the assistant deacons remaining standing, and answering, *Et cum spiritu tuo*, and *Laus tibi Christe*.

9. Towards the end of this, the deacon having received the Missal from the second master of ceremonies, carries

it raised before him to the altar, bowing to the Bishop and to the clergy, and making a genuflection before the lower step, places it in the middle of the altar, goes down, makes a genuflection, goes to the Bishop, kisses his hand, returns to the altar, kneels on the lower step, says, in a low voice, *Munda cor meum*, rises, goes up to take the Missal, comes down, and places himself below the lower step a little towards the Epistle side, with the sub-deacon, who, at the same time, goes to his left, they being exactly in the middle, where they wait. In the meantime, the censer-bearer having gone to the Bishop's seat, with the censer and boat, the incense is put in and blessed, as usual. The censer-bearer, accompanied by the second master of ceremonies, goes behind the deacon; the master of ceremonies behind the sub-deacon; and the two acolytes, with their candlesticks and lighted candles, behind them. At a signal given by the master of ceremonies, they all make a genuflection, bow to the Bishop and to the clergy, and go to the Bishop's seat, walking in the order in which they are, the deacon and the sub-deacon first. Having arrived before the Bishop's seat, they all kneel and remain so; the deacon saying, *Jube Domne, benedicere*, receives the blessing, *Dominus sit*, etc., and kisses the Bishop's hand. Then they all rise, and go to the place where the Gospel is to be sung.

10. The master of ceremonies walks first, after him the censer-bearer, then the two acolytes with the candlesticks, the sub-deacon, and last the deacon. The sub-deacon places himself with his face towards the Epistle side, between the two acolytes, and holds the book resting on his head. The deacon turns towards the book, and the master of ceremonies and censer-bearer are at his side. The deacon sings, *Dominus vobiscum, Sequentia*, etc., making the sign of the cross on the book and himself, etc., incenses the book thrice, towards the middle, the right and the left of the same. The Bishop, at the beginning of the Gospel, rises, without mitre, receives the crosier, which he keeps between both his hands, makes the sign of the cross on himself, bows at the

names of Jesus and Mary, kisses the book, which, after the Gospel, is brought to him by the sub-deacon, and says, *Per evangelica dicta*, etc.; and lastly is incensed by the assistant priest. The deacon and all the others return to their places, making the usual genuflections and bows.

11. If the Bishop preach, he should do it from his throne. But should this be so placed as to prevent the people from seeing or hearing him, the faldstool should be placed on the platform of the altar in the middle, and five other seats, viz., three at the right, and two at the left of the faldstool. The assistant priest sits at his right; near the assistant priest, the deacon of the Gospel; and near him, the first assistant deacon. At the left of the Bishop, the sub-deacon, and near him the second assistant deacon. If the Bishop should not preach, a priest may do it from the pulpit; but first he should go to kiss the Bishop's hand, ask the blessing, saying, *Jube Domne, benedicere*, and ask the Indulgences. After the sermon, the deacon of the Gospel sings the *Confiteor*, near the Bishop, if the Bishop has preached at the altar, otherwise before the lowest step of the Bishop's seat; the assistant priest publishes the Indulgences, and the Bishop, standing without mitre, says, *Precibus et meritis*, then puts on his mitre, and gives the benediction. In case the sermon has been delivered by a priest, the preacher publishes the Indulgences in place of the assistant priest.

12. After the benediction, the Bishop returns to his seat; or if there has been no sermon, after having been incensed, he intones, *Credo in unum Deum*, the assistant priest holding the book till these words are sung; then he gives it to the acolyte, who remains there with the other holding the hand-candlestick, till the Bishop and the assistants have finished the *Credo*, which is also recited by the deacon and sub-deacon, and all the clergy, two by two, at their respective places. At the words, *Et incarnatus*, they all kneel. The Creed being said, they all sit down, and the first assistant deacon puts the plain mitre on the Bishop, and spreads the apron upon

his knees. When the choir sings the words, *Et incarnatus*, the Bishop, with his mitre on, and all the clergy in sacred vestments, uncovering their heads, bow profoundly towards the altar; the rest of the clergy kneel. However, on Christmas day, and on the festival of the Annunciation, the Bishop and all the clergy kneel.

13. After the *Incarnatus* has been sung, the deacon and the sub-deacon rise; the deacon, attended by the second master of ceremonies, goes to the side-table, receives the burse from the master of ceremonies, and, having made the usual bows and genuflections, carries it to the altar, extends the corporal in the middle of it, places the burse on the Epistle side, makes a genuflection, and returns to his place. Then he and the sub-deacon sit down.

14. Towards the end of the Creed all the ministers rise; the Bishop rises when it is ended, the mitre and the apron having been previously taken from him. Then standing, he sings, *Dominus vobiscum* and *Oremus*, and reads the *Offertory* out of the book, which is held before him by one of the acolytes, attended by the other, who holds the hand-candlestick. Afterwards he sits down, the deacon puts on him the precious mitre, the assistant priest takes off his ring, and the deacons his gloves. The two acolytes bring him the basin and ewer to wash his hands, and the towel to wipe them; the assistant priest presents the towel, after he has washed his hands, and having wiped them, puts the ring on his finger. Then the assistant priest having received from the master of ceremonies the Missal with its cushion or stand, attended by the same, carries it to the altar, and puts it, opened at the proper place, near the corporal, on the Gospel side, and waits for the Bishop, retiring to the further corner of the same side of the altar.

15. The Bishop having put on the ring, rises, takes the crosier in his left hand, and between the two assistant deacons, followed by the acolytes of the mitre and of the crosier, goes to the altar, blessing on his way the people and the clergy; when he has arrived before the lower

step, he lays aside the crosier and puts off the mitre, makes a profound bow to the cross, goes up to the altar, assisted by the deacon of the Gospel at his right, and the assistant priest at his left, kisses the altar in the middle, placing his hands on each side. The clergy sit down. The assistant deacons stand on the second step on each side. The crosier and mitre-bearers stand at a certain distance from the lowest step, behind the two assistant deacons.

16. The sub-deacon, after the Bishop has washed his hands, goes to the side-table, attended by the second master of ceremonies and acolytes, who put on his shoulders the long veil, with which the chalice and other things on the table were covered, leaving it to hang lower on his right side. The sub-deacon takes, with his left hand, the chalice with the paten, particle, and pall, extends the longest part of the veil over it, places his right hand on the veil and chalice, lest anything should fall, and thus goes to the altar, followed by the acolyte who carries the cruets with wine and water; when arrived there, at the same time with the Bishop, he places the chalice on the altar at the Epistle side, and removes the veil from it.

17. The deacon receives from the sub-deacon the paten with the particle, kisses it, and gives it to the Bishop, kissing his hand; the Bishop, as usual, raises it before his breast, says, *Suscipe, Sancte Pater*, etc., places the particle on the corporal, and the paten under it at his right. In the meanwhile, the deacon wipes the chalice with the purifier, receives the cruet with the wine from the sub-deacon, who had received it from the acolyte, puts some wine into the chalice, and the sub-deacon, raising the cruet with water a little towards the Bishop, says, *Benedicite, Pater Reverendissime*, and the Bishop having made towards it the sign of the cross, whilst the sub-deacon puts some drops of water into the chalice, says the prayer, *Dues qui humanæ*. Then the deacon gives the chalice to the Bishop, kissing it first, then the Bishop's hand; the Bishop receives it at the knob, with his right hand, and at the foot with his left, and offers

it together with the deacon, who, with his left hand, supports the Bishop's elbow, and with his right the foot of the chalice, saying with the Bishop the prayer, *Offerimus tibi*, etc.; afterwards, the sub-deacon having extended the lower part of the veil hanging on his right on the altar, and put his right hand on it, the deacon gives him the paten, which he covers with a veil, goes down below the steps, and holding the paten raised, remains behind the Bishop till the *Pater* is said.

18. Mass is continued as usual, and after the Bishop has said the words *Benedic hoc sacrificium tuo sancto nomini præparatum*, the censer-bearer goes to the altar; incense is put into the censer, the deacon holding the censer, and saying *Benedicite, Pater Reverendissime*, the Bishop blesses it, saying, *Per intercessionem*, etc.; then, having received the censer from the deacon, the Bishop incenses the *Oblata*, saying, *Incensum istud*—the cross, saying *Dirigatur, Domine*—the relics, saying nothing; and continues the other prayers, as he incenses the altar; which being done, he gives back the censer to the deacon, saying, *Accendat;* then having received the precious mitre from the first assistant deacon, standing at the Epistle corner, he is incensed by the deacon of the Mass, who incenses the assistant priest, the two assistant deacons, the clergy in the sanctuary, according to their rank and order, lastly the sub-deacon; afterwards he gives back the censer to the censer-bearer, who incenses the deacon, then the master of ceremonies, the acolytes, and the people.

19. After the Bishop is incensed, he washes his hands as usual, and then the first assistant deacon takes off his mitre; he continues Mass, the assistant priest and the acolyte with the hand-candlestick remaining by the Missal. The deacon standing on the second step behind the Bishop, being incensed, remains there till the *Sanctus*, then he goes up to the right of the Bishop, and says it with him and the assistant priest. Likewise, all the clergy in the sanctuary, two by two, say the *Sanctus*, at the same time. After the *Sanctus*, the deacon goes down to the second step behind the Bishop.

20. At the *Sanctus*, four or six acolytes, accompanied by the second master of ceremonies, go from the sacristy to the sanctuary, holding in their hand large candles lighted; when they reach the middle of the sanctuary, they make a genuflection, bow to the clergy at each side of the sanctuary, kneel in a line at a convenient distance from one another; those who are at the Epistle side hold their candle in their right, and those at the Gospel side in their left hand, keeping their arm extended, and the end of the candle resting on the floor. They remain there till after the elevation, unless the Bishop give the Communion; in which case they remain kneeling during the Communion of the clergy, which is given at the altar, and accompany the Bishop to the railing, where he gives the Communion to the people. After the Communion, they go back to the sacristy.

21. After the *Sanctus* has been recited by the Bishop and the clergy, all in the sanctuary and in the church kneel down, except the ministers assisting at the altar. When the Bishop says *Quam oblationem*, the deacon goes up to his right during the consecration and elevation, kneels down, raises with his left hand the Bishop's chasuble on his side; after the elevation of the consecrated Host, he rises, uncovers the chalice, kneels again, raises the Bishop's chasuble as before, and after the elevation of the chalice, rises, covers the chalice, and makes a genuflection with the Bishop. The two assistant deacons, the sub-deacon, and the assistant priest remain kneeling at their places during the elevation. The assistant priest, with his right hand, raises the chasuble of the Bishop on his side during the elevation. The master of ceremonies rings the bell at the elevation, and the censer-bearer incenses thrice the Blessed Sacrament at each elevation.

22. During the elevation, nothing should be sung; but some devout and harmonious air may be played on the organ. After the elevation, the choir sings *Benedictus, qui venit*, and all rise, and stand until the Communion. The celebrant continues Mass as usual; the

deacon makes a genuflection and goes to his place behind the Bishop. At the words *Benedicis et præstas nobis*, the deacon goes to the right of the Bishop, makes with him a genuflection, and uncovers the chalice; at the words *Per ipsum*, he places two fingers on the foot of the chalice, and after the words, *Omnis honor et gloria*, he covers the chalice, makes a genuflection with the Bishop, and goes to his place behind him.

23. At the *Pater Noster*, when the Bishop says *Et dimitte nobis*, the deacon and sub-deacon, having made a genuflection, go up to the altar, the deacon to the right of the Bishop, and the sub-deacon to the right of the deacon; there, the sub-deacon, placing his hand on the altar, the deacon uncovers the paten, receives it from the sub-deacon, cleans it with the purifier, kisses it, and puts it into the Bishop's hand, which he also kisses, whilst the Bishop says, *Libera nos quæsumus*, etc. As the Bishop places the paten under the Host, the deacon uncovers the chalice, makes a genuflection, and rises with the Bishop, who puts the particle of the Host in the chalice; the deacon then covers it, and again makes a genuflection. The sub-deacon, having given the paten to the deacon, takes off his veil, gives it to the second master of ceremonies, and having made a genuflection, returns to his place at the foot of the altar; he does not go up to say the *Agnus Dei*, but he goes to the right of the Bishop, whilst the deacon remains at his left, in place of the assistant priest.

24. The assistant priest and the officiating deacon say the *Agnus Dei*, with the Bishop; the rest of the clergy say it at the same time, at their places. After the *Agnus Dei*, the assistant priest and the deacon make a genuflection, exchange places, and again make a genuflection; the deacon remains near the Missal, and the assistant priest kneels down whilst the celebrant says the prayer, *Domine Jesu Christe qui dixisti;* after which, he rises, kisses the altar at the same time with the Bishop, receives from him the *Pax*, approaching his left cheek to the left cheek of the celebrant, placing his two hands under the celebrant's elbows and answering,

Et cum spiritu tuo. Then, rising, he carries the *Pax* to the clergy, giving it to the first of them on each side of the sanctuary; on returning to the foot of the altar, he gives it to the master of ceremonies, by whom he was accompanied, and goes up to the left of the Bishop. The first assistant deacon, after the assistant priest has received the *Pax*, goes to the Bishop's right, and receives it in the same manner; then the second assistant deacon, the officiating deacon, and lastly the sub-deacon.

When the Bishop is to give Communion, after he has received the Precious Blood, the deacon and sub-deacon at his left, kneel on the platform before the Bishop, who, without saying *Misereatur*, etc., or *Ecce Agnus Dei*, etc., gives them Holy Communion. They then receive the *Pax*, kissing the Bishop's left cheek. The officiating deacon then sings the *Confiteor* for the Communion of the clergy.

25. The deacon, after the Communion, goes to the right of the Bishop, receives the cruets from the acolyte, serves the wine for the first ablution, and the wine and water for the second, after which he places the purifier on the Bishop's fingers. After the Bishop has taken the first ablution, the assistant priest carries the Missal, on its cushion or stand, from the Gospel, to the Epistle side, followed by the acolyte with the candlestick. The deacon puts the mitre on the head of the Bishop, who washes his hands, two acolytes having brought the basin and ewer, with water and the towel. The assistant priest takes off his ring, presents him the towel to wipe his hands, and replaces the ring on his finger. Then the officiating deacon takes off the Bishop's mitre. In the meantime, the sub-deacon, having folded the corporal, and put it in the burse, and placed the purifier, paten, pall, and burse on the chalice, carries it to the side-table, and places himself below the lower step behind the deacon, who stands on the middle step, behind the Bishop, who, attended by the assistant priest, and remaining near the Missal, on the Epistle side, reads the Communion, goes to the middle, followed by the

deacon and sub-deacon, says, *Dominus vobiscum*, and finishes Mass as usual. After the last prayer and *Dominus vobiscum*, the Bishop remains turned towards the people, towards whom the deacon also turns, and sings, *Ite Missa est.* Then both turn to the altar towards the Epistle side. The Bishop having said, *Placeat tibi,* etc., gives the solemn blessing, as usual.

If the celebrant is an Archbishop, he gives the blessing without mitre, bowing first to the cross which is held before him. Then he lays his pallium on the altar, and says, *Initium Sancti Evangelii.*

When the Indulgence has not been already published, in consequence of no sermon having been preached, the assistant priest publishes it as usual, from the Epistle side.

26. The Bishop then takes off his mitre, begins the Gospel of St. John, at the Gospel side, puts on the mitre, takes the crosier in his left hand, and continues the Gospel while going to his seat, where he finishes it.

27. The Gospel being ended, the two assistant deacons give their places to the deacon and sub-deacon, and retire to the ministers' bench. The Bishop, having disrobed, washes his hands, and puts on the cappa and pectoral cross; then two acolytes bring the book and candle, and the master of ceremonies brings the Bishop's shoes to his seat, who reads the thanksgiving, whilst the acolytes take off his sandals and put on his shoes. Which being done, and the thanksgiving ended, the clergy and Bishop return to the sacristy, and thence the Bishop is accompanied to his house, or to his room where he may put on his rochet and cape.

CHAPTER VII.

SOLEMN MASS CELEBRATED IN PRESENCE OF THE BISHOP DRESSED IN COPE.

1. On solemn festivals, when the Bishop does not celebrate a Pontifical Mass, it is proper that he should assist at the divine service in mitre and cope. On such occasions, what follows is to be observed:

2. The Bishop's vestments should be placed on the altar, viz., amice, alb, cincture, pectoral cross on a plate, stole and cope; two mitres, one on each side, and the crosier.

On the side-table, besides everything necessary for High Mass, a Missal for the Bishop, the hand candlestick with a candle, the basin and ewer, and a towel on a plate.

3. The celebrant and ministers go to the church before the Bishop, and seat themselves at the bench, waiting for him. The acolytes place their candlesticks on the table, and the thurifer with the holy-water vase stands near the deacon.

4. The Bishop, accompanied by the clergy, goes to the church, and having arrived at the middle of the sanctuary, kneels before the faldstool, rises, after having said a short prayer, and with him all the clergy rise. Then, between the two assistant deacons, preceded by the assistant priest, he goes to his seat, where he puts on all the vestments before mentioned, and sits down. Then the celebrant and ministers go to the altar, having first made the necessary bows. The Bishop rises. The celebrant intones the antiphon and sprinkles the altar as usual, then he rises, and, accompanied by the master of ceremonies and the cleric carrying the holy-water vase, he goes to the throne. The Bishop takes the sprinkle from the celebrant and sprinkles himself, the celebrant and the assistant at the throne; then he hands the sprinkle to the celebrant, who, having made a profound

bow, (which he also does while the Bishop is sprinkling him,) returns to the altar and sprinkles the ministers, who then rise. The rest is done as prescribed in Part III, Chap. II, Art. VII, page 176, n. 4.

When the celebrant and ministers return from the bench to the altar they await the Bishop, a little at one side.

5. The Bishop, with mitre and crosier, goes to the altar, takes off his mitre, bows to the cross, the others making a genuflection, and, having the celebrant on his left, the assistant deacons standing immediately behind him, and the deacon and sub-deacon of the Mass to the left and behind the celebrant, and the acolytes with the mitre and crosier behind the assistant deacon, he makes the Confession, saying, as usual, *In nomine Patris,* etc., the celebrant and the ministers answering. After the prayer, *Indulgentiam, absolutionem,* the Bishop makes a profound bow, receives the mitre and the crosier from the first assistant deacon, and returns to his seat; the celebrant having bowed to the Bishop, goes to the middle and continues Mass.

6. The Bishop, on arriving at his seat, lays aside the crosier and sits with his mitre on; then the censer-bearer, presenting the censer, and giving the boat to the assistant priest, the Bishop puts incense into the censer, and blesses it, as usual. The celebrant incenses the cross and altar, as usual; then he is incensed with two swings only, by the deacon, who gives the censer to the censer-bearer, by whom it is carried to the Bishop's seat, and given to the assistant priest, who is below the lowest step, where he incenses the Bishop with three swings. Afterwards, the Bishop sits, and his mitre is taken off by the second assistant deacon, and the Missal and candlestick are brought before the Bishop by the acolytes, who commences the *Introit,* when the celebrant begins to read it at the altar. After the *Introit,* the Bishop says the *Kyrie* alternately with the assistants and the priests who are present at Mass in the sanctuary dressed in surplices. They go before the Bishop's seat, placing themselves in a semi-circle; after

having bowed to him, they say the *Kyrie* and *Gloria* with the Bishop; at the end of the *Kyrie*, they bow and return to their places. The Bishop, as they bow, gives them his blessing. If the choir has not finished singing the *Kyrie*, the Bishop sits, receives the mitre, and the assistants also sit and cover their heads; otherwise, he remains standing. At the *Gloria*, he rises without his mitre; the book is not held before him during the *Gloria*, but he says it by heart with his assistants, standing. He sits, with his mitre on, after the *Gloria*. During the *Dominus vobiscum* and the Collects, the Bishop stands with his head uncovered. After the Collects, he sits with his mitre on. The sub-deacon, turned towards the Bishop, sings the Epistle, and, having sung it, goes to kiss the Bishop's hand, and to receive his blessing. Then the acolytes come to him with the Missal and candlestick, and the Bishop reads the Epistle and Tract, says, *Munda cor meum*, and reads the Gospel.

7. A little before the Bishop finishes reading the Gospel, the deacon, having placed the Missal on the middle of the altar, goes to kiss the Bishop's hand; he then returns to the altar, and says, kneeling, *Munda cor meum*. In the meantime, the censer-bearer carries the censer, to the Bishop's seat, and the incense is put in, and blessed by the Bishop, as usual. Afterwards, the deacon and sub-deacon, with the master of ceremonies, censer-bearer, and acolytes, go to the Bishop's seat, as has been said elsewhere, and kneel down; the deacon asks and receives the blessing, and sings the Gospel, as usual. After it, the sub-deacon carries the book to the Bishop to be kissed; and the assistant priest incenses the Bishop. The celebrant is not incensed.

If there is a sermon, the preacher asks the Bishop's blessing.

8. At the *Credo*, the Bishop rises, the priests go before his seat, as at the *Kyrie* and *Gloria*, say it with him, and kneel also with him, at the words *Incarnatus est*. The book is not carried to the Bishop, who says the *Credo* by heart. At the Offertory, the Bishop, standing with his head uncovered, reads it out of the Missal, which the

acolyte holds open before him; and then sits with the mitre on. Afterwards he puts incense into the censer and blesses it. The sub-deacon, without leaving the altar, presents the cruet with water to the Bishop, and says, *Benedicite, Reverendissime Pater;* the Bishop then blesses the water. The celebrant incenses the oblation, the cross, and the altar, as usual, then he is incensed twice only by the deacon, who carries the censer to the Bishop's seat; and the assistant priest, coming down to the foot of the throne, receives the censer, incenses the Bishop thrice, returns the censer to the deacon, who incenses the assistant priest, the first and second assistant deacons, and afterwards the clergy in the sanctuary, and the sub-deacon.

9. At the Preface, the Bishop stands with his head uncovered; he recites the *Sanctus* by heart, with the assistants and the priests, who go before his seat as at the *Kyrie* and *Gloria.* After the *Sanctus,* the Bishop goes to the middle of the sanctuary, between the two assistant deacons, and followed by the acolytes carrying the crosier and mitre, and there kneels at the faldstool, till after the elevation, and the sub-deacon will take care to move a little towards the Epistle corner, so as to avoid turning his back to the Bishop; the Bishop then returns to his seat, and stands till after the Communion of the priest.

10. At the *Agnus Dei,* the priests go to the Bishop's seat, and say it with him; then they return to their places. The assistant priest goes to the right of the celebrant, and, with the usual ceremonies, receives from him the *Pax,* and goes to give it to the Bishop, who gives it to the first and second assistant deacons. The celebrant gives it also to the deacon. But the sub-deacon receives it from the assistant priest, and then gives it to the first clergyman on each side of the sanctuary, as in other High Masses. If the celebrant gives Communion, the Bishop kneels as at the elevation; after Communion, the Bishop reads the communion in the Missal, and sits with his mitre on.

11. At the *Dominus vobiscum,* the Bishop and the

clergy rise, and stand during the prayers. The celebrant does not give the blessing, but the Bishop gives it solemnly, as usual; after which the celebrant publishes the Indulgence, and finishes Mass, as usual.

12. After Mass, the celebrant, with the deacon and sub-deacon, and the acolytes, with their candlesticks, having made a genuflection to the cross, and bowed to the Bishop and clergy, go to the sacristy. The Bishop takes off the sacred vestments, puts on the cape and pectoral cross, and having prayed a short time before the altar, retires, accompanied by the clergy.

CHAPTER VIII.

OF SOLEMN MASS,

CELEBRATED IN PRESENCE OF THE BISHOP, NOT DRESSED IN COPE AND MITRE, BUT IN CAPPA MAGNA.

1. EVERYTHING is to be observed as in the preceding chapter, with the following exceptions:

2. The Bishop is incensed only at the Offertory.

3. The celebrant is incensed, as usual, at the beginning of Mass, after the Gospel, and at the Offertory, twice only on each occasion.

4. The Bishop may go from the sacristy to the sanctuary, at the same time with the celebrant, but behind him, immediately preceded by the assistant priest, and having at his side the two assistant deacons; he may likewise return to the sacristy behind the celebrant in the same manner.

[The Bishop cannot assist on his throne at a High Mass or a Solemn Mass wearing only his rochet and mozetta.]

CHAPTER IX.

VESPERS FOR THE DEAD.

CELEBRATED BY THE BISHOP.

1. THE Bishop at these Vespers wears the cape, or the pontifical mantle,* over his rochet. He sits in his stall in the choir, or on his seat, but without assistant priests and deacons.

2. Vespers are begun with the antiphon, *Placebo Domino*, sung by the choir, during which the Bishop and the clergy stand with their heads uncovered. When they begin the Psalm, *Dilexi*, they all sit and put on their caps. When the *Magnificat* is begun, they all take them off, and rise. They sit down again, whilst the choir repeats the antiphon after the *Magnificat;* after which the Bishop says, in an audible voice, *Pater noster*, which is secretly continued and finished by all, kneeling.

3. At the same time, two acolytes, with their candlesticks and lighted candles, and a third one with the book, come before the Bishop, who says, still kneeling, *Et ne nos inducas*, etc., with the other verses, as in the Breviary. When he says *Dominus vobiscum*, he rises, and says the prayer, *Requiem æternam*. Then the chanters sing *Requiescant in pace*.

4. Should the Bishop sit at the usual place, at the *Pater noster*, etc., he kneels before the faldstool, and there finishes the prayers. The same thing is to be observed of Matins.

---

* The *cappa magna* is a full robe with a train.

CHAPTER X.

MATINS AND LAUDS FOR THE DEAD.

CELEBRATED BY THE BISHOP.

1. THE Bishop at these Matins is vested, and sits as at Vespers.

2. Having sat for a short time, the Bishop rises, and with him all the clergy. The choir begins the *Invitatorium: Regem, cui omnia vivunt*, etc., during which, and the Psalm, *Venite exultemus*, all stand. When the Psalm of the first nocturn is begun, they all sit, and put on their caps. After the verses of the first nocturn, they all rise, with their heads uncovered, and say in secret the *Pater noster;* after which the Bishop and the clergy sit down. The Lessons are sung by the clergy in the middle of the sanctuary at the desk. The same is done in the other nocturns.

3. After the ninth response, Lauds are said, the Bishop and the clergy sitting. When the *Benedictus* is begun, they all rise, with their heads uncovered. Whilst the antiphon is repeated after it, they sit and cover their heads.

4. After the antiphon, they rise, the acolytes go with the candlesticks and the book before the Bishop, and everything is done as at Vespers.

CHAPTER XI.

SOLEMN PONTIFICAL MASS FOR THE DEAD.

ARTICLE I.

Things to be Prepared.

1. THE altar should be dresssed in the plainest manner, having on it the cross and six candlesticks with candles of unbleached wax; before it a black antipendium. The veil on the tabernacle, if the Blessed Sacrament is there, should be of purple color.

It is contrary to the Rubrics to put about the altar vestments, stools, or books, any representation of death, or white crosses.*

2. On the side-table, two candlesticks with candles of unbleached wax; the basin and ewer, and a plate with some towels; the Missal, the canon, a vase with holy water and a sprinkle, the chalice, with everything necessary for Mass.

3. On the bench of the ministers, the maniples for the deacon and sub-deacon.

4. On the altar the Bishop's vestments, viz., a black chasuble, dalmatic, tunic, stole, and maniple, cincture, alb, and amice. The pectoral cross and ring on a plate; and a plain white mitre.

The Bishop does not use sandals, gloves, or crosier at this Mass.

The tabernacle may be covered with purple, or not covered.

5. In the sacristy, a black cope for the assistant priest; two black dalmatics, two cinctures, albs, and amices, for the two assistant deacons; also a black dalmatic and stole, with a cincture, alb, and amice, for the officiating

---

* Cæremoniale Episc., chap. xi, lib. ii.

deacon; and a tunic, cincture, alb, and amice, for the sub-deacon. Moreover, as many black copes, chasubles, dalmatics, and tunics, with amices, albs, and cinctures, as may be required for the clergy, who assist in sacred vestments at the Pontifical Mass. Lastly, a cope for the Bishop, to be taken to him by an acolyte after Mass.

6. A black carpet and four candlesticks must be kept ready, in a convenient place, to be extended before the Bishop's seat after Mass, for the absolution, unless a cenotaph or monument be erected in the middle of the church; in this case the processional cross is to be prepared at the Epistle side.

Article II.

From the Beginning to the End of Mass.

1. The Bishop goes to the sacristy as usual.
2. The clergy should put on their respective vestments before the Bishop arrives at the sacristy.
3. They all go from the sacristy to the sanctuary.
4. The Bishop, having arrived at his seat, attended by the deacon and sub-deacon, and the assistant priest (the assistant deacons remaining at the ministers' bench whilst the Bishop is dressing), does not say the anthem, *Ne reminiscaris*, nor the Psalms which follow; but he takes off his cape, reading, from the book which is held open before him by an acolyte, the prayer, *Exue*, etc.; he then washes his hands, puts on the vestments prepared on the altar, as in Art. 1, n. 4, saying the respective prayers, and having received the mitre, sits for a short time; the assistant deacons go to his side, and the deacon and sub-deacon go to put on their maniples.

At this Mass, whenever the ministers give anything to the celebrant, or receive it from him, they do not kiss it, nor the celebrant's hand.

During the Collects, the clergy in the sanctuary, with the exception of the Bishop's assistants, kneel down, as also from the *Sanctus* till the *Pater noster*.

5. The Bishop being vested, he, and the assistants and

ministers, go to the altar, and take their places, as directed above. The Psalm, *Judica*, is not said. After the Confession, he says the usual prayers, goes up to the altar with the assistant priest, deacon and sub-deacon; he then kisses the altar, but not the Missal; neither does he incense the cross or the altar; having kissed the altar, he returns to his seat between the assistant deacons; and the deacon and sub-deacon go to their seat.

6. The Bishop having returned to his seat, takes off the mitre; the acolyte holding the book before him, he reads the *Introit*, and says the *Kyrie*, alternately with his assistants, which last is said likewise by the deacon and sub-deacon, and all the clergy in the sanctuary.

7. After the choir has finished singing the *Kyrie*, the Bishop, rising, his head being uncovered, sings, *Dominus vobiscum*, and the Collect. He then sits with his mitre on. The sub-deacon sings the Epistle as usual; but after it, he does not go to the Bishop to receive his blessing. The Bishop reads the Epistle, and afterwards the Tract and *Sequentia;* says, *Munda cor meum*, etc., but not *Jube Domne*, etc., and reads the Gospel. The deacon and sub-deacon sit at their bench. About the end of the *Sequentia*, the deacon carries the book to the altar, and without going to kiss the Bishop's hand, kneeling on the highest step, says, *Munda cor meum*, etc. The sub-deacon, at the same time, places himself before the lowest step, so as to be at the left of the deacon when he goes down; two acolytes place themselves behind them, without candlesticks. At a signal given by the master of ceremonies, they go to sing the Gospel. The book is not incensed before the Gospel is sung, nor the celebrant after it; nor does the sub-deacon carry the book to the Bishop; who immediately after the Gospel, sings *Dominus vobiscum* and *Oremus*, reads the *Offertory*, and washes his hands.

8. The Bishop, having washed his hands, goes to the altar, and everything is done as before, except, 1st, the sub-deacon, before he puts water into the chalice, does not say *Benedicite*, etc., and the Bishop does not bless it;

2dly, the sub-deacon does not put on the veil, nor hold the paten; 3dly, after having incensed the altar, the Bishop alone is incensed by the deacon.

9. At the *Sanctus*, four acolytes go from the sacristy into the sanctuary with four torches, as directed above, and remain kneeling until after the Communion.

10. The sub deacon, at the elevation, kneels on the lowest step of the altar at the Epistle side, and incenses the Blessed Sacrament.

11. The *Pax* is not given.

12. At the end of Mass, the blessing is not given. The deacon, turned towards the altar, sings, *Requiescant in pace*. The Bishop, having said, *Placeat tibi*, begins, at the Gospel side, the Gospel of St. John, receives the mitre, and continues the Gospel in going to his seat.

13. If candles are distributed, they are given out whilst the *Sequentia* is being sung; they are lighted at the Gospel, at the elevation, and after Mass during the absolution. (*Cær. Ep., lib. II, Cap. XI, n. 6.*)

Article III.

The Absolution after Mass.

1. The Bishop, having finished the Gospel at his seat, takes off the mitre, maniple, chasuble, dalmatic, and tunic, and puts on the cope, previously brought by one of the acolytes from the sacristy, then receives the mitre, and sits down. The deacon and sub-deacon take off their maniples before they help the Bishop to disrobe. If a funeral oration is to be delivered, the preacher, dressed in his cassock, without surplice, after a short prayer before the altar, without asking the Bishop's blessing, but having made a profound reverence to him, goes into the pulpit, which is to be dressed with black hangings; and having there made again a profound bow to the Bishop, he makes the sign of the cross, and begins his discourse.

2. After the funeral oration, or if there be none, after Mass, a large black cloth is spread before the Bishop's

seat, and four candlesticks placed at its corners. In the meantime, the Bishop sits down, and the choir sings *Libera me*, etc.; whilst this response is repeated, two acolytes, one with the censer and boat, the other with the holy-water vase, go to the Bishop, who, whilst the assistant priest holds the boat, puts incense into the censer and blesses it; then he rises, his head being uncovered, and after the last *Kyrie* has been sung, he says the words *Pater noster*, in an audible voice; continues the prayer in silence, and having received the sprinkle from the assistant priest, sprinkles the black cloth three times; he then gives him back the sprinkle and receives the censer, and incenses the cloth thrice also; the assistant deacons holding, during all this time, the extremities of his cope on each side. Two acolytes, with candlesticks and lighted candles, now come to the foot of the Bishop's seat, and another, with the book immediately before him, and the Bishop sings, *Et ne nos*, etc., with the other verses, and the prayer; after which he repeats, *Requiem æternam*, and the chanters sing, *Requiescant in pace*, etc.; the Bishop makes, at the same time, the sign of the cross towards the cloth.

If there be a monument, or cenotaph, in the middle of the church, the absolution should be made there. All go thither in procession in the following order: two acolytes, one with the censer and boat, and the other with the holy-water vase; the sub-deacon carrying the cross between two acolytes with candleticks and lighted candles; then the clergy, two by two, according to their order; the deacon at the left of the assistant priest; the Bishop between the two assistant deacons, followed by the acolytes, who wait on him with the mitre, book, etc.; when they reach the place, the two acolytes, with the censer and holy-water vase, stop at the head of it on the right side, and the sub-deacon, with the acolytes at his side, goes to the foot of the same place; the clergy divide into two lines, one on each side of the monument, and the Bishop sits on the faldstool in the middle, at the head of the same, where he performs what has been directed above.

On particular occasions, for instance at a funeral service for the Pope, etc., besides the Bishop, there are four other prelates or priests, who, after Mass, put on copes, and perform four absolutions before that performed by the Bishop; they walk two by two, immediately before the assistant priest, and when they come to the cenotaph, sit on seats placed at each corner of it. Then all rise, and the assistant priest holds the book before the Bishop, who reads, *Non intres;* the choir afterwards sings the the response, *Subvenite,* and the prelate first in dignity, who is placed at the right corner at the head of the monument, attended by the deacon, puts incense into the censer, blesses it, says, at the proper time, *Pater noster,* sprinkles the monument thrice at each corner, going round it, beginning on his right side, incenses it in the same manner, says, *Et ne nos,* and the verses and prayer as in the Roman Pontifical. Then the prelate second in dignity, who is placed at the left corner, at the foot of the monument, does the same; so also the prelate third in dignity, placed at the left corner at the head of the monument. The same is done by the prelate fourth in dignity, who is placed at the right corner, at the foot of the monument. Last of all, the Bishop performs the same, after the *Libera* has been sung, as is to be found in the Roman Pontifical. But if there are no other prelates present, the Bishop alone is to bless the incense.

CHAPTER XII.

SOLEMN MASS FOR THE DEAD, CELEBRATED IN PRESENCE OF THE BISHOP.

1. THE Bishop may assist at solemn Mass for the dead, either with cappa or with black cope and plain mitre.
2. Should he assist in cope and mitre, his vestments are placed on the altar, and he puts them on, as mentioned above; but he does not use the crosier.

3. He makes the Confession at the beginning of Mass; but he does not say the Psalm, *Judica*.

4. He puts incense into the censer; but he is incensed by the assistant priest at the *Offertory* only, after the deacon has incensed the celebrant twice.

5. At the Collects, he goes to the middle of the sanctuary, and kneels during them at the faldstool between his assistant deacons.

6. After the *Sanctus*, he goes likewise to the middle, and kneels till the *Agnus Dei*, which he says at his seat; but the priests in the sanctuary do not go before his seat.

7. At the *Post Communion*, he goes again to the middle, and kneels as before; he then returns to his seat, but he does not give the blessing.

8. After Mass, he performs the absolution, observing what has been said in the foregoing chapter.

CHAPTER XIII.

PARTICULAR INSTRUCTIONS FOR THE DIFFERENT OFFICERS WHO ATTEND THE BISHOP.

ARTICLE I.

INSTRUCTION FOR THE ASSISTANT PRIEST.

SECTION I.—*His Quality, Dress, and Place.*

1. THE assistant priest, who, in the Pontifical, is sometimes called by the name of archdeacon, is the first amongst all the ministers of the Bishop. Therefore this office should generally be exercised by the most conspicuous clergyman, who holds the first rank in the diocese.

2. His dress, when the Bishop officiates pontifically, is the amice over his surplice (or rochet, if he be entitled to wear it), and the cope.

3. He sits on a stool placed on the platform of the pontifical chair, and at the right of the first assistant deacon; however, should the place not allow this arrangement, he may sit at the left of the second assistant deacon; in either case his stool must not be on the same line with those of the assistant deacons, but a little forward towards the steps of the platform.*

SECTION II.—*His Office in General.*

1. The assistant priest, after the Bishop is dressed, puts the ring on his finger; he also takes it off every time the Bishop is to wash his hands, and puts it on his finger again, and presents to him the towel; he holds the book before the Bishop, whenever he sings anything out of it at Vespers or High Mass; but when the Bishop reads, the book is to be held by an acolyte; he holds the incense-boat, and presents the spoon to the Bishop every time the Bishop is to put the incense into the censer, and says, *Benedicite, Pater Reverendissime;* but at Mass, only when he is at his pontifical chair, for the deacon is to present it when he is at the altar at Mass. He incenses the Bishop when he is at his chair.

SECTION III.—*His Office at Pontifical Vespers.*

1. The assistant priest holds the book before the Bishop when he intones the first antiphon.
2. Standing at his place he intones the third antiphon.
3. He holds the book when the Bishop intones the hymn; after the antiphon of the *Magnificat* has been intoned, he presents the spoon to the Bishop, to put in the incense, kissing, as usual, both the spoon and the Bishop's hand, and saying, *Benedicite,* etc. When the *Magnificat* is begun, he walks before the Bishop to the altar; on arriving there, after the Bishop has kissed it, he gives him the censer with the usual kisses; after the

---

*The Ceremonial says: "He should sit on a stool near and in front of the Bishop, on his right, or, if the place will not permit, on his left; but his regular place is on the Bishop's right."

incensing, he takes it back, and gives it to the censer-bearer; returns to the Bishop's seat, walking before him, and there standing below the lowest step, he incenses the Bishop with three swings, goes up to his seat, is incensed with two swings, holds the book before the Bishop whilst he sings the prayer, then returns to his place, and after Vespers takes off his cope as usual.

SECTION IV.—*The Office of the Assistant Priest at Pontifical Mass.*

1. As the assistant priest particularly attends the Bishop at the book, it is his duty to prepare, find, and mark, with the usual ribbons in the Missal, the Mass of the day, the commemorations, and whatever is to be read or sung by the Bishop, to whom he is to point out everything, and suggest what he has to sing or read.

2. The assistant priest puts on the cope over the amice, which he puts over the surplice, or rochet, if he be entitled to wear it. Whilst the Bishop reads the Psalms for the preparation of Mass, standing near the first or second assistant deacon, he answers together with them, and alternately with the Bishop; then he offers the towel to the Bishop, when he washes his hands; holds the book before the Bishop at the prayer of Tierce; puts the ring on the Bishop's finger after he is vested, offers the spoon, when the Bishop puts incense into the censer, walks to the high altar at the right of the officiating deacon, places himself near the Bishop, and at his right below the lowest step, makes a genuflection, answers to the confession, making a profound bow to the Bishop, when he says *Et tibi Pater*, and *Et te Pater*.

3. When the Bishop has kissed the altar, the assistant priest holds the Missal, which the sub-deacon offers to the Bishop, and he retires on the Gospel side, below the the steps, during the incensing; after it, he walks to the Bishop's chair before him; there he stands at his place, whilst the Bishop reads the *Introit* and *Kyrie*, to which he answers with the assistant deacons; after it he sits. He holds the Missal whilst the Bishop sings *Gloria in*

excelsis Deo; gives it to the acolyte after the Bishop has sung those words; holds it again before him whilst he sings the prayers; and incenses the Bishop after the Gospel. During the sermon, if the Bishop preaches at his seat, he sits at his usual place; but if he preaches at the altar, he sits at the right of the Bishop, and the deacon at the left. After the deacon has sung the *Confiteor*, the assistant priest publishes the Indulgences. But if the assistant priest preaches (for he that preaches at the Pontifical Mass, ought to perform the office of assistant priest), after the Gospel, having incensed the Bishop, he asks his benediction, saying, *Jube, Domne benedicere*, kisses his hand, preaches dressed as he is in cope, and after the *Confiteor*, sung by the deacon from the pulpit, publishes the Indulgences. He holds the Missal whilst the Bishop sings the *Credo*.

4. The Bishop having read the Offertory, the assistant priest attends him with the towel, when he washes his hands, puts the ring on his finger, carries the Missal to the altar, goes to the altar walking before the Bishop; in case, for greater convenience, the Missal was carried thither by an acolyte, the assistant priest attends the Bishop, standing at his left near the book, and turns the leaves, when necessary; when the Bishop incenses the sacred offerings and the altar, the assistant priest takes the Missal with its stand from the altar, and retires with it to the Gospel side, below the steps; after the incensing, he puts it back in the same place; assists at the washing of the hands, presenting the towel as usual, and remains near the Missal to attend the Bishop. He says *Sanctus*, with the Bishop, kneels only at the elevation, and makes a genuflection whenever the Bishop makes it. He says with him, *Agnus Dei;* after it, he exchanges place with the deacon, and when the Bishop says the first prayer, *Domine Jesu Christe*, he kneels at his right; after it, he rises, kisses the altar at the same time with the celebrant, receives from him the *Pax*, approaching his left cheek to the celebrant's left cheek; and when he has said *Pax tecum*, the assistant priest answers, *Et cum spiritu tuo*. Then he makes a genuflection, and attended

by the master of ceremonies, gives the *Pax* to those of the clergy on each side of the sanctuary who occupy the first places or stalls on each row, making no reverence before he gives it, but only after he has given it. Lastly, he gives it to the master of ceremonies, by whom he was accompanied.

5. The assistant priest, after having given the *Pax* to the master of ceremonies, returns to his place, at the left of the Bishop; after the ablution, he carries the Missal from the Gospel side to the Epistle side, attends the Bishop, when he washes his hands, presenting to him the towel, goes near the book at the right of the Bishop, and when the Indulgences have not been published, if there has not been any sermon, he publishes them after the Bishop has given the blessing.

SECTION V.—*The Office of the Assistant Priest, when the Bishop does not celebrate himself, but only assists at Mass or Vespers celebrated by others.*

1. When the Bishop does not celebrate, but assists, either in cope, or in his large mantle or cappa, the assistant priest attends him in his usual choral dress, viz., in surplice, or in rochet, if he be entitled to use it.

2. The assistant priest presents the incense-boat to the Bishop, incenses him, if he assists in cope and mitre, after the Introit, after the Gospel, and at the Offertory; after the *Agnus Dei*, he goes to the altar, kneels, rises, kisses the altar, receives the *Pax* from the celebrant, gives it to the Bishop, who gives it to his assistant deacons, and on returning to his seat he gives it to the sub-deacon, by whom it is given to the clergy; but if Mass be celebrated by a prelate who has his own assistant priest, the latter receives it from the Bishop's assistant priest, and gives it to the others.

Article II.

INSTRUCTIONS FOR THE TWO ASSISTANT DEACONS.

SECTION I.—*Their Office, Dress and Place.*

1. Whenever the Bishop officiates pontifically, either for Mass or for Vespers, two clergymen, the highest in dignity next to him that performs the office of assistant priest, ought to attend the Bishop.

2. They ought to be dressed in rochet or surplice amice and dalmatic; they wear neither maniples nor stoles. Custom permits them to wear albs, instead of rochet or surplice; and this use prevails throughout this country; it may, therefore, be followed.

3. The assistant deacons sit on each side of the Bishop, on two stools placed on the platform, whereon stands the Bishop's chair. They walk at his side, and if he is dressed in cope, they raise it, each on his own side.

4. A Bishop officiating out of his diocese is not entitled to have the two assistant deacons.

SECTION II.—*The Office of the Two Assistant Deacons at the Pontifical Vespers.*

1. Whenever the Bishop kneels before the altar at the faldstool, the assistant deacons adjust the sides of his cope.

2. The second assistant deacon, at the Bishop's left, takes off the mitre, and gives it to the acolyte; the first assistant deacon at his right takes off his cap, and gently presses down his hair, every time the Bishop is to take off his mitre.

3. The first assistant deacon, at the Bishop's right, having first put on his cap, puts the mitre on him, and the second assistant deacon helps him, and fixes behind him the mitre-bands every time the Bishop is to put on the mitre. Every time the Bishop raises his hand, either to make the sign of the cross on himself, or to bless some person or thing, or to put incense into the censer, or to strike his breast, or to incense the altar, or to do

anything else, the first assistant deacon raises the celebrant's cope on his side; likewise, whenever the Bishop raises both his hands, when he has to read anything out of the book, or to give the solemn blessing, both assistant deacons, on each side of him, raise his cope. Whenever the Bishop sings, or reads anything from the book, the two assistant deacons, on each side, put their hands on the book, the first assistant deacon turns the leaves of the book, and the second points out what he has to sing or read.

SECTION III.—*The Office of the Assistant Deacons at the Pontifical Mass.*

1. The assistant deacons go to the side of the Bishop, as soon as he is dressed for Tierce, and sit there till the chapter is sung. Then they rise, the second assistant deacon takes off the Bishop's mitre, and they both attend him standing till Tierce is finished; then they give their places to the deacon and sub-deacon. When the Bishop has put on all the vestments for Mass, they return to his side, walk with him to the altar, where, being arrived, the second assistant deacon takes off his mitre, and they make a genuflection; the first assistant deacon gives his place to the assistant priest, the second assistant deacon to the officiating deacon, and retiring each behind him to whom he gave way, remain there answering, and bowing profoundly at the *Confiteor;* during the incensing, they go up to the second step, the first assistant deacon towards the Epistle side, and the second assistant deacon towards the Gospel side, and remain there till it is finished; then the first assistant deacon puts the mitre on the Bishop; after the Bishop has been incensed, they both go at his side to the pontifical chair, the second assistant deacon takes off his mitre, they both attend him standing whilst he reads the *Introit* and *Kyrie,* to which they answer; then the first assistant deacon (if the choir have not done singing the *Kyrie*) puts on him the mitre, and both seat themselves. The *Kyrie* being sung, they rise; the second assistant deacon

takes off the Bishop's mitre; they attend him whilst he reads the *Gloria*, and when he has finished it, and seated himself, the first assistant deacon puts the mitre on him. After the *Gloria* has been sung by the choir, they both rise, the second assistant deacon takes off the Bishop's mitre, and both attend him, whilst he sings the prayer and the Collects; after which, the first assistant deacon puts on him the mitre, and they both sit, whilst the Epistle is sung; they rise after it, and, standing, attend the Bishop, whilst he reads the Epistle, Tract, etc., and Gospel, and whilst he puts the incense into the censer; they then sit; when the Bishop has given the blessing to the deacon, and the latter is about to begin the Gospel, they both rise; the second assistant deacon takes off the Bishop's mitre, and they stand whilst the Gospel is sung; after the Bishop has been incensed, if there is a sermon, the first assistant deacon puts the mitre on him, and they sit during the sermon; after it the second assistant deacon takes off the Bishop's mitre before he sings the absolution; after it, the first assistant deacon puts the mitre on him; at the blessing, they both bow profoundly and make the sign of the cross on themselves; after the blessing, the second assistant deacon takes off the Bishop's mitre; they both standing attend him, and with him say the *Credo;* they kneel at the *Incarnatus;* the Creed being ended, the first assistant deacon puts the mitre on the Bishop; whilst the *Incarnatus* is sung, they make a profound bow. The Creed being sung, they rise, the second assistant deacon takes off the Bishop's mitre, and standing they attend him whilst he says the Offertory; after it, the first assistant deacon puts the mitre on him, takes off his glove from his right hand, and the second assistant deacon from his left, and they give them to the master of ceremonies. After he has washed his hands, they go at his side to the altar, but the officiating deacon takes off the mitre, they make a genuflection, go up to the second step, remain there whilst the Bishop is at the altar; the first assistant deacon puts on him the mitre before he is incensed, and takes it off after the incensing; at the elevation they both kneel down at their place, and likewise the blessing. After the assistant priest has received the *Pax*, they go to the Bishop's right, make a genuflection without kissing the altar, and receive from the Bishop the *Pax*. Mass being ended, they accompany the Bishop to his seat, where, having made him a profound bow, they give their places to the deacon and sub-deacon, go to the sacristy, disrobe, put on their surplices, and go to accompany the Bishop to his house, or to the sacristy.

SECTION IV.—*The Office of the Assistant Deacons when the Bishop does not celebrate.*

1. In this case, they attend the Bishop in their choral dress, viz., in surplice, or rochet if they have the privilege of using it; they do what has been said in the preceding article, with regard to the mitre, the incense, and the place where they must remain. When the Bishop, at Mass, goes to kneel down before the faldstool or desk, in the middle of the sanctuary, they go with him, and kneel at his side.

The two assistant deacons are to attend only the Bishop in his own diocese; not even Legates have the right of their attendance. However, if the Ordinary should be willing to confer this honor on any Bishop, whom he has invited to officiate in his place, he may give him the two assistant deacons.

ARTICLE III.

INSTRUCTION FOR THE OFFICIATING DEACON.

1. The officiating deacon puts on all the sacred vestments belonging to his order, except the maniple.
2. During Tierce, he sits at his usual place, at the right of the sub-deacon, until the Bishop has read the Psalms and prayers for the preparation of Mass.
3. After the Bishop has read the prayer above mentioned, the officiating deacon goes with the sub-deacon to the Bishop's seat, and having made to him a profound bow, goes to his right, and there standing, after he has

washed his hands, receives every one of the Bishop's vestments from the acolytes who carry them, and vests the Bishop, assisted by the sub-deacon.

4. The Bishop being vested, the deacon returns, with the sub-deacon, to the bench, where they remain till after Tierce is over.

5. After Tierce, the officiating deacon goes again with the sub-deacon to the Bishop's seat, and at his right takes off from him the cope, and puts on him the other vestments for Mass; then he returns with the sub-deacon to the bench, and puts on his maniple.

6. The officiating deacon goes to the altar for the beginning of Mass; if Tierce has been sung, and the Bishop has put on the sacred vestments in the chapel, prepared for this purpose, he walks in procession to the high altar, at the left of the assistant priest, immediately before the Bishop; otherwise, from the bench, he goes before the last step of the altar, at the left of the Bishop, and there answers him at the Confession as usual; goes up to the altar, and standing at the Bishop's right, presents the incense-boat and the spoon, with the usual kiss of the latter, and of the Bishop's hand, and says, *Benedicite, Pater Reverendissime*, receives the censer from the censer-bearer, gives it to the Bishop, kissing the upper part of the chain, which he puts into the Bishop's left hand, and the lower part near the cover into his right hand, which he kisses, attends the Bishop, kneels whenever he kneels, and makes a profound bow when the Bishop bows, raises with his left hand the Bishop's chasuble on his side, and supports his arm whenever he makes a genuflection. After the incensing, he receives with the usual kiss the censer from the Bishop, goes below the last step on the Epistle side of the altar, and after making a profound bow to the Bishop, he incenses him with three swings, and makes again a profound bow to him.

7. When the Bishop goes to his chair, the officiating deacon returns to the bench, where he stands till the Bishop has said *Kyrie eleison*, which he also says alternately with the sub-deacon. Then he sits, rises when the Bishop says, *Gloria in excelsis Deo*, which likewise the

officiating deacon continues together with the sub-deacon. Having finished it, he sits. He rises at the *Pax vobis*, or *Dominus vobiscum;* stands during the prayer and collects, and sits again during the Epistle sung by the subdeacon.

8. Whilst the choir sings the gradual, or *Alleluia*, the officiating deacon receives from the master of ceremonies the Missal, carries it shut before his breast to the altar, saluting the clergy, making a profound bow to the Bishop, and a genuflection on the last step; lays it on the middle of the altar; goes to the Bishop, making the usual reverences, kisses his hand, returns to the altar, kneeling on the lowest step, in the middle, says with a low voice, *Munda cor meum*, rises, takes the book from the altar, returns to the Bishop at the right of the sub-deacon, after having made a genuflection, and salutes the clergy, first on the Epistle side, then on the Gospel side, kneels down with the sub-deacon and acolytes, and say *Jube, Domne, benedicere*. After receiving the blessing, he goes to the place where the Gospel is sung, puts the book open into the hands of the sub-deacon, and turned towards the wall of the sanctuary, on the Gospel side, with his hands joined before his breast, sings *Dominus vobiscum;* when he says *Sequentia*, or *Initium S. Evangelii*, he makes with his thumb the sign of the cross on his forehead, mouth, and breast. Whilst the choir answers, *Gloria tibi*, etc., he receives the censer from the master of ceremonies or the censer-bearer, incenses the book with three swings, one in the middle, the second on the right, the third on the left side of the book, gives back the censer, and, with his hands joined, sings the Gospel.

9. The officiating deacon, having sung the Gospel, and made a genuflection before the altar, returns to his place. If the Bishop preaches from the altar, immediately after the sermon, the officiating deacon, at the left of the Bishop, bowing a little towards him, sings the *Confiteor*, and at the words *Et tibi Pater*, and *Et te Pater*, makes a profound bow. But when any other besides the Bishop preaches, the officiating deacon goes to the Bishop's chair, and standing below the lowest step, sings the *Confiteor*, as before directed.

10. At the *Credo*, the officiating deacon rises, and continues it together with the sub-deacon, reciting it at the same time with the Bishop, and kneeling likewise with him at *Incarnatus est;* and whilst the same verse is sung by the choir, he remains profoundly inclined; then he goes to the side-table, takes the burse with the corporal, which he carries to the altar supported by both his hands, raising it to the height of his eyes, walking slowly, and saluting the clergy, making a bow to the Bishop, and a genuflection, to the cross, he goes up, spreads the corporal in the middle, places the burse on the Gospel side, makes a genuflection, returns directly by the side steps to his place, and sits down.

11. After the Creed has been sung, the officiating deacon goes to the altar at the same time with the Bishop, places himself at his right, takes off his mitre, makes a genuflection, goes up to the altar with him, raising a little his vestments in front, goes to the corner of the altar at the Epistle side, takes off one of the particles from the paten, gives the paten with the other particle, after having kissed it, to the Bishop, kissing also his hand.

12. Whilst the Bishop says *Suscipe, Sancte Pater*, the officiating deacon takes the chalice, wipes it with the purifier, puts wine into it, and after the sub-deacon has put in some drops of water, he wipes with the purifier all the drops that may be within on the sides of the chalice, kisses the foot of the chalice, holding it with his left hand, and the knob under the cup with his right; gives it to the Bishop, kissing his hand, then supporting the Bishop's arm with his left hand, and touching the chalice with his right, he says with the Bishop, *Offerimus tibi Domine*, etc., and when the Bishop has placed the chalice on the corporal, the officiating deacon covers it.

13. When the censer-bearer comes to the altar, the officiating deacon receives from him the incense-boat, attends the Bishop whilst he puts in the incense, gives him the censer, assists him at the incensing, as directed above; observing, moreover, at the incensing of the

sacred offerings, to hold with his left hand the Bishop's vestments, to prevent their embarrassing him, or touching the offerings, and with his right the foot of the chalice; which he also removes from the middle, at the incensing of the cross, and replaces afterwards.

14. After the Bishop has incensed the altar, the deacon receives from him the censer, and incenses him as directed in n. 6; then he incenses the assistant priest, the first and second assistant deacons, with two swings (but in case other Bishops and prelates are present in the sanctuary, they should be incensed with three swings immediately after the Bishop who celebrates); afterwards he incenses with one swing, the clergy in the sanctuary. On returning to the altar, he incenses the sub-deacon with two swings, gives the censer to the censer-bearer, goes to his place on the highest step behind the Bishop, turns towards the censer-bearer, by whom he is incensed.

15. The officiating deacon remains there till after the Preface is sung; then he goes up to the right of the Bishop, and says with him, *Sanctus*, etc., after which he returns to his place. At the words *Quam oblationem*, he goes up to the right of the Bishop; if there be a pyx with small particles to be consecrated, he places it before the Bishop, and uncovers it, kneels on the edge of the platform during the consecration and elevation of the Host, raising the Bishop's chasuble; and when he has placed the Host on the altar, the officiating deacon rises at the same time with him; he covers the pyx, and places it behind the chalice, uncovers the chalice, kneels again, and raises the chasuble during the elevation. When the Bishop lowers the chalice on the altar, the officiating deacon rises, covers it, makes a genuflection with him, and returns to his place behind him. Every time the Bishop makes the sign of the cross, either on the sacred offerings or on himself, the officiating deacon takes care that his vestments should not touch the offerings.

16. When the Bishop says *Benedicis et præstas nobis*, the officiating deacon goes up to his right, uncovers the chalice, making a genuflection every time he uncovers it,

with the Bishop, before and after. When the Bishop makes the sign of the cross on the sacred offerings, saying *Per ipsum et cum ipso*, the officiating deacon puts two fingers of his right hand on the foot of the chalice; and when the Bishop puts the host on the corporal, he covers the chalice, and returns to his place behind the Bishop.

17. Towards the end of the *Pater*, when the Bishop says *Et dimitte nobis*, the officiating deacon goes up to his right, having previously made a genuflection; receives from the sub-deacon the paten, wipes it with the purifier, kisses it, and when the Bishop says *Libera nos*, puts it into his right hand, which he kisses; when the Bishop places the paten under the Host, the officiating deacon uncovers the chalice, and covers it again, after the Bishop has put into it the small part of the Host, making a genuflection, which he always does when at his side.

18. The officiating deacon says the *Agnus Dei*, with the celebrant, then makes a genuflection, exchanges place with the assistant priest, by going to the Bishop's left; there he makes a genuflection, and attends the Bishop at the Missal. If the officiating deacon does not receive Communion, after the second assistant deacon has received the *Pax* from the Bishop, he goes to receive it, making a genuflection first at the Bishop's left, then at his right; but he does not kiss the altar. Having received the *Pax*, he returns to his place, making a genuflection on each side of the Bishop.

19. When the assistant priest returns to the Bishop's left, after having given the *Pax* to the clergy, the officiating deacon returns to the Bishop's right. There he presents wine for the ablution of the chalice, and wine and water for the ablution of the Bishop's fingers, and puts the purifier on his fingers over the chalice.

20. But if Communion is to be given by the Bishop, and if the deacon and sub-deacon are to receive it, immediately after the Bishop has consumed the Precious Blood, the officiating deacon covers the chalice, makes a genuflection, places the pyx with the consecrated Hosts before the chalice, uncovers it, makes a genuflection, kneels at the right of the sub-deacon on the edge of the platform,

receives from the Bishop first the *Pax*, and answers, *Et cum spiritu tuo*, then the Communion, rises, goes to the Epistle side, bows somewhat, having his face turned to the Gospel side, and sings the *Confiteor*, making a profound bow towards the Bishop at the words *Et tibi Pater*, and *Et te Pater*. When he does not receive Communion, he says the *Confiteor* before the celebrant takes the first ablution, as directed above; after the celebrant has said *Indulgentiam*, etc.; he changes place with the subdeacon, and going to the Gospel side, he makes a genuflection in the middle; takes the paten, holds it under the sacred Host, and accompanies the hand of the Bishop, as he gives the Communion, going with the paten to the railing, if the people are to receive the Communion; after it he returns to the altar, goes to the Epistle side, and presents the wine and water for the ablutions.

21. After the ablutions, the officiating deacon puts the mitre on the Bishop, and, after he has washed his hands, takes it off, and goes behind him, follows him to the middle, and then back to the Epistle side, he returns again behind him to the middle, and when the Bishop has sung *Dominus vobiscum*, after the last prayer, the officiating deacon, turned to the people, sings *Ite, Missa est*, or, if the Mass so require, remaining turned to the altar, he sings *Benedicamus Domino*.

22. Before the Bishop gives the solemn blessing, the officiating deacon puts the mitre on him; unless the celebrant be an Archbishop, who does not wear it. In this case, after the Archbishop has given the blessing, and the Indulgences have been published, the officiating deacon takes off the pallium, and lays it on the altar. He kneels and receives the blessing,[*] accompanies the Bishop to the Gospel side, where he begins the Gospel of St. John, or reads it entirely, goes below the steps of the altar, makes a genuflection; accompanies the Bishop to his seat, and assists him in taking off the sacred vestments. When the Bishop has washed his hands, he puts

---

[*] All kneel at the blessing, except Canons and Prelates, who bow profoundly.

on him the cape, gives his place to the first assistant deacon, or to one of the two other clergymen who come to the side of the Bishop, and returns to the sacristy, where he disrobes, and then retires.

Article IV.

Instruction for the Sub-deacon Officiating at Pontifical Mass.

1. The sub-deacon, at a proper time, puts on all the vestments belonging to his order, except the maniple.

2. During Tierce, he sits at the bench as usual, at the left of the deacon, until the master of ceremonies comes to invite him to go to the side-table; he lays his cap on the bench, takes the plate on which are the Bishop's stockings and sandals, carries them, covered with a veil, and raised to the height of his eyes, and, assisted by some acolytes, puts them on the Bishop's right and left foot. Then he returns to the bench, and remains there till the Bishop has read the Psalms and prayers of the preparation for Mass.

3. After the Bishop has read them, the sub-deacon goes with the deacon to the Bishop's seat, and having made to him a profound bow, goes to his left, and there standing, after he has washed his hands, helps the deacon to vest the Bishop.

4. The Bishop being vested, the sub-deacon returns with the deacon to the bench, and remains there till after Tierce is over.

5. After Tierce, the sub-deacon goes again with the deacon to the Bishop's seat, and standing at his left, assists the deacon to take off the Bishop's cope, and to put on him the other vestments for Mass; then he returns with the deacon to the bench, and puts on his maniple.

6. When the Bishop is ready to proceed to the altar, the sub-deacon receives from the master of ceremonies the Missal, with the Bishop's maniple in it, and carrying it shut before his breast, walks to the altar before the deacon, either from the chapel or *Secretarium* in procession, or from his bench goes to the Gospel side; at the

left of the deacon, but a little behind him, makes a genuflection, gives the Missal to the master of ceremonies, answers the Bishop at the confession, as usual, making him a profound bow at the words *Et tibi Pater*, and *Et te Pater;* and while the Bishop says *Indulgentiam*, etc., takes the Bishop's maniple from the book, kisses it on one side, and offers it to the Bishop to kiss, puts it on his left arm, and kisses the Bishop's hand. When the Bishop goes up to the altar, he follows him with the Missal, and on the Gospel side, with the help of the assistant priest, offers the Bishop the Missal open, and pointing out the beginning of the Gospel of that day to be kissed. The sub-deacon gives it to the master of ceremonies, remains at the left of the Bishop, and attends him, whilst he puts incense into the censer, and incenses the altar, raising with his right hand the Bishop's chasuble on his side, and making a genuflection every time he passes before the middle.

7. After the incensing of the altar, the sub-deacon goes below the steps by the Epistle side, and remains at the left of the deacon, whilst he incenses the Bishop, making with him the usual bows; then he goes with him to the bench, stands there at his left, whilst the Bishop reads the *Introit*, and says the *Kyrie*, which he says alternately with the deacon; sits till the *Kyrie* is finished by the choir; rises at the *Gloria in excelsis*, says the rest of it together with the deacon; afterwards he sits at the same time as the deacon, and all the others, whilst it is sung; makes a bow, and takes off his cap at the words *Adoramus, gratias, suscipe, Jesu Christe;* at the end of it, he rises, and stands during the Collect. When the Bishop says *Per Dominum nostrum,* or the words of the conclusion of the last prayer, the sub-deacon receives the Missal from the master of ceremonies, goes to the middle, holding it with both his hands, and leaning it towards his breast, he makes a genuflection to the altar, a profound bow to the Bishop, and a moderate bow to the clergy, first on the Gospel side, then on the Epistle side; goes to his place below the last step, and turned to the Bishop, without turning his back to the altar, he

sings the Epistle, supporting with both his arms the open book.

8. After the Epistle, the sub-deacon goes again to the middle, makes a genuflection to the altar, a bow to the Bishop, and to the clergy on the Epistle side, and the Gospel side, goes to the Bishop, kneels before him, rests the book on his knees, and kisses his hand, as he puts it on the book, rises, returns to the bench, and gives the book to the master of ceremonies; then he goes to the middle, at the left of the deacon, makes a genuflection, salutes the clergy at the Epistle side, and at the Gospel side, walks, at the left of the deacon, to the Bishop's seat, and makes a profound bow. On arriving before it, he kneels whilst the deacon says, *Jube Domne*, etc., and during the blessing; then he rises, makes a profound bow to the Bishop, walks to the place where the Gospel is sung, receives the book in his hand, and supports it on his head before the deacon; and whilst the deacon sings, he remains without moving.

9. When the deacon has done singing the Gospel, the sub-deacon, still holding the book open, without making any bow, carries it to the Bishop to kiss the beginning of the Gospel. When the Bishop has kissed it, the sub-deacon shuts the book, bows to the Bishop, and returns to the bench, making a genuflection to the altar as he passes before it.

10. At the *Credo*, the sub-deacon, rises, says it together with the deacon, and at the same time with the Bishop, kneels at the *Incarnatus;* and having finished the *Credo*, sits with the rest of the clergy. Whilst the *Incarnatus* is sung, the sub-deacon remains profoundly inclined. After the *Incarnatus*, he rises, standing, waits till the deacon returns from the altar, and sits.

11. At the *Offertory*, the sub-deacon rises, goes to the side-table, puts on his shoulder the long veil, and lets it hang lower on his right side, takes hold of the chalice with his left hand, covers it with the longest part of the veil hanging on his right, and places his right hand open over it; then he goes to the altar, whither he should arrive at the same time with the Bishop, uncovers the

chalice, gives it to the deacon, then he gives also to the deacon the wine-cruet which he has received from the acolyte, and having received the water-cruet, he presents it to the Bishop, saying, *Benedicite, Reverendissime Pater*, and puts a few drops of water into the chalice.

12. After the oblation of the chalice, the sub deacon receives the paten from the deacon in his bare hand, and covers it with the longest part of the veil hanging on his right; then he goes down below the lowest step in the middle, holding the paten against his breast; but when he has arrived there, he keeps it raised to the height of his eyes, supporting his elbow with his left hand. There he remains without moving, except only to kneel in the same place, and on the lowest step, for the elevation. When the celebrant says those words of the *Pater Noster, Et dimitte nobis*, etc., the sub-deacon makes a genuflection, goes up to the altar, at the Epistle side, gives the paten to the deacon, takes off the long veil, makes a genuflection, returns below the steps in the middle, he goes up on the right of the deacon and recites the *Agnus Dei*, then returns to his place. He goes up and receives the *Pax*, from the Bishop after the deacon (unless they are to communicate) and remains on the platform at the Bishop's right, if the deacon be attending to the Missal, whilst the assistant priest gives the *Pax;* if the deacon, however, is on the Bishop's right, the sub-deacon will remain on the deacon's right. When the deacon sings or recites the *Confiteor*, the sub-deacon goes to the Gospel side, and remains turned to the opposite side, till the Bishop has said *Indulgentiam*, etc., then he changes places with the deacon, and goes to the Epistle side, remaining by the Bishop, and accompanying him to the railing for the Communion of the people. Returning to the altar, the sub-deacon goes to the Epistle side, puts wine and water into the chalice for the ablutions; puts the purifier on the Bishop's fingers, unless the deacon has already returned to that side, and is there ready to minister for the ablutions; then he goes to the Gospel side, wipes the chalice, puts on it the puri-

fier, paten, pall, veil, and burse with the corporal; takes hold of it with his left, and places his right hand on it, goes down, makes a genuflection on the last step, and carries it to the side-table, returns to his place, below the last step, behind the Bishop, whom he follows, when he goes to the middle. At the blessing the sub-deacon goes up on the highest step, and receives it kneeling, takes in his hand the book, or the altar card, and presents it to the Bishop, to read the Gospel of St. John. After the Bishop has read this, the sub-deacon goes to his left side and helps the deacon to disrobe him. Which being done, he goes to the sacristy, puts off the sacred vestments, and retires.

Article V.

Instruction for the Inferior Ministers who attend the Bishop at Pontifical Mass and other Functions.

Section I.—*The Master of Ceremonies.*

1. There should be two masters of ceremonies; the first, if possible, should be either a priest, or at least in sacred orders.

2. The office of the first master of ceremonies, is to direct and conduct the whole ceremony; he should, therefore, be perfectly acquainted with what is to be done by the celebrant and all the officers. He ought to be familiar with all the instructions given in the present work, which he ought to read frequently; and especially he ought to refresh his memory, by looking at the particular ceremonies to be performed, the day before.

3. He ought to take especial care of what is to be performed by the Bishop, either at his seat or at the altar, or in any other place, and always be near him.

4. The second master of ceremonies assists the first; he ought to be likewise well conversant with this book; and his particular duty is to attend the ministers, and he should therefore remain near them.

5. During Mass, the masters of ceremonies never sit, except during the sermon. They must stand, with their

heads uncovered, whilst the rest of the clergy sit, the first master of ceremonies below the steps of the Bishop's seat, the second near the bench of the ministers; and a little before a reverence is to be made, or a genuflection, they ought to give a signal to the clergy. At the *Incarnatus*, and at the blessing, they kneel down.

6. At the procession, and when the clergy go from the sacristy to the church, and from the church to the sacristy, the masters of ceremonies never wear their caps, neither do they carry them.

7. At Vespers they may sit during the Psalms; but they must rise before the *Gloria Patri*, to give the signal to the clergy to bow.

8. The second master of ceremonies, at the altar, gives the Bishop's vestments to the acolytes when he is to be vested, and receives them back likewise at the altar, when he takes them off.

SECTION II.—*Instruction for the Crosier-bearer.*

1. The crosier-bearer, when the Bishop celebrates Mass, or Vespers, pontifically, may be dressed in surplice and cope; at least, he must be in surplice.

2. He holds continually in his hand the Bishop's crosier, whenever the Bishop does not use it. He must watch the time, in which he is to give or receive the crosier, and be always ready.

3. The crosier-bearer sits either on the steps of the Bishop's chair, or at any other convenient place near it. He must stand whenever the Bishop stands.

4. When the Bishop walks, either from the chair to the altar, or from the sacristy to the sanctuary, the crosier-bearer walks after him, at the right hand of the mitre-bearer; he likewise stands at the right of the mitre-bearer, at a certain distance from the lowest step, when the Bishop is at the altar, and kneels there at the elevation and Communion.

5. In processions, when the Bishop uses the crosier, and carries it, the crosier-bearer walks behind him; but at the procession of the Blessed Sacrament, when the Bishop does not carry the crosier, and on similar occa-

sions, the crosier-bearer walks alone in the middle, immediately before the clergy, dressed in sacred vestments, and carries the crosier erect with both hands.

SECTION III.— *Instruction for the Mitre-bearer.*

1. The mitre-bearer may wear the cope over his surplice, when the Bishop celebrates Mass or Vespers pontifically; at least, he ought to be in surplice, and wear a long white silk veil, hanging from his neck; with the lower part of which he covers his hands, whenever he holds the mitre.

2. He goes to receive it at the altar, from the master of ceremonies, when the Bishop is to be dressed; goes with the others before him to his seat, and carries it back to the altar, after the Bishop is disrobed.

3. He sits either on the steps near the Bishop's chair or in any other convenient place; he holds the mitre whenever the Bishop does not use it; he must watch the moment in which he is to give or receive it, and be always ready; he gives it to the deacon that is at the Bishop's right hand, and receives it from the deacon that is at his left.

4. The mitre-bearer must stand whenever the Bishop stands. When the Bishop walks, either from his chair to the altar, or from the sacristy to the sanctuary, the mitre-bearer walks after him, at the left hand of the crosier-bearer; he likewise stands at his left, at a certain distance from the lowest step of the altar, and kneels there at the elevation and Communion.

5. As the Bishop generally uses two mitres, the precious and the plain mitre, the mitre-bearer must give the precious mitre whenever the Bishop first puts it on, after having vested; at Vespers, after the first Psalm has been commenced, the mitre-bearer places the precious mitre on the altar, at the Epistle side, and carries the lighter mitre to the deacon. At the beginning of the antiphon, before the *Magnificat*, he carries the lighter mitre to the altar, and the precious mitre to the deacon. At Mass, the mitre-bearer, at the beginning of the *Gloria in excelsis*, carries the precious mitre to the altar, and the lighter

mitre to the deacon, which the Bishop uses till the end of the *Credo*. Then the mitre-bearer carries the precious mitre to the deacon, and the lighter mitre to the altar. The Bishop uses the precious mitre till the end of Mass, whenever he has to put it on; therefore, the mitre-bearer holds it in his hand while the Bishop is at the altar, standing or kneeling, as has been said before. When he holds the mitre, the bands must always be outside, and hang down.

6. In processions, the mitre-bearer walks always behind the Bishop.

SECTION IV.—*Instruction for the Book-bearer.*

1. The book-bearer is dressed in surplice. He should take care that the marks be at the proper place in the Missal, and hold it.

2. He sits in a convenient place by the candle-bearer; watches the moment in which the book is necessary, and at the first token given by the master of ceremonies, he carries it to the Bishop. When the Bishop reads standing, the book-bearer holds it likewise standing; when the Bishop sings anything out of the book at his chair, the book-bearer gives it to the assistant priest, who is to hold it only during that time; then he receives it back; when the Bishop reads anything sitting, the book-bearer holds it kneeling down. Holding the book, he places the upper end of it on his forehead, and holds the lower on his hands. He never genuflects nor bows whilst he is holding the book before the Bishop.

SECTION V.—*Instruction for the Candle-bearer.*

1. The candle-bearer, who carries and holds the hand-candlestick, which is used whenever the Bishop officiates, is dressed in surplice; he sits, and remains at the right of the book-bearer; accompanies him whenever he carries the book to the Bishop's chair, and remains at his side with the candlestick in his hand, but always standing whilst the Bishop reads or sings anything.

2. The candle-bearer, moreover, goes to the altar, and there, always at the side in which is the Missal, stands by the assistant priest, holding the candle near the book.

PART VI.

Other Solemn Offices,

AT WHICH THE BISHOP OFFICIATES,

OR IS PRESENT.

CHAPTER I.

COMMEMORATION OF ALL THE FAITHFUL DEPARTED.

1. On All-Saints' Day, for the second Vespers, a black altar veil is to be placed under the white one; the latter is to be removed by the acolytes, soon after the solemn Vespers of the day.

2. After these Vespers, the Bishop and the clergy take off the sacred vestments, the Bishop at his seat, and the clergy (as quickly as possible) in the sacristy; the latter return to the sanctuary, and the Bishop goes to his choir-stall.

3. Vespers for the dead are sung as directed in Part V of this book, chapter ix.

4. After Vespers, in Cathedral churches, Matins and Lauds for the dead are sung, as directed in Part V, chapter x.

5. The next day, a Pontifical Mass is celebrated by the Bishop, as in Part V, chapter xi.

6. After Mass, the absolution is made by the Bishop, either at his seat, or at the cenotaph, as directed in Part V, chapter xi.

CHAPTER II.

SUNDAYS IN ADVENT.

1. IF the Bishop officiates on these Sundays, the assistant deacons, the officiating deacon and sub-deacon, instead of dalmatics, use folded chasubles, which have the same form as the usual chasubles, but that part which hangs before is shorter, and does not hang further than the cincture. Where there are none for this purpose, the others may be used, if folded. The same are used by the ministers for all High Masses celebrated either in the presence or in the absence of the Bishop. However, on the third Sunday in Advent, the ministers use dalmatics and tunics of rose color. If the fourth Sunday falls on Christmas Eve, dalmatics of violet color are also used.

2. The Bishop, instead of *Pax vobis*, says *Dominus vobiscum*.

3. The sub-deacon, whilst the celebrant sings the last Collect, takes off his folded chasuble, sings the Epistle without it, and having received the Bishop's blessings, puts on the folded chasuble again.

4. The deacon also, before the first *Alleluia* is sung, takes off his chasuble, puts on the large stole over the other, and remains so till after the celebrant's Communion; he then takes off the large stole, and puts on the folded chasuble.

5. What has been said above, n. 3 and 4, is to be observed also in other High Masses, celebrated either in the presence or in the absence of the Bishop.

CHAPTER III.

CHRISTMAS.

1. On Christmas Eve, the first Vespers are sung as directed, page 272.

2. The following night, Matins are sung as directed, page 278.

3. What follows is to be particularly observed for these Matins.

4. The church and sanctuary must be illuminated with a sufficient number of candles.

5. Another table, besides the usual side-table, is to be prepared, and all the sacred vestments for the Pontifical Mass should be placed on it; also a cope to be worn by the Bishop during the *Te Deum*.

6. At the third nocturn, whilst the choir sings the Psalm, *Misericordias Domini*, the Bishop, attended by the two assistants in surplice, reads the antiphon and Psalms for the preparation of Mass, out of the book, which is held open before him by an acolyte, who has at his side another acolyte with a candlestick; and in the meantime the Bishop's stockings and sandals are put on. The deacon and sub-deacon go also, at the beginning of the third nocturn, to the sacristy, where they put on the sacred vestments. The Bishop ought to finish the preparation in time to be ready to sing, *A vinculis*, etc., before the lessons. The two assistants, after the preparation, return to their seats; but they go again to the side of the Bishop, when he sings the last Lesson; after which, having intoned the *Te Deum*, the deacon and sub-deacon go to his side, and assist at the washing of his hands, and the two assistants go to put on the sacred vestments; the acolytes, with the book and candlestick, go before the Bishop; the master of ceremonies, having given the Bishop's vestments to the acolytes, goes also with them before the Bishop, who, after having put on the stole, receives the cope, and remains standing till

the end of the *Te Deum;* he then sings *Dominus vobiscum* and the prayer; after which he repeats *Dominus vobiscum,* and whilst the singers sing *Benedicamus Domino,* the Bishop takes off the cope, puts on the other vestments for Mass, which he celebrates as usual. During the *Te Deum,* the clergy put on the sacred vestments.

7. At the *Incarnatus,* the Bishop and all the clergy kneel.

8. The Bishop does not take the ablutions because he is to sing the third Mass; he washes his fingers in another chalice or vessel.

9. Lauds are sung as directed, page 280.

CHAPTER IV.

FESTIVALS BETWEEN CHRISTMAS AND CANDLEMAS.

1. THE Bishop may celebrate these festivals with more or less solemnity, as he thinks proper.

2. However, on New Year's day, he ought to assist at Mass in cope, as directed, page 300.

3. On the Epiphany, he ought to celebrate pontifically, as directed, page 281.

On the same day, after the Gospel has been sung, a clergyman in cope goes to the pulpit, and publishes the movable feasts, singing what is prescribed for this purpose in the Roman Pontifical.

4. On other festivals, the Bishop may assist at Mass in cope or in his cappa, as directed, page 304.

CHAPTER V.

CANDLEMAS.

Things to be Prepared.

1. In the sanctuary, between the Bishop's seat and the altar, a table entirely covered with a white linen cloth, and on it a sufficient number of candles for the Bishop and clergy.

2. On the side-table, besides everything necessary for High Mass celebrated in presence of the Bishop, the holy-water vase, the basin, ewer, towels on a plate, and some slices of bread on another plate, for cleansing the Bishop's hands; an apron beautifully embroidered, to be put on the Bishop's knees at the distribution of the candles.

3. Near the side-table, the processional cross; and in a convenient place the censor with the incense-boat, a chafing-dish, with fire and tongs.

4. In front of the altar, a violet veil over another of a white color, to be removed after the procession, unless the Mass be not of the Blessed Virgin.

5. On the altar, the Bishop's ornaments, viz., the violet cope and stole, the pectoral cross, the cincture, alb, amice, and mitre, besides the crosier at the angle between the altar and the steps.

6. In the sacristy, a violet cope for the assistant priest, two violet chasubles folded, with two cinctures, albs, and amices for the assistant deacons, and violet vestments for all the clergy, as before directed.

7. The clergy put on their vestments in the sacristy; the Bishop goes thither as before directed.

They go out from the sacristy to the sanctuary, as directed, page 284.

The Bishop is vested as prescribed at page 286.

8. The Bishop being vested, takes off the mitre, and rises; the acolytes go before him with the book and the

candlestick, and the Bishop, standing turned a little towards the candles, blesses them, singing in the ferial tone what is prescribed in the Missal for this purpose. When he begins the last prayer, the two acolytes go before him with the censer and incense-boat, and the holy-water vase.

9. After the prayer, the Bishop puts incense into the censer and blesses it; then having received the sprinkle from the assistant priest, he sprinkles the candles three times; afterwards he incenses them also thrice, after which he sits, and puts on the mitre. Then the priest first in dignity, having been previously invited by the master of ceremonies, goes before the Bishop, makes a bow to him, and gives him the candle, which he kisses as well as the hand of the Bishop, who gives the candle to the master of ceremonies to be kept by one of the acolytes.

10. Then the apron, prepared for the purpose, is put on the Bishop's knees. One of the acolytes brings the candles to be distributed, gives them, one by one, to the second assistant deacon, who presents them to the Bishop, who distributes them, first to the priest from whom he received the candle, then to the assistant priest, the assistant deacons, and all the clergy, who go to receive them, according to their order and rank; all receive them kneeling, and kiss the candle and the Bishop's hand. In the meantime, the candles are distributed to the people by one or two priests; and during the distribution the choir sings, *Lumen ad revelationem.*

11. After the distribution, the Bishop washes his hands. The antiphon, *Exurge,* having been repeated, the Bishop takes off his mitre, rises and sings *Oremus;* the first assistant deacon sings *Flectamus genua,* and the second, *Levate,* only after Septuagesima, but not on Sunday, and the Bishop sings the prayer, *Exaudi quæsumus,* after which he sits, puts on the mitre, puts the incense into the censer, and blesses it.

12. In the meantime, the candles are lighted, and everything is arranged for the procession around the

church. The censer-bearer, with the censer, goes to the middle of the sanctuary, behind the sub-deacon, in his folded chasuble, carrying the cross, and having the acolytes, with their candlesticks and lighted candles, at his side. The first assistant deacon sings *Procedamus in pace*, the choir answers, *In nomine Christi, Amen.* Then the procession moves from the sanctuary in the following order: first, the censer-bearer, then the cross-bearer with the acolytes, afterwards the clergy, two by two, according to their order, all carrying their candles; lastly, the Bishop, between the assistant deacons, carrying the candle in his left hand, and blessing the people with his right.

13. During the procession, the priest who is to sing Mass, and the deacon and the sub-deacon, go to the sacristy, and put on their respective vestments—white, if Mass is of the Blessed Virgin; violet, if of the Sunday. Also the violet altar-veil is removed, if Mass is of the Blessed Virgin.

14. After the procession, the clergy take off their sacred vestments in the sacristy, and extinguish their candles. The Bishop goes to his seat, takes off the violet cope and stole, and puts on the white, which an acolyte should bring thither in time. But if Mass is of the Sunday, the Bishop does not change his vestments.

15. Then the celebrant, preceded by the deacon and sub-deacon, goes to the altar, and Mass is celebrated as directed, page 300.

16. The clergy hold in their hands lighted candles, from the beginning to the end of the Gospel, and from the consecration to the Communion, except the Mass of Sunday be said.

CHAPTER VI.

ASH-WEDNESDAY.

ARTICLE I.

Things to be Prepared.

1. ON the side-table, besides everything necessary for High Mass, the following should be prepared: the holy-water vase, the ewer with the basin, a plate with some towels, another with slices of bread to cleanse the Bishop's hands, a towel to be placed on the Bishop's knees during the distribution of the ashes, a Missal for the Bishop, the candlestick, and a large stole for the deacon.

2. On the altar, the Bishop's vestments, viz., a violet cope and stole, pectoral cross, cincture, alb, amice, mitre, and crosier; also a vase containing the ashes to be blessed, made of branches blessed on Palm Sunday the year preceding.

3. In the sacristy, the sacred vestments for the celebrant, deacon, and sub-deacon (the two latter make use of folded chasubles), also two folded chasubles for the assistant deacons, a cope for the assistant priest, and a sufficient number of sacred vestments for the clergy, according to their order and dignity, the censer with the incense-boat, a chafing-dish, with fire and tongs.

ARTICLE II.

From the entrance of the Bishop into the sacristy, to the end of the blessing and distribution of the ashes.

1. The Bishop goes to the sacristy, attended as before directed. The clergy put on their vestments in the sacristy; they go out from the sacristy to the sanctuary, as directed, page 284, except that the celebrant, preceded by the deacon and sub-deacon, walks immediately before the assistant priest.

2. On arriving at the sanctuary, the clergy go to their usual places, the celebrant, with the deacon and sub-deacon, to their bench, and the Bishop, with his assistants, to his seat, after having respectively made the usual genuflections and bows. The Bishop is vested as directed, page 286.

3. The sub-deacon, attended by the second master of ceremonies, goes up to the altar, and taking, with both hands, the vase containing the ashes, carries it, raised before his face, to the throne, and holds it there, kneeling at the right of the Bishop, till the end of the blessing.

4. The acolytes, with the book and the candlestick, go before the Bishop, who, sitting with the mitre on, reads the antiphon, *Exaudi nos;* which being repeated after the Psalm by the choir, the Bishop rises, with his head uncovered, and sings, in the ferial tone, *Dominus vobiscum, Oremus,* and the four prayers as in the Missal.

5. After the prayers, the Bishop puts incense into the censer and blesses it, sprinkles and incenses the ashes three times.

6. Then he sits with his head uncovered; the celebrant, accompanied by the master of ceremonies, goes to the Bishop, and having bowed to him, puts ashes on his head, saying, *Memento homo,* etc.

7. The Bishop puts on the mitre, the apron is placed on his knees, and he puts ashes on the head of the celebrant, who kneels before him;* to whom he says *Memento,* etc.

8. Then the Bishop puts ashes on the heads of the assistant priest, assistant deacons, officiating deacon, and all the clergy, who go for this purpose to receive them, according to their respective rank and order, kneeling whilst the ashes are put on. Last of all, he puts ashes on the people at the railing; in doing which, he may be assisted by a priest, if the number of people is great.

9. Afterwards, he returns to his seat and washes his hands as usual; then rises, with his head uncovered, and

---

* Only canons bow profoundly, the rest kneel.

sings, *Dominus vobiscum*, and the prayer as in the Missal, during which two acolytes remain before him, with their candlesticks and lighted candles.

10. After the prayer, the clergy go to take off the sacred vestments; the Bishop keeps his on, and assisted and vested as before, does everything at Mass as directed, page 300, observing what follows.

11. At the Collects, the Bishop kneels at the faldstool or praying desk, in the middle of the sanctuary, between his assistants. Again, he kneels in the same place, but with his mitre on, during the whole verse, *Adjuva*, sung by the choir. Also the celebrant, with his ministers, kneels before the altar during the same.

12. The deacon and sub-deacon observe what has been said before.

13. The preacher, after the Gospel has been sung, goes to ask the Bishop's blessing, and announces the Indulgences.

14. The Bishop, having said the *Sanctus*, kneels as for the Collects, till the *Per omnia sæcula*, before the *Agnus Dei*. So also all the clergy in the sanctuary. At the Post Communion, the Bishop kneels in the same manner; after the celebrant has sung the last *Oremus*, the deacon, turned towards the people, sings, *Humiliate capita*, etc. The rest is done as usual. What has been said in particular for this Mass, is to observed in all ferial Masses during Advent and Lent.

CHAPTER VII.

SUNDAYS IN LENT.

1. For the Sundays in Lent, everything is to be observed as directed for Sundays in Advent.

2. What has been said for the third Sunday in Advent, is to be observed also for the fourth Sunday in Lent.

3. Before the first Vespers of Passion Sunday, all the crosses and images on the altar and in the church are to be covered.

CHAPTER VIII.

PALM SUNDAY.

ARTICLE I.

Things to be Prepared.

1. On the altar, the Bishop's vestments, as directed, page 282.

2. On the side-table, everything as there directed; also the large stole for the deacon.

3. By the side-table, as there stated. The processional cross is to be covered with a violet veil.

4. Between the Bishop's seat and the altar, a table covered all over with a white linen cloth, and on it the palms to be blessed, and that of the Bishop adorned with flowers.

5. In the sanctuary, on the Gospel side, three stands for the deacons who are to sing the Passion.

6. In the sacristy, the sacred vestments for the celebrant, deacon, and sub-deacon, as directed in chap. vi. Also three violet stoles and maniples, with three cinctures, albs, amices, and books, for three deacons who are to sing the Passion.

ARTICLE II.

From the entrance of the Bishop and Clergy into the Church to the beginning of Mass.

1. The Bishop goes to the sacristy, attended as directed, page 284.

2. The clergy put on their vestments in the sacristy.

3. All go out from the sacristy to the sanctuary.

4. The Bishop puts on the sacred vestments. All is done as directed, page 285.

5. The Bishop being vested, the choir sings *Hosanna*, etc., which the Bishop reads in the meantime, and then sings, in a ferial tone, *Dominus vobiscum*, and the prayer as in the Missal. The sub-deacon sings the Epistle with the usual ceremonies, and the Bishop reads it as well as the Gradual, *Munda cor meum*, and the Gospel. The deacon sings the Gospel with the usual ceremonies. After the Gospel, the sub-deacon carries the book to the Bishop, who kisses it, and is afterwards incensed by the assistant priest.

6. Then the Bishop sings *Dominus vobiscum*, and the prayer, *Auge*, as in the Missal, and after it the Preface; which being ended, the choir sings, and the Bishop says the *Sanctus*. Afterwards the Bishop sings the five prayers, as in the Missal. Whilst he is singing the last prayer, two acolytes go before him with the censer and incense-boat, and with the holy-water and sprinkle. The last prayer being ended, the Bishop puts incense into the censer, blesses it, sprinkles thrice the palms, saying, *Asperges me*, without the Psalm, and incenses them thrice. Then he sings *Dominus vobiscum*, and the prayer, *Deus qui Filium, tuum;* and having finished it, he sits down, and puts on the mitre.

7. The first in dignity amongst those who are present on invitation from the master of ceremonies, goes to the Bishop, and gives him the palm, kissing it and the Bishop's hand. The apron, prepared for this purpose, is then put on the Bishop's knees, and one of the acolytes furnishing, one by one, the palms to the second assistant deacon, the deacon gives them to the Bishop, who distributes them, first to the priest from whom he received it, then to the assistant priest and assistant deacon, to the deacon and sub-deacon, and all the clergy, who go to receive them, two by two, and kiss both the palm and the Bishop's hand, making the usual reverences. The choir, during the distribution, sings, *Pueri Hebræorum*.

8. After the distribution, the Bishop washes his hands. Then two acolytes, with their candlesticks and lighted candles, go before the Bishop, who, standing with his head uncovered, sings *Dominus vobiscum*, and the prayer,

Omnipotens sempiterne Deus; at the end of which he sits down, puts on the mitre, and puts incense into the censer, as usual.

In the meanwhile, everything is prepared for the procession. The first assistant deacon sings, *Procedamus in pace.* They all carry the palms in their hands. The Bishop, between the assistant deacons, holds the palm in his left, and blesses the people with his right. The officiating deacon walks at the left of the assistant priest. The choir sings the antiphons as in the Missal.

9. The procession moves out of the church; there they divide and place themselves as directed, page 228; two or four of the singers remain within the church; the doors are shut, the *Gloria, laus,* is sung, and after it, when the sub-deacon knocks at the door with the foot of the cross, it is opened, the procession enters the church, the choir singing *Ingrediente Domino.*

10. The procession having returned to the sanctuary, the Bishop goes to his seat, and remains for Mass in his sacred vestments; but the others take them off. The celebrant comes from the sacristy to the sanctuary, and Mass is celebrated, as directed in page 230 and page 300.

11. What follows, is particularly to be observed at Mass.

12. When the sub-deacon, at the Epistle, sings the words, *Ut in nomine Jesu omne genu flectatur,* the Bishop and all the clergy kneel till after the words, *Et infernorum.*

13. Whilst the Epistle and Tract are sung, three deacons go to the sacristy, put on amices, albs, cinctures, maniples, and stoles, and at the end of the Tract, preceded by the master of ceremonies, go to the sanctuary in the following order, carrying the Book before their breast: First the deacon, who sings the words of the Evangelist; second, he who sings the words of the crowd; third, he who sings the words of Christ. They are followed by three acolytes, without candlesticks, and without the censer; after having made the usual genuflection and bows, they go to kiss the Bishop's hand,

without asking the blessing. They go to the place where the Passion is to be sung, and place themselves as directed, page 231, the acolytes holding the books.

14. When they begin to sing the Passion, the Bishop and all the clergy rise, with their heads uncovered, and stand with the palms in their hands till the end of it. The celebrant reads it at the Epistle side, and when he has done reading, he turns towards the deacons of the Passion, and stands at the corner of the altar, the deacon also on the middle step, and the sub-deacon before the lowest step, with palms in their hands; at the words *Emisit spiritum*, the Bishop and all the clergy kneel at their places.

15. After the Passion, the Bishop sits, says *Munda cor meum*, and reads the Gospel; the deacon takes off his folded chasuble, puts on the large stole, carries the book to the altar, kisses the Bishop's hand, goes to the altar, kneels, and says *Munda cor meum*; at the same time, the Bishop puts incense into the censer as usual; then the deacon and sub-deacon, with the censer-bearer, and two acolytes, without candlesticks, go to the Bishop's seat, the deacon asks his blessing, the Gospel is sung as usual, and the Bishop, having kissed the book, is incensed by the assistant priest.

16. At the elevation, the Bishop alone holds the palm in his hand. The rest is done as in other Masses.

CHAPTER IX.

MATINS OF THE TENEBRÆ.

1. For these Matins, everything is to be prepared as directed, page 233, and when the Bishop officiates at them, everything is done as there specified.

2. If the Bishop, occupies his usual seat, he has no other assistant than the master of ceremonies, who sits in some place near; but it is advisable that the Bishop should sit in a choir-stall with the other clergymen.

3. The Bishop rises with the clergy, and kneels and recites the prayer, *Respice.*

4. On Maunday Thursday, and on Good-Friday, for the Tenebræ, the altar, the Bishop's throne, and faldstool should be quite bare.

CHAPTER X.

MAUNDAY THURSDAY.

Article I.

Things to be Prepared.

1. A CHAPEL for the repository.
2. The high altar, as on the greatest festivities, with white altar veil, etc.
3. On the altar, the Bishop's vestments, with the exception of the cope. A chalice, with a purifier, for cleansing the Bishop's fingers.
4. On the side-table, besides everything necessary for the Pontifical Mass, two particles on the paten, one of which should be of a size to fit the chalice in which it is to be placed; a second chalice, with its paten, pall, veil, and a white ribbon to fasten the veil round the chalice; a pyx, with a sufficient number of small particles, for the Communion of the clergy and people; a long linen cloth for the Communion of the clergy.

By the side-table, the processional cross.

5. In a convenient place, in or near the sanctuary, the canopy for the procession.
6. In the sanctuary, in the middle towards the railing, a table covered with fine linen cloth, two candlesticks and candles, and the Pontifical on a cushion or stand on it, on that side which corresponds to the Gospel side. Behind the table, a chair for the Bishop, with three stools for the assistant deacons on each side, and for the

assistant priest on the Gospel side. On each side of the table, six seats, or a bench sufficient for six persons, covered with suitable cloth. Behind the Bishop's chair, placed near the table, seats for the seven deacons and seven sub-deacons, who assist at the consecration of the oils.

7. In the sacristy, besides the usual white vestments for the assistant priest and deacons, and for the officiating deacon and sub-deacon, twelve white chasubles, stoles, and maniples, with as many cinctures, albs, and amices, for twelve priests; also seven white dalmatics, stoles, and maniples, with as many cinctures, albs and amices, for seven deacons, and seven white tunics and maniples, with seven cinctures, albs, and amices, for seven sub-deacons, who are all to assist at the consecration of the oils; besides, a sufficient number of sacred vestments for the other clergy, according to their order and rank, if there be any more. Moreover, two censers and incense-boat, and a wooden clapper. Candles in sufficient number for the procession.

8. In a suitable place, either in the sacristy, or near the baptismal font, three metal vases, large enough to contain a sufficient quantity of oil for all the churches of the diocese. On one of them there should be engraven at least the initials of these words, *Oleum Infirmorum*, on another, *Oleum Catechumenorum*, and on the third, *Sanctum Chrisma*. The first and second should be covered with silk cloth of any color, the third with white silk cloth. Near them, should be prepared two long veils for the deacons, who are to carry the vases containing the oil of catechumens and the chrism. Also near the vase, a plate, and in it a small vessel containing the balsam, and a spatula to mix it.

9. For the washing of the feet, should be prepared the necessary vessels to hold the water, which should be a litte warm; and basins for washing the feet; also, a sufficient number of towels to wipe them; the ewer, basin, and towels for the Bishop to wash and wipe his hands; also a large towel with strings, which the Bishop puts before him, when he washes the feet; two benches,

capable of containing six persons each, higher than usual, before which there should be a step; the book of the Gospel, a violet stole, and cope, for the Bishop; and white dalmatic, tunic, stole, and maniples, for the deacon and sub-deacon; the candlesticks, with lighted candles, for the acolytes, and the censer and incense-boat.

ARTICLE II.

From the entrance of the Bishop and Clergy into the sanctuary, to the beginning of Mass.

1. The Bishop goes to the sacristy as before directed.

2. As soon as the Bishop and clergy arrive at the sacristy, they go into the sanctuary before they put on the sacred vestments. After a short prayer, they all rise, and say *None*, which is not to be sung. The Bishop, at the same time, reads the Psalms for the preparation of Mass, without *Gloria Patri*, and they put on him the stockings and sandals. The Psalms of *None* being ended, the Bishop goes to the middle, kneels before the faldstool, and all the clergy kneel at their places, during *Christus*, *Pater*, and *Miserere*, etc.; at the end of which the Bishop says the prayer *Respice*.

3. The prayer *Respice* being ended, the clergy who have to put on the sacred vestments, go for this purpose to the sacristy. The Bishop goes to his seat; the deacon and sub-deacon, who should take their sacred vestments during *None*, go to the Bishop's side, and help to take off his cape, wash his hands, and put on the sacred vestments as before directed.

ARTICLE III.

From the beginning to the end of Mass.

1. As soon as the clergy have put on their vestments, they go to their places in the sanctuary, and the Bishop being vested, the deacon and sub-deacon put on their maniples, the assistant deacons go to the side of the Bishop, and Mass is celebrated as usual, with the following exceptions.

2. At the Confession the Psalm, *Judica*, is omitted. The organ is not played, nor the bells rung any more after the *Gloria in excelsis*. At the Offertory, the sub-deacon carries to the altar, first the ciborium for Communion, if necessary, and then the chalice; and when the wine and water are put in the chalice, he returns to the side-table and leaves off the veil; as on account of the consecration of the Holy Oils, he does not hold the *paten* during this Mass; he assists at the incensing with the deacon; he remains at the foot of the altar until the *Sanctus*, which he recites with the Bishop, going up to the platform for that purpose; he incenses the Blessed Sacrament at the elevation.

3. Before the Bishop says the words, *Per quem hæc omnia, Domine, semper bona creas*, having made a genuflection to the Blessed Sacrament, he retires to the Epistle side, near the altar, where he washes his fingers in another chalice, and wipes them, the deacon holding the chalice and the sub-deacon pouring the wine on his fingers; he then makes again a genuflection to the Blessed Sacrament, goes to the first step of the altar, puts on the mitre, takes the crosier in his hand, and between the deacon and sub-deacon, preceded by the assistant priest, goes to the seat near the table, prepared as in Art 1, n. 6, of this chapter, sits, turned towards the altar, having the table before him, and his assistants at his side, all the others remaining at their places; the assistant deacons take no part in the blessing of the Holy Oils; hence they retire to one side during the ceremony; then the assistant priest says, with a loud voice, in the tone of a Lesson, *Oleum infirmorum*. Immediately after, one of the seven sub-deacons, having at his side two acolytes, goes to the sacristy, takes the vessel with the oil to be consecrated for the sick, covered as it is, and holding its foot in his right hand, and having his left arm round it, carries it to the Bishop, and gives it into the hands of the assistant priest, saying, *Oleum infirmorum*. The assistant priest presents it to the Bishop, saying the same words, and puts it on the table.

4. The Bishop, with his mitre on, rises, and reads the

exorcisms in a low voice, loud enough, however, to be heard by the priests who are round him; after the exorcisms, the clergy answer, *Amen;* the Bishop, having taken off his mitre, says *Dominus vobiscum,* and reads also, in a low voice, the prayer, *Emitte quæsumus;* after which, the vessel is brought back to the sacristy by the sub-deacon, accompanied by two acolytes. The Bishop puts on the mitre, seats himself, and washes his hands; then, rising with his mitre on, returns to the altar attended by his ministers, and on arriving before the lowest step, takes off his mitre, makes a genuflection, goes up to the altar, and continues Mass from the words, *Per quem hæc omnia,* etc., as far as the Communion of the Sacred Body and Blood inclusively. The deacon goes up to the altar with the Bishop; the sub-deacon remains at the foot of the steps. The sub-deacon does not go up at the *Dimitte nobis;* the *Agnus Dei* is said, but the *Pax* is not given.

5. The Bishop having communicated, places the consecrated Host to be reserved for the following day in the chalice prepared for the purpose, which the master of ceremonies should have previously carried to the altar, with its veil and ribbon; the deacon covers it with the pall and the paten; over them he places the veil, which he fastens with the ribbon round the foot of the chalice, and places in the middle of the altar.

6. Then the deacon sings the *Confiteor,* and the celebrant gives the Communion, first to the deacon and sub-deacon, and afterwards to the rest of the clergy, according to their rank, beginning with the priests, who should wear the stole. To-day, the *Pax* is not given to the deacon and sub-deacon by the Bishop before the Communion.

7. The Communion being ended, the Bishop having taken not only the usual ablutions, but also that which had been previously left in the other chalice, makes a genuflection to the Blessed Sacrament, goes down to the second step, puts on the mitre, takes the crosier, and attended by the ministers as before, goes to the seat near the table.

8. The Bishop having seated himself, the assistant priest, standing near him, says in a loud voice, and in the tone of a lesson, *Oleum ad Sanctum Chrisma*, and immediately after, *Oleum Catechumenorum;* then the Bishop puts incense into the censer and blesses it. This being done, they go to the sacristy for the oils in the following order: the censer-bearer, the two acolytes with their candlesticks and lighted candles, the seven sub-deacons, two by two, and in the third row three; the seven deacons likewise; and, lastly, the twelve priests, also two by two. The Bishop, and his assistants and ministers, remain at their places.

9. The procession comes out of the sacristy in the following order: the censer-bearer, the sub-deacon with the processional cross, between the acolytes with their candlesticks, two chanters singing the verses, *O Redemptor;* six sub-deacons, two by two; five deacons, in the first row two, in the second three; a sub-deacon, carrying the vase with the balsam, two deacons carrying the vases with oil, having a long veil hanging from their neck before their breast, holding the vases with their left arms round them, and covering the lower part of the vases with that part of the veils which hangs on their right; the deacon carrying the oil for the chrism, walks at the right, and he that carries the oil of catechumens at the left; last of all, the twelve priests, two by two. As they move from the sacristy, the chanters begin to sing the verses, *O Redemptor*, etc., which are immediately repeated by the choir; as also after each strophe sung by the chanters.

10. When the procession arrives at the sanctuary, the censer-bearer and the sub-deacon with the cross, between the acolytes, place themselves near the altar at the Epistle side; the twelve priests, six on each side of the assistant deacons, with their faces turned towards the altar, the deacons behind the Bishop, and the sub-deacons behind the deacons. The sub-deacon with the balsam, and the deacons with the oil, stop until the others have taken their places. Which being done, the deacon with the oil for the chrism goes before the Bishop, and

the assistant priest, receiving from him the vase wrapped in the veil, which the deacon had round his neck, presents it to the Bishop, and lays it on the table before him. In the meanwhile, the other deacon holds the vessel of the oil of the catechumens on his arm. Then the sub-deacon with the balsam gives the vase which contains it to the assistant priest, who, having presented it to the Bishop, lays it on the table. The Bishop takes off his mitre, rises, and turned towards the altar, blesses the balsam, saying, *Dominus vobiscum*, and the two prayers, as found in the Roman Pontifical. The second prayer being ended, the Bishop, still standing, puts on the mitre, and mixes in a paten, or in another vessel, the balsam with some oil, which is taken from the vase, saying the third prayer.

11. After the third prayer, the clergy having answered, *Amen*, the Bishop standing, with his mitre on, breathes thrice in the form of a cross over the mouth of the vase, which is yet kept wrapped in the veil. Then the twelve priests breathe over it in the same manner as the Bishop, one after another, making genuflections to the Blessed Sacrament on the altar, and bowing to the Bishop both before and after. Which being done, the Bishop rises, and, with his mitre on, reads the exorcism; at the end of which, he takes off his mitre, and with his hands extended before his breast, he sings the Preface as in the Pontifical, and having concluded it with the words, *Per eumdem Dominum*, etc., which he reads, the clergy answer, *Amen*.

12. Then the Bishop puts into the vase for the chrism, the mixture of balsam and oil, saying, *Hæc commixtio*, etc., and the deacon, who carried the vase of the chrism, removes from it the long veil in which it was wrapped. Then the Bishop bowing, sings, *Ave, Sanctum Chrisma*, three times, but the second time he raises his voice a tone higher, and the third he raises it another tone higher. After the third time, he kisses the border of the vessel, sits down and puts on his mitre.

13. The twelve priests, one after the other, make a genuflection to the Blessed Sacrament and a reverence

to the Bishop, kneel on both knees, in the middle, at a distance from the table, and sing, *Ave, Sanctum Chrisma*, then rise, go nearer the table, kneel again, sing, *Ave, Sanctum Chrisma*, a tone higher; rise, approach the table, kneel, sing *Ave Sanctum Chrisma*, another tone higher; then rise and kiss the border of the vase. They then return to their places, having made a genuflection to the Blessed Sacrament on the altar, and a bow to the Bishop. This being done by the twelve priests, the vase with the chrism is placed on one side of the table.

14. The deacon who holds the vase of the oil of catechumens goes before the Bishop, and gives it (without the veil, which he retains) to the assistant priest, who, having shown it to the Bishop, places it on the middle of the table before the Bishop who immediately after rises, and breathes over it thrice in the form of a cross, and sits down. The twelve priests, one after the other, breathe over it in like manner. Then the Bishop rises, with his mitre on, and reads in a low voice, the exorcisms; at the end of which, the clergy answer, *Amen*. The Bishop takes off his mitre, and standing, says, in a low voice, *Dominus vobiscum*, etc., *Oremus*, and the prayer, *Deus, incrementorum*, for the blessing of the oil of catechumens, which being ended, the clergy answer, *Amen*. Afterwards, the Bishop sings thrice, *Ave Sanctum Oleum*, as has been said, n. 12, for the chrism, and kisses the brim of the vase; the same is done likewise by the twelve priests, as directed in n. 13.*

15. All this being done, the deacons take the vases in their arms, and the procession is arranged as in n. 9, to bring back to the sacristy the consecrated oil and the chrism, the chanters singing the verses, *Ut novetur*, and the choir repeating after each strophe, *O Redemptor*.

16. Whilst they go to the sacristy, the Bishop, sitting, washes his hands, returns to the altar, and continues Mass as usual; but every time he goes to or from the

---

* Mgr. Martinucci says that the twelve priests should not genuflect in this case, but only make a bow towards the oil of catechumens. The Pontifical says, *Reverenter salutant Oleum*.

middle of the altar, he makes a genuflection to the Blessed Sacrament, and when he says *Dominus vobiscum*, does not not turn his back to the Blessed Sacrament, but draws back a little towards the Gospel side. After the *Ite, Missa est*, the Bishop standing, without mitre, on the Gospel side, without turning completely round, gives the solemn blessing. But the Indulgences are to be published in the chapel of the repository.

17. The Bishop, at the words *In principio erat Verbum*, should not make the sign of the cross, as usual, on the altar, but only on himself.

Article IV.

The Procession to the Repository.

1. After the Gospel of St. John, he goes to his seat, takes off the sacred vestments as far as the stole exclusively, and puts on a white cope. In the same time, another sub-deacon in tunic, takes the processional cross, covered with a violet veil, and the acolytes their candlesticks; candles are distributed to the clergy, and lighted; the canopy is brought outside of the railing, and given to those who are to carry it.

2. The Bishop, at his seat, with his mitre on, puts incense into the two censers, but he does not bless it, neither does the assistant priest kiss the spoon, nor the Bishop's hand. Then the Bishop, with his assistants, goes to the altar, takes off his mitre, and kneeling on a cushion on the lowest step of the altar, he incenses thrice the Blessed Sacrament; the long veil is put on his shoulders, and fastened before his breast. The first assistant deacon goes up to the altar, and after the usual genuflections, takes the Blessed Sacrament, and, standing, presents it to the Bishop, kneeling down on the highest step; who, having received it, rises, and the deacon makes a genuflection, and the choir begins to sing *Pange Lingua*. The assistant deacons, on each side of the Bishop, raise the extremities of his cope, and the master of ceremonies raises up his vestments in front, when he goes up or down the steps. The procession

walks to the repository in the following order: the sub-deacon between the acolytes with their candlesticks, the chanters, the inferior clergy, the acolyte carrying the crosier, the sub-deacons, the deacons, the priests in chasubles, the deacon and sub-deacon, the assistant priest, the two censer-bearers, moving slowly and regularly their censers; the Bishop, between the two assistant deacons under the canopy, followed by the acolytes, with the mitre, book, candle, etc.

3. The cross-bearer and the acolytes, on arriving near the door of the chapel, retire a little on one side to make way for the procession, and remain there standing and turned towards the procession. Those of the clergy who walk next to the cross-bearer stop, the first on each side of the chapel, and those who follow stop next to them, so that the clergymen who walked the last may be the nearest to the altar of the repository, and divide into two lines, and the Bishop, with the assistant ministers, passes between them. The censer-bearers, on entering the chapel, keep their censers motionless. Those who carry the canopy, stop at the door of the chapel.

4. The Bishop, on arriving at the highest step of the altar, stops, and the deacon kneeling down, receives from him the Blessed Sacrament, and immediately places It in the urn, or tabernacle, prepared for the purpose, leaving the door opened. Then the Bishop goes down to the second step, puts incense into the censer, kneels down, and incenses thrice the Blessed Sacrament. The deacon shuts the door of the urn, and the Bishop goes up to the altar, makes a genuflection, kisses the altar, takes in his left hand the crosier, and standing at the Gospel side, without mitre, gives the solemn blessing; after which the assistant priest publishes, as usual, the forty-days' Indulgences.

5. The procession returns to the sanctuary in the same order as it came; the Bishop, on arriving at his seat, takes off the sacred vestments. The clergy take theirs off in the sacristy. Then Vespers are recited, and the altars stripped.

Article V.

The Mandatum, or Washing of the Feet.

1. At a convenient hour, the Bishop and clergy meet in the place prepared for the washing of the feet. The Bishop puts on the amice, alb, cincture, with a violet stole and cope, and plain mitre. The deacon and sub-deacon, with the assistant priest, put on white vestments as for Mass.

2. Thirteen poor men, or thirteen clergymen, sit on high benches, with a high step in front; the covering of their right feet should be so arranged as to make it easy to remove it, when they are to be washed.

3. The Bishop, attended as usual by his assistants, at his seat or faldstool, puts incense into the censer and blesses it. Then the deacon holding the Missal before his breast, with the sub-deacon, the two acolytes carrying their candlesticks, go before the Bishop, kneel down, and the deacon asks the blessing, saying, *Jube Domne*, etc., which the Bishop gives him as usual, saying *Dominus sit*, etc. The Gospel is afterwards sung with the usual ceremonies; the book is carried to the Bishop by the sub-deacon, and the Bishop is incensed by the deacon.

4. After the Gospel, the choir sings *Mandatum novum*, and what follows as in the Missal; the Bishop takes off his cope, receives the *gremiale*, and with his mitre on, goes before the first poor man, or clergyman, kneels on a cushion, which for this purpose is moved by an acolyte, as he passes on, and the ewer and basin being brought by the attending clergymen, the Bishop washes the right foot, wipes it with a towel, and kisses it; and if a poor man, he gives him some alms. He does in like manner to the other twelve.

5. After having washed their feet, the Bishop returns to his seat, washes his hands, takes off the *gremiale*, which he had tied on him, puts on the cope, and takes off his mitre. The two acolytes with their candlesticks, and a third one with the book, and a fourth with the candle-

stick, go before him, and rising, he says, *Pater Noster*, etc., *Et ne nos*, etc., with the following verses and prayers as in the Missal. After which, the Bishop, raising his hands, makes the sign of the cross towards those who are present. Lastly, he takes off the sacred vestments, and retires.

CHAPTER XI.

GOOD FRIDAY.

ARTICLE I.

What is to be Prepared.

1. THE altar, the seat intended for the Bishop, the sacred ministers's bench, and all the sanctuary, should be quite bare, without any ornaments.

2. On the altar, the cross, covered with a black veil, but in such manner as to render it easy to uncover its different parts successively; six plain candlesticks, with unbleached wax candles; the Bishop's vestments, viz., an amice, alb, and cincture, with a black maniple, stole, dalmatic, tunic, and chasuble, the pectoral cross, and the plain white mitre. The sandals, gloves, and crosier are not used on this day.

3. On the small table should be spread a linen cloth, which ought not, however, to hang down; and on this table should be placed the ewer and basin, with a towel on a plate; the cruets, a book-stand with a Missal, another Missal, an altar-cloth folded, a large black stole for the deacon, a black burse with a purifier and a corporal, a black veil for the chalice, two candlesticks, with unbleached wax candles, for the acolytes.

4. In the sacristy, the sacred vestments for the deacon and sub-deacon, viz., two amices, albs, and cinctures, and a stole; a black cope for the assistant priest; also two folded chasubles of the same color, with cinctures, albs,

and amices, for the two assistant deacons. Likewise, a sufficient number of sacred vestments for the clergy. Also, three amices, albs, cinctures, with as many black maniples and stoles, and three Missals, for the deacons who have to sing the Passion. Two censers with incense-boats, a chafing-dish with fire and tongs, the tapers and candles for the procession.

5. At the Gospel side in the sanctuary, a violet carpet, with a long white veil, and a violet velvet cushion, adorned with gold-lace and embroidery, for the veneration of the cross. Also, three bare book-stands or desks, for those, who are to sing the Passion.

6. Before the middle of the altar, and at the foot of the lowest step, the praying-desk bare, and five cushions, to be placed on the highest step of the altar, for the prostration of the Bishop's assistants and ministers, three on the Epistle side, and two on the Gospel side.

7. In any convenient place, the processional cross, covered with a violet veil, and the wooden clapper.

8. At the chapel of the repository, besides the canopy, the white veil on the side-table, and the key of the tabernacle on the altar; also near it, the steps (if necessary) to reach the door of the tabernacle.

9. On the minister's bench, the folded chasubles, and maniples for the deacon and sub-deacon.

Article II.

From the entrance of the Bishop and clergy into the sanctuary, to the beginning of the Office.

1. The Bishop goes to the sacristy as directed in the first part of this book.

2. From the sacristy, the clergy, before they put on the sacred vestments, go with the Bishop to the sanctuary: only the deacon and sub-deacon remain in the sacristy, and put on the sacred vestments, the folded chasubles and maniples excepted. The Bishop and clergy having entered the sanctuary, kneel, pray for a short space of time, and rise. The Bishop goes to his

seat; they all say *Pater* and *Ave*, in a low voice, and when the Psalm *Mirabilia* is begun, they sit down, and continue *None*. At the end of this canonical hour, the Bishop goes to the praying-desk, and, with the clergy, kneels during the *Christus* and *Miserere ;* the Bishop says the prayer *Respice,*. at the end of which they all rise; the Bishop goes to his seat; the deacon and sub-deacon come from the sacristy, go to his side and assist him to put on his vestments.

At the same time, the clergy put on their sacred vestments in the sacristy. The two assistant deacons go to the side of the Bishop, and the deacon and sub-deacon go to their bench, and put on their maniples and folded chasubles.

ARTICLE III.

From the beginning of the Office to the end of it.

1. The Bishop, being vested, goes to the middle, and taking off his mitre, kneels before the praying desk; at the same time the assistant priest and deacons, with the officiating deacon and sub-deacon, prostrate themselves on the cushions, which the acolytes place on the steps as directed above. All the clergy kneel, and remain praying for some time. Meanwhile, two acolytes unfold the altar-cloth.

2. The Bishop and ministers rise, go up to the altar, and kiss it. An acolyte places the faldstool on the platform, at the Epistle side, and the Bishop sits on it, turned towards the Gospel side (for to-day he does not go to his seat, before the end of the Office); the assistant priest sits on the first step, at the feet of the Bishop, and behind him, on the same step, the deacon and sub-deacon; and near. these, the two assistant deacons. The clergy sit at their usual places.

3. One of the clergy, attended by the master of ceremonies, having made the usual genuflection and reverences, goes to the place where the Epistle is usually sung, and there sings the Lesson in the tone of a

Prophecy. He does not kiss the Bishop's hand; but, leaving the book in the hands of the master of ceremonies, makes the usual genuflection and reverences, and returns to his place. Whilst the Tract is sung by the choir, the Bishop, still sitting, reads the Lesson and the Tract from the book, which an acolyte holds before him; but he is not accompanied by the other, nor do the acolytes carry the candlesticks on this day. The Bishop's assistants and ministers stand by him whilst he reads.

4. After the Tract, the Bishop takes off his mitre, rises, and turning towards the altar, sings *Oremus*. The deacon sings *Flectamus genua;* and the sub-deacon, *Levate;* standing, one after the other, behind the Bishop. At the words, *Flectamus*, etc., all, except the Bishop, kneel, and at the word *Levate* they rise. Then the Bishop sings the prayer; during which the sub-deacon takes off his folded chasuble, and at the end of the prayer sings the second Lesson in the tone of the Epistle, during which the Bishop, with his assistants and the clergy, sit as before. After the Epistle, the sub-deacon does not kiss the Bishop's hand; but he resumes his chasuble, and returns to his place. The Bishop sits, and whilst the choir sings the Tract, he reads the Epistle and the Tract, attended as usual.

5. Whilst the Tract is sung, the three deacons, who are to sing the Passion, go to the sacristy, put on the sacred vestments, and towards the end of the Tract go out to the sanctuary, and sing the Passion. Everything is done as at page 349, except that they do not kiss the Bishop's hand.

The Bishop, attended by his assistants, reads the Passion out of the Missal placed on the altar at the Epistle side, and makes a genuflection there at the words *Et inclinato capite*.

6. After the Passion, the Bishop and the clergy seat themselves; the officiating deacon takes off his chasuble, puts on the large stole, carries the book to the altar, kneels, says, *Munda cor meum*, takes the book, and, without asking the blessing, goes with the sub-deacon, and the acolytes without candlesticks, and without the

censer, to sing the last part of the Passion, in the tone of the Gospel; which being done, they all return to their places.

7. If there is a sermon, the preacher accompanied by the master of ceremonies, goes to the Bishop, and asks the Indulgences, without, however, asking the blessing; and having made the usual genuflection and reverences, goes to the pulpit and preaches. The Bishop sits at the Epistle side, but turned towards the preacher. All the clergy sit during the sermon. After the sermon, the preacher publishes the Indulgences. Then the Bishop immediately takes off the mitre, and rises; the chair is removed, and the prayers are sung as in the Missal; the Bishop singing *Oremus*, the deacon *Flectamus genua*, and the sub-deacon, *Levate*. Whilst the last prayers are sung, the acolytes spread the carpet on the steps of the altar, and put the cushion on the lower steps, and over it the veil on which the cross is to be laid.

8. After all the prayers, the Bishop takes off his chasuble, goes to the back corner of the altar, at the Epistle side, and turns towards the people. The sacristan, taking the cross from the altar, gives it to the deacon, and the deacon to the Bishop, who, having received it respectfully, with his right hand uncovers the top as far as the cross-piece, and raising it with both hands, sings, *Ecce lignum Crucis*, out of the book which the assistant priest holds before him; the deacon being at the Bishop's right and the sub-deacon at the left. All rise with their heads uncovered; the Bishop, assisted by the ministers, continues to sing, *In quo salus mundi pependit;* and the choir and all the clergy, the Bishop only excepted, kneeling on both knees, and bowing their heads, answer, *Venite, adoremus;* after which, the Bishop, with the assistant priest and ministers, goes up to the platform, and stops at the Epistle side, where he uncovers the right arm and head of the crucifix, and raising his voice one tone higher, sings again, *Ecce lignum Crucis;* and everything is done as before. Afterwards he goes to the middle of the altar with all his assistants; there he uncovers the whole cross, giving the veil to the sub-

deacon, by whom it is given to an acolyte, who carries it to the small table; and the Bishop then sings, one tone still higher than the second time, *Ecce lignum Crucis;* and everything is done the third time as before.

The Bishop goes alone to the place prepared for the cross, carrying it raised up with both hands, and lays it on the cushion. He then goes to the faldstool, takes off his shoes, and without mitre, goes between the two assistant deacons to venerate the cross, kneeling the first time near the communion-rail, and praying a little; the second time, at half the distance from it to the place where the cross is; and the third time, close to the cross, which he reverently kisses, after having prayed, and returns to the faldstool, where he puts on his shoes, chasuble, and mitre. He afterwards sits and reads, *Popule meus*, etc.

9. After the Bishop, the assistant priest, the two assistant deacons, the deacon and sub-deacon, and all the clergy, according to their respective order and dignity, go to venerate the cross, in the same manner as the Bishop. During the veneration of the cross, the choir sings the *Improperia;* and about the end of it the candles are lighted. The deacon and sub-deacon unfold the linen cloth, which had been extended by the acolytes on the altar. The deacon carries from the small table to the altar the corporal and the purifier, and having taken the corporal out of the burse, unfolds it in the middle of the altar; the master of ceremonies carries the book-stand and the Missal to the altar, and places it at the Gospel side. The veneration being ended, the deacon carries back the cross to the altar, without making any reverence, and all the clergy kneel as he passes. The Bishop sits down and washes his hands, and puts incense in the thurible.

10. Then the procession is arranged in the following order: the two censer-bearers with their censers and incense-boat; the cross-bearer in sub-deacon's vestments, between the two acolytes with their candlesticks; the clergy; the assistant priest between the deacon and sub-deacon, and the Bishop between the two assistant deacons. As they move from the middle of the altar, they all make a genuflection to the cross.

11. When the procession arrives at the repository, all place themselves as yesterday; the Bishop, on arriving at the door or entry of the chapel, takes off his mitre; on coming to the altar, he kneels, with all the clergy; and, having prayed for some time, the Bishop rises; the assistant priest presents to him the incense-boat. The Bishop puts incense into the censers; but does not bless the incense; the sacristan, if in Holy Orders, opens the tabernacle, and the Bishop having knelt down, incenses the Blessed Sacrament thrice; the long veil is put on the Bishop's shoulders, and the first assistant deacon takes the Blessed Sacrament from the tabernacle, and gives it to the Bishop, who is yet kneeling. The deacon makes a genuflection, and the Bishop, having covered the chalice with the veil hanging from his shoulders, holds it with both hands, rises, and all go in procession, as yesterday, to the altar; at the same time the choir sings, *Vexilla Regis*, etc. Those, who carry the canopy, stop at the chancel, the others form a double semi-circle before the altar, and kneel down till after Communion, holding the lighted candles in their hands.

12. The Bishop, on arriving at the steps of the altar, standing, gives the Blessed Sacrament to the officiating deacon, who receives it kneeling, and places it on the altar. The Bishop, having taken off the veil, kneels on a cushion, on the lowest step. He afterwards rises, and being attended by the assistant priest, puts incense into the censer without blessing it. He incenses the Blessed Sacrament thrice, goes up to the altar, takes the Blessed Sacrament out of the chalice, and taking care not to touch It, places It on the paten which is held by the officiating deacon; and having received the paten from the hands of the same, lays the Sacred Host on the corporal, without saying anything. If he happen to touch the Blessed Sacrament, he washes his fingers in some vessel prepared for this purpose; the deacon puts wine into the chalice, and the sub-deacon water, which is not blessed by the Bishop, who does not say the usual prayer; but having received the chalice from the deacon, places it on the altar, and the deacon covers it with the pall.

13. The Bishop, having received the incense-boat from the assistant priest, put incense into the censer, without blessing it, and incenses first the sacred offerings, saying, *Incensum istud;* secondly, the cross, and thirdly, the altar, saying, *Dirigatur, Domine,* etc., making a genuflection before and after, and every time he passes before the Blessed Sacrament; and having incensed the altar, he gives the censer to the deacon, saying, *Accendat in nobis, Domine,* etc. The Bishop is not incensed.

14. After the incensing, the Bishop retires a little towards the Epistle side beyond the altar, and washes his hands, without saying anything; then he goes to the middle of the altar, bows, and joins his hands, saying, *In spiritu humilitatis;* afterwards receding a little towards the Gospel side, he turns towards the people, and says, *Orate, fratres,* taking care not to make a complete circle, turning his face towards the people, and back again, towards the altar. He immediately sings in a ferial tone, *Oremus, Præceptis salutaribus moniti,* etc., and having said in a low voice, *Amen,* says the prayer, *Libera nos,* etc., in the same tone of voice in which he said the *Pater.* Having finished it, he makes a genuflection, puts the paten under the Blessed Sacrament, and taking the latter in his right hand, raises It so that It may be seen by the people; then he divides the Sacred Host in three parts as usual, and puts the smallest of them into the chalice, without making the sign of the cross. He does not say *Pax Domini,* nor *Agnus Dei;* neither does he give the *Pax.*

15. The Bishop, having put the particle into the chalice, makes a genuflection, and having said only, *Perceptio corporis,* makes again a genuflection, takes the paten with the Blessed Sacrament, says, *Panem cœlestem accipiam,* etc., signs himself with the Blessed Sacrament, saying, *Corpus Domini nostri,* etc., and communicates; he immediately consumes the wine with a part of the Host in the chalice, without saying anything; afterwards he washes his fingers (the deacon pouring, as usual, the wine into the chalice), takes the ablution, and bowing, with his hands joined, in the middle of the altar, says

only, *Quod ore sumpsimus, Domine,* etc. After this, he goes to the Epistle side, puts on the mitre, washes his hands, and goes to his seat; where, having taken off his vestments and put on the cape, he says Vespers with the clergy, who have by this time taken off the sacred vestments and put on their surplices. The candles are extinguished, and after the antiphon of the *Magnificat* has been repeated, the Bishop goes to the middle, kneels at the faldstool during the *Christus* and the *Miserere;* after which he says the prayer, *Respice,* and retires, as usual.

CHAPTER XII.

HOLY SATURDAY.

Article I.

Things to be Prepared.

1. The church, the high altar and the baptismal font should be prepared as directed, page 256. Likewise, the triple candle, the paschal candle, the new fire, the grains of incense, and everything else, as there directed.

2. In the sacristy, the sacred vestments should be prepared as usual for the assistant priest, the two assistant deacons, the deacon and sub-deacon; for the clergy according to their order and dignity; with this difference, that to-day violet vestments must be prepared; the deacon and sub-deacon make use of folded chasubles. Under the violet, white vestments must be prepared.

3. On the altar, two front veils, white and purple; the sacred vestments for the Bishop must be double, that is, white vestments should be placed immediately upon the altar, and over them violet vestments.

4. The Bishop's chair should be adorned with white ornaments, and then covered with purple cloth.

Article II.

The Blessing of the New Fire.

1. The Bishop having entered the sanctuary, prays before the high altar for a short time and goes to the throne; he takes off his cappa and receives the amice, alb, etc., and cope of violet. Meanwhile, the new fire is brought in and placed near the throne. The Bishop rises, and in a low tone says *Dominus vobiscum* and the three ensuing prayers. Near the end of the third prayer the thurifer puts some of the new fire in the censer. The Bishop then blesses the grains of incense, and sitting down, he puts incense in the censer; then he rises and receives the sprinkle from the assistant priest, and sprinkles the fire and incense, reciting meanwhile the *Asperges;* then he incenses them. The acolytes leave and the Bishop unvests, assisted by the ministers; then the assistant deacons put on him the cappa, and he sits down.

Article III.

The Exultet, and the Blessing of the Paschal Candle.

1. The Bishop, dressed in cappa, sits on his pontifical chair, having at his side the two assistant deacons and the assistant priest, and puts incense into the censer and blesses it, the assistant priest presenting to him the incense-boat.

2. The sub-deacon, in violet folded chasuble, taking the processional cross, goes with the deacon, who is habited in a white dalmatic, with a sufficient number of attending clergymen, to the place where the triple candle and other necessary things have been prepared. The Bishop, with his assistants, remains at his seat, and the rest of the clergy in the sanctuary.

3. The master of ceremonies walks first; then the censer-bearer, having at his left an acolyte; after them a sub-deacon carrying the cross; the deacon follows; and lastly four acolytes, two by two.

4. On arriving at the place prepared, the master of ceremonies lights a candle from the new fire; the deacon takes the triple candle, and one of the acolytes the plate with the grains of incense; after this, they go back in the following order: first, the acolyte, carrying with both hands the plate with the grains of incense; on his left the censer-bearer, swinging the censer gently; second, the sub deacon, carrying the cross; third, the deacon with the triple candle, and on his left the master of ceremonies with the lighted candle; lastly, the four acolytes, two by two.

5. As the deacon enters the church, he lowers the triple candle, that one of the branches may be lighted by the master of ceremonies; then he raises it again, and he, as well as all the others in the procession, except the sub-deacon carrying the cross, together with the Bishop and all the clergy, kneel on one knee, when *Lumen Christi* is sung by the deacon, and rise when *Deo gratias* is answered by the clergy. The same is done a second time when they arrive at the middle of the church, and a third time when they arrive before the altar; but the deacon, at each time, raises his voice one tone higher.

6. Then the Bishop and all in the sanctuary sit down. Those of the procession rise, and place themselves as directed, page 261. The deacon having left the triple candle in the hands of one of the acolytes, receives from the master of ceremonies the Missal; and having made the usual genuflection to the altar, and reverences to the Bishop and the clergy, goes to the Bishop, and without kissing his hand, says, *Jube, Domne,* etc.; the Bishop makes the sign of the cross towards him, using the accustomed form, *Dominus sit,* etc., saying, however, *Paschale præconium,* instead of *Evangelium.*

7. The deacon, having received the blessing, goes from the Bishop's seat to the middle before the altar, between the cross-bearer and the acolyte, who carries the triple candle, and having there made a genuflection and the usual reverences, he goes to sing the *Exultet;* he first incenses the book. The sub-deacon, with the cross turned towards the Bishop, and the thurifer stand on his

right, and the acolyte with the triple candle and the one with the grains of incense on his left.

8. When the deacon commences, the Bishop and all the clergy in the sanctuary rise, and during it stand with their heads uncovered.

Article IV.

From the end of the Exultet to the Benediction of the Baptismal Font.

1. The *Exultet* being ended, the deacon shuts the Missal, leaves it on its stand, goes to the bench of the sacred ministers, takes off his white maniple, dalmatic, and stole, and puts on the violet stole; the sub-deacon leaves the cross by the side-table, and takes off his folded chasuble and maniple, and with the deacon goes to the Bishop's seat, and the acolyte places the triple candle on its stand at the Gospel side.

2. The Bishop and all the clergy, standing with their heads uncovered, say, *Pater et Ave*, secretly, and then sit down, and *None* is recited. After the last Psalm, the Bishop kneels at the faldstool, the clergy kneeling likewise during the *Christus* and the *Miserere;* after which, the Bishop says the prayer, *Respice*. Then having returned to his seat, he reads the Psalm, *Quam dilecta*, etc., with the *Gloria Patri*, and the other verses with the following prayers; at the same time he puts on the white sandals; after the prayers he washes his hands, and puts on the pontifical vestments of violet color, including the maniple and the plain mitre, reading the appropriate prayers. The clergy likewise put on their sacred vestments; and the Bishop being vested, the two assistant deacons in violet folded chasubles, and the assistant priest in violet cope, go to the Bishop's chair, and the deacons to their bench, where they put on their violet chasubles and maniples, and sit down.

3. The Bishop rises, takes the crosier in his left hand, and attended by his assistants, and the deacon and sub-deacon, goes up to the altar, which he kisses, after

having taken off his mitre. Then having made a reverence to the cross, he puts on the mitre, takes the crosier in his left hand, and attended by the assistant deacons and priest, goes to his chair, where he sits; the deacon and sub-deacon go to their bench. All in the sanctuary sit down.

4. A book-stand is placed in the middle of the sanctuary; an acolyte or chanter, attended by the master of ceremonies, goes to it, makes a genuflection to the altar, and the usual reverences to the Bishop and to the clergy, on each side of the sanctuary, and reads the first prophecy, without the title. In the meantime, the Bishop reads the same prophecy out of the book, which an acolyte holds open before him. Whilst he reads, his assistants stand near him. The singer, having finished the prophecy, and made the usual genuflection and reverences, goes to kiss the Bishop's hand. Then the Bishop rises, sings *Oremus*, and the first assistant deacon says or sings, *Flectamus genua*. At these words, all in the sanctuary (the Bishop only excepted) make a genuflection, and the second deacon sings, *Levate;* then all rise, and the Bishop sings the prayer out of the book, which the assistant priest holds open before him. The same is done in regard to all the other prophecies, with the exception, that after the fourth, eighth, and eleventh prophecies, the choir sings the Tract, and the Bishop reads it. After the twelfth prophecy, *Flectamus genua* and *Levate* are not sung.

ARTICLE V.

Blessing the Baptismal Font.

1. After the prayer which follows the last prophecy, the Bishop takes off the maniple, chasuble, dalmatic, and tunic, and puts on a violet cope; then, with his mitre on, and the crosier in his left hand, preceded by the cross, carried by the sub-deacon and all the clergy, arranged as directed at page 264, between two assistant deacons he goes to the baptismal font, the assistant

priest walking immediately before him at the right of the deacon, and he does everything as directed in the same place, and in the Roman Missal.

2. If any child or adult is to be baptized, the Bishop baptizes them, as directed in the Roman Ritual.

3. After the blessing of the font, they return to the sanctuary in procession, in the same order as they came to the font.

ARTICLE VI.

From the Benediction of the Font to the beginning of Mass.

1. The Bishop, on arriving at the high altar, takes off his cope and mitre, and kneels, leaning on the faldstool; the assistants, deacon and sub-deacon, and all the clergy, likewise kneel; and the Litany is sung by two chanters kneeling before two stools behind the Bishop.

If there is an ordination, those who are to be ordained prostrate themselves during the Litany, which the singers interrupt at the proper place when the Bishop is to say, *Ut hos electos,* etc.

2. When the chanters sing the verse, *Per mysterium sanctæ incarnationis tuæ,* the deacon and sub-deacon go to the sacristy, take off their violet vestments, and put on white, and come out immediately.

3. At the verse, *Peccatores,* the Bishop rises with the assistant deacons and priests; the latter go to the sacristy to take off the violet vestments and put on white; the Bishop, standing in the same place, assisted by the deacon and sub-deacon, takes off the violet vestments and puts on the white; all the clergy in sacred vestments do the same. In the meanwhile, the acolytes remove from the altar the violet front-veil, and from the tabernacle the canopy of the same color, and from the small table the violet veil that covered the white; the candles are lighted, the relic cases are placed between the candlesticks, and the carpet is spread. The chanters should take care to sing the Litany very slowly from the verse, *Peccatores.*

Article VII.

From the beginning to the end of Mass.

1. The Bishop, having put on the white vestments, when the singers begin *Kyrie*, makes the Confession with his ministers, saying the Psalm *Judica* and the *Gloria Patri;* goes up to the altar, kisses both it and the book of the Gospels; puts incense into the censer and blesses it; incenses the cross and altar, and is incensed, as usual, by the deacon. Then he goes to his seat, where, having said the *Kyrie*, he sings, *Gloria in excelsis Deo*. Then all the bells are rung, and the organ is played.

2. After the hymn, *Gloria in excelsis*, the Bishop rises without mitre, turns towards the people, and sings, *Pax vobis*, and the prayer, *Deus, qui hanc sacratissimam noctem*, etc. The rest is done as usual.

3. The sub-deacon, having sung the Epistle, leaves the Missal in the hands of the master of ceremonies, and forthwith going to the Bishop, says in a clear voice, *Reverendissime Pater, Annuntio vobis gaudium magnum, quod est Alleluia*, and kisses his hand; then, either the sub-deacon or chanter intones *Alleluia* to the Bishop, who, rising without mitre, sings thrice, *Alleluia*, raising every time his voice one tone higher, and the choir every time repeats it; and after the third *Alleluia*, sings the verse, *Confitemini;* then the Bishop sits down and continues Mass as usual.

4. At the Gospel, the acolytes do not carry the candlesticks, but the book is incensed as usual, and the deacon asks the blessing. *Pax Domini sit semper vobiscum* is said; but the *Pax* is not given. *Agnus Dei* is not said, neither the *Communio*.

5. The Bishop, after the Communion and the usual ablutions, washes his hands, goes to his seat, seats himself, and the choir begins *Alleluia*, in place of Vespers. At the *Magnificat*, the sub-deacon intones the antiphon to the Bishop, which he repeats, standing; then he sits with his mitre on, puts incense into the censer, and when

the *Magnificat* is begun, he goes to the altar, takes off his mitre, makes a bow to the cross, kisses the altar, incenses the cross and the altar, returns to his seat, is incensed, as well as all the clergy, as usual, and stands till the end of the *Magnificat*. Whilst the antiphon is repeated, he sits, puts on the mitre, returns to the altar at the end of the antiphon, sings *Dominus vobiscum*, and the prayer; the deacon sings, *Benedicamus Domino, Alleluia, Alleluia;* the Bishop gives the solemn blessing, and the Indulgences are published.

Then the Bishop disrobes and retires, as usual.

CHAPTER XIII.

CEREMONIES TO BE OBSERVED IN PROVINCIAL COUNCILS.*

ARTICLE I.

What is to be done before it opens.

1. PREVIOUS notice should be given of the celebration of the Provincial Council to all the Bishops of the province, and others who are to attend.

2. On the feast of the Epiphany, when the movable feasts are published, as directed in the Roman Pontifical, Part III, *Tit. De publicatione festorum mobilium in Epiphania Domini,* adding to the usual formula before the publication of the movable feast, immediately following the day of the celebration of the Council, these words, *Die ... mensis ... hujus anni, quæ erit dominica ... Concilium provinciale Deo adjuvante in Metropolitana Ecclesia ——— inchoabitur.*

3. On the three Sundays immediately preceding the opening of the Council, it should be published from the

---

* Ex Cæremoniali Episcoporum, L. i, c. 31 et ex Pontificali Romano, Part III, Tit. Ordo ad Synodum.

pulpit before the sermon, in all the churches of the province, and the prayers of the people requested for its success. It is usual on such occasions that the Bishop of each diocese order the Collect, *De Spiritu Sancto*, to be added at Mass every day till the conclusion of the Council.

ARTICLE II.

How the Metropolitan Church is to be adorned and arranged.

1. The Metropolitan, or any other church in which the Council is to be celebrated, should be adorned as for the greatest festivals. On the evening before, the bells, with festive peals, should announce the opening of the Council.

2. The Archbishop's seat is placed at the altar; those of the Bishop's on each side of the sanctuary: those nearest to the altar are to be occupied by the senior Bishops, according to priority of consecration; they should be raised on a platform by one or two steps. The other clergymen may sit against the railing of the sanctuary; the vicars-general of any diocese, if present, taking precedence, according to priority of ordination; next, the superiors of clerical congregations; next, the provincials of religious orders; next, the theologians, according to priority of ordination. The first place is on the Gospel side. This arrangement is not quite conformable to that prescribed by the Roman Pontifical, in which it is required that the Bishops should sit in a semicircle before the Archbishop, and behind them the priests; but we have adapted ours to suit best the sanctuary of our churches.

3. The Archbishop's usual chair should be likewise prepared and adorned as on great festivals, with stools on each side for two assistant deacons; also a third one for the assistant priest.

4. The seats for the deacon and sub-deacon are to be placed, as usual, at the Epistle side, where also the side-table should be placed.

5. On those days on which one of the Bishops sings High Mass, a faldstool should be prepared on the Epistle side, on a small platform, where the officiating Bishop will sit, with his face turned towards the people; on the same side, near the side-wall of the sanctuary, and in the same direction with it, a bench should be placed, where the deacon and sub-deacon with the asssistant priest sit.

ARTICLE III.

THE OPENING OF THE COUNCIL.

SECTION I.—*What is to be prepared for it.*

1. In one of the rooms of the Archbishop's house, the following vestments are to be prepared:

For the Archbishop, sandals and stockings, amice, alb, cincture, with red stole and cope, crosier, and mitre.

For the Archbishop's assistant priest, a red cope, which he puts over his surplice or on his rochet, if he is entitled to use it.

For the Archbishop's assistant deacons, red vestments suitable to their order.

For each of the Bishops, an amice, cope, and mitre; they put the amice over their rochet.

For the officiating deacon and sub-deacon, the sacred vestments of their order.

For priests, sacerdotal vestments.

If other deacons and sub-deacons be present, besides those who officiate, a sufficient number of sacred vestments suitable to their order.

For the Archbishop on the altar, a chasuble, the dalmatic, and tunic and gloves, which he puts on immediately before he begins Mass, having taken off the cope; also the pallium.

If the Archbishop does not celebrate Mass, he remains in cope and assists at the Mass celebrated by the senior Bishop of the Province—who, in this case, puts on the pontifical dress in the Archbishop's house, and is attended by the deacon and sub-deacon, and an assistant priest.

Section II.—*The Procession.*

1. All the prelates and clergy being dressed, the procession moves from the Archbishop's house in the following order:

The censer-bearer and the second master of ceremonies.

The cross-bearer, between the acolytes carrying their candlesticks.

The inferior clergy in surplices, two by two.

Those in sacred orders in dalmatics, two by two.

The priests in chasubles, two by two.

The Bishops in mitre and cope, two by two, according to the time of consecration, those last consecrated going before.

The senior Bishop—pontifically dressed to celebrate Mass, proceded by his assistant priest, and between the deacon and sub-deacon, in case the Archbishop does not sing it—should walk after the other bishops.

The sub-deacon.

The assistant priest at the right of the deacon.

The Archbishop's cross.

The Archbishop between the two assistant deacons, and followed by the crosier and mitre bearers.

2. During the procession, the bells ring continually, and the clergy sing psalms.

3. The organ is played as the procession enters the church.

4. The clergy, as they arrive at the sanctuary, make a genuflection, bow to each other, and go to their places, where they remain standing.

5. When the Archbishop has arrived at his seat, all the clergy sit down; and he takes off his cope, and puts on the other vestments for Mass, if he celebrate.

Section III.—*Mass.*

1. The Mass is to be of the Holy Ghost, with *Gloria* and *Credo*, without any commemoration of the current Feast, or Sunday; the last Gospel is that of St. John. The Archbishop wears the pallium.

2. The Mass is sung as usual. The Bishops and priests in sacred vestments do not kneel at the Confession; they make it two by two; the one that is at the right, begins, the other at the left answers, at the Confession, and at the *Kyrie*. They bow to one another before they begin, and after they have finished, not only for the Confession and *Kyrie*, but also for the *Gloria, Credo, Sanctus*, and *Agnus Dei*, which they recite together. After the subdeacon has kissed the celebrant's hand, the second assistant deacon removes the Archbishop's mitre, and the chanters begin the *Veni Sancte Spiritus*, etc., during which all kneel. Then the celebrant rises, receives the mitre and reads the Epistle and the rest as in other Masses.

3. The deacon incenses the Bishops with three swings, and the priests in sacred vestments with two, in the order that will be pointed out for the *Pax* in the following number.

4. The *Pax* is carried by the assistant priest, first to the senior Bishop, who sits first at the Gospel side, then to the second senior Bishop, who sits first at the Epistle side; afterwards to the priest who sits first at the Gospel side, then to the other, who sits in the first place at the Epistle side.

5. The Archbishop does not give the blessing at the end of Mass, but, as it will be said below, at the end of the Session.

SECTION IV.—*The Ceremonies for the first Session, or the Opening of the Council.*

1. It is more convenient that the sermon, which is chiefly intended for the instruction of the people, should be preached after Mass; during this time the Archbishop takes off the chasuble and tunic, and puts on the cope, either in the sacistry, or in the church at his seat.

2. The faldstool is prepared below the lowest step of the altar, in the middle. The Archbishop, attended by the assistant priest and deacon, goes to the middle, salutes the Bishops on each side, and kneels before the faldstool; having taken off his mitre, he intones the antiphon,

Exaudi nos, Dominie, which is continued and chanted by the choir; after the antiphon, the chanters intone the 68th Psalm,* *Salvum me fac, Deus, quoniam intraverunt aquæ usque ad animam meam*, which is alternately sung by the clergy. After the first verse, all rise, the Archbishop sits on the faldstool, which is placed in the middle of the platform of the altar, having at his side the two assistant deacons and the assistant priest at the right of the first assistant deacon, the book-bearer and the candle-bearer holding respectively the book and the candle before him. The Bishops likewise, with their mitres, and the clergy with their caps on, sit during the Psalm.

3. After the Psalm is ended, and the anthem *Exaudi* repeated, all rise, and the Archbishop and Bishops take off their mitres. The Archbishop, turned towards the altar, sings the prayer, *Adsumus, Domine Sancte Spiritus*, etc., at the end of which the clergy answer, *Amen*. Then the Archbishop sings *Oremus*, and the prayer, *Omnipotens, sempiterne Deus;* after which the clergy answer, *Amen*.

4. Then the Archbishop, with his mitre on, kneels before the faldstool; the Bishops likewise kneel with their mitres on, and all the clergy kneel at their places. The two chanters, kneeling in the middle of the sanctuary, sing the Litany of the Saints, to which the clergy answer.

5. When the chanters have sung the verse, *Ut omnibus fidelibus defunctis*, etc., and the clergy answered, *Te rogamus, audi nos*, the Archbishop alone arises, takes the crosier in his left hand, and turned towards the clergy, sings, *Ut hanc præsentem Synodum visitare, disponere, et benedicere digneris;* the clergy answer, *Te rogamus, audi nos*. The chanters continue the Litany to the end, viz., as far as *Kyrie eleison, Christe eleison*, and *Kyrie eleison*, inclusively.

6. The Litanies being ended, they all rise, the Archbishop and Bishops take off their mitres, the Archbishop, turned towards the altar, sings *Oremus;* the first deacon,

---

* It is found at the beginning of Matins of the V. Feria.

Flectamus genua, and the second, *Levate*. The Archbishop sings the prayer, *Da, quæsumus ecclesiæ tuæ*, etc.

7. The prayer being ended the Archbishop goes up to the altar, sits on the chair or faldstool placed in the middle, turning his back to the altar. The clergy sit in the meantime, and the Archbishop puts the incense into the censer and blesses it, as usual. The deacon carries the Missal, and lays it on the altar, kneels, says, *Munda cor meum*, asks the Archbishop's blessing, and goes with the sub-deacon, master of ceremonies, censer-bearer, and acolytes, to the place where the Gospel is usually sung; having first made the genuflection to the altar, and bowed to the Archbishop, Bishops, and clergy, he sings in the usual manner the Gospel, which is taken from St. Luke, c. 9, from v. 1 to 6.

8. After the Gospel, the sub-deacon carries the Missal to the Archbishop, who kisses it; and the deacon incenses him, as usual.

9. After the Archbishop has been incensed, he takes off his mitre, and kneels before his chair, or faldstool; the Bishops likewise, having taken off their mitres, and all the clergy, kneel at their places. The Archbishop intones the hymn, *Veni Creator Spiritus*, and the choir continues to sing it; after the first strophe, they all rise, and stand till the end of the whole hymn.

10. After the hymn, all sit, and the Archbishop makes a Latin allocution to the Council, either as it is in the Roman Pontifical, or any other, as he pleases. Should he choose to have another discourse addressed to the Council by some one else, it may be made at this time.

11. The Archbishop addresses the Fathers of the Council to this effect: *Reverendissime Patres, venerabiles fratres, placetne vobis ad Dei gloriam et honorem, et ad Catholicæ Ecclesiæ amplificationem Councilium provinciale . . . . legitime convocatum, et hic congregatum hodierno die aperiri et inchoari.* The Bishops severally reply, *Placet aperiatur.* Then the Archbishop, in his own name and that of his colleagues, turning towards the people, says, *Christe nomine invocato, decernimus*

Sanctam Synodum provincialem .... *esse apertam et ita judicamus.**

12. The Archbishop then orders his secretary to read the names of those whom he proposes as officers of the Council; which being read, he says, *Placetne vobis venerabiles fratres, hosce in Concilii officiales eligendos.* The Bishops severally answer, *Placet.* The Archbishop's secretary then reads the Decree in these words: *Reverendissimus D. Archiepiscopus* .... *una cum Episcopis in hoc sacro Concilio Provinciali congregatis decernit hosce Reverendos viros in officiales hujus sancti Concilii eligendos esse, et legitime jam electos, nempe Promotorem* .... *Secretarios* .... *Magistros Cæremoniarum* .... *Cantores.*

13. The Promoter addresses the Archbishop: *Illustrissime ac Reverendissime Domine, peto ut legantur Sacro-sancti Concilii Tridentini decreta de Professione fidei, et de residentia.* The Archbishop, addressing the Bishops, says: *Venerabiles fratres, placetne vobis ut legantur decreta Concilii Tridentini de Professione fidei et de residentia?* The Bishops severally reply, *Placet legantur.* Then the Archdeacon reads the decrees.

14. Then, such of the Bishops as have not in a former Council made the profession of faith, approach to the front of the altar, take off their mitres, make a genuflection on the lowest step, salute the Archbishop, and kneeling on the step, simultaneously recite the Profession of Faith, as in the Roman Pontifical. In saying the last words, *Sic me Deus adjuvet,* etc., each Bishop places his right hand on the Book of the Gospel. After having made the usual genuflection and salutation, they retire to their places.

15. The Archbishop then gives the solemn pontifical blessing, which the Bishops receive standing, with their heads uncovered, and profoundly inclined. After this, they all retire as usual to the sacristy, where they disrobe.

---

* Ex Concil. Rhemensi, an. 1583.

Article IV.
Mode of Procedure of the Council.

1. Each day, two meetings, called Congregations, are usually held; the one private, consisting of the Bishops alone, with the secretaries of the Council, in the sacristy of the Metropolitan church, or in the Archbishop's house, in the morning, from about nine till twelve; the other public, in the afternoon, held in the Metropolitan church, from about four to six. To this latter are invited the Theologians of the Archbishop and Bishops, with the Superiors of the Religious Orders and Clerical bodies, and all the officers of the Council. The chief matters, which each prelate intends to submit to the consideration of the Council, are usually made known by him to the Archbishop, within a reasonable time before the holding of the Council, and by the Archbishop communicated to the Bishops generally. The Promoter, after the opening of the Council, appoints select committees, called also Congregations, of the inferior clergy there assembled, to whom such matters as the Bishops deem proper are referred for examination. They assemble in the morning at convenient places to investigate the matters submitted to them respectively, and their written reports are read in the public Congregations; after the reading of the reports, the Promoter suggests that any clergyman who dissents therefrom, or who wishes to propose any amendment, or to make any observation, may freely, but respectfully, deliver his sentiments. If no one rises to speak, the Promoter proposes that the report be referred to the Bishops for private consideration. Should any one choose to speak, the reference is made after the sentiments have been delivered. In speaking, the clergy follow the order in which they are seated. No clergyman speaks a second time on the same subject, unless he obtains special leave.

2. In the private Congregations of the Bishops, the matters to be submitted to the consideration of the clergy are designated; the reports of the clergy are subsequently

read, and the matters finally decided. Each prelate, according to priority of consecration, is free to express his sentiments on the respective mattters treated of in the Council. After the matters have been canvassed, the question is put by the Archbishop, and the decision made by the majority of suffrages, which are given according to the order of consecration.

3. It is usual in Councils, that all propositions be expressed in the Latin language and given in writing, and that the decrees be in the first instance drawn up in that language.

4. No special exercise of devotion is prescribed for the various Congregations. It is usual, however, to begin by the recital of the hymn, *Veni Creator Spiritus*. The evening Congregation is opened by the recital of the *Veni, Sancte Spiritus*, etc., and closed by reciting the *Sub tuum præsidium*. In this article we have stated the usages of the Baltimore Councils.

Article V.

Second Solemn Session.

1. On some day during the holding of the Council, a second solemn session is celebrated; High Mass for the deceased Bishops and clergy is sung by one of the prelates, the other prelates assisting in their pontifical robes; a discourse is usually pronounced after Mass, by a prelate or priest appointed for that purpose.

2. A faldstool or chair for the celebrant is placed on a small platform in front of the altar, at the Epistle side, so that the celebrant when sitting has his face towards the people. A bench for the assistant priest, deacon, and sub-deacon, is placed near the faldstool, parallel to the side-wall of the sanctuary. The assistant priest takes his seat on it, nearest to the Bishop's left hand; next to him sits the deacon on the same bench; the sub-deacon sits at the side of the deacon.

3. The prelates vest in the sacristy, and proceed thence to the church, in the same order as on the first

day, except that the celebrant with his assistants follows the other prelates, and walks immediately before the Archbishop.

4. The prelates go to their respective seats, and the celebrant with his assistants, having made a genuflection before the altar, salutes the Archbishop and the prelates, and then begins Mass as usual.

5. The ceremonies of the Mass are the same as on other occasions, with the following exceptions: After the Confession the Bishop ascends to the altar and kisses it, and then, having received the mitre, makes a profound bow to the cross, and goes directly, *per breviorem*, to the faldstool, where the sub-deacon, having taken off the mitre, the celebrant and assistants standing with their faces turned to the altar, the celebrant reads the Introit, and says the *Kyrie;* he turns to the people to say, *Dominus vobiscum*, and turns again to the altar to say the prayer. He sits whilst the sub-deacon sings the Epistle, which being terminated, he himself reads it with the Tract, *Sequentia, Munda cor meum*, and the Gospel. The Offertory is read by him standing with his face towards the altar, which posture is observed whenever he reads or sings anything standing.

6. At the end of the Mass, the celebrant with his assistants retires to the sacristy, and the Archbishop from his chair performs the absolution of the dead as usual.

7. After the absolution, the black ornaments are laid aside, and the prelates put on copes. The ceremonies of the session are performed as prescribed in the Roman Pontifical,—for the second day of the synod, beginning with the anthem, *Propitius esto peccatis nostris, Domine, nequando dicant gentes: ubi est Deus eorum?* and the Psalm 78, *Deus, venerunt gentes in hæreditatem tuam*, etc., which may be found in the Breviary, at Fer. V. ad Matutin. The prelates and clergy kneel while the anthem and first verse of the Psalm are sung, and then the prelates resume their mitres, and sit until the end of the Psalm, as directed in the first session. The prayers are then sung by the Archbishop, after which he resumes his seat

on the platform of the altar, and puts in and blesses the incense, and gives the blessing to the deacon; then all the prelates and clergy rise, and stand with their heads uncovered, while the deacon sings the Gospel, *Designavit Dominus*, Luke x, from the 1st verse to the 9th inclusive, with the usual ceremonies.

8. Afterwards, all kneel with their heads uncovered, whilst the first verse of the hymn, *Veni, Creator Spiritus*, is sung, which being intoned by the Archbishop, is continued by the choir and clergy. After the first verse, all rise, and stand until the termination of the hymn. Then all resume their seats, and the Archbishop addresses them in the words of the Pontifical, or others, if he thinks proper. Such decrees, as have been already agreed on, may be then read, and the assent of the Fathers asked, after which the pontifical blessing is given, and all depart

ARTICLE VI.

Third Solemn Session.

1. On the last day of the Council the third solemn session is held. The prelates wear copes and mitres as in the other sessions. Solemn Mass is celebrated by the Archbishop, or by one of the Bishops.

2. When one of the Bishops celebrates, he proceeds before the Archbishop to the sanctuary, as before expressed, and observes the other peculiar ceremonies stated in the preceding article. On ascending to the altar, after the Confession, he makes the usual incensing, and then, having received the mitre, he stands at the Epistle side of the altar, with his face turned towards the side-wall, and is incensed by the deacon. He then retires to his faldstool and reads the Introit. The censer-bearer, in the meantime, carries the censer to the assistant priest of the Archbishop, who incenses the Archbishop. After the Gospel, the celebrant is incensed by the deacon, and then the Archbishop by his assistant priest. After the Offertory, the celebrant is incensed by

his deacon, the Archbishop by his assistant priest, and the prelates by the deacon, with three swings, the clergy in sacred vestments, with two, and the inferior clergy with one.

3. The *Pax* is given by the celebrant, first to the assistant priest of the Archbishop, who, advancing to the altar, kneels down as usual, whilst the previous prayer is recited. The deacon and sub-deacon then receive the *Pax* from the celebrant. In the meantime, the assistant priest of the Archbishop gives the *Pax* to the Archbishop, who immediately gives it to his assistant deacons. The assistant priest of the celebrant, after the deacon and sub-deacon have received the *Pax*, goes to the assistant priest of the Archbishop, and from him receives the *Pax*, which he subsequently gives to the first prelate on each side, and to the first among the clergymen. The Bishop, who receives from him the *Pax*, gives it to the next, and so on.

4. The celebrant does not give any blessing at the end of Mass, but having secretly said the prayer, *Placeat*, etc., recites the Gospel of St. John, and, with his attendants, retires to the sacristy.

5. The Archbishop advances towards the altar and kneels by his faldstool below the lowest step. He begins the anthem, *Exaudi nos, Domine, quoniam benigna est misericordia tua, est secundum multitudinem miserationem tuarum respice nos, Domine;* which is chanted as the Psalm, *Salvum, me fac, Deus,* on the first day. Then three prayers are sung by the Archbishop, and the Gospel is sung, taken from the xviii chap. of St. Matthew, from the 15th to the 22d v. The hymn, *Veni, Creator,* is sung as in the preceding sessions. The Archbishop, seated on his faldstool on the platform of the altar, addresses his brethren in the words of the Pontifical, or in such other terms as he deems expedient. A sermon is delivered by a prelate, or priest, appointed by the Council, unless it has been already delivered during Mass, or subsequently. The secretary of the Council, by order of the Archbishop, reads the decrees which have been prepared in the private Congregations

of the prelates, and the Promoter solicits that they be publicly approved of and confirmed by the Council, in these words: *Reverendissime Pater, ego N. hujus Sancti Concilii promotor, peto ut decreta hæc quæ lecta sunt, a patribus hujus Concilii approbentur et confirmentur, ad ecclesiæ Catholicæ augmentum.* Then the Archbishop proposes them to the judgment of the prelates, in these words: *Placetne vobis, Venerabiles Fratres, hæc quæ lecta sunt decreta approbare et confirmare.* The Bishops severally reply, *Placet, approbamus, confirmamus.* Then the secretary reads the decree in these words: *Nos. N. N. Archiepiscopus aliique episcopi in hoc Sacro Concilio adunati, decreta hæc, quæ mox lecta sunt, approbamus, et confirmamus.* Then the prelates sign the decrees, which are placed by the secretary on the altar; the Archbishop first suscbribes, in these words, *Ego N. Archiepiscopus .... definiens subscripsi.* The Archbishop, having retired from the altar to his seat, the other Bishops, according to priority of consecration, successively advance towards the high altar, and, having made a genuflection and saluted the Archbishop, severally subscribe the decrees in these words, *Ego N. epis. N. definiens subscripsi.*

6. The Archbishop having returned to the faldstool, on the platform of the altar, the Promoter solicits that the Council be terminated, in words of this import: *Reverendissime Pater, Ego N. hujus S. Concilii Promotor, peto ut huic Concilio Provinciali finis jam fiat.* The Archbishop inquires into the wishes of the Fathers in words to this effect: *Venerabiles Fratres, placetne vobis ad Dei Omnipotentis laudem hujus Concilii Provincialis finem jam fieri.* The Fathers severally answer, *Placet.* The secretary then reads the decree in these terms: *Nos. N. Archiepiscopus . . . . . aliique Patres, qui huic Concilio Provinciali intersumus, cum absoluta sint, quæ pro temporis ratione agi gerique posse videbantur, cumque pastoralis cura ad ecclesiarum nostrarum status et pastorales vigilias revocet, propterea huic Sancto Concilio finem imponi censuimus.*

7. The prayer, *Nulla est, Domine*, as in the Roman Pontifical, is then sung by the Archbishop.

8. Afterwards the Acclamations are sung by the archdeacon, the prelates and clergy singing the responses.

9. After the Acclamations the *Te Deum* is sung, and after it the prayer, *Pro gratiarum actione; Deus cujus misericordiæ non est numerus*, etc. The Archbishop then having returned to his seat, gives the *Pax* to each of the Bishops; each of them, as he advances to receive it, retaining his mitre, salutes the Archbishop. Each Bishop subsequently gives the *Pax* to all of his brethren in their respective places.

The Session closes with the solemn blessing of the Archbishop. The deacon sings, *Recedamus in pace*, and the clergy respond, *In nomine Christi. Amen*. They then return to the sacristy, and disrobe as usual.

CHAPTER XIV.

CEREMONIES TO BE OBSERVED IN DIOCESAN SYNODS.

1. THE priests and clergymen of every grade, who by right or custom are bound to come to the Synod, assemble in the city, or such other place as the Bishop may prescribe.

2. On the first day of the Synod, at a very early hour in the morning, the Bishop in his ordinary episcopal dress (*cappam indutus*), accompanied by all the clergy in surplice, goes to the church, puts on the pontifical vestments at his seat, celebrates the Mass of the Holy Ghost, and gives communion to the clergy. At the end of Mass the faldstool or seat is placed on the floor of the sanctuary, near the lowest step, about the middle of the altar; and another seat on the platform of the altar; (the faldstool, however, may suffice, and be placed on the platform at the proper time).

3. The Bishop, over his rochet, or over his surplice, if he be a regular, puts on the amice, stole, red cope, and precious mitre, and bearing his pastoral staff, goes before the altar; the deacon and sub-deacon, in red ornaments, such as they use at Mass, accompanying him, one on each side. Kneeling there before the faldstool, and having laid aside the mitre, he begins the antiphon, *Exaudi nos, Domine*, etc., which the choir continues. The Psalm 68, *Salvum me fac Deus*, is then sung. After the first verse, the Bishop sits with the mitre, and so remains until the antiphon is repeated, after the conclusion of the Psalm.

4. The Bishop rises, and turning towards the altar, after the mitre has been taken off, says the prayer, *Adsumus Domine*, etc., to which all reply, *Amen*. He then says, *Oremus, Omnipotens sempiterne Deus*, etc., as in the Pontifical.

5. At the end of this latter prayer, the Bishop, having put on the mitre, kneels, leaning on the faldstool, and all the clergy kneel, whilst the chanters sing the Litany. After the verse, *Ut omnibus fidelibus defunctis*, etc., the Bishop rises, and holding his crosier in his left hand, standing with his face towards the Synod, says, *Ut hanc præsentem Synodum visitare, disponere, et benedicere digneris, R. Te rogamus, audi nos*. In saying this, he makes the sign of the cross over all; and then he again kneels as before until the end of the Litany.

6. The Litany being sung, all rise, and the Bishop, laying aside his mitre, says, with his face turned towards the altar, *Oremus*. The deacon says, *Flectamus genua;* the sub-deacon, *Levate*. Then the Bishop recites the prayer, *Da, quæsumus*, etc. This being finished, he resumes the mitre, ascends to the seat prepared for him on the platform of the altar, and sits with his back towards the altar. He puts incense into the censer, and blesses it, as usual. The deacon, in red dalmatic, preceded by the censer-bearer and acolytes, and by the sub-deacon in tunic, after the pontifical blessing, sings the Gospel, Luke ix, 1, 6. The sub-deacon then presents the book of the Gospels to the Bishop to kiss, and the

deacon subsequently incenses him. The Bishop then putting off his mitre, kneels before the seat, with his face towards the altar, and all the others kneel at the same time, in their respective places. The hymn, *Veni, Creator Spiritus*, is begun by the Bishop, and continued by the choir. After the first verse, the Bishop rises, and stands without his mitre, and with his face towards the altar, until the end of the hymn; and in like manner all the others rise with the Bishop. Then all sit, and the Bishop having resumed the mitre, and seated himself on the platform of the altar, addresses them in the words of the Pontifical, or others, at discretion.

7. After the address, or before, as the Bishop may think proper, a discourse is delivered by some learned priest, who in it treats of ecclesiastical discipline, of the divine mysteries, and of the correction of abuses, according as the Bishop may think fit. After the discourse, any complaints that the clergy may think fit to put forward may be made.

8. Then the Archdeacon reads aloud from the pulpit the Decrees of the Council of Trent, regarding residence and the profession of the faith, which all who are bound to it make in the hands of the Bishop, according to the form prescribed in the Pontifical.

Finally, all are charitably admonished to conduct themselves with edification in all respects during the Synod. The Bishop, after the admonition, gives the solemn blessing.

9. On the second day of the Synod, the clergy assemble again in the church, and Mass being ended, the Bishop, dressed as on the first day, proceeds to the foot of the altar, accompanied by the deacon and sub-deacon, who likewise are dressed as on the preceding day; then kneeling before the faldstool, and having laid aside his mitre, he begins the antiphon, *Propitius esto*, which is continued by the choir. The LXXVIII Psalm, *Deus, venerunt gentes*, is then sung. After the first verse the Bishop sits down, resumes his mitre, and remains seated, until the antiphon is repeated at the end of the Psalm.

10. The antiphon having been repeated, the Bishop

lays aside the mitre, rises, and turning towards the altar, says the prayer, *Nostrorum tibi*, etc., and the other prayers marked in the Pontifical.

11. Then the Bishop ascends to the seat prepared for him on the platform of the altar. After this, the deacon presents the censer. The Bishop puts incense into the censer, then gives his blessing to the deacon, who afterwards proceeds to sing the Gospel, with the accustomed ceremonies; the Bishop having taken off his mitre, stands at his seat turned towards the deacon.

12. When the Gospel has been sung, the Bishop kisses the book, and is incensed. Then the Bishop kneels before his seat, and the clergy kneeling also at their places, he intones the hymn, *Veni, Creator*, which is continued by the choir till the end, as on the first day. After the first verse the Bishop rises, and stands with the mitre on, his face being towards the altar; the clergy likewise stand until the end of the hymn. The hymn being sung, they sit in silence. Then the Bishop being seated, and having received the mitre, addresses the clergy in the words of the Pontifical; or others, at his discretion.

13. After the address, or before it, if the Bishop thinks proper, a discourse is delivered by some learned priest, who treats of ecclesiastical discipline, or of other subjects at the pleasure of the Bishop. After this the Archdeacon reads the decrees of the Holy See, or of Provincial Councils, which have not yet been promulgated, or any others the Bishop may direct. Afterwards the Diocesan Constitutions are read, which are to be approved of by the Synod. Then the suffrages are taken, and those which are approved of are confirmed. This being done, the Bishop rises, and gives his solemn blessing, as on the preceding day. Then all retire.

14. On the third day, the clergy being assembled in the church, at the end of Mass, the Bishop dressed as on the preceding days, accompanied by the deacon and subdeacon, makes a genuflection on the lowest step, in the middle of the altar, and laying aside his mitre, commences the antiphon, *Exaudi nos, Deus*, which is con-

tinued by the choir. Then is intoned the LXVIII Psalm, *Salvum me fac, Deus,* as on the first day, and the antiphon is repeated at the end of it. After the first verse the Bishop takes his seat in the middle of the altar, resumes his mitre, and remains sitting until the antiphon is repeated. When this is sung, he puts aside his mitre, rises, and turning towards the altar, says, *Oremus. Ad te, Domine,* and the other prayers mentioned in the Pontifical. When these are said, he resumes his mitre, and sits on the faldstool prepared for him. Then the deacon, with the censer-bearer, comes to him, and the Bishop puts incense into the censer. Then he gives his blessing to the deacon, who proceeds to sing the Gospel at the accustomed place, with the usual ceremonies; the Bishop standing before his seat, without his mitre, and turned towards the deacon.

15. After the Gospel, the book is brought to the Bishop to be kissed, and the deacon incenses him. The Bishop, having taken off his mitre, kneels before his seat, turned towards the altar, and all the others likewise kneeling, he intones the hymn, *Veni, Creator Spiritus,* which is continued by the choir to the end. The first verse having been sung, the Bishop rises, turned towards the altar, without his mitre, and remains standing till the end. The hymn being ended, all sit in silence. Then the Bishop, being seated with his mitre, addresses the Synod, if he pleases, in the words which follow—*Venerabiles, et dilectissimi fratres,* etc.; or he may direct that some learned priest should deliver a discourse on the topics herein mentioned.

16. Then the constitutions are read which are to be approved by the clergy; which being approved, if it seems good to them, and all things being concluded, the Bishop being seated, and having his mitre on, recommends himself to the prayers of all. When the names of those who ought to be present are read out, each one rises and answers *Adsum.* A suitable penalty is inflicted on the absent. Then the Bishop, being still seated with his mitre on, admonishes those who are present, in the words of the Pontifical, *Fratres dilectissimi,* etc., or in other words at discretion.

17. Then the Bishop lays aside his mitre, and, rising, turned towards the altar, says the prayer, *Nulla est*, etc.; afterwards, he gives his solemn blessing. After this, the Archdeacon, standing by his side, says, *Recedamus in pace*, to which all answer, *In nomine Christe. Amen.* Then all rise, and accompany the Bishop to his house.

18. If either on the first or second day all the business of the Synod be terminated, the Synod may be concluded in the manner here prescribed for the third day.

CHAPTER XV.

SOLEMN ADMINISTRATION OF THE SACRAMENT OF CONFIRMATION.

Article I.

Things to be Prepared.

1. On the Gospel side of the sanctuary, the Bishop's chair raised on a platform by two or three steps, with a canopy over it and hangings behind it.

2. On the altar, the Bishop's vestments, viz., the amice, stole, cope, mitre and crosier.

3. On the side table, the Pontifical book, the candlestick with a candle, the vessel containing the holy chrism, on a small plate, a sufficient quantity of cotton to wipe the forehead (this cotton should be divided in small balls for greater convenience), a ewer and basin, to wash the Bishop's hands, clean towels on a plate, some slices of bread, neatly cut and arranged on another small plate, for the same purpose.

4. Outside of the sanctuary, but near the rails, some benches for those who are to be confirmed; all the men at the Epistle side, and the women at the Gospel side.

5. Those, who are to be confirmed, should have been

previously instructed and prepared by the Sacrament of Penance; and it is advisable that they receive on the same day the Holy Communion, which may be done either at the Bishop's Mass, or at the High Mass, as may be deemed most convenient. Each ought to have a ticket, on which should be written the Christian and family name, which each should hold in the hand, when he kneels to receive Confirmation, and give to the clergyman who attends the Bishop. This will answer the double purpose of suggesting the Christian name to the Bishop, and of recording it, together with the family name, in the Register.

6. Where it is customary to have sponsors, these should be placed behind the persons to be confirmed, and should be no more than one for each, and of the same sex as the person to be confirmed.

7. It is customary in some places to add another name on this occasion, especially if that which they have be not of some saint. The adopted name ought to be written after the name received at baptism, and called with it by the Bishop.

8. It is proper that the solemn administration of Confirmation should be made at High Mass, either before it commences, or, as it seems more convenient, especially if the persons to be confirmed receive Communion at it, after Mass.

9. There should be four boys dressed as those who usually attend at High Mass, one to hold the mitre, another the crosier, another the book, and another the candlestick.

Article II.

The Administration of the Sacrament of Confirmation.

1. At the stated hour, the Bishop, attended by the clergy and preceded by the acolytes, goes to the church; on arriving before the altar, he makes a genuflection, kneels on the lowest step, and prays for awhile with the clergy; then he goes to his seat; there he takes off his cape, washes his hands, puts on the above-mentioned

vestments, which are carried before him by the acolytes, puts on the mitre, and having taken the crosier in his left hand, goes to the altar.

If Confirmation be given after High Mass, the Bishop might assist at it in mitre and cope; in this case, after he has been vested, he goes to the altar to begin Mass; the priest who celebrates Mass ought to come to the sanctuary in his vestments, walking immediately before the Bishop; having made a genuflection, when the Bishop goes to his chair, the celebrant should go to his seat, and remain there sitting, until the Bishop is vested, then he goes to the altar, places himself at the left of the Bishop, and does everything as directed for High Mass celebrated in presence of the Bishop.

2. On arriving at the altar, the Bishop kneels, and although it is not prescribed by the Pontifical, the hymn, *Veni, Creator Spiritus*, and the prayer, *Deus qui corda fidelium*, may be sung. Then, either the Bishop, or some other clergyman, if the Bishop chooses, gives an instruction on the holy sacrament of Confirmation.

3. After the instruction, the persons to be confirmed are directed to kneel at the rails, holding the tickets in their hands; then the Bishop, turned towards them, takes off his mitre, and says, or sings, *Spiritus Sanctus*, etc., and all the rest as in the Roman Pontifical, with the prayer, *Omnipotens, sempiterne, Deus*, extending his hand towards those who are to be confirmed.

4. The prayer being ended, the Bishop puts on the mitre, takes the crosier in his left hand, and goes to the rails,* where he anoints the foreheads of the persons whom he confirms, and having said, *In nomine Patris*, etc., and touched the cheek, says, *Pax tecum. Et cum spiritu tuo* is not said. One of the assistants, at his right, holds the vessel with the chrism, the other, at his left, wipes the foreheads of those who have been confirmed, with the cotton, which an acolyte holds on a

---

* If there are only a few to be confirmed, or if it be more convenient, the persons to be confirmed may kneel before the Bishop sitting on the faldstool.

plate near him; and either he or another clergyman takes the tickets from the hands of the persons to be confirmed, and suggests their Christian name to the Bishop. While each person is being confirmed, the sponsor places his right hand on the right shoulder of the recipient. The rubric prescribes: *Adulti ponant pedem suum super pedem dexterum patrini sui;* but this is difficult, if not impossible, to observe.

5. When the Bishop has confirmed the men at the Epistle side, and as he continues to confirm the women at the Gospel side, if there be more than one row of them, the men already confirmed are directed to retire, walking one after the other, behind the last row, and those of the second row take the place of the first at the rails, those next to them advancing forward; the same is done when the women at the Gospel side are confirmed; and so on successively.

6. The Bishop having confirmed all those who were to be confirmed, goes to his seat; the acolytes carry to him the ewer with the basin, the towel and the plate with slices of bread; he washes his hands, and in the meanwhile the choir sings, *Confirma, hoc Deus,* etc., or if there be no choir, the Bishop's attendants read it; then he returns to the altar, and turned towards it, sings, or says, the verses, *Ostende,* etc., the prayer, *Deus qui apostolis,* etc.; afterwards, he turns towards the confirmed, blesses them, as in the Pontifical, gives them the admonitions suggested by the Roman Pontifical, and tells them to say once, *I believe in God, Our Father,* and *Hail Mary,* which he may recite with them.

7. The Bishop returns to his seat, takes off the sacred vestments, puts on the cape, and accompanied by the clergy, after a short prayer before the altar, retires.

CHAPTER XVI.

EPISCOPAL VISITATION OF PARISHES.*

ARTICLE I.

The Bishop's Reception, when he visits the Parishes of his Diocese.

1. As it would be inconvenient in this country to make the solemn procession as directed in the Roman Pontifical, the essential part of the ceremony might be performed when the Bishop goes to the church to administer Confirmation, or the first time the faithful meet in it after his arrival in the parish.

2. He proceeds, accompanied by the clergy, from the priest's house, if near the church, or from the sacristy to the church. On entering it, the clergy or the choir sing the response, *Ecce Sacerdos magnus, qui in diebus suis placuit Deo*, etc., in the office, *Confessoris Pontificis;* and the priest offers to the Bishop the sprinkle with holy water; the Bishop having received it, first applies it to his own forehead, and then sprinkles the others; then the priest presents to him the boat, and the Bishop puts incense into the censer, and the priest incenses him. Afterwards, they all go before the high altar, there the Bishop kneels before the faldstool, or the praying-desk, placed below the steps, in the middle; the clergy likewise kneel, and pray for a short time. In the meantime, the priest standing with his head uncovered, at the corner of the altar, on the Epistle side, sings what follows:

V. Protector noster, aspice, Deus.
R. Et respice in faciem Christi tui.
V. Salvum fac servum tuum.
R. Deus meus, sperantem in te.

---

* Ex. Pont. Rom., Part. 3.

V. Mitte ei, Domine, auxilium de Sancto.
R. Et de Sion tuere eum.
V. Nihil proficiat inimicus in eo.
R. Et filius iniquitatis non apponat nocere ei.
V. Domine, exaudi orationem meam.
R. Et clamor meus ad te veniat.
V. Dominus vobiscum.
R. Et cum spiritu tuo.

OREMUS:

Deus, humilium visitator, qui eos paterna dilectione consolaris, prætende societati nostræ gratiam tuam; ut per eos, in quibus habitas, tuum in nobis sentiamus adventum. Per Christum Dominum nostrum.

3. After the prayer, the Bishop gives the solemn blessing to the people, saying as usual, *Sit nomen Domini benedictum*, etc., and the Indulgences are published.*

4. He then addresses the people, or, if he chooses, after the Gospel at High Mass.

5. High Mass is then celebrated as usual, with the ceremonies to be performed when the Bishop is present.

6. After Mass, the Bishop puts on the amice, alb, cincture, and the black stole and cope, with the plain mitre, and standing near the altar, turned towards the people, intones the anthem, *Si iniquitates*, and says alternately with the clergy, the Psalm, *De profundis*, etc., and after it, *Requiem*, etc., repeats the anthem, *Si iniquitates observaveris, Domine, Domine, quis sustinebit?* Then having taken off the mitre, he says:

Kyrie eleison.
Christe eleison.
Kyrie eleison.

Pater noster, etc., which is continued secretly, and during which he sprinkles and incenses thrice before himself.

Et ne nos inducas in tentationem.

---

* The Pontifical does not prescribe that the antiphon or prayer of the patron saint should be said.

R. Sed libera nos a malo.
V. In memoria æterna erunt justi.
R. Ab auditione mala non timebunt.
V. A porta inferi.
R. Erue, Domine, animas eorum.
V. Requiem æternam dona eis, Domine.
R. Et lux perpetua luceat eis.
V. Domine, exaudi orationem meam.
R. Et clamor meus ad te veniat.
V. Dominus vobiscum.
R. Et cum spiritu tuo.

OREMUS.

Deus qui inter Apostolicos Sacerdotes famulos tuos pontificali fecisti dignitate vigere; præsta quæsumus, ut eorum quoque perpetuo aggregentur consortio. Per Christum Dominum nostrum. R. Amen.

7. The prayer being ended, if the grave-yard be adjacent to the church, the Bishop, preceded by the cross, the acolytes with the candlesticks, and two others with the censer, and the holy-water vase and sprinkle, and all the clergy, two by two, go in procession to the grave-yard; but if it be not convenient to the church, they go to the middle of the church, where a cenotaph, with at least four candles, is placed, and the Bishop makes the absolution of the dead. The choir and clergy, while going, sing, *Qui Lazarum resuscitasti a monumento fœtidum, Tu eis, Domine, dona requiem et locum indulgentiæ.* V. *Qui venturus es judicare vivos et mortuos, et sæculum per ignem, Tu eis,* etc. Then the anthem *Si iniquitates* is intoned, the Psalm *De Profundis* is sung, and the anthem repeated.

8. On arriving at the grave-yard, or at the cenotaph, the response *Libera me Domine* is sung, and repeated as usual; the Bishop puts incense into the censer; after the *Kyrie eleison* has been sung thrice, the Bishop sings *Pater noster*, which is continued secretly, sprinkles and incenses as usual, and says:

Et ne nos inducas in tentationem.

R. Sed libera nos a malo.
V. In memoria æterna erunt justi.
R. Ab auditione mala non timebunt.
V. A porta inferi.
R. Erue, Domine, animas eorum.
V. Requiem æternam dona eis, Domine.
R. Et lux perpetua luceat eis.
V. Domine, exaudi orationem meam.
R. Et clamor meus ad te veniat.
V. Dominus vobiscum.
R. Et cum spiritu tuo.

OREMUS.

Deus qui inter Apostolicos Sacerdotes famulos tuos Sacerdotali fecisti dignitate vigere, præsta quæsumus ut eorum quoque perpetuo aggregentur consortio.

Deus veniæ largitor, et humanæ salutis amator, quæsumus clementiam tuam, ut nostræ congregationis fratres, propinquos, et benefactores, qui ex hoc sæculo transierunt, Beata Maria semper Virgine intercedente, cum omnibus sanctis tuis, ad perpetuæ beatitudinis consortium pervenire, concedas.

Deus, cujus miseratione animæ fidelium, requiescunt, famulis et famulabus tuis omnibus, hic et ubique in Christo quiescentibus, da propitius veniam peccatorum, ut, a cunctis reatibus absoluti, tecum sine fine lætentur. Per Christum Dominum nostrum. R. Amen.

V. Requiem æternam dona eis, Domine.
R. Et lux perpetua luceat eis.

Then two singers sing *Requiescant in pace.* R. *Amen.*

The Bishop, raising his hand, makes the sign of the cross on the grave-yard, or on the cenotaph, puts on his mitre, and returns to the sanctuary, saying alternately with the clergy the Psalm *Miserere.*

9. On arriving before the altar, the Bishop takes off the mitre, makes a genuflection on the lowest step, and standing before it in the middle, turned towards the altar, says:

Kyrie eleison.
Christe eleison.
Kyrie eleison.
Pater noster, etc.
Et ne nos inducas in intentionem.
R. Sed libera nos a malo.
V. A porta inferi.
R. Erue, Domine, animas eorum.
V. Domine, exaudi orationem meam.
R. Et clamor meus ad te veniat.
V. Dominus vobiscum.
R. Et cum spiritu tuo.

OREMUS.

Absolve, quæsumus, Domine, animas famulorum, famularumque tuarum ab omni vinculo delictorum, ut in resurrectionis gloria inter sanctos et electos tuos resuscitati respirent. Per Christum Dominum nostrum. R. Amen.

10. This being ended, the Bishop takes off his black cope and stole, and puts on a white cope and stole, and begins the visitation by the tabernacle, where the Blessed Sacrament is kept; then proceeds to the baptismal font, to the place where the sacred oils are kept, also to that where the relics are kept; visits and inspects the altars, chapels, sacristy, the sacred vestments, the confessionals, and everything relating to the divine worship; also the parish registers, the grave-yard, etc.

THE THINGS SUBJECT TO THE EPISCOPAL VISITATION ARE THE FOLLOWING:

Of the Holy Eucharist.

Tabernacle.	Veil of ciborium.	Processional canopy.
Veil, and how many.	Particles.	Pyx, for the sick.
Interior lining.	Fragments.	Burse, etc., for Communion of the sick.
Corporal spread out.	Renewed, how often.	Monstrance.
Ciborium: bowl silver, gilt within.	Key.	Throne, for benediction.
Vessel for purifying the fingers.	Lamp, always burning.	Portable lanterns.
	Umbrellino for processions.	Humeral-veil.

Of the Baptistery.

Font.	Water.	Holy oils.
Cover.	Drain.	Salt.
Halls.	Shell.	Cloths.

Of the Holy Oils.

Ambry on the Gospel side of Sanctuary.	Vessel for holy oils.	How brought from the cathedral.
Inscription (exterior and interior.)	Cotton wet with oil, dry cotton above.	Renewal.
	Purple burse, or cover.	Burning the old.

Of the Confessionals.

In a public position.	Thick veil.	Doors with bolt.
Pierced grating.	Pictures.	Purple stole.

Of the Holy Relics.

Ambry.	Names.	Key.
Lining.	Approbation.	Proper Offices.
Reliquaries.	Exposition.	Festivals.

Of the Altars.

High Altar.	Candlesticks.	Canopy.
Steps up to it.	Statues.	Predella.
Steps upon it.	Pictures.	Credence.
Stone Altar.	Altar-cards.	Piscina.
Consecration.	Covering.	Screen, or rails.
Wax-cloth.	Cloths for changing.	Bell.
Altar-cloths.	Antependiums, and how many.	Endowment.
Their blessing.		Obligations.
Crucifix.		

Of the Church itself.

Choir.	Alms-chests.	Use of bells.
Large Crucifix, in a prominent place.	Holy-water stoups.	Subterranean chapels.
Bishop's throne, steps, and canopy.	Doors.	Patron.
	Churchyard.	Improper epitaphs.
Nave and aisles.	Cross therein.	Burying-place for the clergy
Walls.	Trees.	And for children.
Images of saints.	Bell-tower.	Titulars of church.
Pulpit.	Bells.	Dedication.
Windows.	Their blessing.	Both festivals.
Vaults.	Ladders, ropes.	Office, how held.
Seats.	Roof.	Other festivals.
Division of sexes.	Spire.	Indulgences.
Roof.	Weathercock.	Forty hours Prayer.
Pavement.	Pavement.	Benediction, how often.
Ambry.	Door.	Lights, how many.
	Key.	

Of the Sacristy.

Ambries.	Chalices.	Lavabo-dishes.
Lavatory.	Patens.	Bells.
Towels.	Purificators.	Thurible and boat.
Kneeling-desk.	Corporals and Palls.	Processional Cross.
Prayers before and after Mass.	Veils.	Holy-water vessel and aspersory.
Prayers for vesting.	Burses.	Pax.
Altar-cloths.	Amices.	Banners.
Finger-cloths.	Albs.	Flower-vases.
Communion-cloths.	Girdles.	Triangular candlestick.
Altar-breads, where made	Stoles, maniples and chasubles, of five colors, for feast-days, for ferias.	Paschal candlestick.
Cottas.		Door.
Missal-markers.	Dalmatics.	Key.
Bier.	Tunics.	Safe.
Pall.	Copes of different colors.	Pavement.
Book-stands.	Humeral veils.	Windows.
Books.	Altar-cushions and book-stands.	Wall.
Supplement to Missal.		Roof.
Ordo celebrandi.	Devout images.	Table of obligations.
Ritus servandus.	Cruets.	Inventory of the aforesaid
Missals, binding.		

INDEX OBSERVANDORUM IN VISITATIONE PERSONARUM.

Name.	Proper feasts.	Given in private houses.
Surname.	Customs.	Godfathers and godmothers.
Country.	Monthly conferences.	
Age.	Servers at Mass.	Confessions, where, at what time.
When appointed.	Blessing of ashes, candles, palms.	
Profession of faith.		Instructions for first communion.
Income.	Holy Week.	
Obligations satisfied.	Blessing houses.	Sick persons, and how often.
Divine office.	Holy Sepulchre.	
Faculties.	Blessing font and Paschal candle.	Visiting sick, commendation.
Parish books and papers.		
Residence.	Pious pictures.	Marriages, how, where.
Mass, how often.	The long litanies.	Other functions.
Sermons.	Ceremonies in High and Low Mass.	Lent sermons.
Publication of feasts, fasts, pastorals.		Funerals.
	The administration of the Sacraments.	Moral and dogmatic theology.
Catechism.		
Vespers.	Baptism, how long delayed.	Books, what studied.
Processions.		

11. He gives Confirmation at the time he deems most convenient, as directed in the foregoing chapter.

12. When the Bishop has completed the visitation, he goes in his usual dress to the church, and standing before the altar, at the Epistle side, he says the Psalms *De profundis, Requiem æternam*, the anthem, *Si iniquitates, Pater noster.*

Et ne nos inducas in tentationem.
R. Sed libera nos a malo.
V. A porta inferi.
R. Erue, Domine, animas eorum.
V. Requiescant in pace.
R. Amen.
V. Domine, exaudi orationem meam.
R. Et clamor meus ad te veniat.
V. Dominus vobiscum.
R. Et cum spiritu tuo.

OREMUS:

Deus cujus miseratione animæ Fidelium requiescunt, famulis et famulabus tuis omnibus hic et ubique in Christo quiescentibus, da propitius veniam peccatorum, ut, a cunctis reatibus absoluti, tecum sine fine lætentur. Per Christum Dominum nostrum.
R. Amen.

APPENDIX.

CHAPTER I.

FORTY HOURS' EXPOSITION.

ARTICLE I.

Things to be Prepared for the Mass of the Exposition.

1. THE picture or image of the high altar, as well as the walls near it, should be covered with precious drapery; bu trepresenting nothing profane.

2. The altar ought to be prepared as well as possible. No statues or relics of saints should be placed on or about it. The figures of angels bearing candelabra need not be covered. In the most conspicuous place of it, should be erected the throne, or exposition place for the Blessed Sacrament, with a pall or corporal on it. It should be surrounded with a sufficient number of candles near it, besides those that are on the steps of the altar. The cross may be left, or taken away. The front altar-veil must always be white, although the Mass may require another color.

3. On the side-table, besides what is usually necessary for High Masses, should be a cope of the color of the vestments for the celebrant, the book containing the Litany and prayers, the remonstrance covered with a white veil, and a stole for the priest, who is to expose the Blessed Sacrament.

4. In the sanctuary, a bench covered with a cloth or carpet for the clergy who remain at the adoration.

5. In the sacristy, the usual vestments for the celebrant and ministers.

6. In any convenient place, the processional canopy, the ombrellino, the processional cross, two censers, with their boats, candles for the procession, and two books with the Litany for the chanters.

Article II.

Of the Mass for the Exposition.

1. The Mass for the exposition and reposition, is to be sung at the altar where the exposition is made. The Mass should be the solemn *Votiva* of the Blessed Sacrament, with the *Gloria* and *Credo*, and with the commemoration of the Sunday, and of the feasts of either double or semi-double rite.* But on Sundays of first or second class, on festivals of double rite of first or second class, on Ash Wednesday, on Monday, Tuesday, and Wednesday in Holy Week, during the whole octave of Easter, Pentecost, and Epiphany, on the vigils of Christmas and Pentecost, and within all privileged octaves, that exclude the celebration of festivals of first and second class, either translated or falling on those days, the Mass of the Blessed Sacrament cannot be sung, but the Mass occurring on that day is to be celebrated with the prayer of the Blessed Sacrament, *Sub unica conclusione*, with the Preface, *de Nativitate*, if the Mass of the day has not a proper preface; and should those festivals fall on Sunday, the prayer of the Blessed Sacrament is to be said, *Sub unica conclusione*, with that of the Saint, and the commemoration of the Sunday is to be made afterwards under its proper conclusion.

2. This Mass is celebrated as other High Masses, having nothing particular, except that another large particle is to be consecrated with that of the Mass.

---

* This apparent anomaly in admitting commemorations in a solemn Votiva Mass *Pro re gravi*, arises from the fact that there is no Conventual Mass of the day celebrated here, and hence such commemorations must be made.

3. The acolytes, who hold the candles for the elevation, must not leave the sanctuary, before the consecrated Host is placed in the remonstrance; and before they go, they must make a genuflection on both knees.

4. The acolytes should light all the candles of the altar, prepared for the exposition before the elevation.

5. After the celebrant has consumed the Precious Blood, the deacon and sub-deacon make a genuflection, exchange places, make another genuflection; the master of ceremonies carries the remonstrance to the altar; and the celebrant, assisted by the deacon, places the sacred Host in the remonstrance, the deacon shuts it and places it in the middle of the corporal; the deacon and sub-deacon again exchange places. During the remaining part of the Mass, the ministers omit the usual kisses in giving or receiving anything from the celebrant.

6. The celebrant in the usual place makes the ablution of his fingers; after which the ministers make a genuflection and exchange places; the sub-deacon wipes the chalice, and covers it as usual, leaving the corporal spread on the altar, taking care to retire a little, whilst the celebrant sings, *Dominus vobiscum;* he then makes a genuflection on the platform, and on the lowest step, as he passes before the Blessed Sacrament, and having brought the chalice to the side-table, goes to his place behind the deacon.

7. The celebrant having given the chalice to the sub-deacon, makes a genuflection, and goes to read the *Communio;* then he returns to the middle, makes a genuflection with the deacon, kisses the altar, turns to the people from the Gospel side, so as not to turn his back to the Blessed Sacrament; sings, *Dominus vobiscum,* makes again a genuflection with the ministers, goes to sing the prayers; after having sung them, returns to the middle, makes a genuflection with the ministers, kisses the altar, turns to the people as before, sings, *Dominus vobiscum;* in the meanwhile, the deacon makes another genuflection, turns to the people in the same manner as the celebrant, and sings, *Ite, missa est.* Then the celebrant and the ministers make a genuflection; the cele-

brant says, *Placeat*, etc., and the ministers kneel on the platform for the benediction.

8. The celebrant having said the *Placeat*, kisses the altar, says, *Benedicet vos ;* instead of bowing, makes a genuflection, turns as for the *Dominus vobiscum*, blesses the people, without completing the circle, and without making another genuflection, turns on his left, says the Gospel, does not make the sign of the cross on the altar, but he makes it on his forehead, mouth, and breast, and saying, *Et verbum caro,* he makes a genuflection to the Blessed Sacrament.

9. After Mass, the ministers go up to the platform at the side of the celebrant, and having made a genuflection on one knee, they all go directly by the side steps to the bench.

10. Towards the end of Mass, the acolytes give the candles to the clergy and light them; the two censer-bearers prepare their censers, and whilst the celebrant reads the last Gospel, the latter go to the altar and make a genuflection on both knees.

Article III.

Of the Procession for the Exposition.

1. The celebrant and the ministers, on arriving at the bench, take off their maniples; the celebrant, moreover, takes off his chasuble and puts on the cope, puts incense in both censers, without blessing it, the deacon presenting the incense-boat, and goes with them to the middle, below the steps, where he makes with them a genuflection on both knees, kneels on the lowest step, and incenses the Blessed Sacrament, with three throws.

2. In the meantime, the master of ceremonies brings from the side-table the long veil, and puts it on the celebrant, after he has given the censer to the deacon. The censer-bearers go to each side of the altar, and the acolytes give the canopy to those who are to carry it.

3. The celebrant, having incensed the Blessed Sacrament, goes up to the second step with the deacon and

sub-deacon; the celebrant and the sub-deacon kneel, and the deacon goes up to the altar, makes a genuflection on one knee, takes the Blessed Sacrament without bowing, and standing gives it to the celebrant; then the deacon makes a genuflection, and at the same time bows, goes to the celebrant's right, who, with the ministers, goes up to the platform, and they turn towards the people in such a manner that the deacon be at the right, and the sub-deacon at the left of the celebrant, whose cope they raise on each side; a priest in surplice holds the ombrellino opened over the Blessed Sacrament, and the singers intone the *Pange, lingua.*

4. The procession moves in the following order: the cross-bearer, in surplice, having on each side the acolytes with their candlesticks, goes to the lower part of the sanctuary near the railing, and stands turned to the altar. When the chanters intone the *Pange Lingua*, they turn towards the people, without making any genuflection and begin to move; the clergy, two by two, make a genuflection on both knees, follow them, carrying their candles outside—that is, those who are at the right carry them in their right hand, and those at the left side, in their left hand.

5. The celebrant, between the deacon and sub-deacon, who raise his cope on each side, preceded by the two censer-bearers, who gently swing their censers, and surrounded by four or six acolytes, who carry lighted candles on each side of the canopy, walks in the last place, reciting, in a low voice, psalms and hymns alternately with the ministers, and the choir continues to sing the *Pange Lingua.*

6. The procession having returned, the acolytes put their candlesticks on the side-table, and the cross-bearer leaves the cross at its place, the clergy divide in two lines at each side of the altar, and as the Blessed Sacrament approaches, they all kneel down. The censer-bearers, on arriving near the altar, do not swing their censers any more, but stop at each side of it, and remain there standing. The celebrant stops at the lowest step of the altar, and there standing, gives the Blessed

Sacrament to the deacon, who receives it kneeling on both knees, and turned a little to the Epistle side. Then the celebrant kneels, and takes off the long veil. The deacon places the ostensorium on the altar, if there be no other priest to place it on the throne; otherwise the deacon himself places it thereon, makes a genuflection on the platform, without bowing his head, and goes down by one side to the right of the celebrant.

7. Those who carried the canopy, having left it at a convenient place, receive candles and kneel down, forming a semicircle before the altar, if they be clergymen: but if laymen, they kneel outside of the chancel.

8. After the deacon has placed the Blessed Sacrament on the throne, and returned to the right of the celebrant, the chanters intone *Tantum ergo*. At the verse *Genitori*, the celebrant rises with the ministers, puts incense into the censer, without blessing it, the deacon presenting the incense-boat, and the sub-deacon raising the celebrant's cope at his right, while he incenses the Blessed Sacrament with three throws. After the incensing, the censer-bearer, having received the censer from the deacon, goes to the middle, makes a genuflection, with the second censer-bearer, and both carry their censers back to the sacristy.

9. After the *Tantum ergo*, the chanters do not sing the verse *Panem de Cœlo*, but they go in the middle, kneel, and sing the Litany. At the end of it the celebrant intones *Pater noster*, the rest of which being recited secretly, the chanters intone the Psalm *Deus in adjutorium;* after it, the celebrant, kneeling, sings in a ferial tone the verses from the book which the ministers hold on each side; he then rises, and standing, sings with his hands joined, *Dominus vobiscum*, and the prayers that follow; these being ended, he kneels, says *Domine exaudi orationem meam*, and the chanters, *Exaudiat nos omnipotens et misericors Dominus;* the choir answers, *Et custodiat nos semper, Amen;* the celebrant subjoins, *Fidelium animæ*, etc., without making the sign of the cross; the choir answers, *Amen;* Then all the clergy pray for a short time in silence; the

acolytes go to the middle with their candlesticks, kneel on both knees, rise, and walk to the sacristy, followed, as usual, by the clergy and the sacred ministers, who all make in the middle a genuflection on both knees; the latter, when at a proper distance from the Blessed Sacrament, put on their caps.

If, for want of a sufficient number of persons, or for any other cause, the procession cannot be made, the celebrant, and the deacon and sub-deacon, after Mass, go to the bench, as has been said above, take off their maniples, the celebrant taking off also his chasuble, and putting on the cope, go to the altar, make a genuflection on both knees below the last step, then kneel on it, and after a short prayer, rise; the celebrant puts incense into the censer, and kneeling, incenses with three throws the Blessed Sacrament; then the deacon, or another priest in surplice and stole, making the usual genuflections, places the remonstrance on the throne; the choir sings *Pange, lingua;* at the verse *Genitori* the celebrant puts incense again into the censer, and incenses, as usual, the Blessed Sacrament. After the hymn is finished, the chanters sing the Litany immediately. The same is to be done at the reposition of the Blessed Sacrament, except that the hymn, *Pange, lingua* is sung after the verse, *Domine, exaudi orationem meam,* and the benediction is given as usual.

10. After the clergy have left the sanctuary, the bench or stool prepared for the purpose is placed near the last step of the altar in the middle, and the two clergymen destined to begin the adoration, dressed in surplice (and stole if they be priests), kneel before it, and remain there for the space of an hour, after which two others go to take their place, and so on till the exposition is finished.

11. There should be constantly, day and night, during the exposition, at least twenty lights; and when the church is shut in the night, at least ten of them should be candles and ten lamps.*

---

* The privilege granted in this country with regard to the discontinuance of the exposition during the night makes this unnecessary.

Article IV.

Of the Mass pro pace.

1. Everything is to be prepared for this Mass as for others, but the color of the vestments is to be violet.

2. This Mass ought to be sung on the second day of the forty hours' exposition, with the assistance of deacon and sub-deacon. It should not be sung at the altar where the Blessed Sacrament is exposed, or where it is usually kept in the tabernacle. However, as in most of our churches in this country, there is but one altar, the Mass here spoken of must necessarily be celebrated at the altar of the exposition. The assistance of the deacon and sub-deacon must be dispensed with where there is only one clergyman.

3. The Mass, *pro pace*, is sung without *Gloria* and *Credo*, and with the commemoration of the Blessed Sacrament, *sub unica conclusione*, and according to the rules given above for the votive Mass of the Blessed Sacrament. However, if it is celebrated on a Sunday, the *Credo* is to be said.

4. The days on which this Mass, *pro pace*, cannot be said, are the same as mentioned above for that of the Blessed Sacrament, n 1, art ii. When any other is said in its place, the prayer, *pro pace*, is to be said, *sub unica conclusione*, with that of the current Mass, and the commemoration of the Blessed Sacrament is then said *sub propria conclusione*, should the rite of the day allow it.

5. All private Masses celebrated during the exposition are of the current office, with the commemoration of the Blessed Sacrament after the others prescribed for that day by the Rubrics; and if a feast of the first or second class be then celebrated, the commemoration of the Blessed Sacrament is omitted; the little bell is not to be rung;* if, on the days of the exposition, votive Masses are permitted by the Rubrics, it is proper that all private Masses should be of the Blessed Sacrament, without *Gloria* and without *Credo*, with the Preface *de Nativitate*.

---

* However, if Mass is celebrated at the altar of exposition, there does not seem to be any reason for not ringing the bell. This prohibition was made in order that the minds of the faithful might not be distracted from the main place—the altar of exposition.

Article V.

Things to be prepared for the Mass of the Reposition.

1. In the sacristy and on the side-table, everything as for the first day.
2. On the altar, the key of the tabernacle, the Missal on its stand, the cards and the cross, according to the established custom. All the candles are to be lighted before Mass.
3. In the sanctuary, the bench or stools placed in the middle for the adoration are to be removed.

Article VI.

Of the Mass for the Reposition.

1. We think it proper to mention here some general rules, before we speak of the ceremonies to be observed in Masses celebrated at the altars on which the Blessed Sacrament is exposed.
2. These rules are the following: During Mass, the genuflections are made only on one knee, except when the priest first arrives at the altar, and when he leaves it to return to the sacristy; in both these cases, he makes the genuflection on both knees.

The usual reverences to salute the clergy are omitted, by the celebrant and ministers, and by every one else.*

The ministers and all others in giving anything to the celebrant, or receiving it from him, do not kiss it or his hand; but the sub-deacon, after the Epistle, kisses the hand in receiving his blessing; likewise the deacon when he goes to receive his blessing before he sings the Gospel; at the Offertory, when he presents the paten and chalice to the celebrant, he kisses both the paten and chalice, and his hand, as also when he gives him the paten at the end of the *Pater noster*. The celebrant, at the end of the Gospel, sung by the deacon, kisses the Missal, as usual.

---

* The deacon, however, salutes the choir before incensing them.

3. The sacred ministers being vested, go from the sacristy to the sanctuary as usual; the acolytes arriving before the altar, make a genuflection on both knees, and a profound bow, retire on each side, and wait for the ministers. The clergy, as they arrive at the middle make likewise a genuflection on both knees, with a profound reverence, and go to their respective places, without bowing to each other. The sacred ministers uncover their heads, as soon as they can see the Blessed Sacrament, carry their caps till they enter the sanctuary, then they give them to the master of ceremonies, and, on arriving before the last step of the altar, they, with the acolytes and the master of ceremonies, make a genuflection on both knees, and a profound bow, and Mass is begun as usual.

4. Having made the confession, they go up to the altar, without making a genuflection, where they make a genuflection on one knee. The deacon and sub-deacon should observe, that in making the genuflections, they must not place their hands on the altar, this being allowed only to the celebrant. When the latter has said, *Oramus te Domine,* they retire a little to the Gospel side, turned to the Epistle side, to put incense into the censer; and before the censer-bearer goes up for this purpose, he makes below the last step a genuflection, bending one knee; the deacon does not kiss the spoon, nor the celebrant's hand, as has been observed before for all similar cases.

5. The incense having been blessed, the censer-bearer retires to his place, making a genuflection, and the celebrant and ministers go down to the second step, taking care not to turn their backs to the Blessed Sacrament; on which account the celebrant and the sub-deacon go down by the Gospel side, and the deacon by that of the Epistle, kneel on the edge of the platform; there the celebrant, having received the censer from the deacon, without the usual kisses, and made a profound bow, incenses the Blessed Sacrament with three throws, the ministers raising in the meanwhile, his chasuble on each side. Then they rise, go up to the altar, making a genuflection on one knee, and incense the altar, as usual.

If, according to the custom established in some churches, the cross has been placed on the altar, it must not be incensed. (*Decr. S. R. C.*, 29 Sept., 1738.)

6. After the incensing, the celebrant goes down to the first step, or below them all, according to the construction of the altar, and there, turned towards the people, is incensed by the deacon, who turns towards him. Then he goes to read the Introit, etc.

7. After the choir have done singing the *Kyrie*, the celebrant with the ministers goes to the middle as usual, makes with them a genuflection, and intones the *Gloria;* the ministers make again a genuflection, go to his side, recite the rest of the hymn, make a genuflection, and by the side steps go to the bench, where they sit without their caps; after it is sung, they go to the middle, make a genuflection below the steps, and go, one behind the other, without making any other genuflection. The celebrant, after arriving on the platform and kissing the altar, genuflects, and turned a little towards the Gospel side, sings the *Dominus vobiscum;* then he returns to the middle, makes a genuflection with the ministers, and goes to sing the prayers as usual; after which, the sub-deacon sings the Epistle, having made the usual genuflections before the altar, then asks the celebrant's blessing, kisses his hand, and carries the Missal to the Gospel side, as usual.

8. During this time, the celebrant says the *Munda cor meum*, makes a genuflection before and after, then reads the Gospel; and the deacon takes the book to the altar, having made a genuflection in the middle on the lowest step, and again on the platform.

9. When the celebrant has read the Gospel, he turns in his place, and puts in the incense as at n. 4; then all three go to the middle on the platform, the sub-deacon descends to the bottom of the steps, and the deacon kneels to say the *Munda cor meum*. The celebrant, at the proper time, gives the deacon his blessing, who, having kissed his hand, rises, both make a genuflection, the celebrant goes to the Epistle side, the deacon goes to the floor, makes a genuflection with the others, and pro-

ceeds as usual to sing the Gospel. At the end, the subdeacon takes the Missal to the celebrant to kiss, without making a genuflection before, comes down from the altar (which he must do without turning his back to the Blessed Sacrament), and the deacon incenses the celebrant as usual.

10. After incensing the celebrant, all three go to the middle, one behind the other, make a genuflection, and the celebrant intones the *Credo;* at the end, the ministers make a genuflection, and go to recite it with the celebrant. Then all three make a genuflection and go to the bench, as was mentioned at n. 7.

11. At the *Crucifixus*, the deacon takes the burse from the side-table, bows to the celebrant only, goes to the middle, makes a genuflection on the lowest step, and again on the platform, and spreads the corporal in the usual manner, makes a genuflection, and returns by the side of the altar to the right of the celebrant.

12. At the end of the *Credo*, the ministers go to the altar, as at n. 7. The celebrant sings the *Dominus vobiscum*, makes a genuflection, and sings *Oremus*. After which the deacon and sub-deacon make a genuflection, and go, the first to the celebrant's right, and the other to the side-table, in the usual manner, for the chalice, which he brings to the altar, making there a genuflection. The deacon presents the paten and chalice with the usual kiss. In like manner the sub-deacon presents the cruets, then takes the paten, and makes a genuflection, first on the platform, and again on the lowest step.* He does not, however, make a genuflection when the celebrant kneels on the platform to incense the Blessed Sacrament. (*S. C. R.*, 11 Feb., 1764.)

13. After the oblation of the chalice, the deacon gives the incense as at n. 4. And the celebrant, without making a genuflection, incenses the offerings; the deacon does not remove the chalice from the middle of the corporal. When this is done, they descend to the second step, kneel on the edge of the platform, and incense the

---

* The sub-deacon does not kiss the cruets.

Blessed Sacrament, the altar as at n. 5, and the celebrant as at n. 6, and he washes his hands according to the Rubric of the Missal on Good Friday, and the S. C. R., 22d August, 1682; then he returns to the middle, makes a genuflection, and says the *Suscipe, Sancta Trinitas*, etc.

14. When the deacon has incensed the celebrant, he incenses the choir as usual, then the sub-deacon, who makes a genuflection, and then turns for this purpose a little towards the Gospel side. This done, the deacon gives the censer to the censer-bearer, goes up to the second step, makes a genuflection, and turns in the same manner as the sub-deacon, to be incensed, and again makes a genuflection.

15. When the celebrant has said the *Suscipe, Sancta Trinitas*, he kisses the altar, makes a genuflection, and turns, as at the *Dominus vobiscum*, to say the *Orate, Fratres;* but he does not make a perfect circle; then he returns to the middle, makes a genuflection, and continues Mass.

16. At the *Sanctus*, the acolytes approach with torches, and without bowing, kneel down till after Communion, as they did on the first day. From this to the end of Mass, they observe exactly what is prescribed for the first day, and make preparations toward the end for the procession.

ARTICLE VII.

From the Litany to the end of the Forty Hours.

1. At the end of Mass, the celebrant goes to the bench with the ministers, receives the cope, and without putting in incense, returns to the middle, makes a genuflection on both knees, and kneels on the lowest step; then the chanters sing the Litany, as on the first day, to *Domine, exaudi orationem*, etc., inclusive.

2. At *Peccatores*, the acolytes give the candles to the clergy, and light them; the censer-bearers prepare their censers, and approach the altar with the usual genuflections.

3. After the celebrant has said the *Domine, exaudi*, etc., he rises with the ministers, puts incense into the censers, without blessing it, and kneeling, incenses three times the Blessed Sacrament; and the master of ceremonies gives him the veil.

4. After incensing the Blessed Sacrament, the censer-bearers place themselves on each side of the altar, and the deacon or a priest with surplice and stole, with the usual genuflections, takes It from the throne; if it is the deacon, without placing It upon the corporal, he places It in the celebrant's hands, who receives It after a genuflection; and as soon as he has delivered It, the deacon makes in turn a genuflection. If another priest takes It from the throne, he places It upon the corporal, makes a genuflection and retires; then the deacon goes upon the platform, and takes It as said above, and as to the remainder, observes what is prescribed in the ceremonies and rite of the procession.

5. When the procession has returned, and the celebrant has arrived at the lowest step of the altar, the deacon makes a genuflection, receives from him the Blessed Sacrament; the celebrant then immediately makes a genuflection, and the veil is taken off. The deacon places the remonstrance on the corporal, in the middle of the altar, and returns to the right of the celebrant, making the usual genuflections.

6. As soon as the deacon returns to the right of the celebrant, the singers intone the *Tantum ergo;* at the *Genitori* incense is given, and the Blessed Sacrament is incensed; and after the verse *Panem de cœlo* (to which an *Alleluia* is added during paschal time, and the octave of *Corpus Christi*, according to the Decree, S. C. R., 10 Jan., 1705), the celebrant rises without making another genuflection, or saying *Dominus vobiscum* (Decree, S. C. R., 16th June, 1663; 28th Sept., 1675; 2d Aug. and 6th Sept., 1698), and sings the prayers with his hands joined, and the ministers hold the book.

7. After the prayers, he kneels, and after saying *Fidelium animæ*, as on the first day, the deacon adjusts the veil on his shoulders, and the sub-deacon ties it in

front. Then the celebrant with the ministers goes up to the altar and gives the Benediction of the Blessed Sacrament in the usual manner. The celebrant and subdeacon go down to the foot of the altar (the deacon, if there is no assisting priest, remaining on the *predella* to replace the Blessed Sacrament) and genuflect, and the master of ceremonies removes the humeral-veil. The deacon immediately, or a priest with a stole, observing the usual ceremonies, puts the Blessed Sacrament in the tabernacle, which must be on the altar where the exposition is made, and the consecrated Host must be consumed during Mass, either the same morning or the following. (*Instruct. Clement.*)

8. Whilst the Blessed Sacrament is put away, the acolytes take their candles from the side-table, and go to the middle; the master of ceremonies takes the ministers' caps, and at the end of the function gives them a signal to rise; all make a genuflection together on the floor; he presents the caps, and they go, preceded by the censer-bearers and acolytes, to the sacristy, to disrobe as usual.

As it frequently happens that not the celebrant, but a Bishop, terminates the function, it may be necessary to point out what is to be observed after Mass. At the end of the last Gospel, the celebrant, with the ministers at each side of him, goes to the middle of the altar, makes a genuflection on one knee, without bowing the head, and then goes down to the floor, in such a manner as not to turn his back to the Blessed Sacrament. When they are at the bottom of the steps, they all make a genuflection together on both knees, together with a prostration; the acolytes with their candles, and the master of ceremonies, do the same as they did in the beginning of Mass. Then they all depart with their heads uncovered, and do not take their caps until they are out of sight of the Blessed Sacrament. When they arrive in the sacristy, the ministers take off their maniples; and if they are to assist the Bishop, and their vestments be not white, they take them off and put on white. (Decree, S. C. R., 20th Sept., 1806.) Then they assist the Bishop to vest, and proceed to the altar, proceded by the acolytes with their candles, and followed by the train-bearer and mitre-bearer. When they come in sight of the Blessed Sacrament, the deacon takes off the Bishop's mitre, and after making a genuflection on both knees, both kneel on the first step, on which the master of ceremonies will put a cushion for the Bishop. The function is then continued as prescribed above, and the mitre-bearer during the benediction kneels down.

9. The greater part of the ceremonies prescribed in this chapter, have been taken from the 6th volume of the Collection of Decrees of the S. C. R., Part II, in which Gardellini explains the instructions of Clement XI on the Forty Hours.

CHAPTER II.

DIFFERENT INTONATIONS FOR VESPERS AND SOLEMN MASS.

IT was deemed advisable to add, at the end of this Manual, the different intonations for Vespers and Solemn Mass.

It may be well to remark that the priest who officiates or celebrates, if capable of regulating his voice, or intoning *Deus in adjutorium,* &c., or in commencing a prayer, &c., should take a moderate pitch, neither too high nor too low—such a note, for instance, that would answer that of *sol* or *la* of the organ, would suit the generality of voices of the choir that is to sing the responses.

DEUS IN ADJUTORIUM, &c.

For Festivals.

V. De-us in ad-ju-to-ri-um me-um in-ten-de.

R. Do-mi-ne ad ad-ju-van-dum me fes-ti-na.

Glo-ri-a Pa-tri, et Fi-li-o, et Spi-ri-tu-i

Sanc-to Si-cut e-rat in prin-ci-pi-o, et nunc

et semper, et in sæc-u-la sæc-u-lo-rum. Amen.

Al-le-lu-ia.

FOR VESPERS AND SOLEMN MASS.

During Septuagesima and Lent.

La-us ti-bi Do-mi-ne, rex æ-ter-næ glo-ri-æ.

Ferial Intonation.

V. De-us in ad-ju-to-ri-um me-um in-ten-de.

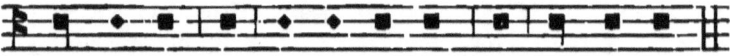
Do-mi-ne ad ad-ju-vandum me fes-ti-na.

Glo-ri-a Pa-tri, &c. Al-le-lu-ia.

Laus tibi Domine, as above.

THE CHAPTER.

is sung on the note *Do, recto tono,* all the way through, except the last word, which is sung on *la, sol, la.*

Ec-ce sa-cer-dos magnus, &c. et in tem-po-re

i-ra-cun-di-æ fac-tus est re-con-ci-li-a-ti-o.

R. De-o gra-ti-as.

THE VERSES

Immediately after the Hymn.

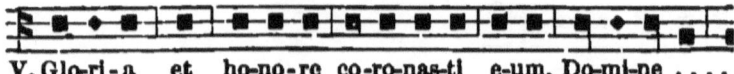
V. Glo-ri-a et ho-no-re co-ro-nas-ti e-um, Do-mi-ne ....

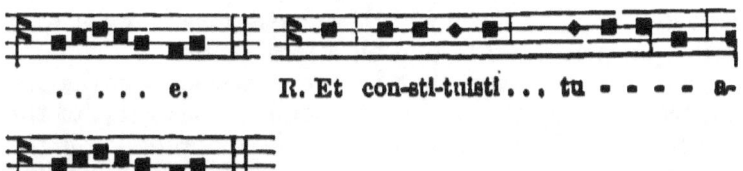

..... e.   R. Et con-sti-tuisti... tu - - - a-

- - - rum.

The Verses

For the Commemorations.

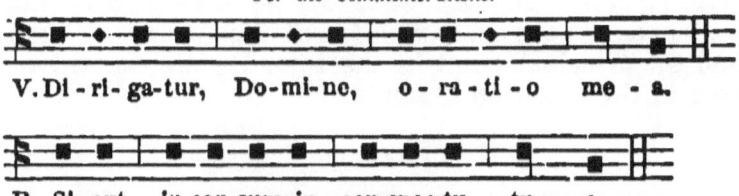

V. Di - ri - ga - tur, Do - mi - ne,   o - ra - ti - o   me - a.

R. Si - cut   in - cen - sum in   con - spec - tu   tu - o.

The tones for *Dominus vobiscum* and for the prayers are marked hereafter at page 425: and, as the different intonations for *Benedicamus* are to be found in every missal, we abstain from noting them here.

After the *Deo gratias*, in response to the *Benedicamus*, the priest sings in the low note *do, Fidelium animæ*, in the following manner:

V. Fi - de - li - um   a - ni - mæ ... in   pa - ce. R. A - men.

After the prayer that follows the Antiphon of the Blessed Virgin, the officiating priest sings, in a low note of voice:

V. Di - vi - num au - xi - li - um   ma - ne - at   semper no - bis - cum.

A - men.

In a Festival tone the prayers are sung on one note, *do*, with the exception of two variations, *do, si, la, do, do,* and *do, si*. The former of these variations is made on a principal point, the second on a semi-point. It will be observed that in every prayer there is the address to God, the petition through the mystery, or the intercession of a saint whose Mass is celebrated, and the conclusion. The end of the address is generally marked by a semicolon; and on the word preceding it the principal point is sung. If in the petition, the sentences are divided so as to admit a semicolon, the semi-point is then sung on the last word of the first part of the sentence. In the conclusion the semi-point is sung first, and the principal point in the second place, as will be seen in the following example:

PRAYERS.

qui te-cum vi-vit et reg-nat in u-ni-ta-te Spi-ri-tus Sancti De-us, per om-ni-a sæc-u-la sæc-u-lo-rum. A-men.

FERIAL TONES.

THE ferial tone is more simple, and is used in the prayers of ferial Masses, and in the Mass of Requiem. The inflection is from *Do* to *Re*, and is made at the end of the prayer, and at the conclusion. When there is more than one prayer, the inflection is made at the end of the first, at the end of the last, and at the conclusion.

Example.

Con-ce-de, mi-se-ri-cors De-us, fra-gi-li-ta-ti nos-træ præ-sid-i-um.... Re-sur-ga-mus. Per e-undem Christum Do-minum nostrum. A-men.

EPISTLE.

THE Epistle is intoned and continued throughout on the note *Do*. A prolonging of the voice is made on the fourth, fifth, or sixth syllable before the end of a period, according as the accents may require an inflection of the voice, from *Do* to *Si*. Another inflection, sanctioned by custom, may be made at the end, as it may suit the accents.

FOR VESPERS AND SOLEMN MASS.   427

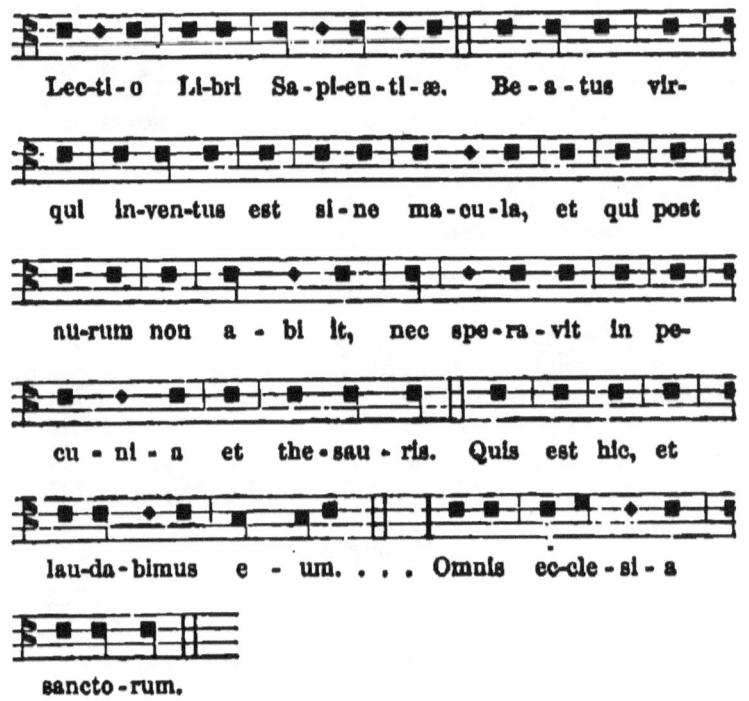

THE GOSPEL

is sung on the note *Do*, as its dominant, with three variations. At the end of a period the voice is lowered to *La* in the fourth, fifth, or sixth syllables, returning immediately to *Do*. The interrogation point is sung as at the Epistle. At the close of the Gospel the voice descends to *La* on the fourth, fifth, or sixth last syllable, which are sung on three notes, *La, Si, Do*, the remaining syllable being sung in *Do*.

Example.

Se-quen-ti-a Sancti E-van-ge-li-i se-cundum Mattheum. Glo-ri-a ti-bi Do-mine. In il-lo tem-po-re dix-it Jesus dis-ci-pu-lis su-is: vos es-tis sal ter-ræ. Quod si sal e-va-nu-e-rit, in quo sa-li-e-tur?.. Hic magnus vo-ca-bi-tur, in reg-no cœ-lo-rum. La-us ti-bi Christe.

CONFITEOR.

Con-fi-te-or De-o om-ni-po-ten-ti, Be-a-tæ Ma-ri-æ semper Vir-gi-ni, be-a-to Michae-li Archan-ge-lo be-a-to Jo-an-ni Baptis-tæ, sanctis, A-pos-to-lis Petro et Paulo, om-ni-bus sanctis et ti-bi Pa-ter: qui-a pec-ca-vi ni-mis

(Martinucci Manuale Sac. Cærem., Lib. I, Cap. XXXV.)
DEFECTUUM QUI FREQUENTIUS IN MISSÆ CELEBRATIONE ADMITTI SOLENT, DEMONSTRATIO.

I. Ut majoris emolumenti flant documenta, quæ pro celebratione Missæ tradidimus, defectus seu menda quæ præcipue in re divina conficienda incidere solent, enumerare juvat, quibus aute oculos ordinatim propositis, ea quæ superius descripta sunt, in mentem revocari facile poterunt.

II. Nisi qua justa caussa adsit Matutinum saltem et Laudes non recitasse ante Missam defectus est.

III. Item convenientem præparationem in Ecclesia et in Sacrario, bono etiam aliorum exemplo, non præmittere, præsertim si in Sacrario adsint laici homines, in quibus admiratio gigni possit,

IV. Post præparationem commorari in Sacrario tempus terendo sermonibus futilibus, loquendo de nugis aut novitatibus, multo autem magis alios obtrectando præcipue hiemis tempore circa focum.

V. Lavare manus antequam Missam in Missali reperiat, aut postquam Calicem disposuerit, vel etiam postquam se paraverit.

VI. Non præparare Calicem per seipsum, aut saltem, si jam in promptu esset, non inspicere an regulariter præparatus sit.

VII. Ponere corporale extra bursam vel super aut infra ipsam ac tali modo ad Altare afferre illud et referre in Sacrarium.

VIII. Loqui cum aliis dum sacra paramenta induet sibi.

IX. Se paramentis induere capite cooperto, Calici vel Missali imponere linteolum, birotum, pileolum, conspicilla.

X. Inclinationem facere priusquam sibi imponat amictum, aut se crucis signo munire cum amictu ipso.

XI. Sinistram sibi albæ manicam primo induere, deinde dexteram; partem dexteram amictus et stolæ non super-imponere sinistræ; adjicere *Amen* ad unamquamque orationem statutam pro paramentis, quum ad ultimam tantum id præscribatur.

XII. Linteolum coloratum et sordidum cingulo alligare, idque adeo negligenter ut extra planetam appareat.

XIII. Manipulum ad cubitum apponere; stolam dejicere per humeros, non eam aptare circa collum, ut crux, quæ est in medio, prodeat e planeta.

XIV. Albam aut planetam osculari.

XV. Nescire orationes secretas, quæ in Missa sunt memoriter recitandae.

XVI. Vagari in Sacrario quum paramentis indutus sit tam ante, quam post Missam.

XVII. Reverentiam efficere ad crucem vel ad imaginem præcipuam Sacrarii biretum manu gestando; biretum ipsum capiti detrahere quum genuflectendum sit ante SS. Sacramentum in tabernaculo reconditum, vel quum reverentia facienda sit ad Altare maximum transeundo ante ipsum.

XVIII. Calicem ferre nimium sublime ferme ad oris altitudinem, aut nimium demissum et non ad pectus, vel eam sustinere sinistra tantum, non superimposita dextera. Ire aut redire ab Altari citato gradu oculis sublimibus.

XIX. Post genuflexionem ad Altare, in quo adsit SS. Sacramentum, reverentiam quoque ad Crucem adjicere.

XX. Sinistra manu applicare bursam ad candelabrorum gradum; jubere aut permittere ministro ut Missale aperiat et occludat: corporale super mensa non totum explicare, sed unam vel plures partes plicatus relinquere.

XXI. Morari in medio Altari intuendo Crucem aut orando priusquam de gradibus in planum descendat ad Missam exordiendam.

XXII. Tergum ad Crucem vertere, eo quod pigeat paullum recedere versus cornu Evangelii, in descendendo tum in principio Missæ tum in fine.

XXIII. Non servare debitam gravitatem, tergere oculos, scalpere aures, nasum, capillos aptare atque his similia.

XXIV. Missam incipere antequam sint accensæ candelæ, aut sinere ut extinguantur antequam perlectum sit Evangelium ultimum.

XXV. Quum manus jungendæ erunt, non extendere et conjungere digitos, nec pollicem dexterum sinistro super-imponere in modum crucis.

XXVI. Se signare signo crucis extra seipsum aut dimidiato et imperfecto.

XXVII. Negligere inclinationum qualitatem *profundam*, *mediocrem* et *simplicem* et alteram pro altera exsequi.

XXVIII. Non pati ut minister responsiones suas ex toto compleat, neque eum opportuno tempore de inconsiderantiis et mendis admonere.

XXIX. Addere particulam *et* in repetenda antiphona *Introibo* post psalmum *Judica me, Deus*.

XXX. Pectus ad *Confiteor* percutere cum strepitu et vehementer; se vertere ad ministrum in dicendis verbis *vobis fratres* et *vos fratres;* respondere *Amen* postquam ille recitaverit *Confiteor;* addere verbum *omnibus* vel *omnium* in precibus *misereatur* et *Indulgentiam*, aut dicere in hac *peccatorum vestrorum* pro *nostrorum*.

XXXI. Ad orationem *aufer a nobis* non inclinari tempore præscripto, aut post osculatum Altare inclinationem facere priusquam perveniat ad librum.

XXXII. Exsequi cæremonias ante aut post tempus assignatum.

XXXIII. Legere aut recitare nimium festinanter et verba etiam per syncopem contrahere; alta voce proferre quod secreto dicendum est et vicissim.

XXXIV. Simulare Altare osculari, nec reipsa osculari, vel osculari e latere, non vero in medio aut osculandi gratia contorquere membra vel caput.

XXXV. Incipere *Kyrie Eleison* priusquam se sistat in medio Altaris, et præscriptas inclinationes omittere.

XXXVI. Convertere se ad populum dum dicit *Dominus vobiscum* manibus disjunctis, intuendo adstantes, non depositis conspicillis.

XXXVII. Dicere *Oremus* antequam veniat ad Missale, duplicare literam *O* ita ut pro *Oremus* dicat fere *O oremus*. Intueri crucem dicendo *Oremus*.

XXXVIII. Recitare orationes non junctis manibus aut non apertis ante pectus manibus, aut uti ad legendum

APPENDIX.

parvo conspicillo, quo in casu manus non possent esse apertæ.

XXXIX. Oculos ad Crucem aut in cœlum non intendere quum a rubrica præscribitur, contra autem attollere quum non præscribitur.

XL. Ad *Munda cor meum* dicere *Jube Domne* pro *Jube Domine*, aut osculari Altare post hanc precationem.

XLI. Manibus insistere Altari ad *Munda cor meum*, ad *Sanctus* et ad *Agnus Dei*.

XLII. Incipiendo Evangelium manum sinistram non imponere Missali, ut Crucis signum super textum signet, nec, quum se pollice signabit, manum eamdem infra pectus ponere, nec digitos tenere extensos.

XLIII. Inclinationem facere versus Crucem in legendo Evangelio, aut genuflectere Crucem non librum versus, quum genuflexio præscripta sit.

XLIV. Ad *et incarnatus* genuflectere utroque genu, vel morari in genuflexione, aut caput etiam inclinare.

XLV. Inchoare Crucis signum prius quam verba *et vitam venturi sæculi*.

XLVI. Detegere Calicem dum recitatur *Credo* aut quum legitur *offertorium*.

XLVII. Recitare eumdem versum extensis manibus.

XLVIII. Dum Hostiæ fiet oblatio intueri Crucem, aut tres digitos inferiores sub patena non extendere.

XLIX. Detecto Calice, velum post ipsum utcumque implicare.

L. Calicem tergere violenter, aut dum e medio Altari transibit in cornu Epistolæ: incipere orationem *Deus qui humanæ substantiæ* dum vinum in Calicem infundet, aut priusquam ampullam vini deponat.

LI. Patenam cum Hostia vel Calicem in offertorio nimis elevare, aut utrumque demisse nimis sustinere.

LII. Inclinare caput proferendo nomen *Jesu* et *Mariæ* in oratione *suscipe Sancta Trinitas*, itemque in reliquis ante communionem orationibus.

LIII. Crucis signa super Hostiam et Calicem efficere aut flectendo digitos in ducendis lineis ad illa efficienda, aut manu fere clausa, vel eadem efficiendo saltuatim.

LIV. Elata voce dicere *Orate fratres*, aut non secreto

dicere *ut meum*, etc., aut subsistere contra populum praedicta verba proferendi gratia; respondere *Amen*, aut continuare secreta priusquam responsio *Suscipiat* a ministro compleatur.

LV. Ad *Sursum corda* clausas attollere manus aut palmis non ad invicem sed ad Altare conversis.

LVI. Inclinare caput ad *ubique gratias agere* aut ad verba *per Christum Dominum nostrum* in praefatione, vel alio etiam loco praeterquam post *Memento* defunctorum.

LVII. Pectus percutere dicendo *Sanctus* aut non mediocri voce dicere ipsum; recitare voce intelligibili totum Canonem aut aliquot ejus partes, quum omnia secreto dicenda sint.

LVIII. Non jungere manus priusquam signa Crucis faciat, aut suspensam tenere sinistram, dum dextera actionem aliquam exsequitur.

LIX. Digitos saliva conspergere ad evolvenda Missalis folia.

LX. Immorari nimis in memento, vel nimia brevitate conficere, aut alta voce proferre *Memento Domine*, etc.

LXI. Pollices supponere palmis manuum dicendo *Hanc igitur oblationem*, etc.

LXII. Abstergere digitos, antequam accipiat Hostiam, non extremo sed medio corporali prope Hostiam.

LXIII. Imponere brachium sinistrum Altari sustinendo Hostiam ante Consecrationem ad verba *benedixit, fregit*, etc.

LXIV. Insistere et incurvari indecenter super Altare proferendi caussa Consecrationis verba.

LXV. Proferendo verba Consecrationis gesticulari capite aut contorquere corpus; non proferre illa secreto, eadem verba repetere, dicere sufflando, aut pedem dexterum suspensum tenere ut statim possit genuflecti.

LXVI. Non removere de Altari cubitos nec ferre manuum articulos versus frontem Altaris post Consecrationem, ut commodius genuflectatur.

LXVII. Post elevationem Hostiae detegere Calicem, postea genuflectere.

LXVIII. Accipere Calicem ad verba *Accipiens et hunc*

præclarum Calicem manu dextera tantum, os et nasum Calici imponere, aut inclinare cum ad se vel Altari applicatum tenere.

LXIX. In elevatione non sequi oculis Hostiam et Calicem aut elevare et demittere nimis festinanter, aut plus æquo sustinere sublime in conspectum adstantium, aut nimis attollere extensis monstruose brachiis, aut tam parum attollere ut conspici non possint, aut elevando super caput ponere, aut Calicem osculari.

LXX. Verba *Hæc quotiescumque*, etc., tempore elevationis dicere, non post Consecrationis verba dum genuflectitur.

LXXI. Non genuflectere usque in terram, vel genuflectere inconcinne et properanter.

LXXII. Non tenere pollices et indices junctos a Consecratione usque ad purificationem, aut Hostiam tangere digitis inferioribus, aut digitos istos non extendere quum Hostiam accipiet.

LXXIII. Ponere manus junctas super Altare omnino intra corporale post Consecrationem non sequendo præscriptiones a rubrica expressas una in perpetuum vice sine ulla distinctione aut limitatione.

LXXIV. Pausam facere in commemoratione defunctorum antequam dicatur *qui nos præcesserunt*, etc., aut alta voce dicere *Memento etiam, Domine*, aut reliquas *Ipsis, Domine*, etc.

LXXV. Pectus non digitis tribus inferioribus percutere, et reliquis junctis tangere casulam ad *Nobis quoque peccatoribus*, ad *Agnus Dei*, ad *Domine non sum dignus*.

LXXVI. Inclinare caput dicendo *Nobis quoque peccator.bus*, aut alta voce dicere etiam *famulis tuis* cum suspirio, vel dicere *Amen* ante *Per quem hæc omnia*.

LXXVII. Caput etiam inclinare ad *Præceptis salutaribus*, aut recitare illa apertis manibus, aut oculos non defigere in Sacramentum quum recitabitur *Pater noster*, aut patenam de corporali deducere eamque abstergere priusquam minister responderit *Amen*, aut non abstergere manu tantum dextera, sed adjuncta etiam sinistra.

LXXVIII. Non applicare sinistram infra pectus quum signo Crucis se muniat.

LXXIX. Osculari patenam in parte inferiori aut in margine, vel abstergere super planetam aut in alia parte postquam illam osculatus sit.

LXXX. Purificare digitos fragmentis terendo unum post alterum in labro Calicis.

LXXXI. Se vertere ad alterutram partem dicendo *Domine, non sum dignus,* aut brachium sinistrum imponere Altari.

LXXXII. Crucis signum Hostia efficere extra limites patenæ et frontis suæ in Communionis actu, aut expuere dum sumpturus est, vel etiam osculari S. Hostiam antequam sumat.

LXXXIII. Nimia vel modica diligentia peccare in colligendis fragmentis, et collectis intra Calicem injiciendis.

LXXXIV. Sumere Calicem strepondo labiis aut oculis sublatis, aut sensim et similia.

LXXXV. Pallam patenæ imponere antequam transeat in cornu Epistolæ ad accipiendam ablutionem, aut eam purificatorio abstergere.

LXXXVI. Accipiendo purificationem ponere Calicem super Altare, aut extra Altare illum ministro porrigere nulla cogente necessitate.

LXXXVII. Extergere labia aut os digitis jam ablutis vino et aqua antequam purificatorio extergantur.

LXXXVIII. Corporale complicare elato in altum Calice, bursam ponere non versa ante pectus apertura ejus, et relinquere velum ex parte anteriori sublatum.

LXXXIX. Sinere ut minister, quamquam Clericus, multo pejus si laicus sit, Calicem cooperiat et accomodet.

XC. Missale non claudere, ut præscribitur, et conclusionem ultimæ orationis absolvere veniendo ad medium Altare.

XCI. Se inclinare ad populum dicendo *Ite missa est,* aut dicendo *Benedicamus Domino* se inclinare ad Altare aut convertere ad populum.

XCII. In discessu de Altari accipere biretum antequam reverentiam vel genuflexionem efficiat, aut illud sibi de capite detrahere priusquam reverentiam fecerit ad Crucem vel imaginem præcipuam Sacrarii.

XCIII. Paramenta acervatim deponere in exuendo se, non osculari stolam, manipulam, amictum, aut sibi albam detrahere ex adverso.

XCIV. Sermones conserere et confabulari in Sacrario, aut ex illo et Ecclesia discedere quin tempus conveniens intercesserit pro debita gratiarum actione.

XCV. Quod ad defectus spectat in rubricis generalibus pluribus capitibus notatos, quum de rebus agatur, quas omnis Sacerdos novisse et probe scire tenetur, quasque potest unusquisque in Misssali legere et perpendere, potius quam eadam capita retractemus, in totum silentio praeterire operae pretium visum est.

INDEX.

Absolution after Mass for the dead, 310.
Acolytes, Instruction for the, at the High Mass, 146; at Solemn Vespers, 188.
A Cunctis, What Saint to be named in, 13, *n.*
Adorna thalamum, 91.
Advent, Sundays in, when Bishop officiates, 337.
All Souls, Vespers of, 208; when Bishop officiates, 337.
Altar, Mode of Kissing, 11, *n.*
Altar Veil, 87.
Ambry, 2, *n.*
Antependium, what, 1, *n.*
Archbishop, 288; vesting of, 284.
Ash-Wednesday, necessary preparations, 92, 217, 343; blessing of Ashes, 92, 217; Mass, 95, 221; when Bishop officiates, 344.
Asperges, when there is but one priest, 67.
Assistant Deacon, Instructions for, 318; their quality, dress, and place, 318; at Pontifical Vespers, 318; at Pontifical Mass, 319; when the Bishop does not celebrate, 321.
Assistant Priest, his quality, dress, and place, 313; his office in general, 314; his office at Pontifical Vespers, 314; at Pontifical Mass, 315; when the Bishop does not celebrate, 317.

Baptism of Infants on Holy Saturday, 266.
Benediction with the Blessed Sacrament, 79; ceremonies when but one Priest, 80; when assisted by another Priest, 83; when assisted by deacon and sub-deacon, 200; by Bishop, 275.
Bench in Sanctuary, 136, *n.*
Bishop, what, to be named in memento, 20, *n.*; serving of, at Low Mass, 60; when there is but one chaplain, 65; Mass in presence of, 46; Solemn Mass celebrated in presence of, when in cope, 300; Solemn Mass in presence of, when in Rochet and Cappa Magna, 304; Vespers solemnly celebrated by, 270; Solemn Vespers in presence of, 276; Complins by, 277; Matins, 278; Lauds, 280; Matins and Lauds for the Dead, 306; Solemn Pontifical Mass, 281; Seat of, 281; Vespers for the Dead by, 305; Instructions for officers who attend, 313; on All Souls, 336; Sundays in Advent, 337; Christmas, 338; Festivals between Christmas and Candlemas, 339; Candlemas, 340; Ash-Wednesday, 343; Sundays in Lent, 345; Palm Sunday, 346; Maunday-Thursday, 350; the Mandatum, or washing of the feet, 360; Good Friday, 361; what to be prepared for, *ib.*; to the beginning of the

office, 362; the office, 363; Holy Saturday, 369; what to be prepared for, 369; Solemn Administration of Confirmation, 395; Visitation of Parishes, 399.
Blessed Sacrament, how often to be renewed, 30, *n.*; Low Mass, when it is exposed, 44; Solemn Vespers, when it is exposed, 202; when exposed, no bow made to any one in Sanctuary, 204.
Book-bearer, Instruction for, 335.
Bows, 6, *n.*, 54; not made to Sanctuary boys, 68, *n.*
Burse, 32, 53.

Calotte, what, 137, *n.*
Candle-bearer, Instructions for, 335.
Candlemas, blessing of Candles, 86, 213; distribution, 89, 213; procession, 90, 215; when Bishop officiates, 340; Mass after the procession, 92, 217.
Canon, what, 60, *n.*
Cappa Magna, 305, *n.*
Celebrant, at High Mass, Instruction for the, 176; at Vespers, 198.
Censer-bearer, Instruction for, at High Mass, 142; at Solemn Vespers, 190.
Ceremonies of Low Mass, 1; High Mass, 67; Pontifical High Mass, 281; High Mass for the Dead, 183; Pontifical Mass for the Dead, 307; for the principal Festivals, 211.
Chapter, Intonation for, 428.
Choir, Rules for Clergy in, at High Mass, 135; at Vespers, 187; order to be observed, 136; internal dispositions, 138; order in going from, 140.
Christmas, when Bishop officiates, 338; Festivals between Christmas and Candlemas, 339.
Ciborium, Veil of, 17, *n.*; Purification of, 51.
Cincture, how made, 5.
Commemoration of all the faithful departed, 208, 336.
Communion at Masses for the dead, 43, *n.*; general rules for Communion at Mass, 48; at other times, 51; at High Mass, 139.
Complins, when Bishop officiates solemnly, 277.
Confirmation, Solemn Administration of, 395; things to be prepared for, *ib.*; the administration of the Sacrament, 396.
Confiteor, Intonation for, 428.
Corporal, what, 4, *n.*
Corpus Christi, Procession on, and its octave, 206; Benediction during procession, 207, *n.*
Cope-bearers, Instruction for the, at Solemn Vespers, 195; Vespers without, 72.
Credence, what, 2, *n.*
Credo, generally omitted in Votive Masses, 30.
Crosier-bearer, Instructions for, 333.
Cross, Veneration of, on Good Friday, 112, 247.
Cruets, to be of glass, not of silver, 2, *n.*
Cum appropinquaret, 99.

Deacon, Instruction for the officiating, 166; deacon at Pontifical Mass, 321.

INDEX. 441

Dead, Low Mass for the, 42; High Mass, 183; Vespers for the, 208
Defectuum Elenchus. Append. *in fine.*
Deus in adjutorium, Intonation, 422.
Dies iræ, when said, 43.
Diocesan Synods, Ceremonies to be observed in, 390.

Epistle, Intonation for, 426.

Faldstool, what, 283.
Ferial tones, 426.
Font, Blessing of the, 129, 264.
Forty Hours' Exposition of the Blessed Sacrament, 406; things to be prepared, *ib.*; of the Mass of the Exposition, 407; of the Procession for the Exposition, 409; of the Mass, *pro pace,* 413; things to be prepared for the Mass of the Reposition, 414; of the Mass of the Reposition, 414; from the Litany to the end of the Forty Hours, 418.

Genuflection, how made, 54.
Gloria in Excelsis, in what votive Masses omitted, 36.
Good Friday, what is to be prepared, 110, 243; when Bishop officiates, 361; Office to the uncovering of the Cross, 111, 244; uncovering and veneration of the Cross, 112, 247; Procession, 118, 250; remaining part of the office, 120, 252; from the entrance of the Bishop to the beginning of the office, 362; the office, 363.
Gospel, Intonation for the, 427.

High Mass, without deacon or sub-deacon, 67; vesting, 68; ceremonies, 69; rules for clergy in choir, 135; order to be observed, 136; internal dispositions, 138; receiving Holy Communion, 139; going from Choir, 140; Preparation for, 141; Instructions for the officers at, 142; Instruction for celebrant, 176; incensing, 143. (*See Pontifical Mass, Solemn Mass.*)
High Mass for the Dead, what to be observed particularly at, 183; Pontifical, 307.
Holy Saturday, things to be prepared, 123, 256; when Bishop officiates, 369; office, 125, 258; Benediction of the new fire, 125, 258; by Bishop, 370; Exultet, 128, 261, 371; Blessing of the Paschal Candle, 128, 261; by Bishop, 371; Prophecies, 128, 263; Blessing of the Font, 129, 264; by the Bishop, 373; Baptism of Infants, 131; Litany, Mass, 132, 267; Vespers, *ib.*; bringing back the Pyx to the Altar, 133; to the beginning of Mass, when Bishop officiates, 374; Mass, 375.
Holy Week and other Festivals, Ceremonies for, 86, 211.
Host, how broken, 27.

Incense-boat, 86.
Incensing, manner of, 144, *n.*
Incensing, candles at Candlemas, 89; ashes, 94; palms, 98; the Blessed Sacrament in the Repository, 107, 241; on Holy Saturday, 126, 258; at Benediction of the Blessed Sacrament, 81, 84; at High

442   INDEX.

Mass, 180; in High Mass for the Dead, 185; at Solemn Vespers, 190, 199; Corpus Christi, 203.
Inferior ministers, at Pontifical Mass, instructions for, 313.
Intonation for Mass and Vespers, 423.

Lætare and Gaudete Sundays, 222.
Lauds, when the Bishop officiates, 280; for the Dead, 306.
Lent, Sundays in, 345; when the Bishop officiates, 345.
Low Mass, Ceremonies of, 1; what to be prepared for, 1, 2; from Commencement to Introit, 9; Introit to the Epistle, 11; Epistle to the Offertory, 13; Offertory to the Canon, 15; Canon to the Consecration, 20; Consecration to the Pater Noster, 24; Pater Noster to the Communion, 26; Communion to the end of Mass, 32; Low Mass for the Dead, 42; when the Blessed Sacrament is exposed, 44; in the presence of Prelates, 46; manner of serving at, 54; Bishop at Low Mass, 60.

Mandatum, or Washing of Feet, 360.
Mass, Preparations for, 3; Ceremonies for Low Mass, 1; Votive Masses, 34; Mass pro Sponso et Sponsa, 35; Low Mass for the Dead, 42; High Mass, 141; High Mass for the Dead, 183; Pontifical Mass, Solemn, 281; for the Dead, 307.
Mass, Solemn, in presence of the Bishop, 300, 304.
Masses for the Dead, classed among Votive Masses, 37; when prohibited, 38; when allowed, 38; Dies iræ, when said, 43; Low Mass for the Dead, 42; Communion at, 43; High Mass, 183; Pontifical, 307; things to be prepared, ib.; the Mass, 308; absolution after Mass, 310.
Master of Ceremonies, duty of, at High Mass, 150; at Solemn Vespers, 192.
Matins, when the Bishop officiates, 273; for the Dead, 306; of Tenebræ, 349.
Maunday-Thursday, Preparation, 103, 235; Mass, 104, 236; Procession, 106, 239; removal of the Pyx, 108; Vespers, 241; stripping of the Altar, 109, 241; when the Bishop officiates, 350; repository, how prepared, 103, 350.
Mitre-bearer, Instruction for, 334.
Monstrance, 80.
Mozetta, 271, n.

Newly ordained priest, the three Masses of, 87.

Obtulerunt Domine, 91.
Officers, Instructions for the, at High Mass, 141; censer-bearer, 142; acolytes, 146; master of ceremonies, 150; sub-deacon, 153; deacon, 166; celebrant, 176; instruction for officers who attend Bishop, 313.
Officiating deacon, Instruction for, 166; at Pontifical Mass, 321.
Ordo, to be observed by priest celebrating in another church, 89.
Umbrellino, 202, n.

INDEX.   443

Pall, what, 4, *n.*
Palm Sunday, Preparation for, 96, 222; blessing of the palms, 97, 223; distribution of, 98, 226; procession, 99, 227; Mass and Passion, 230; when Bishop officiates, 346.
Parishes, Episcopal visitation of, 399.
Paschal Candles, Blessing of, 127, 261.
Pax, how given, 138.
Peace, instrument of, 47.
Pontifical mantle, 305.
Pontifical Mass, Solemn, 281; things to be prepared, *ib.*; vesting of the clergy and Bishop, 284; the Pontifical Mass, 288: for the Dead, 307; things to be prepared, *ib.*; the Mass, 308; absolution after Mass, 310.
Popule meus, 114.
Prelates, what, 46.
Priest, preparation for Mass, 3; at Low Mass, 6; after Mass, 34; instruction for, at High Mass, 67; assistant priest, 313.
Procession at Candlemas, 90; Palm Sunday, 99, 227; Maunday-Thursday, 106, 239; Good Friday, 118, 250; Corpus Christi and its octave, 206; at Provincial Councils, 379.
Prophecies on Holy Saturday, 128, 263.
Provincial Councils, Ceremonies to be observed in, 376; how the Metropolitan Church is to be adorned and arranged, 377; opening of the Council, 378; procession, 379; Mass, 379; Ceremonies for the first session or opening of the council, 380; Mode of procedure, 384; second Solemn Session, 385; third Solemn Session, 387.
Purification, Feast of the, necessary preparations, 86, 211; from the Vesting to the distribution of the candles, 86, 212; to the Procession, 90, 213; the Procession, 90, 215.
Purificator, what, 4, *n.*
Pyx, of the removal of the, 108; bringing back to the altar, 133.

Quarant 'Ore, 406.

Remonstance, see *Monstrance*.
Repository, how prepared, 104, 236; procession to, on Maunday-Thursday, 106, 239; on Good Friday, 118, 250.
Requiem Masses, 37; Communion at, 43.
Rose Colored Vestments, 222.

Sacred Species, Renewal of, 30, *n.*
Sanctuary, Chairs in, 136, *n.*; rules for clergy in, 135, 187; when sacristy is behind altar, how to enter, 34, *n.*
Serving Mass, Low Mass, 54; Vesting, 55; the Mass, 56; Bishop's Low Mass, 60.
Sign of the Cross, how made, 9, *n.*
Solemn Mass, in presence of Bishop in mitre and cope, 300; when in rochet and cappa, 304; Intonations for, 425.
Solemnities when Bishop officiates, 336.
Stole, Use of, 73, *n.*
Sub-deacon, Instruction for, at High Mass, 158; Pontifical Mass, 323.

Tenebræ, Office of, 233; when Bishop officiates, 349.
Two Masses on the same day, Order of, 40.

Unrobing after Mass, 84.

Vespers, without cope-bearer, 72; Solemn, 186; things to be prepared *ib.*; general rules for the clergy in the sanctuary, 187; instruction for cope-bearers, 195; for the celebrant, 198; Solemn Vespers, the Blessed Sacrament being exposed, 202; for the Dead, on November 1st, 208; things to be prepared, *ib.*; peculiar ceremonies, 209; on Maunday-Thursday, 241; Solemn Pontifical, 270; things to be prepared, *ib.*; from the entrance to the beginning of Vespers, 271; to the end of Vespers, 272; Solemn Vespers in the presence of the Bishop 276; All Souls, when the Bishop officiates, 305; Christmas, 338; intonations for, 422.
Vesting priest at Low Mass, 55; Bishop, 60.
Vexilla regis, 119.
Visitation of the Parishes, 399; things subject to the Episcopal visitation, 403.
Votive Masses, 34; Solemn, when can it be said, 35; what Preface to be said at, 36; prayers at, *ib.*; certain Masses not to be said as Votive, 36.

Water, what quantity to be poured into chalice, 17, *n.*
Wax candles, only two at Low Mass of priests, 1.

www.ingramcontent.com/pod-product-compliance
Lightning Source LLC
Chambersburg PA
CBHW032004300426
44117CB00008B/894